ASIAN DEVELOPMENT
OUTLOOK 2017
UPDATE

SUSTAINING DEVELOPMENT THROUGH PUBLIC–PRIVATE PARTNERSHIP

50 YEARS

ADB

ASIAN DEVELOPMENT BANK

ISBN 978-92-9257-959-3 (Print), 978-92-9257-960-9 (e-ISBN)
ISSN 1655-4809
Publication Stock No. FLS179053-3
DOI: http://dx.doi.org/10.22617/FLS179053-3

The views expressed in this publication are those of the authors and do not necessarily reflect the views and policies of the Asian Development Bank (ADB) or its Board of Governors or the governments they represent.

ADB does not guarantee the accuracy of the data included in this publication and accepts no responsibility for any consequence of their use. The mention of specific companies or products of manufacturers does not imply that they are endorsed or recommended by ADB in preference to others of a similar nature that are not mentioned.

By making any designation of or reference to a particular territory or geographic area, or by using the term "country" in this document, ADB does not intend to make any judgments as to the legal or other status of any territory or area.

Notes:
In this publication, "$" refers to US dollars.
Corrigenda to ADB publications may be found at http://www.adb.org/publications/corrigenda

Contents

Foreword   iv
Acknowledgments   v
Definitions   vi
Abbreviations   vii

ADO 2017 Update—Highlights   ix

Part 1   Confident resurgence in developing Asia   1

Trade strength lifts regional prospects   4
Risks from unwinding quantitative easing   23
Gauging Asia's business cycles   29
Annex: Solidifying global recovery   36

Part 2   Sustaining development through public–private partnership   47

Applying public–private partnership to Asia's infrastructure challenge   50
Hurdles to public–private partnership   72
Financing public–private partnership   91
Toward better-performing partnership   111

Part 3   Economic trends and prospects in developing Asia   127

Central Asia   129
East Asia   141
South Asia   153
Southeast Asia   175
The Pacific   202

Statistical appendix   215

Foreword

The outlook for developing Asia supports optimism. Rather than the slight growth moderation forecast in *Asian Development Outlook 2017* in April, this *Update* envisages a slight uptick this year. Growth in the region is set to pick up from 5.8% in 2016 to 5.9% this year and 5.8% in 2018. Excluding the high-income newly industrialized economies, the region is expected to expand by 6.4% in 2017 and 6.3% in 2018. An upturn in global trade is backed by strengthening recovery in the United States, the euro area, and Japan. Robust investments in developing Asia and higher growth in the People's Republic of China contribute to the healthy outlook.

Risks to developing Asia's outlook have become more balanced since April. The US Federal Reserve announced its plan to begin winding down the assets it purchased in the wake of the global financial crisis of 2008–2009. Analysis in the *Update* notes that clear communication from the Fed has avoided market overaction to the policy change, but authorities in developing Asia nevertheless need to prepare for tighter global liquidity. In an analysis of the business cycle, this *Update* notes that many economies are still in the accelerating phase of their growth cycles, but that the pace of growth is weaker than the average of recent upturns. Additional policy support to remove constraints on productivity by, for example, closing infrastructure gaps may be needed to boost future output potential.

Asia's infrastructure needs amount to $1.7 trillion per year until 2030. However, even factoring in funds saved through public finance reform or received from multilateral agencies, a significant financing gap remains. The theme chapter in this *Update* explores how public–private partnership (PPP) can help to fill the infrastructure gap. The success of the approach depends on governments identifying projects suitable for it, engaging qualified private partners, and instituting the right process. The Asian Development Bank is a frontrunner in supporting the development of PPP in the region. Experience has shown that, if the three conditions are met, all stakeholders in PPP projects can expect a fair share of the benefits.

TAKEHIKO NAKAO
President
Asian Development Bank

Acknowledgments

Asian Development Outlook 2017 Update was prepared by staff of the Asian Development Bank (ADB) in the Central and West Asia Department, East Asia Department, Pacific Department, South Asia Department, Southeast Asia Department, and Economic Research and Regional Cooperation Department, as well as in ADB resident missions. Representatives of these departments constituted the Regional Economic Outlook Task Force, which met regularly to coordinate and develop consistent forecasts for the region.

The authors who contributed the sections are bylined in each chapter. The subregional coordinators were Dominik Peschel and Fatima Catacutan for Central Asia, Akiko Terada-Hagiwara for East Asia, Masato Nakane for South Asia, Kwang Jo Jeong and Dulce Zara for Southeast Asia, and Rommel Rabanal and Cara Tinio for the Pacific.

A team of economists in the Economic Research and Regional Cooperation Department, led by Joseph E. Zveglich, Jr., director of the Macroeconomics Research Division, coordinated the production of the publication, assisted by Edith Laviña. Technical and research support was provided by Shiela Camingue-Romance, Cindy Castillejos-Petalcorin, Marthe Hinojales, Nedelyn Magtibay-Ramos, Pilipinas Quising, Aleli Rosario, Dennis Sorino, and Mai Lin Villaruel. Additional research support was provided by Emmanuel Alano, Raymond Gaspar, Jade Laranjo, and Michael Timbang. The economic editorial advisors Robert Boumphrey, Joshua Greene, Srinivasa Madhur, Richard Niebuhr, and Reza Vaez-Zadeh made substantive contributions to the country chapters and regional outlook.

The theme chapter benefited from the insightful comments from the Office of Public–Private Partnership and the public–private partnership thematic group, and in particular Amr Qari, Alexander Jett, Srinivas Sampath, Takeo Koike, and Weonho Yang. The valuable support and guidance of Bambang Susantono, Yasuyuki Sawada, Juzhong Zhuang, and Joseph E. Zveglich, Jr. throughout the production process is gratefully acknowledged. Josef Yap provided editorial advice on the theme chapter.

Peter Fredenburg advised on ADB style and English usage. Alvin Tubio handled typesetting and graphics generation, in which he was assisted by Heili Ann Bravo, Elenita Pura, and Azaleah Tiongson. Art direction for the cover design was by Anthony Victoria, with artwork from Design Muscle. Support for the printing and publishing of the report was provided by the Printing Services Unit of the ADB Office of Administrative Services and by the Publishing and Dissemination Unit of the ADB Department of External Relations. Fermirelyn Cruz and Rhia Bautista-Piamonte provided administrative and secretarial support. The Department of External Relations, led by Satinder Bindra, Omana Nair, and Erik Churchill, planned and coordinated the dissemination of *Asian Development Outlook 2017 Update*.

Definitions

The economies discussed in *Asian Development Outlook 2017 Update* are classified by major analytic or geographic group. For the purposes of this publication, the following apply:

- **Association of Southeast Asian Nations** comprises Brunei Darussalam, Cambodia, Indonesia, the Lao People's Democratic Republic, Malaysia, Myanmar, the Philippines, Singapore, Thailand, and Viet Nam.
- **Developing Asia** comprises the 45 members of the Asian Development Bank listed below.
- **Newly industrialized economies** comprises the Republic of Korea, Singapore, Taipei,China, and Hong Kong, China.
- **Central Asia** comprises Armenia, Azerbaijan, Georgia, Kazakhstan, the Kyrgyz Republic, Tajikistan, Turkmenistan, and Uzbekistan.
- **East Asia** comprises the People's Republic of China, the Republic of Korea, Mongolia, Taipei,China, and Hong Kong, China.
- **South Asia** comprises Afghanistan, Bangladesh, Bhutan, India, Maldives, Nepal, Pakistan, and Sri Lanka.
- **Southeast Asia** comprises Brunei Darussalam, Cambodia, Indonesia, the Lao People's Democratic Republic, Malaysia, Myanmar, the Philippines, Singapore, Thailand, and Viet Nam.
- **The Pacific** comprises the Cook Islands, Fiji, Kiribati, the Marshall Islands, the Federated States of Micronesia, Nauru, Palau, Papua New Guinea, Samoa, Solomon Islands, Timor-Leste, Tonga, Tuvalu, and Vanuatu.

Unless otherwise specified, the symbol "$" and the word "dollar" refer to US dollars. *Asian Development Outlook 2017 Update* is generally based on data available up to **4 September 2017**.

Abbreviations

ADB	Asian Development Bank
ADO	Asian Development Outlook
ASEAN	Association of Southeast Asian Nations
CPEC	economic corridor linking Pakistan with the PRC
E&E	electrical and electronic equipment
FDI	foreign direct investment
FSM	Federated States of Micronesia
FY	fiscal year
GDP	gross domestic product
Lao PDR	Lao People's Democratic Republic
LNG	liquefied natural gas
M1	money that includes cash and checking accounts
M2	broad money that adds highly liquid accounts to M1
M3	broad money that adds time accounts to M2
mbd	million barrels per day
MDB	multilateral development bank
NIE	newly industrialized economy
NPL	nonperforming loan
OECD	Organisation for Economic Co-operation and Development
OPEC	Organization of the Petroleum Exporting Countries
PNG	Papua New Guinea
PPF	project preparation facility
PPP	public–private partnership, purchasing power parity
PRC	People's Republic of China
PRI	political risk insurance
QE	quantitative easing
saar	seasonally adjusted annualized rate
SOE	state-owned enterprise
SPV	special purpose vehicle
US	United States

ADO 2017 Update—Highlights

Growth prospects for developing Asia are looking up, bolstered by a revival in world trade and strong momentum in the People's Republic of China. The region is forecast to expand by 5.9% in 2017 and 5.8% in 2018, a slight upgrade from *Asian Development Outlook 2017*. Excluding the newly industrialized economies, the region is expected to grow by 6.4% this year and 6.3% in 2018.

Rebounds in international food and fuel prices are gentler than expected, helping to contain consumer price pressures. Inflation is likely to dip to 2.4% in 2017, or 0.1 percentage points off the 2016 rate, and pick up to 2.9% in 2018.

Risks to the outlook have become more balanced, as the advanced economies have so far avoided sharp, unexpected changes to their macroeconomic policies. Further, the fuel price rise is providing fiscal relief to oil exporters but is measured enough not to destabilize oil importers.

Looking ahead, developing Asia must mobilize $1.7 trillion annually to meet its infrastructure needs. Public–private partnership can help fill the financing gap by allocating risk to the party best able to manage it. The success of the approach depends on governments identifying projects suitable for it, engaging qualified private partners, and instituting the right process.

Yasuyuki Sawada
Chief Economist
Asian Development Bank

Confident resurgence in developing Asia

Trade strength lifts regional prospects

■ **The short-term growth outlook for developing Asia is heartening.** This *Update* looks forward to stable economic growth, not the growth moderation forecast in April in *Asian Development Outlook 2017 (ADO 2017)*. Gross domestic product (GDP) in the region is now expected to grow by 5.9% in 2017, a slight uptick from 5.8% in 2016 and 0.2 percentage points higher than the earlier forecast. The region is benefiting from a rebound in global trade, which is supported by firm recovery in the major industrial economies, and by strong domestic investment demand. Growth in the People's Republic of China (PRC) that exceeds expectations is also lifting regional prospects. Developing Asia is forecast to maintain its growth momentum in 2018, expanding by 5.8% as strong trade linkages reinforce gains stemming from domestic demand. The forecast for growth excluding the newly industrialized economies is adjusted up by 0.1 percentage points to 6.4% in 2017 and 6.3% in 2018.

　» **Recovery in the industrial economies beats earlier expectations.** The forecast for aggregate growth in the United States, the euro area, and Japan is revised up by 0.1 percentage points to 2.0% for both 2017 and 2018. With rising consumption, US growth in the second quarter more than doubled the first quarter pace. Growth in Japan exceeded expectations, spurred by improving consumer confidence and business sentiment. Absent a major interruption of global trade, growth should expand further this year and next. Recovery in the euro area appears to be broadly supported by expansive fiscal and monetary policies, easing political uncertainty, and robust market confidence, which should keep growth momentum going through 2018.

　» **Growth has picked up slightly more than expected in the PRC.** GDP growth is now forecast 0.2 percentage points higher, at 6.7% in 2017 and 6.4% in 2018, with growth led by expansionary fiscal policy and unanticipated external demand. Supply-side reform is moving forward, but eventual success hinges on a careful balancing of the role of the market and the state during the current economic transition.

　» **Transitory challenges temper India's strong growth prospects.** With sluggish consumption and dampened business investment, GDP growth is now expected to dip from 7.1% in 2016 to 7.0% in 2017. Demonetization last November suppressed small businesses and private credit, and adjustment to a new national goods and services tax muted manufacturing. However, short-term disruption is expected to dissipate, allowing these initiatives to generate growth dividends over the medium term. Expansion is forecast to accelerate to 7.4% in 2018.

　» **Growth in Southeast Asia strengthened in the first half of 2017.** First-half performances in the subregion vary across economies but remain solid. The growth forecast is upgraded for Singapore and Malaysia, boosted by rising electronics exports, and for the Philippines, on the strength of higher domestic demand. Projections for Indonesia and Thailand are retained as first-half 2017 performance met earlier expectations, but weakness in mining triggers a slight downward adjustment for Viet Nam. Southeast Asia as a whole is expected to grow by 5.0% in 2017, or 0.2 percentage points higher than *ADO 2017* forecasts, and by 5.1% in 2018.

» **External factors lift Central Asia as growth stalls in the Pacific.** This *Update* revises up growth forecasts for Central Asia this year and next amid moderately rising oil prices, improving prospects for the Russian Federation, and increasing remittances. Meanwhile, the Pacific outlook is retained for 2017 but adjusted slightly downward for 2018 as prospects for two of the larger Pacific economies—Papua New Guinea and Timor-Leste—are unchanged.

■ **Inflation remains broadly in check amid firming oil prices.** This *Update* revises downward the forecast for average inflation in the region, from 3.0% to 2.4% in 2017 and from 3.2% to 2.9% in 2018. Stable oil prices in the first half of 2017 helped to soften domestic fuel prices in the region, prompting downward revisions to inflation projections for some of the larger commodity importers. The inflation forecast is revised up for Central Asia, boosted by further currency depreciation in Azerbaijan and Uzbekistan. Inflationary pressures are largely contained elsewhere in the region.

■ **Developing Asia and the rest of the world enjoy a revival in trade.** The dollar value of the region's exports surged by 11% in the first 5 months of 2017 over the same period in the previous year, and the value of its imports rose by 17%. The pickup follows 2 consecutive years of contracting export values caused by falling commodity prices and subdued external demand for manufactures. Excluding the PRC, the eight largest regional developing economies saw real manufacturing exports rebound, particularly in electronics, where foreign direct investment has been strengthening. The strong showing for exports comes hand-in-hand with a surge in intermediate goods moving through cross-border manufacturing supply chains. Further, as the PRC rebalances toward domestic demand, supply chains have evolved with some processes shifting to other regional manufacturing hubs, consequently boosting trade within the region.

■ **Yet the regional current account surplus is set to contract.** Developing Asia's current account surplus is forecast to narrow from 2.3% of GDP in 2016 to 1.5% in 2017 and 1.4% in 2018. This is because the regional rebound in import values so far in 2017 has been higher than that of exports. In particular, imports to the PRC and India, which together receive 38% of developing Asia's total, grew by 23% in the first 5 months of 2017. However, the projected moderate rise in oil prices will help net oil importers in the region keep external balances under control.

■ **Risks to the outlook become more balanced, upside and down.** Oil prices are lower than the baseline forecast in *ADO 2017*. More softening would benefit oil importers but deliver a further fiscal hit to oil exporters. Sudden changes in US monetary policy could induce large capital outflows from developing Asia, but advance communication from the Federal Reserve (Fed) of its intentions has helped avert market overreaction. The path of US fiscal policy remains uncertain. While tax reform and spending on public works could have positive global spillover, political stalemate over budget details could unsettle business plans.

Finally, economic disruption from a geopolitical or weather-related disaster, though less than likely, could impede the recent trade rebound, particularly for high-tech goods that depend heavily on global production chains.

Risks from unwinding quantitative easing

- **The Fed will start normalizing its balance sheet in October 2017.** From November 2008 to October 2014—bookends for the US Federal Reserve bond-purchasing program—the Fed's securities holdings ballooned from under $0.5 trillion to $4.2 trillion. In March 2017, the Fed had indicated that it would start to unwind the mass of debt securities added to its balance sheet, though the pace would be contingent on continued macroeconomic strength. Balance sheet normalization is part of a broader US monetary policy of normalization, which has so far included four modest interest rate hikes since December 2015.

- **Market response to the Fed's planned normalization has been muted.** In the "taper tantrum" of May–June 2013, volatility hit global and Asian financial markets in the wake of the Fed's unexpected hint that it would taper down its securities purchases. To cite one resulting imbalance, while yields on 10-year government bonds issued by the US shot up by 81 basis points during that episode, those issued by India soared by 163 basis points. The Fed's clear and transparent communication this time about its normalization plans allows markets to prepare. Bond yields in the US and Asia alike reacted much less in February–April 2017.

- **Policy makers still need to brace for the end of easy global liquidity.** Data suggest that the Fed's asset unwinding may drain capital from the region, which would challenge Asia's financial stability in different ways. Tighter global liquidity could push down asset prices and thus strain the balance sheets of banks and corporations in the region. Further, higher bond yields in the US may spill over into Asia, pushing up the region's long-term financing costs. Finally, higher rates in the US will strengthen the US dollar and likely cause even more capital outflow from the region. The debt that piled up in Asia during the recent period of low global interest rates may pose a risk to financial stability. Because long-term interest rates in many Asian economies are closely linked to those in the US, policy makers need to strengthen their financial positions further and monitor debt levels and asset prices.

Gauging Asia's business cycles

- **Many Asian economies are in an upturn phase of the business cycle.** Knowing where an economy is in its cycle helps determine whether macroeconomic stimulus is needed or if it would cause overheating. Analysis of emerging Asian economies with sufficient data shows that since 1993 all have experienced multiple cycles, defined as fluctuations in output around the trend. The duration of the current upturn, which started after 2013, has so far been shorter than past episodes for Malaysia and Taipei,China, but has already stretched beyond the past average for India, Indonesia, the Republic of Korea, the Philippines, and Thailand. However, the pace is slower than the average in previous episodes for all economies except the Philippines.

- **Monetary policy has sought to minimize the cycle's ups and downs.** The same analysis pointed out that different national monetary authorities have, however, targeted different macroeconomic indicators in the last decade. In Indonesia, the Republic of Korea, and the Philippines, monetary policy has responded mostly to price fluctuations. In Taipei,China, monetary policy stabilized vacillations in the growth rate. In India, Malaysia, and Thailand, monetary policy was used to stabilize prices and output simultaneously.

- **Room for additional policy support varies across the region.** A boost from accommodative policy designed to spur activity would be welcome to make the expansion less tepid. Some economies, like Indonesia, Malaysia, Thailand, and Taipei,China, retain room for policy maneuver. In others, such as the Republic of Korea and the Philippines, the case for stimulus may be less clear because the growth upturn is protracted and price pressures are intensifying. One option is to aim to raise the output trend by removing constraints on productivity improvement, notably by closing infrastructure gaps. Apart from purely government initiatives, the private sector should be encouraged to participate in infrastructure development through public–private partnership.

Outlook by subregion

- **The outlook is improving for most large economies in developing Asia.** Growth forecasts are upgraded from projections in *ADO 2017* for 22 of the 45 regional economies. Better prospects for Central Asia, East Asia, and Southeast Asia more than offset the downward revision in the growth outlook for South Asia, while the Pacific remains largely on track to meet projections.

- **East Asia benefits from a rebound in global trade.** GDP in the subregion will expand by 6.0% in 2017 and 5.8% in 2018, higher than forecast in *ADO 2017*. On top of the unexpected boost to the subregion from export demand, expansionary fiscal policy in the PRC will push growth there to 6.7% in 2017 and 6.4% in 2018. Government spending is similarly boosting growth in the Republic of Korea and Taipei,China, while rising business confidence is strengthening the outlook in Hong Kong, China. The growth forecast is upgraded for Mongolia, bolstered by rising coal production and mining-related services. Inflation in East Asia will be lower than forecast in April, at 1.7% in 2017 and 2.3% in 2018. The PRC will see prices rise by 1.7% in 2017 and 2.4% in 2018, less than previously forecast because recovery will likely be slow for sharply lower food prices. In contrast, the inflation forecast is revised up for the Republic of Korea on higher growth, lingering drought, and impending wage hikes.

- **South Asia's economic recovery is delayed until 2018.** The subregional growth forecast is downgraded to 6.7% in 2017, 0.3 percentage points lower than envisaged in *ADO 2017* but the same rate as in 2016. Growth remains strong in India despite temporary drag from adjustments to policy reform. Manufacturers there sold off inventory in response to a goods and service tax introduced in July 2017, which moderates growth in that sector. Most other South Asian economies are expected to meet or exceed April growth forecasts, but not Sri Lanka, because of adverse weather, or Bhutan, where geological problems have constrained construction on two large hydropower projects. Growth in

Nepal surged in fiscal 2017 on earthquake recovery but is slowing as the pace of reconstruction eases and agriculture struggles following floods. In 2018, a pickup in Indian growth to 7.4% will buoy expansion in South Asia to 7.0%, which is still 0.2 percentage points off the earlier forecast. The subregional inflation forecast is lowered to 4.2% for 2017 and 4.7% for 2018. Expectations of favorable global commodity prices, generally good harvests, and prudent macroeconomic policy are all in play.

- **Southeast Asia is poised to surpass earlier growth forecasts.** Projections for subregional growth are revised up to 5.0% for 2017 and 5.1% for 2018, both higher than the *ADO 2017* projections of 4.8% and 5.0%. Some common growth drivers across the subregion are a pickup in global electronics trade, stronger inflows of foreign direct investment, and higher agricultural production. Broad expansion in demand underpins faster growth in Malaysia and the Philippines, while stronger exports spur higher growth in Singapore. Elsewhere, growth rates are sustained in line with forecasts by strengthening investment and exports in Indonesia and by higher exports and foreign direct investment in Cambodia, the Lao People's Democratic Republic, and Myanmar. Mining sector weaknesses cloud prospects for Brunei Darussalam and Viet Nam. Unexpectedly modest increases in international fuel and food prices help the subregion keep average inflation at 3.1% this year and next, less than the *ADO 2017* forecasts of 3.3% and 3.5%. However, inflation will be slightly higher than foreseen in Viet Nam, which hiked administered prices and minimum wages, and in Malaysia following a spike in transport prices.

- **Central Asia sees growth boosted by better prospects in Kazakhstan.** This *Update* raises the 2017 growth forecast for Central Asia from 3.1% in *ADO 2017* to 3.3% as stable oil prices, a better outlook for the Russian Federation, and rising remittances improve projections for Kazakhstan, the largest economy in the subregion, as well as Armenia, Georgia, the Kyrgyz Republic, and Tajikistan. In contrast, cuts in oil production are delaying recovery in Azerbaijan. The factors supporting the growth upgrade in 2017 look set to continue, so the subregional forecast for 2018 is raised as well, from 3.5% in *ADO 2017* to 3.9%. Inflation in a few economies is picking more sharply than expected in April, taking the inflation forecast for Central Asia up by 1.1 percentage points to 8.9% in 2017 and by 0.5 percentage points to 7.8% in 2018. Foreign exchange restrictions and expectations of further currency depreciation have stoked inflation in Azerbaijan, and the large currency devaluation in Uzbekistan in September 2017 will push up prices for traded goods.

- **Pacific growth forecasts are on track despite mixed prospects.** The growth forecast of 2.9% for 2017 is unchanged from *ADO 2017*, but the pickup forecast for 2018 is adjusted down slightly to 3.2%. Papua New Guinea, the predominant economy in the subregion, remains on track to meet its *ADO 2017* growth projection. In Fiji, the second largest economy, recovery in sugar production in 2017 slightly lifts the forecast for this year, but the higher base will marginally reduce the rate in 2018. In Palau, growth this year is now expected to be considerably lower than projected in April because of a decline in tourism and delays affecting public investment projects. Domestic supply constraints in some economies will push inflation in the Pacific to 5.4% in 2017, marginally higher than previously forecast. Inflation will maintain that pace in 2018.

Sustaining development through public–private partnership

Applying public–private partnership to Asia's infrastructure challenge

■ **Asia's infrastructure needs dwarf traditional sources of finance.** Over 400 million Asians live without electricity, 300 million without safe drinking water, and a staggering 1.5 billion without basic sanitation. The region will need to invest an estimated $1.7 trillion annually through 2030 to maintain its growth momentum, reduce poverty, and respond to climate change. Further, the financing gap to meet these investment needs currently approaches $500 billion per year. While state funds currently finance 92% of the region's infrastructure investment, some economies struggle to meet these needs, constrained by high fiscal deficits and deepening public debt. Even factoring in funds saved through public finance reform or received from multilateral agencies, a significant infrastructure financing gap remains.

■ **Public–private partnership has potential to fill the infrastructure gap.** Bridging the infrastructure gap demands improved infrastructure delivery. Public–private partnership (PPP) transforms how the public and private sectors collaborate to deliver public infrastructure and services. PPP effectively marshals the private sector's most valued strengths—incentivized finance, operational efficiency, and capacity to innovate—to meet public sector objectives. Moreover, PPP can be a conduit for infrastructure finance by institutional investors such as insurance funds and pensions.

» **Where appropriately implemented, PPP yields superior results.** Private partners innovate when risk-sharing provides incentive to avoid failure and deliver, in a timely and cost-effective manner, high-quality infrastructure and associated services. Other modalities lack this incentive.

» **PPP improves access to infrastructure.** Doubling PPP investment from 0.5% of GDP in 2015 to 1.0% could bring safe drinking water to 12 million people among the 300 million who currently lack it and provide electricity to 14 million of the 400 million without. Improving access to infrastructure, when coupled with public sector reform, enhances productivity and competitiveness across the economy. The same doubling of the ratio of PPP investment to GDP is projected to add 0.1 percentage points to GDP growth per capita across Asia and the Pacific.

■ **Project delivery through PPP rose fourfold in Asia in 25 years.** Analysis of the Private Participation in Infrastructure database shows that the number of PPP projects in developing Asia grew by 11% annually from 1991 to 2015. The region accounts for half of all projects in 139 developing economies worldwide, followed by Latin America and the Caribbean with 30%. However, the distribution of PPPs is uneven across economies and sectors within the region.

» **PPP transactions are heavily concentrated in East and South Asia.** More than 70% of PPPs in developing Asia are in East and South Asia, and 90% of that portion are in the PRC and India. PPPs are gaining ground in Southeast Asia, however, particularly in the larger economies of Indonesia, Malaysia, the Philippines, Thailand, and Viet Nam. Central Asia and the Pacific together account for only 2% of the region's PPPs.

» **PPPs in the two largest economies reveal different approaches.** In the PRC, energy sector projects make up 50% of the transactions, followed by water supply and sanitation projects with 34%. Local governments and banks often partner with state-owned enterprises. In India, more than half of the PPP transactions are in the transport sector. Though PPP transport investments declined significantly after 2013, recent initiatives to mitigate revenue uncertainty are expected to boost these transactions again.

» **More than half of PPPs are in energy, and a third in transport.** This concentration of PPP projects in two sectors reflects the region's development needs. A similar sectoral distribution is found in Latin America and the Caribbean.

» **Most PPPs in developing Asia literally break new ground.** Such new infrastructure projects, so-called greenfield projects, account for almost 70% of all PPPs in terms of both the number of projects and their committed investment. Projects that improve and expand existing assets, so-called brownfield projects, account for only 23% by number.

■ **If successfully pursued, a PPP offers something for everyone.** Different as their motives and needs may be, all stakeholders in PPPs can expect a fair share of benefits. The state expands its capacity through a flexible development mechanism, the private sector gets profitable investment opportunities, and end users enjoy adequate and efficient infrastructure and services.

Hurdles to public–private partnership

■ **Terminated PPP contracts create large losses in efficiency.** This disruption may discourage private investment and disrupt the delivery of infrastructure and services. From 1991 to 2015, PPP projects with $41.6 billion in initial committed investment were cancelled, affecting 6.3% of all committed PPP investment in developing Asia. Project survival is more assured with socioeconomic stability, government support through subsidies and guarantees, and strategies for proper planning, preparation, and implementation.

■ **Governance remains a stumbling block.** In its *Global Competitiveness Report, 2016–2017*, the World Economic Forum found developing Asia scoring low on the quality of its legal and institutional environment. According to businesses in the region, the most pressing issues were lapses in law and order, governmental inefficiency, corruption, and instability.

■ **Institutional structures and capacity are lacking.** More than half of the economies in developing Asia lack dedicated PPP units. The World Bank reports a high positive correlation between efficient national PPP units and successful PPP programs.

■ **PPP laws and policies are inadequate.** Hindering the whole PPP process are legal gaps, incoherent policies, redundant processes, and laws and regulations that discriminate or change unpredictably. These problems confuse and discourage investors. Robust regulatory and market institutions are important starting points for the development of successful PPP programs. Further, ratings agencies consider the adequacy of the national legal framework when rating a country's investment potential and thereby determining how attractive it is to investors.

■ **Country and sovereign risks hamper PPP financing.** Infrastructure investors are concerned about the creditworthiness of PPP projects, so they are less likely to be implemented where country and sovereign risks are high. In developing Asia, 59% of economies are unrated and would therefore be considered risky by international lenders. Another 26% are rated below investment grade, leaving only 15% at or above investment grade.

Financing public–private partnership

■ **The success of PPP depends on the optimal allocation of risk.** Project finance for infrastructure extends beyond construction and well into the useful life of the asset. It depends entirely on cash flow generated by the project through user charges or revenues paid by the government. By allocating risk to the party best able to manage it, project finance aligns private profit incentive with the public interest. This makes project finance the preferred financing and governance structure for successful PPP.

■ **The main sources of project finance are equity and debt.** The choice of financing method depends on project requirements and risks, the amount of capital available for direct investment as equity, and the quality of the financing consortium. Debt is the largest component of PPP financing, commonly more in the form of bank loans than bonds. Bonds are more desirable, though, as they allow for long-term financing. More financing can become available for infrastructure PPPs if bond issues allow access to abundant institutional savings, but this requires that project risks be appropriately mitigated.

■ **The infrastructure financing gap is essentially a risk gap.** The large infrastructure gap in Asia coexists with a substantial pool of long-term savings that can be mobilized if offered the appropriate balance of risk and return. Credit enhancement mechanisms can mitigate certain risks from PPPs to make them more attractive to a wider range of capital providers. These instruments include partial credit or revenue guarantees, off-take guarantees, subordinated debt, pooling and tranching, and infrastructure debt or equity funds. Multilateral development banks can do much more to promote credit-enhancement products, unlock potential in private capital markets around the world, and bridge the risk gap.

Toward better-performing partnership

■ **PPP success depends on the Three Ps: Project, Partner, and Process.** Projects considered for selection must stand to benefit from the strengths of PPP, be pursued by partners possessing complementary abilities, and adhere to a process that reinforces strengths and mitigates risks toward ensuring that all stakeholders enjoy their intended benefits.

» **Implement PPP only if the project is suitable.** Not all projects can be implemented through PPP, nor are all projects best implemented through PPP. Key features must exist for a project to be appropriate for PPP. A suitable project should provide net social benefit to all stakeholders. It should have scope for innovation and real efficiency gains in service delivery, as well as performance indicators that can be stipulated in the contract, readily measured, and rectified as needed. A project should be ring-fenced to manage risk effectively, uphold service provider accountability, and ensure viability.

» **Engage only qualified private partners.** A qualified partner should possess, in addition to traditional skills connected with construction, operation, and technology, higher-level skills in contracting, finance, and good corporate governance. Prospective partners should have access to private finance through banks and capital markets. A winning partner should emerge from a competitive process. Because the PPP approach is predicated on the optimal allocation of risk, prospective private partners should be sufficiently large, experienced, and reputable to bear risk credibly and reliably.

» **Institute the right process.** Governments should ensure a level playing field to encourage competitive private participation. An effective regulatory process must ensure that contracts are effective, binding, and enforceable with regard to technical, safety, and economic safeguards. Public institutions must monitor PPPs vigilantly to ensure that performance targets are met and risks appropriately allocated to the party best suited to manage them. PPPs to procure infrastructure should not be pursued as an easy way of financing off budget. Fiscal rules must be established to maintain sound and stable fiscal management. Putting together successful PPPs requires a dedicated unit able to help design effective contracts and serve as the intermediary between the government and the market. Appropriate mechanisms to provide guarantees, manage contingent liabilities, and resolve disputes as appropriate through negotiation, mediation, or arbitration can help bridge the last mile between prudent private investment and durable public benefit.

■ **PPP can be an innovative tool to meet Asia's infrastructure needs.** In sum, a suitable project, pursued with qualified private partners, and overseen through the right processes is the surest combination for the efficient and effective delivery through PPP of public infrastructure and the services it enables.

GDP growth rate and inflation, % per year

	Growth rate of GDP					Inflation				
	2016	2017		2018		2016	2017		2018	
		ADO 2017	Update	ADO 2017	Update		ADO 2017	Update	ADO 2017	Update
Central Asia	**2.2**	**3.1**	**3.3**	**3.5**	**3.9**	**11.0**	**7.8**	**8.9**	**7.3**	**7.8**
Armenia	0.2	2.2	3.8	2.5	3.0	−1.4	1.2	1.2	1.8	1.8
Azerbaijan	−3.8	−1.1	−1.3	1.2	1.0	12.4	9.0	14.0	8.0	10.0
Georgia	2.7	3.8	4.2	4.5	4.5	2.1	4.2	5.7	4.5	4.0
Kazakhstan	1.1	2.4	2.7	2.2	3.0	14.6	8.0	8.0	7.0	7.0
Kyrgyz Republic	3.8	3.0	4.0	3.5	4.0	0.4	5.0	3.5	4.0	5.0
Tajikistan	6.9	4.8	5.0	5.5	5.5	6.1	8.0	8.0	7.0	7.5
Turkmenistan	6.2	6.5	6.5	7.0	6.5	6.0	6.0	5.7	6.0	5.5
Uzbekistan	7.8	7.0	6.8	7.3	7.5	8.0	9.5	11.5	10.0	12.0
East Asia	**6.0**	**5.8**	**6.0**	**5.6**	**5.8**	**1.9**	**2.3**	**1.7**	**2.6**	**2.3**
China, People's Rep. of	6.7	6.5	6.7	6.2	6.4	2.0	2.4	1.7	2.8	2.4
Hong Kong, China	2.0	2.0	3.6	2.1	3.2	2.4	2.0	1.7	2.1	1.8
Korea, Rep. of	2.8	2.5	2.8	2.7	2.8	1.0	1.7	1.8	1.8	1.9
Mongolia	1.0	2.5	4.0	2.0	3.0	1.1	3.5	3.0	3.9	3.4
Taipei,China	1.5	1.8	2.0	2.2	2.2	1.4	1.3	1.1	1.2	1.2
South Asia	**6.7**	**7.0**	**6.7**	**7.2**	**7.0**	**4.5**	**5.2**	**4.2**	**5.4**	**4.7**
Afghanistan	2.0	2.5	2.5	3.0	3.0	4.4	5.5	5.5	5.8	5.8
Bangladesh	7.1	6.9	7.2	6.9	6.9	5.9	6.1	5.4	6.3	6.0
Bhutan	6.4	8.2	6.9	9.9	8.0	3.3	4.9	4.3	5.4	5.4
India	7.1	7.4	7.0	7.6	7.4	4.5	5.2	4.0	5.4	4.6
Maldives	3.4	3.8	4.2	4.1	4.4	0.5	2.1	3.1	2.3	2.8
Nepal	0.0	5.6	6.9	5.4	4.7	9.9	6.0	4.5	6.5	6.5
Pakistan	4.5	5.2	5.3	5.5	5.5	2.9	4.0	4.2	4.8	4.8
Sri Lanka	4.4	5.0	4.5	5.0	5.0	4.0	6.0	7.0	6.0	4.0
Southeast Asia	**4.6**	**4.8**	**5.0**	**5.0**	**5.1**	**2.1**	**3.3**	**3.1**	**3.5**	**3.1**
Brunei Darussalam	−2.5	1.0	0.0	2.5	1.0	−0.7	0.1	−0.3	0.1	0.1
Cambodia	7.0	7.1	7.1	7.1	7.1	3.0	3.4	3.0	3.5	3.2
Indonesia	5.0	5.1	5.1	5.3	5.3	3.5	4.3	4.0	4.5	3.7
Lao People's Dem. Rep.	6.8	6.9	6.9	7.0	7.0	1.6	2.5	1.5	3.0	1.5
Malaysia	4.2	4.4	5.4	4.6	5.4	2.1	3.3	3.7	2.7	2.7
Myanmar	5.9	7.7	7.7	8.0	8.0	6.8	7.0	7.0	7.5	7.5
Philippines	6.9	6.4	6.5	6.6	6.7	1.8	3.5	3.2	3.7	3.5
Singapore	2.0	2.2	2.7	2.3	2.7	−0.5	1.0	1.0	1.5	1.5
Thailand	3.2	3.5	3.5	3.6	3.6	0.2	1.8	0.7	2.0	1.5
Viet Nam	6.2	6.5	6.3	6.7	6.5	2.7	4.0	4.5	5.0	5.5
The Pacific	**2.4**	**2.9**	**2.9**	**3.3**	**3.2**	**4.5**	**5.2**	**5.3**	**5.4**	**5.3**
Cook Islands	8.8	5.0	5.0	5.0	5.0	−0.1	0.5	−0.1	1.2	0.5
Fiji	0.4	3.5	3.6	4.0	3.9	3.9	2.5	3.5	2.5	2.5
Kiribati	1.8	2.0	2.0	1.5	2.3	0.7	2.0	2.0	2.0	2.0
Marshall Islands	1.9	4.0	4.0	2.5	2.5	−1.5	1.5	0.5	1.5	1.0
Micronesia, Fed. States of	−0.1	2.5	2.0	2.5	2.0	−1.0	1.5	1.5	2.0	2.0
Nauru	10.4	4.3	4.0	−4.5	−4.0	8.2	5.7	6.0	1.8	2.0
Palau	1.9	3.0	0.5	5.5	3.5	−1.3	1.5	1.5	2.0	2.0
Papua New Guinea	2.0	2.5	2.5	2.8	2.8	6.7	7.5	7.5	7.5	7.5
Samoa	7.1	2.0	3.0	1.5	1.0	0.1	2.0	1.4	2.0	2.0
Solomon Islands	3.2	3.0	3.0	2.8	3.0	1.1	1.8	0.5	2.2	1.0
Timor-Leste	5.4	4.0	4.0	6.0	6.0	−1.4	1.2	1.2	3.0	3.0
Tonga	3.1	2.6	2.8	2.6	3.5	2.5	2.5	2.5	2.5	2.5
Tuvalu	4.0	3.0	3.2	3.0	3.0	3.5	2.0	2.9	2.0	2.5
Vanuatu	4.0	4.3	4.5	3.8	4.0	0.8	2.4	2.8	2.6	3.3
Developing Asia	**5.8**	**5.7**	**5.9**	**5.7**	**5.8**	**2.5**	**3.0**	**2.4**	**3.2**	**2.9**
Developing Asia excluding the NIEs	**6.3**	**6.3**	**6.4**	**6.2**	**6.3**	**2.7**	**3.2**	**2.5**	**3.5**	**3.1**

Note: The newly industrialized economies (NIEs) are the Republic of Korea, Singapore, Taipei,China, and Hong Kong, China.

1

CONFIDENT RESURGENCE IN DEVELOPING ASIA

Confident resurgence in developing Asia

The growth outlook for developing Asia over the short term is remarkably healthy. This *Update* expects slightly higher growth than forecast in *Asian Development Outlook* (*ADO 2017*) in April. Gross domestic product (GDP) in the region is expected to grow by 5.9% 2017 and 5.8% in 2018, slightly up from 5.8% in 2016 (Figure 1.0.1). A synchronized export recovery has emerged from solid recovery in the major industrial economies, including a small second-quarter rebound in the United States, along with strong investment growth in the region. Developing Asia is expected to maintain its growth momentum into 2018 as strong trade reinforces gains from domestic demand. The key growth drivers remain healthy consumer demand amid rising incomes and spillover from global commodity price increases in the past year, though these are likely to dissipate.

Risks to the outlook are more contained and broadly balanced than in April. Sustained improvements in global trade and stable oil prices around current levels provide upside potential for the region. However, any suddenly unannounced changes to US monetary policy could induce capital outflows from developing Asia. Possible tax cuts and higher infrastructure spending in the US would, if implemented, help developing Asia, but political stalemate over budget details could unsettle business plans. Geopolitical and weather-related disasters pose unlikely but significant downside risks, as they could abruptly interrupt growth momentum in trade, particularly in the high-tech manufactures that led the recent trade surge and depend heavily on global production chains.

Most of Asia's economies are currently in an upswing stage of their business cycle, but with variation across the region. A notable norm is that the pace of the upswing is slower than the average in the past. Knowing where each economy is in the business cycle can inform policy makers on the desirability of policy stimulus. Moreover, despite the slower pace of the upswing, business sentiment across major trading regions seems to be optimistic.

1.0.1 GDP growth outlook for developing Asia and the industrial economies

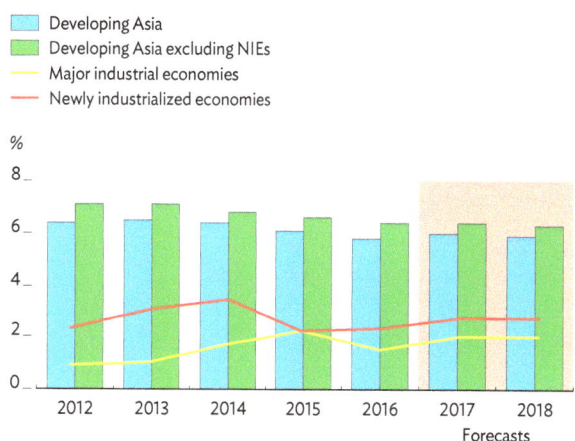

Note: The major industrial economies are the United States, the euro area, and Japan. The newly industrialized economies (NIEs) are the Republic of Korea, Singapore, Taipei,China, and Hong Kong, China.
Source: *Asian Development Outlook* database.

This chapter was written by Valerie Mercer-Blackman, Donghyun Park, Arief Ramayandi, Madhavi Pundit, Shu Tian, Benno Ferrarini, Shiela Camingue-Romance, Cindy Castillejos-Petalcorin, Marthe Hinojales, Nedelyn Magtibay-Ramos, Pilipinas Quising, and Dennis Sorino of the Economic Research and Regional Cooperation Department, ADB, Manila.

Trade strength lifts regional prospects

Developing Asia is projected to grow by 5.9% this year and 5.8% in 2018, as headwinds that stymied global activity last year are likely to dissipate this year (Figure 1.1.1). Excluding the region's newly industrialized economies (NIEs), growth should reach 6.4% in 2017 and 6.3% in 2018. Helping the acceleration in growth is the continued implementation across the region of countercyclical policies to ease drag from external and domestic factors and, starting in the fourth quarter of 2016, the resurgence in trade to its highest value since 2011. Thanks to the favorable global trade environment, higher exports underpin the region's growth prospects for the remainder of 2017. Supporting the pickup in external demand, the outlook for the major industrial economies has improved, with the US, the euro area, and Japan collectively forecast to expand by 2.0% in 2017 and 2018, an uptick of 0.1 percentage points from *ADO 2017* forecasts for both years (Box 1.1.1).

Gathering momentum

Developing Asia is expected to perform better this year than earlier forecast in large part because growth exceeded expectations in the first half of 2017 in some of the region's larger economies (Figure 1.1.2). Projected growth in the PRC is revised up on a strong first half for consumption and continued fiscal support. Better growth prospects for Southeast Asia and solid expansion in the NIEs will further lift growth in the region. The forecast for growth in the region's second-largest economy, India, is trimmed, reflecting unexpectedly slower expansion in the first quarter of FY2017 (ending 31 March 2018). India notwithstanding, the region is expected to enjoy a growth resurgence in 2017 that is broadly based on stronger demand at home and abroad.

The higher growth forecasts for developing Asia primarily reflect unexpected momentum in export-oriented economies, especially for suppliers of semiconductors and other high-technology products (Figure 1.1.3). Forecasts for 2017 have risen for 22 of the region's 45 economies, with another 13 retaining their April projections. The significant revisions are in Central, East, and Southeast Asia. Growth forecasts for East and Southeast Asia are now revised up by 0.2 percentage points for 2017, with a similar revision for East Asia in 2018, while the Southeast Asian increment is 0.1 percentage points. Meanwhile, the

1.1.1 GDP growth forecasts for developing Asia, 2017 and 2018

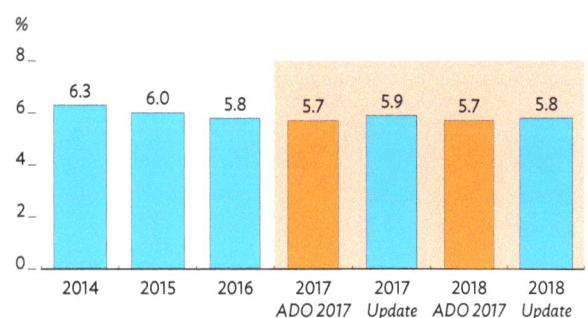

Source: Asian Development Outlook database.

1.1.2 2017 GDP forecasts in *Asian Development Outlook 2017* versus first half results

ASEAN-5 = Indonesia, Malaysia, the Philippines, Thailand, and Viet Nam, HKG = Hong Kong, China, IND = India, INO = Indonesia, KOR = Republic of Korea, MAL = Malaysia, NIE = newly industrialized economy, PHI = Philippines, PRC = People's Republic of China, SIN = Singapore, TAP = Taipei,China, THA = Thailand, VIE = Viet Nam.
Note: For India, data are for the first quarter of FY2017 (April–June).
Source: Asian Development Outlook database.

1.1.1 Clear recovery by mid-2017

Growth in the major industrial economies of the US, the euro area, and Japan is now seen to be stronger than anticipated in *ADO 2017* (box table).

GDP growth in the major industrial economies (%)

Area	2015 Actual	2016 Actual	2017 ADO 2017	2017 Update	2018 ADO 2017	2018 Update
Major industrial economies	2.3	1.5	1.9	2.0	1.9	2.0
United States	2.9	1.5	2.4	2.2	2.4	2.4
Euro area	1.9	1.7	1.6	2.0	1.6	1.8
Japan	1.1	1.0	1.0	1.5	0.9	1.1

ADO = Asian Development Outlook.

Notes: Average growth rates are weighted by gross national income, Atlas method. More details in Table A1.1 on page 36.

Sources: US Department of Commerce, Bureau of Economic Analysis, http://www.bea.gov; Eurostat, http://ec.europa.eu/eurostat; Economic and Social Research Institute of Japan, http://www.esri.cao.go.jp; Consensus Forecasts; Bloomberg; CEIC Data Company; Haver; World Bank, Global Commodity Markets, http://www.worldbank.org; ADB estimates.

GDP in the US expanded by a seasonally adjusted annualized rate (saar) of only 1.2% in the first quarter, revised down from the 1.4% reported earlier in the year because of technical revisions to the GDP series. An unusually warm winter having trimmed first-quarter expansion, US growth rebounded in the second quarter to 3.0% saar. All domestic demand components picked up in the second quarter, most notably government consumption, which had suffered a slow start in the protracted transition to a new administration. Consumer confidence and retail sales also improved steadily in the first half of 2017, while fixed investment recorded strong growth at an average of 5.9% saar. Unemployment remains low, and labor market improvement is evident in a 2.6% rise in average weekly earnings in the first 8 months of 2017.

Headline inflation nevertheless continued to slow, reaching in July a 12-month rate of 1.6% as core inflation fell to 2.0%. These numbers led the US Federal Reserve to raise its federal funds rate more gradually than earlier anticipated. Nonetheless, as the labor market continues to strengthen, the Fed is expected to proceed with its normalization of monetary policy.

Although the growth rebound is expected to continue, surprisingly slow growth in first half prompts a downward revision to the 2017 growth forecast for the US from 2.4% to 2.2%. The forecast for 2018 remains at 2.4%.

The euro area sustained its growth momentum in the second quarter of 2017 after a strong first quarter. The region grew by 2.6% saar on improvements both domestic and external. Expansion in the region finds broad support. Industrial production expanded by 0.3% in the second quarter after near stagnation in the first, and despite a dip in June. Businesses appear more optimistic thanks to higher new orders and robust job growth. The European Central Bank left its rates unchanged at its July meeting. Inflation in the year to date stood at 1.6% to July, not much below the central bank's target of 2.0%, and recent movement in core inflation suggests that price pressures may be resurfacing.

Reflecting positive developments in recent months, the forecast for growth this year is revised up to 2.0% from 1.6% in April. Investment has benefitted from a calming of political uncertainty that earlier in 2017 had firms holding off on investment decisions.

Japan has seen economic growth exceed expectations. The economy expanded for a sixth consecutive quarter, recording its fastest growth in over 2 years in the second quarter, at 2.5% saar. While business investment has risen occasionally in recent quarters, an unexpected boost to growth came from private consumption, which surged by 3.4% in the second quarter as consumers bought more durable goods. Robust consumption comes against a backdrop of falling unemployment, which remained at a low of 2.8% in July. Government fiscal stimulus on top of a rise in spending for the 2020 Tokyo Olympics further supported growth. Exports and imports alike seem to be increasing, but imports at a much faster clip, by 5.7% in the second quarter.

With wage and price pressures contained, inflation remained low at 0.4% in July. In its July 2017 meeting, the Bank of Japan stuck to its expansionary monetary policy with the aim of achieving stable consumer price index inflation above 2%. With output growth in the first half of 2017 higher than expected and indications of resilient domestic demand in the coming quarters, the growth forecast for Japan is revised up to 1.5% in 2017, moderating to 1.1% in 2018.

forecasts for South Asia are downgraded by 0.3 percentage points for 2017 and 0.2 points for 2018. The forecasts are unchanged for the Pacific in 2017 but slightly down for next year (Figure 1.1.4).

East Asia is now expected to expand by 6.0% in 2017, up from April largely in tandem with a higher forecast for the PRC, the region's principal growth driver. Developments in this important economy are discussed in more detail below. Growth is expected to remain elevated even with weather-related disruptions, slowing investment, and a squeeze on demand from government efforts to drive down debt. The 0.2 percentage point upgrade to projected PRC growth in 2017 and 2018 bodes well for economies with strong trade links to the PRC, particularly exporters of primary products such as Mongolia. The growth forecast for the Republic of Korea is also raised largely on higher global demand but on a fiscal spending jolt as well from a $9.85 billion supplementary budget approved in July. Taipei,China and Hong Kong, China are also expected to perform well this year and next as external demand remains strong, with growth in Hong Kong, China much higher this year on a stellar first half.

Southeast Asia is now expected to grow by 5.0% after 3 years of respectable but lackluster growth, with three of the subregion's ten economies now forecast to outperform their earlier projections and only two forecast to underperform. Growth projections have been raised for Malaysia, the Philippines, and Singapore on surprisingly strong performances in the first half with broad revisions for domestic and external demand. Malaysia surged in the first half thanks to a notable expansion in private consumption and investment and a huge rebound in exports. Singapore gained steam as rising shipments of electronics buoyed manufacturing, a key driver of growth, and rising business confidence boosted services. The upgrade for the Philippines reflects stronger exports, rising remittances, higher investments, and continued credit expansion.

Growth projections are retained for Indonesia and Thailand as first-half performances met earlier forecasts. Indonesia is expected to see higher investment supported by additional public investment spending, an improving investment climate, and a continuation of the positive trend for exports in the first half. Thailand will build on a solid recovery in agriculture and higher electronics exports in the first half of the year to maintain growth as forecast in April. Similarly, growth forecasts for Cambodia, the Lao People's Democratic Republic (Lao PDR), and Myanmar are unchanged from April, reflecting solid private consumption growth in Cambodia, robust public and foreign investment in the Lao PDR and Myanmar, and rising tourism in Cambodia and Myanmar. Meanwhile, the projection is trimmed for Brunei Darussalam on account of the continued slump in global demand for oil and gas, and for Viet Nam for weak mining and quarrying output. The subregion is expected to grow faster in 2018 as the slower growth in Brunei Darussalam and Viet Nam will be more than offset by stronger expansion in Malaysia, the Philippines, and Singapore, and as growth in the remaining five economies in the subregion meets the April forecasts.

Projected growth is higher for Central Asia as the subregion's larger economies are set to benefit from stable oil prices, improving prospects in the Russian Federation, and rising remittances.

1.1.3 Exports growth, selected developing Asian economies

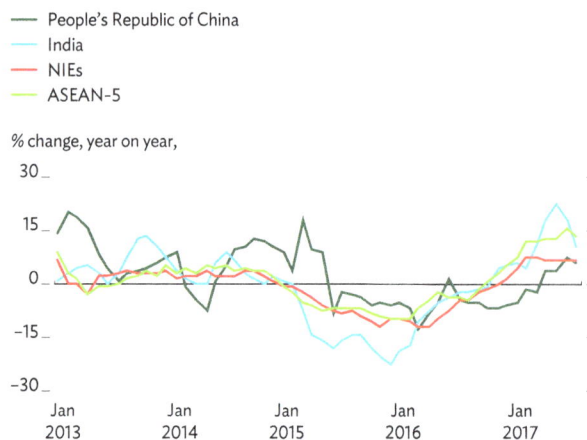

— People's Republic of China
— India
— NIEs
— ASEAN-5

% change, year on year,

ASEAN-5 = Indonesia, Malaysia, the Philippines, Thailand, and Viet Nam, NIEs = Republic of Korea, Singapore, Taipei,China, and Hong Kong, China.
Source: Haver Analytics (accessed 26 August 2017).

1.1.4 GDP growth by subregion

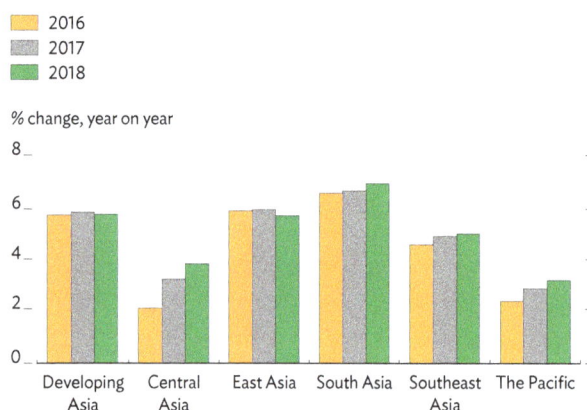

2016
2017
2018

% change, year on year

Source: Asian Development Outlook database.

Growth is now projected at 3.3% in 2017 and 3.9% in 2018, with higher growth in five of the larger economies, the largest increments being in the Kyrgyz Republic at 1.0 percentage point and in Georgia at 0.4 percentage points. Georgia has benefitted from higher infrastructure spending that is expected to continue through 2018, while the Kyrgyz Republic will see gold production rise this year. Growth in the Kyrgyz Republic is accelerating as well on improved remittances from Kazakhstan and the Russian Federation, as in the subregion's two other remittance-receiving economies: Armenia and Tajikistan. Greater expansion in mining and manufacturing and firmer commodity prices raise the growth projection for Kazakhstan, the subregion's largest economy. However, Central Asia's three other oil-producing economies—Azerbaijan, Uzbekistan, and Turkmenistan—will continue to feel the effects of lackluster oil prices despite prices remaining mostly stable.

South Asia is the only subregion with lower aggregate growth forecasts, down by 0.3 percentage points for 2017 and by 0.7 percentage points for 2018, undercut by reduced projections for India and Sri Lanka. The downgraded forecast for India reflects an unexpectedly weak first quarter in FY2017, in which growth was unsettled in the run-up to the July implementation of a goods and services tax while the economy was still recovering from a surprise demonetization last November. Weaker manufacturing and softer credit growth add to the tepid outlook for 2017. Sri Lanka has been weighed down by flooding in May and prolonged drought, which are expected to delay the recovery in agriculture and impair domestic trade, prompting a less favorable growth forecast for 2017. In Bhutan, anticipated negative spillover from India's new goods and services tax on trade and government revenue argue for a similar downward adjustment.

Better crop production and a good monsoon helped to revive agriculture in Bangladesh, Nepal, and Pakistan, while higher tourist arrivals stimulated activity in Maldives. Growth in these economies should accelerate by 0.1–1.3 percentage points in 2017 on these factors and a pickup in investment with faster implementation of key infrastructure projects in Bangladesh, reconstruction in Nepal after its 2015 earthquake, higher tourism infrastructure construction in Maldives, and the implementation of infrastructure projects under an economic corridor program linking Pakistan to the PRC.

Growth forecasts for the Pacific are retained for 2017 but slightly downgraded for 2018 with unchanged outlooks for the largest Pacific economies, Papua New Guinea and Timor-Leste. Papua New Guinea can expect to see mining and agriculture recover from disruption caused by weather and operational issues in recent years. However, as large investments in mining will likely be delayed until the third or fourth quarter of 2018, growth forecasts are retained. The growth projection for Timor-Leste is also unchanged as higher government spending on wages and purchases of goods and services will be offset by a planned slowdown in capital expenditure.

Updates to prospects for some of the smaller economies are mixed. The growth forecast is down for the Federated States of Micronesia and more so for Palau on account of investment bottlenecks and lower tourist arrivals, as well as in Nauru as prices for phosphate exports drop.

Projections for Fiji and Samoa are raised on strong agriculture output, and an improved outlook for Tonga reflects higher remittances and earnings from tourism and exports. Some domestic drags on Pacific economies are expected to persist into 2018, pulling down the subregional growth forecast slightly to 3.2%.

Sustained pickup in demand

Developing Asia is projected to see a sustained rise in domestic activity. Of the 11 economies in the region with quarterly data, 7 posted expansion in the first half of 2017 above the full-year forecast in *ADO 2017* (Figure 1.1.2 above), an improvement from only 5 last year. In 2016, these 11 economies provided 95% of developing Asia's aggregate GDP. NIEs recorded the largest rebounds, followed by modest increases in some Southeast Asian economies.

Among the 11 economies with demand-side data, 8 recorded private consumption as their dominant source of growth. In the Republic of Korea, the pickup came largely from fixed investment, while in Singapore the buildup of inventories and exports supported growth. Taipei,China is the only economy where consumption and investment contributed equally to growth in the first half (Figure 1.1.5). The pickup in consumption came mainly from higher wages in the PRC and in Hong Kong, China (in the latter, from a tighter labor market); expanding employment and rising incomes in Malaysia, the Philippines, and Viet Nam; and recovery in agriculture and a subsidized loan program in Thailand. By contrast, consumption was evidently squeezed in Singapore as concerns lingered over the likely impact of higher interest rates on heavily indebted households.

Investment in almost all the 11 selected economies contributed significantly to growth, though to vastly varying degrees. Fixed investment rose in most, while stocking by firms in anticipation of higher domestic activity later in the year picked up more in Singapore and Thailand. In three of the nine economies with sector aggregation, a large portion of investment came from the private sector. Housing-related construction raised fixed investment in Hong Kong, China, while investment in machinery and equipment, mostly for semiconductor manufacturing, led the recovery in the Republic of Korea and Malaysia. Higher imports of raw materials and capital goods helped to boost investment in most of the larger economies, largely in response to activity in the semiconductor supply chain in recent months. Many East and Southeast Asian economies, including the PRC, Malaysia, the Philippines, Singapore, Thailand, Viet Nam, and Taipei,China, have sizable electronics sectors. Some of the pickup is in preparation for the planned launches of new mobile phone models later in the year, but it is not clear how much. Overall, recent growth in total investment remains below the 10-year average from 2000 to 2010 in some economies, but it exceeds the average in Indonesia, Malaysia, the Philippines, and, though just slightly, Singapore (Figure 1.1.6).

1.1.5 Demand-side contributions to growth, selected economies

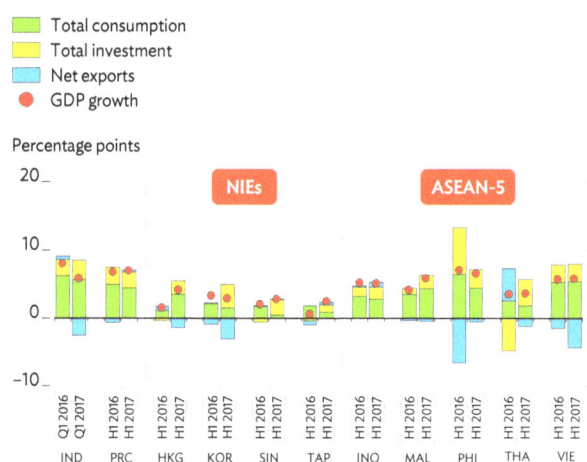

ASEAN-5 = Indonesia, Malaysia, the Philippines, Thailand, and Viet Nam, H = half, HKG = Hong Kong, China, IND = India, INO = Indonesia, KOR = Republic of Korea, MAL = Malaysia, NIE = newly industrialized economy, PHI = Philippines, PRC = People's Republic of China, Q = quarter, SIN = Singapore, TAP = Taipei,China, THA = Thailand, VIE = Viet Nam.
Note: For India, data are for the first quarter of FY2017 (April–June). For the PRC, data on private consumption also cover government consumption.
Source: Haver Analytics; CEIC Data Company (accessed 26 August 2017).

1.1.6 Total investment, % of GDP in selected economies in developing Asia

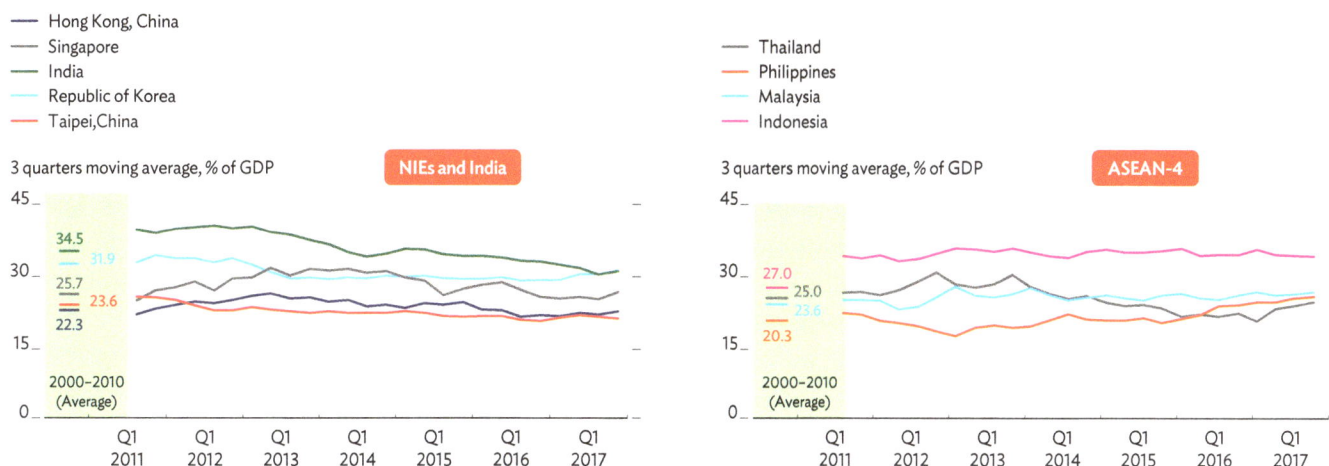

— Hong Kong, China
— Singapore
— India
— Republic of Korea
— Taipei,China

— Thailand
— Philippines
— Malaysia
— Indonesia

3 quarters moving average, % of GDP   **NIEs and India**

```
45
        34.5
        31.9
30      25.7
        23.6
        22.3
15
        2000–2010
        (Average)
0
          Q1    Q1    Q1    Q1    Q1    Q1    Q1
         2011  2012  2013  2014  2015  2016  2017
```

3 quarters moving average, % of GDP   **ASEAN-4**

```
45
        27.0
30              25.0
                23.6
        20.3
15
        2000–2010
        (Average)
0
          Q1    Q1    Q1    Q1    Q1    Q1    Q1
         2011  2012  2013  2014  2015  2016  2017
```

Q = quarter.
Sources: Haver Analytics (accessed 13 September 2017); ADB estimates.

Buoyed by accommodative fiscal and monetary policies and the bullish outlook for the region, consumer confidence returned to optimistic territory in most economies in the first 7 months of 2017, foretelling stronger private consumption in the near term (Figure 1.1.7). It has consistently trended upward in the PRC, Indonesia, and the Philippines as consumers have become ever more optimistic about the economy, wages, and the labor market. Though the index slid a bit in Indonesia from June to August 2017, largely on concerns about the effect on prices of a rollback of government energy subsidies, the index reached 125.9 in May, its highest since 2000s. The steady increase in the PRC is worth noting as the index reached in July its highest since June 2013. The Republic of Korea saw huge improvements as the index started low then quickly reversed in the second quarter. It jumped to a 3-year high in the Republic of Korea following a presidential election in May 2017, before sliding in July and August as sentiment was buffeted by worries about the government's latest measures to cool housing debt and flaring tensions on the peninsula.

Elsewhere, the pickup has been relatively modest. Confidence improved in Malaysia, Thailand, and Taipei,China, albeit falling short of the threshold of optimism. In January, confidence in Taipei,China had fallen to its lowest in 4 years amid stagnation in the domestic economy. Confidence has since picked up thanks to a strong first half and a booming stock market that saw prices breach the 10,000 mark in mid-May for the first time in 17 years and continued to rise on strong foreign institutional buying of highly capitalized high-tech stocks. Likewise, a more upbeat outlook for the economy in Malaysia helped to raise confidence, with manufacturing rising alongside exports, but the index remained below 100 on lingering concerns about the rising cost of living and high household debt. Consumer sentiment in Hong Kong, China lagged its neighbors, reflecting apprehension about the economy this year, but still improved compared with the same period in 2016.

1.1.7 Consumer confidence and expectations, selected economies in developing Asia

People's Republic of China
Hong Kong, China
Republic of Korea
Taipei,China

Indonesia
Malaysia
Thailand
Philippines

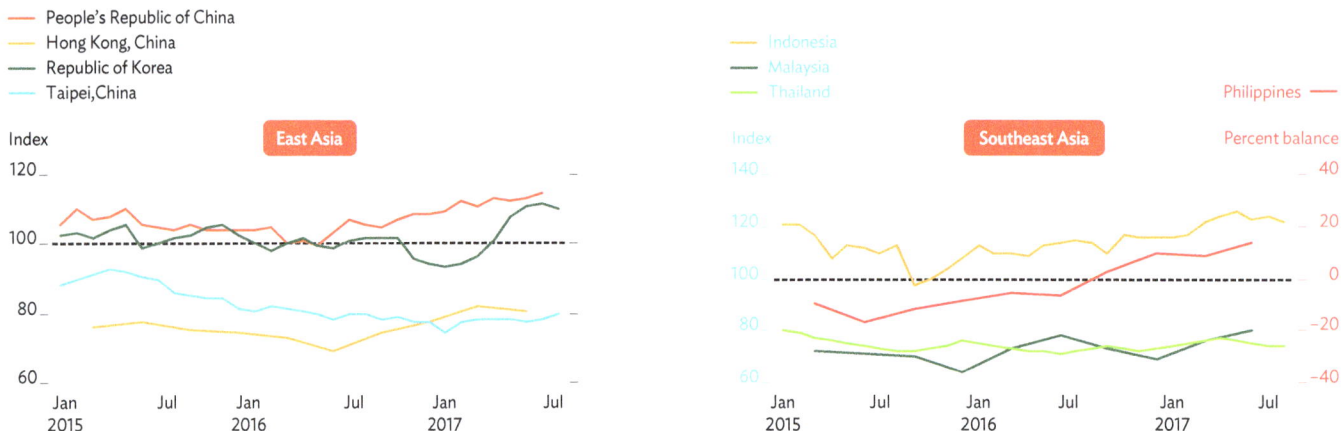

Notes: Data for Malaysia, the Philippines, and Hong Kong, China are quarterly. A rating above 100 indicates rising optimism, and a score below 100 means deepening pessimism. Data for Hong Kong, China use January 2000 as the base year. For the Philippines, the index refers to consumer expectations, computed as the percentage of households that expressed a favorable view less the percentage that expressed an unfavorable view.
Source: Haver Analytics (accessed 26 August 2017).

1.1.8 Retail sales, selected economies in developing Asia

People's Republic of China
Hong Kong, China
Republic of Korea
Taipei,China

Indonesia
Malaysia
Singapore
Thailand
Viet Nam

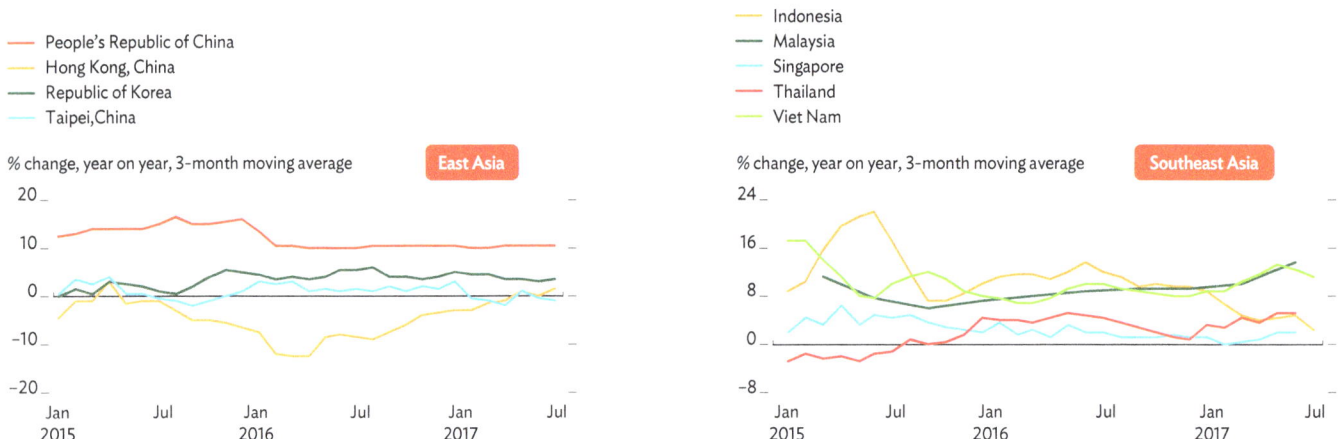

Note: Data for Malaysia refer to quarterly percentage change year on year.
Source: Haver Analytics (accessed 26 August 2017).

Retail sales were mixed but remained broadly positive (Figure 1.1.8), supported by rising consumer confidence. Retail sales in the PRC remained strong, rising by 10% from January to July 2017 on higher spending on automobiles, clothing, and appliances. They rose steadily in Hong Kong, China as tourist arrivals from the PRC rebounded, and in Malaysia as rising incomes and government income-support measures helped to boost household spending. Meanwhile, retail sales picked up in Singapore and Thailand largely on higher motor vehicle sales in both economies, though growth compared unfavorably to last year in Singapore because of weaker sales in some retail segments in February.

Retail sales started strong in Indonesia and Taipei,China but slowed as the year progressed with lower purchases of motor vehicles, electronic products, and household equipment in Indonesia and of food and beverages,

1.1.9 Industrial production, selected economies in developing Asia

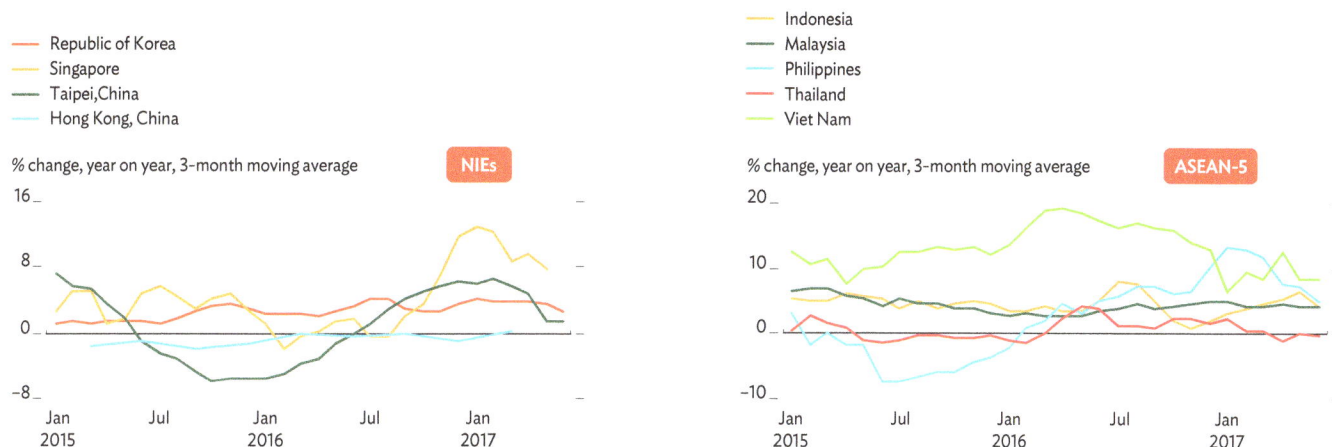

ASEAN-5 = Indonesia, Malaysia, the Philippines, Thailand, and Viet Nam, HKG = Hong Kong, China, INO = Indonesia, KOR = Republic of Korea, MAL = Malaysia, NIE = newly industrialized economy (Republic of Korea, Singapore, Taipei,China, and Hong Kong, China), PHI = Philippines, SIN = Singapore, TAP = Taipei,China, THA = Thailand, VIE = Viet Nam.
Note: Data for Malaysia refer to quarterly percentage change year on year.
Sources: CEIC Data Company; Haver Analytics (both accessed 26 August 2017).

clothing, and household appliances in Taipei,China. Household appliances and general merchandise in Taipei,China were hit by lower household spending, while the hospitality industry suffered from lower tourist arrivals from the PRC. In Indonesia, automobile retailers were hit by sluggish credit approvals caused by stricter conditions set by leasing companies to limit loan defaults, while electronics retailers suffered unusually lower sales at the end of Ramadan. In the past 4 years, sales of electronics sometimes grew by 30% year on year during this period.

Industrial production trends improved in the first half of 2017 over the same period last year in the NIEs but mainly held steady in Southeast Asia, except in Thailand and Viet Nam (Figure 1.1.9). Growth was particularly strong in the first half of 2017 in Singapore and Taipei,China, and above the average trend in the Republic of Korea, largely on huge increases in the production of semiconductors and other electronic products, machinery, and equipment. The semiconductor industry has enjoyed double-digit increases so far this year, with increases in every major regional market and semiconductor product category.

High growth with reform in the PRC and India

India's economic performance has been rockier so far in FY2017 (ending 31 March 2018) than in recent years as shocks from a series of reforms hit production and investment, particularly manufacturing. The forecast for GDP growth in FY2017 is revised down by 0.4 percentage points to 7.0%, though this is still one of the highest growth rates in developing Asia. The underlying growth driver, as forecast in *ADO 2017*, is consumption. On the positive side, a healthy monsoon, buoyant consumer confidence, and a strong pickup in trade bode well for FY2017. On the other hand, the introduction of a goods and services tax has significantly hit manufacturing orders. The Nikkei purchasing managers' index dipped in July to 47.9, its lowest since the global financial crisis of 2008–2009 and well into contraction territory below 50 (Figure 1.1.10). Industrial production has also been volatile, ticking up earlier in the year but then falling in the second quarter, in contrast with other major Asian economies. This possibly reflects firms' destocking and reductions in production over concerns about the goods and services tax. Still, it is possible that, with greater clarity about the tax implications for manufacturers, the outlook may improve by the end of FY2017. Consumption is expected to remain buoyant following a wage hike for government workers in 2016. Total private consumption contributed 3.6 percentage points to growth in the first quarter FY2017, while investment contributed 2.9 points.

The demonetization of about 86% of Indian currency in circulation, by value, was successfully completed despite a very short period between the announcement of the policy and its implementation. The surprise demonetization targeted off-the-books cash transactions, but the results of the exercise suggest that most were legitimate. At the end of August, the Reserve Bank of India reported that 99% of the old bills had been deposited into the banking system by the December 2016 deadline. Nevertheless, the government is convinced that a long-term benefit will be the formalization of the economy, as many small merchants were forced to open bank accounts to make the deposits necessary to redeem their old cash. A slow adjustment to the national goods and services tax temporarily disrupted firms' credit and investment plans, including many tied to small suppliers, which affected manufacturing output. Nonetheless, unexpectedly strong tax revenues reported midyear suggest that simplified administration helped improve collections. The effect of the tax on growth seems to be temporary, and it could have positive effects on long-term growth trends. Now that the tax implementation is behind them, the owners of small businesses may become more confident. Over the medium term, the government has stated its commitment to structural reform, which will help to maintain or lift potential GDP growth.

Growth in the PRC has been decelerating steadily since 2010, slowing from 6.9% in 2015 to 6.7% in 2016 as part of the long-term strategy of rebalancing growth toward domestic demand. Growth in 2017 will remain at 6.7%, an upward revision from 6.5% projected in *ADO 2017* as external demand has stimulated trade amid healthy domestic consumption.

Growth in domestic demand in the first half of 2017 was in line with *ADO 2017* projections. Consumption contributed almost 5 percentage points to growth, making it the largest contributor as net exports subtracted from growth. Consumer confidence in August is still on the positive side but not as high as in the second quarter. Still, consumption is expected to be the main growth driver as incomes rise. PRC retail trade and transport services boomed, fueling growth in services at 7.7% year on year in the first half. Industrial production growth held steady at 10.0% as growth in consumer durables compensated for lower

1.1.10 Production indicators

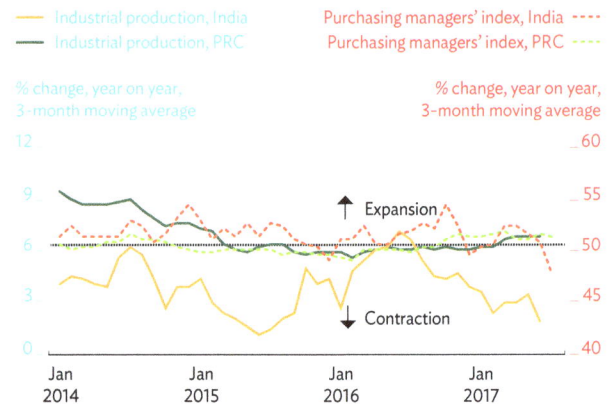

PRC = People's Republic of China.

Note: A survey reading of above 50 for the purchasing managers' index shows expansion and below 50 contraction.

Sources: CEIC Data Company; Bloomberg (both accessed 27 August 2017).

production in heavy industry. Despite pockets of labor-shedding in heavy industry, the labor market remained tight overall, even placing some upward pressure on wages.

Business confidence has improved so far in 2017, as corporate profits and the ability to service debt improved in the PRC. Investment is not expected to be as important going forward because capital-intensive heavy industries will need to shed excess capacity. Investment in consumer and service-oriented industries is growing, particularly foreign direct investment. Government spending has perked up under expansive fiscal policy. Although revenues strengthened on higher land sales, corporate profits, and external trade, expenditure by local governments on health, education, and social services was even higher.

Inflation broadly in check amid stable oil prices

Inflation remains subdued across developing Asia, with the average rate in the region anticipated to remain below its 10-year average of 3.9%. In 26 economies that publish monthly data on inflation, 19 had lower inflation in the year to date than forecast in *ADO 2017* (Figure 1.1.11). Global oil prices eased, declining from a 20-month high of $55/barrel in February 2017 to below $50/barrel in June. The average price of Brent crude oil to mid-September 2017 is just below $52/barrel, the forecast for the year and about half of the price at its last peak in June 2014. Global food prices continued to decline from June 2016 all the way to August 2017. This was despite disruption to food supply in some economies that saw their food prices rising until mid-2017 and large currency devaluations in Central Asia. Regional inflation is now forecast at 2.4% in 2017, rising to 2.9% in 2017 but still lower than the 3.0% regional average in 2014 (Figure 1.1.12). Excluding the NIEs, regional inflation is higher at 2.5% in 2017 and 3.1% in 2018 but lower than earlier projections.

The milder inflationary environment is mostly attributed to softer global commodity prices since the beginning of the year, and to country-specific measures to reduce prices.

In contrast, Central Asia will see double-digit inflation in two of its largest economies this year and next, prompting a huge upward revision for the region.

East Asia will see inflation in most of its economies decline this year. All economies except the Republic of Korea undershot expectations, and the forecast is for prices to remain low toward the end of the year. Sharp declines in food prices in the PRC and expectations of lower increases for nonfood items prompted a huge downward revision for inflation this year from the April forecast. This pulls the forecast subregional average in 2017 down to 1.7%, with a slight rise in 2018, as consumer demand rises and price deregulation continues. Weak inflationary pressures will keep prices in Mongolia and Taipei,China from rising beyond

1.1.11 Inflation forecasts in *Asian Development Outlook 2017* versus year-to-date results

░ *Asian Development Outlook 2017* forecast
○ Year-to-date 2017

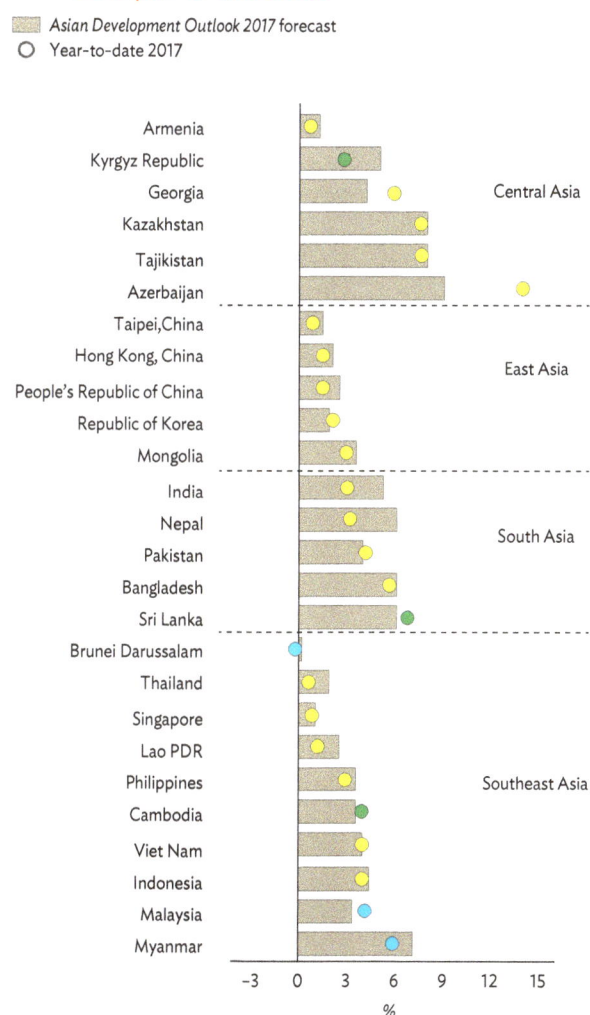

Lao PDR = Lao People's Democratic Republic.
Note: Yellow colored dots indicate data covering up to July 2017, blue to June 2017, and green to May 2017.
Source: Asian Development Outlook database.

what was forecast in April. Depressed consumer demand will keep consumer prices in check in Hong Kong, China, but the opposite trend will stoke inflation in the Republic of Korea this year and next.

Subregional inflation in South Asia is downgraded to 4.2% from 5.2% in April and to 4.7% in 2018, in both cases largely reflecting a huge downward revision in India. Inflation in India is now forecast to rise by only 4.0% in 2017, a large downgrade from April, on sharp decreases in food and other prices and on the lingering effects of demonetization. Concerns over the possible inflationary impact of the implementation of the landmark national sales tax begun on 1 July, and salary hikes for state employees later in the year that have yet to be announced will push prices in 2018 to 4.6%, but still less than forecast in April. The inflation forecast for Afghanistan is maintained, and those for Bangladesh, Bhutan, and Nepal are downgraded as price increases were suppressed by lower commodity prices, adjustments to administered prices, ample food supply, and subdued Indian inflation. Meanwhile, the forecast has been revised up for Pakistan, motivated by the expected rise in domestic activity and a revival in agricultural output this year, and for Sri Lanka because food supplies were disrupted by bad weather.

Southeast Asia will see inflation lower than earlier forecast, at 3.1% both this year and next, chiefly on subdued inflation in half of the economies in the region: Brunei Darussalam, Cambodia, Indonesia, the Lao PDR, the Philippines, and Thailand. For Indonesia, the inflation forecast for 2017 is lowered to 4.0% largely because of the delay in the planned increase in administered prices and fresh government measures to better manage food prices, with the forecast lowered further to 3.7% next year. In Thailand, the projection for 2017 is slashed on lower-than-anticipated trends in the first half, and because state price controls and subsidies will likely put a lid on price increases in the second half of the year. It is also lowered for the Philippines both this year and next on account of subdued international oil prices and augmented domestic food supplies. It is unchanged for Myanmar, though a one-time drop in food prices lowered inflation in the initial months of this year. Elsewhere, inflation forecasts are raised for Malaysia because of a one-time pickup in transport prices, for Viet Nam with planned increases for public social services fees and the minimum wage, and for Singapore because of higher transportation costs. Consumer prices are declining again in Brunei Darussalam, with pervasive deflation prompting a downward revision in the forecast for this year.

Central Asia is the only subregion in which inflation will greatly surpass the April projection. The forecast is now revised to 8.9% in 2017, up by 1.1 percentage points because of large revisions for Azerbaijan, Georgia, and Uzbekistan (the forecast is unchanged for the subregion's largest economy, Kazakhstan, but high). Tighter foreign exchange restrictions paired with expectations of further domestic currency depreciation and price deregulation have pushed inflation up in Azerbaijan, while higher government spending will continue to create inflationary pressure in Uzbekistan this year and next. A downward

1.1.12 Subregional inflation

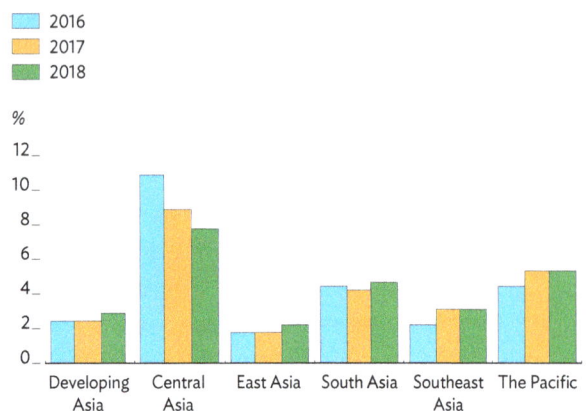

Source: *Asian Development Outlook* database.

revision for the Kyrgyz Republic largely reflects deflation in January and February and expectations of lower prices for commodities later in the year. The slightly lower forecast for Turkmenistan takes into account administrative price controls and ample supplies of consumer and industrial goods.

Average inflation in the Pacific is seen to accelerate, but only mildly, to reach 5.3% in 2017, or 0.1 percentage points higher than projected in April. This reflects significant supply disruptions in Fiji, increased economic activity in Tuvalu and Vanuatu, and expensive imports from Australia in Nauru. Soft international food and fuel prices, which brought lower-than-expected inflation in the Marshall Islands and Solomon Islands, and even deflation in the Cook Islands and Samoa, failed to lower aggregate inflation in the subregion.

Consistent with the pickup in domestic activity across the region, producer prices in almost all of the 19 economies with monthly data rose in the first 7 months of the year (Figure 1.1.13). They rose by more than half of the pace of consumer price inflation in the PRC, even as factory gate prices dropped in the period from February to July on tumbling prices for raw materials. The recent drop has prompted concerns of a likely disconnect between sluggish producer prices and improving economic growth, as it follows almost 6 years of falling factory gate prices that turned positive year on year only in September 2016. In Azerbaijan, producer prices shot up following a 16% increase in electricity tariffs and measures to deregulate other administered prices. In both Azerbaijan and Kazakhstan, pass-through from currency depreciation in 2016 seems to have played out. Except in Malaysia, producer prices picked up, though less than consumer prices, because of higher factory prices for intermediate materials, supplies and components, and finished goods. Meanwhile, producer prices declined in the Philippines, though less than they did last year, along with lower prices for basic manufactures.

As prices in the region are now rather subdued, most governments in developing Asia have maintained policy interest rates consistent with a low-inflation environment.

1.1.13 Consumer and producer price inflation, January to July 2017

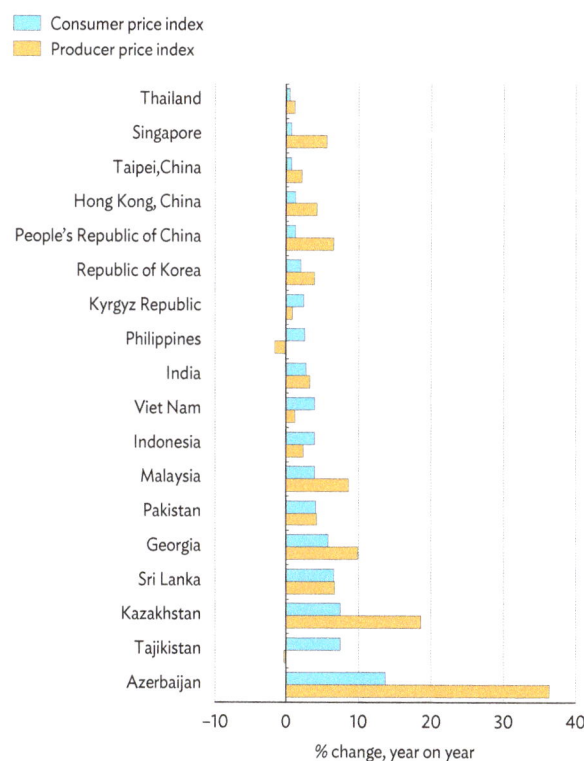

Sources: CEIC Data Company and Haver Analytics (both accessed 1 September 2017); ADB estimates.

Trade soared, slightly narrowing current account balances

External trade in developing Asia performed remarkably well in the first 5 months of 2017. Regional exports grew in value terms by 10.9%, after an equally significant drop in the previous 2 years. The turnaround started in the fourth quarter of 2016. In volume terms, exports from the 10 largest economies (which comprise 93% of developing Asia's exports) grew by 3.2% in the first half of 2017 after dropping by 2.6% in the first half of the previous year, while real import growth reached 6.9% in the first half of 2017 after falling by 2.3% in the first half of 2016. Trade improved for other regions and groups outside of Asia,

1.1.14 Change in export and import values

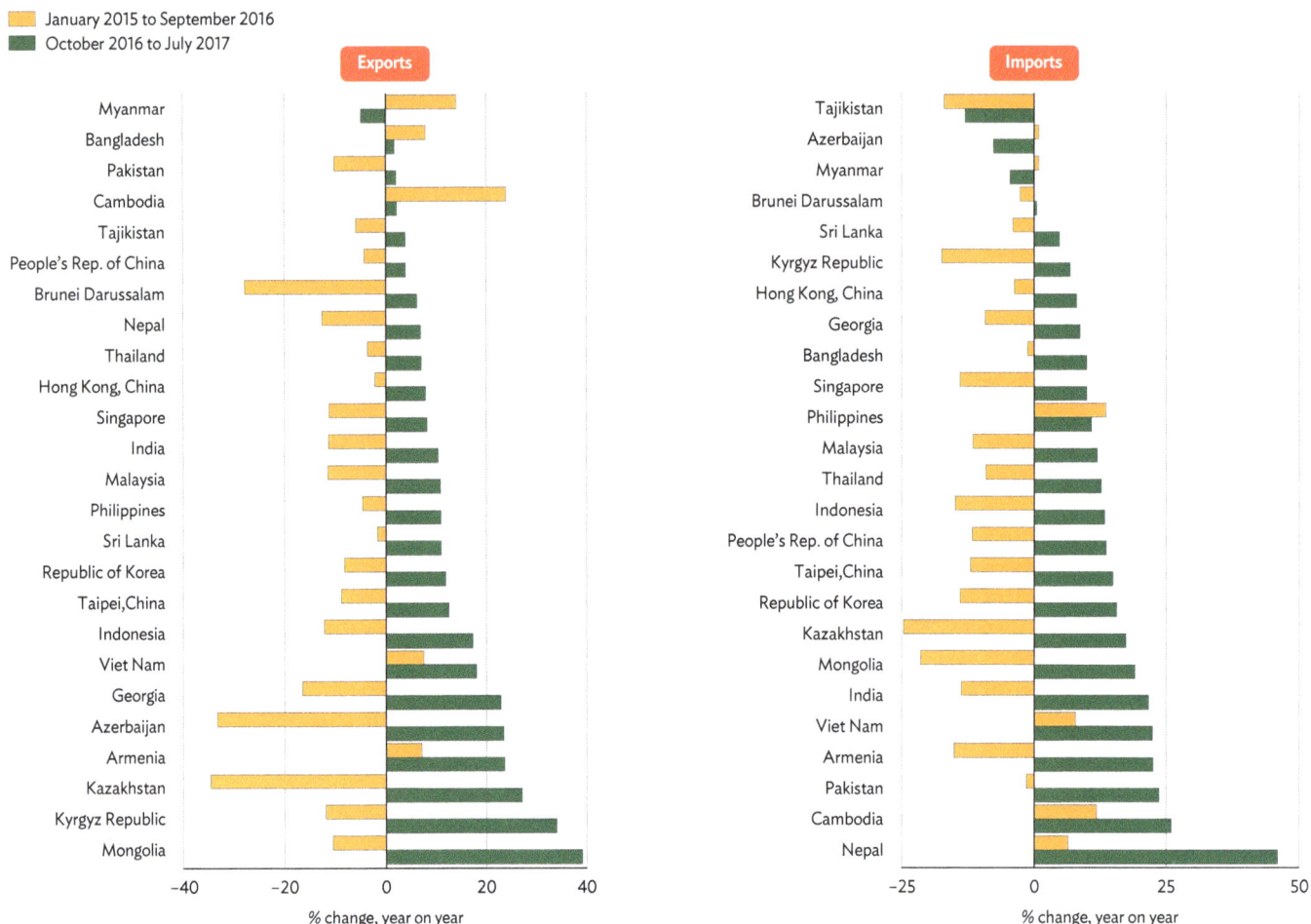

■ January 2015 to September 2016
■ October 2016 to July 2017

Exports

Myanmar
Bangladesh
Pakistan
Cambodia
Tajikistan
People's Rep. of China
Brunei Darussalam
Nepal
Thailand
Hong Kong, China
Singapore
India
Malaysia
Philippines
Sri Lanka
Republic of Korea
Taipei,China
Indonesia
Viet Nam
Georgia
Azerbaijan
Armenia
Kazakhstan
Kyrgyz Republic
Mongolia

−40   −20   0   20   40
% change, year on year

Imports

Tajikistan
Azerbaijan
Myanmar
Brunei Darussalam
Sri Lanka
Kyrgyz Republic
Hong Kong, China
Georgia
Bangladesh
Singapore
Philippines
Malaysia
Thailand
Indonesia
People's Rep. of China
Taipei,China
Republic of Korea
Kazakhstan
Mongolia
India
Viet Nam
Armenia
Pakistan
Cambodia
Nepal

−25   0   25   50
% change, year on year

Note: Data for most economies end in July 2017, except in Brunei Darussalam (which end in June), the Kyrgyz Republic (April), and Cambodia and Myanmar (May).
Sources: CEIC Data Company and Haver Analytics (both accessed 15 September 2017); ADB estimates.

particularly for the advanced economies, which receive 27% of their imports from developing Asia. With few exceptions, the trade turnaround was widespread and synchronized (Figure 1.1.14).

The trade pickup follows a notable 5-year decline in the openness indicator of developing Asia—defined as the sum of exports and imports of goods and services as a share of GDP—which had risen steadily from 2000 to 2008 and then picked up temporarily in 2010 after a pause for the global financial crisis of 2008–2009 (Figure 1.1.15). The openness of the PRC fell in the same 5 years from 48% to 32%, or $1.77 trillion, equal to almost 1.5 times the decline in the US dollar value of trade in the rest of developing Asia. This meant that the other economies compensated somewhat, but not completely, for the drop in PRC trade in 2011–2016. The forecast pickup in the openness indicator in 2017 is driven mostly by trade-intensive economies in developing Asia, with the PRC expected to continue dropping.

1.1.15 Trade openness indicator

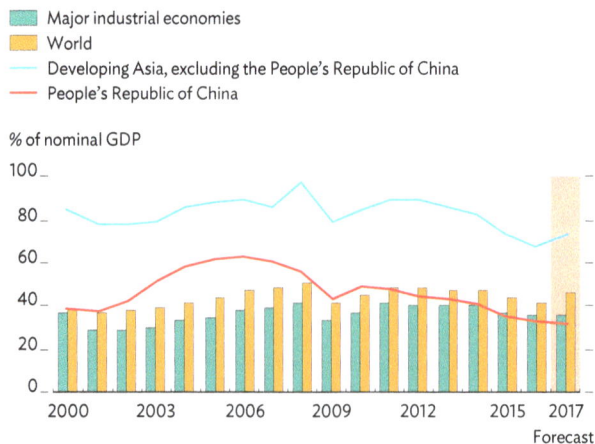

■ Major industrial economies
■ World
— Developing Asia, excluding the People's Republic of China
— People's Republic of China

% of nominal GDP

100
80
60
40
20
0

2000   2003   2006   2009   2012   2015   2017
Forecast

Note: The major industrial economies are the US, the euro area, and Japan. Trade openness is defined as the sum of exports and imports of goods and services in US dollars.

Sources: Haver Analytics and Netherlands Bureau for Economic Policy Analysis, https://www.cpb.nl/en (both accessed 15 September 2017); Asian Development Outlook database; ADB estimates.

The lull in trade before the recent pickup was not limited to Asia. The fall in both global import demand, adjusted for trade intensity, and relative prices explained about 75% of the gap compared with historical averages (IMF 2016). A small part of the gap could be explained by slower growth in global value chain participation and higher trade costs.

More data are needed to understand the nature of the trade rebound, given its novelty, but evidence to date suggests that it is robust and likely to continue, albeit at a slower pace as the base effects wear out. A closer look at export and import growth in the context of structural production changes corroborates this.

Revival in exports

Eight of the ten largest economies for which detailed data are available saw a revival of real merchandise exports in the first 6 months of 2017, both of primary products and manufactures (Figure 1.1.16). Indonesia's exports were hit by a one-time event that has to do with a high holiday season. Manufacturing exports soared in high-tech sectors such as machinery and transportation equipment, and in electrical and electronics equipment (E&E), in nine of the ten economies, excepting the PRC.

These dynamic sectors depend heavily on foreign direct investment, which picked up significantly in 2015 and 2016 as a share of GDP, particularly through mergers and acquisitions, though most foreign direct investment goes to other sectors. Figure 1.1.17 shows a steady rebound over the past 3–5 years, particularly in electronics and business services. While 70% of US dollar foreign direct investment in electronics went to the PRC and India in 2016, by far the fastest-growing destinations were the NIEs, Malaysia, and Viet Nam, where the pickup in exports has been the largest.

High-tech trade has been changing to reflect the productive structures of modern manufacturing and services. Table 1.1.1 reports a measure of the value added in E&E created domestically, either directly or indirectly, from exports of a particular country (VAX_B). The value is a measure of the spillover effect on domestic production from export demand, indicating a positive trade externality of sorts. It is reported as a share of the economy's exports. E&E is by far the largest sector in terms of total trade in developing Asia. In 2016, E&E constituted 12% of world exports, 20% of total exports of selected economies in developing Asia, and 23% of PRC exports. Because transport costs are so low, intermediate goods in this industry move back and forth across national borders many times before being finalized, and these transactions typically occur within the E&E sector. Business services, which are key exports for India and the Philippines, also produce important spillovers, even though they comprise only 4% of developing Asia's total exports.

1.1.16 Growth in nominal and real exports, primary and manufactures, selected economies in developing Asia

Nominal primary products
Nominal manufactures
Real primary products
Real manufactures

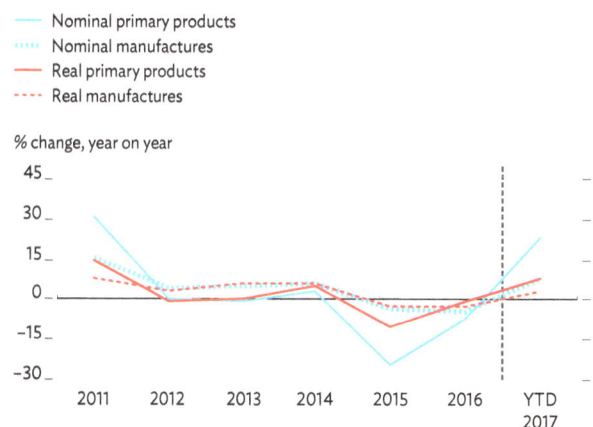

Note: Selected economies in developing Asia include the People's Republic of China, India, Indonesia, the Republic of Korea, Malaysia, the Philippines, Singapore, Thailand, Taipei,China, and Hong Kong, China.
Sources: CEIC Data Company, Haver Analytics (both accessed 1 September 2017); ADB estimates.

1.1.17 Foreign direct investment in developing Asia

Mergers and acquisitions
Greenfield
Total investment in electronics
Total investment in electronics and business services

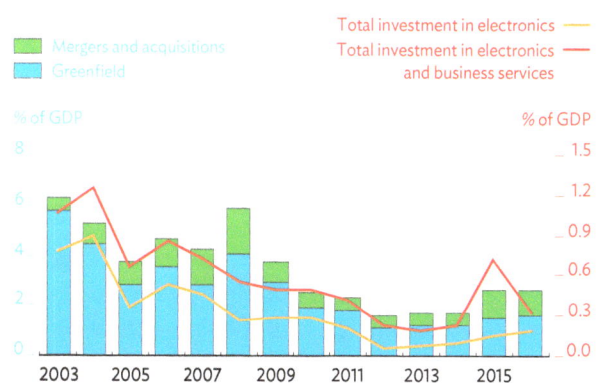

Note: 2015 spike reflects large investment in Hong Kong, China.
Sources: fDI Markets. *The Financial Times.* https://www.fdimarkets.com; ADB estimates.

1.1.1 Contribution of electrical and electronics equipment, and business services to value added by exports and total exports, 2016

Country/region	Value-added contribution to exports through backward linkages, VAX_B, as a share of country/region exports (%)		Exports of sector, as a share of country/region exports (%)	
	Electrical and electronics equipment	Business services	Electrical and electronics equipment[a]	Business services[a]
Malaysia	7	1	12	1
Philippines	9	15	18	16
Thailand	8	2	15	2
Taipei,China	15	1	26	1
Republic of Korea	13	2	19	3
India	2	12	3	13
People's Republic of China	16	3	23	4
Selected developing Asia	13	3	19	4
World	**8**	**7**	**12**	**8**

[a] Developing Asia totals in the last 2 columns include Hong Kong, China and Singapore.

Note: Economies included in the total but not shown separately are Bangladesh, Bhutan, Brunei Darussalam, Cambodia, Fiji, Indonesia, Kazakhstan, the Kyrgyz Republic, the Lao People's Democratic Republic, Maldives, Mongolia, Nepal, Pakistan, Sri Lanka, and Viet Nam.

Sources: Asian Development Bank. 2017. Key Indicators 2017; ADB estimates.

The recent pickup in the production and export of electronics since mid-2016, particularly for the PRC, the Republic of Korea, Malaysia, and Taipei,China, is impressive. Unlike in the past decade, when electronics were used in just a few products and were therefore susceptible to boom and bust, they are now used in all kinds of products, including robotics for medical and industrial equipment. This increased ubiquity is dampening the electronics cycle as measured by the lower volatility in the billings series (Figure 1.1.18). This will alleviate investor uncertainty about the sector, which will continue to grow by 15%–20% annually until 2020, according to Manyika et al. (2015). A semiconductor industry projection sees the production of semiconductor manufacturing equipment growing by 19.8% in 2017 and 7.7% in 2018 (North American Semiconductor Equipment Industry 2017).

1.1.18 Total semiconductor billings, by region

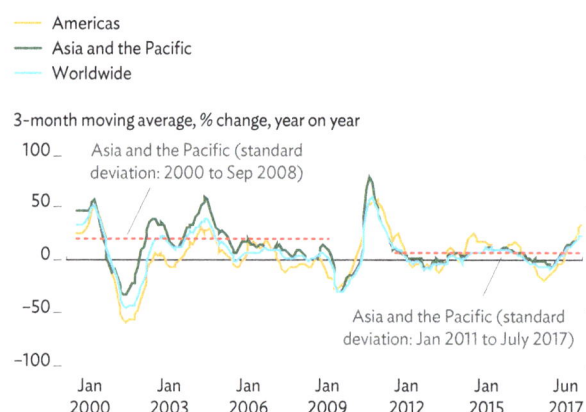

— Americas
— Asia and the Pacific
— Worldwide

3-month moving average, % change, year on year

Source: World Semiconductor Trade Statistics. https://www.wsts.org (accessed 11 September 2017).

Pickup in imports

Developing Asia's imports picked up in volume terms for both manufactured and primary goods (Figure 1.1.19). Real imports of primary products grew by double-digits in the PRC, Indonesia, the Republic of Korea, and Taipei,China, where public infrastructure investment is picking up. Real imports of manufacturing goods rose by 5.9% on average to all economies except the PRC, where real imports of manufacturing goods declined by 2.5% in the first half of 2017. This followed the trend for the past 5 years in line with the localization of production in the PRC that has been observed in the data. A growing portion of PRC indirect domestic value added in forward-linked exports suggests that output is increasingly being used as intermediaries for local production, rather than being exported for use in production abroad. It is thus a reasonably reliable indicator of localization (ADB 2017).

The sensitivity of imports to growth in developing Asia has increased. Figure 1.1.20 presents simple import demand elasticities for developing Asia. As expected, the average elasticity (defined as the percentage change in real imports as a result of a 1 percentage point change in GDP) was much higher before the global financial crisis of 2008–2009, equal to 2.22 globally and 1.33 for selected economies in developing Asia. In the period immediately before the recent spike, import elasticities were much lower, at 1.24 globally and 0.41 for developing Asia. If 2011–2016 elasticity were applied over the last 3 quarters starting in the fourth quarter of 2016 to projected import demand, real imports should have grown by 2.4% in developing Asia. Instead, actual growth was more than 3 times higher, at 8.9%, leaving a large gap to be explained. This suggests a positive externality coming from the synchronized nature of trade seen so far in 2017. Two main reasons explain why this may signify a break from the past.

First, improving investment is fueling demand for imports. Investment is the most trade-intensive component of domestic demand, with an import content of about 30% on average globally from 2011 to 2015 (IMF 2016). The contribution of investment to GDP improved. For India, Indonesia, the Republic of Korea, Malaysia, and the Philippines, ambitious public infrastructure programs have added to the sharp rise in imports.

Second, rebalancing in the PRC contributed to a shift and expansion of trade in intermediate goods to elsewhere in Asia. The gradual structural shift of productive activity from the PRC to other economies in developing Asia—the result of the PRC growth rebalancing strategy toward more domestic demand and localized production chains—has come hand-in-hand with a geographic shift of intermediate goods exports within Asia. Domestic demand in the PRC is becoming much more sophisticated and more consumer-oriented toward a growing middle class. Consequently, low-cost manufacturing centers geared for import and export, in particular, have shifted to other economies in developing Asia, which are more open than the PRC (with higher ratios of trade to GDP).

Meanwhile, developing Asia's intraregional trade excluding the PRC has increased as a share of the total, from 28% in 2000 to 32% in 2016. Trade within developing Asia is composed of about 70% intermediate goods, 15% capital goods, and the rest consumer goods. Exports within developing Asia excluding the PRC increased by 4 times (Figure 1.1.21). Relative to the PRC, the production processes of other economies in developing Asia are much more trade-intensive, as illustrated in the right panel of Figure 1.1.21.

1.1.19 Growth in nominal and real imports, primary and manufactures, selected economies in developing Asia

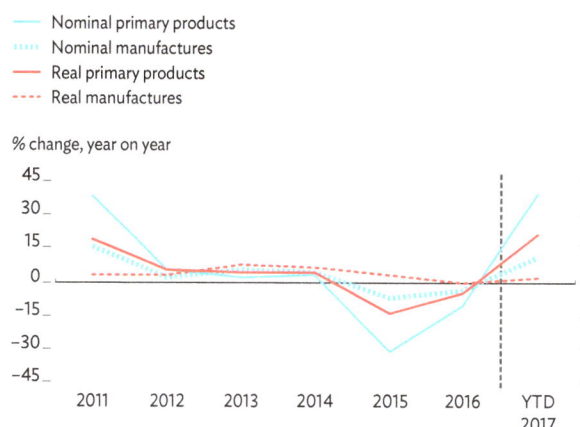

YTD = year to date.

Note: Selected economies in developing Asia include the People's Republic of China, India, Indonesia, the Republic of Korea, Malaysia, the Philippines, Singapore, Thailand, Taipei,China, and Hong Kong, China.

Sources: CEIC Data Company, Haver Analytics (both accessed 1 September 2017); ADB estimates.

1.1.20 Import elasticity, selected economies in developing Asia

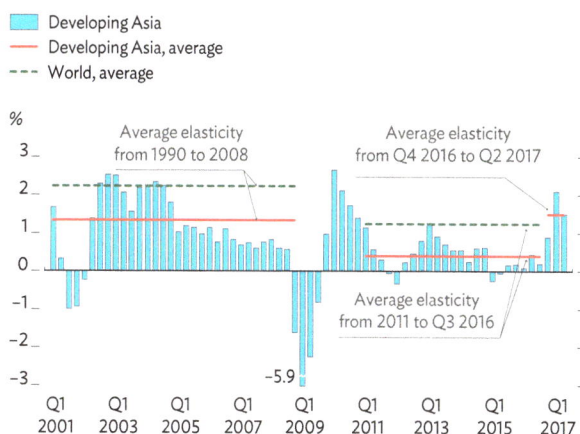

Q = quarter.

Note: Selected economies in developing Asia include the People's Republic of China, India, Indonesia, the Republic of Korea, Malaysia, the Philippines, Singapore, Thailand, Viet Nam (starting Q1 2012 only), Taipei,China, and Hong Kong, China.

Sources: Asian Development Outlook database and Haver Analytics (accessed 14 September 2017); ADB estimates.

1.1.21 Developing Asia's export to the world

Developing Asia excluding the People's Republic of China
Major industrial economies
Middle East and North Africa
Sub-Saharan Africa
People's Republic of China
Latin America
Rest of the world

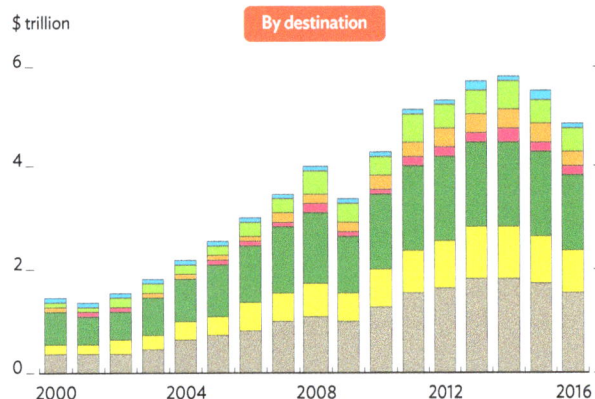

Capital
Intermediate
Consumption
Others

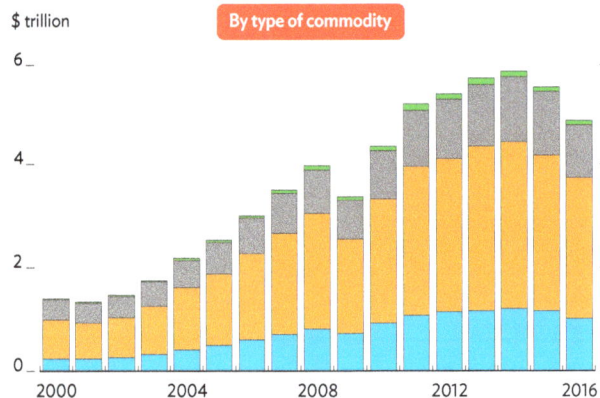

Notes: Commodities are grouped based on classification by broad economic category (BEC). The following are classified as intermediate goods: primary and processed food and beverages mainly for industry (BEC codes 111 and 121); primary and processed industrial supplies (codes 21 and 22); primary fuels and lubricants (code 31); other processed fuels and lubricants (code 322); parts and accessories of capital goods except transport equipment (code 42); and parts and accessories of transport equipment and parts (code 53). The following are consumption goods: primary and processed food and beverages mainly for household consumption (codes 112 and 122); other nonindustrial transport equipment and parts and accessories thereof (522); and all consumer goods (code 6). Capital goods include: capital goods except transport equipment (code 41) and other industrial transport equipment and parts and accessories thereof.

Source: United Nations Statistics Division. UN Comtrade Database. Available: https://comtrade.un.org/data (accessed 15 August 2017).

Current account balances

In most economies, demand for imports was even stronger than for exports. As a result, the forecast for the regional current account surplus is 0.4 percentage points narrower than the *ADO 2017* forecast, equal to 1.5% of GDP in 2017 and 1.4% in 2018.

Central Asia (excepting Azerbaijan) and South Asia are expected to have larger current account deficits in 2017 and 2018. South Asia's current account deficit is expected to double from 0.9% of GDP in 2016 to 1.6% in 2017 as the Sri Lanka and Pakistan deficits widen, and then widen further to 1.8% in 2018. In the Pacific, strong imports are expected to send the current account into deficit in 2017 and 2018 (Figure 1.1.22).

Stronger growth in Southeast Asia and the concomitant rise in imports is shrinking the current account surplus more than foreseen in *ADO 2017*, but the subregion will continue to post surpluses this year and next. As a share of GDP, the subregion's combined current account surplus is now expected at 3.0% of GDP this year and 2.8% next year. In many Southeast Asian economies, notably Viet Nam, export growth in the first half of the year was more than offset by import growth. Malaysia's current account surplus, on the other hand, will be larger this year than expected in April on a surge in exports.

1.1.22 Current account balance, developing Asia

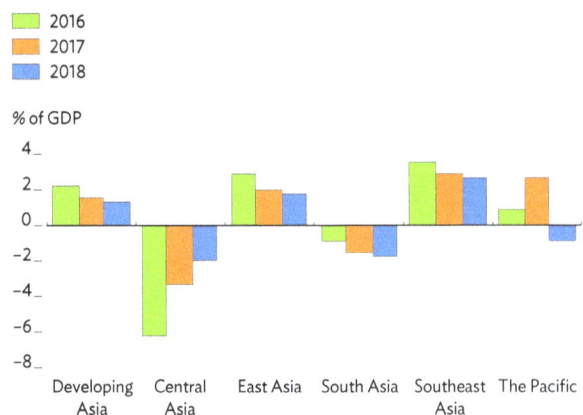

2016
2017
2018

Source: Asian Development Outlook database.

1.1.23 World current account balance

- United States
- Russian Federation
- Japan
- People's Republic of China
- Middle East
- Other industrial countries
- Rest of the world
- Rest of developing Asia

% of World GDP

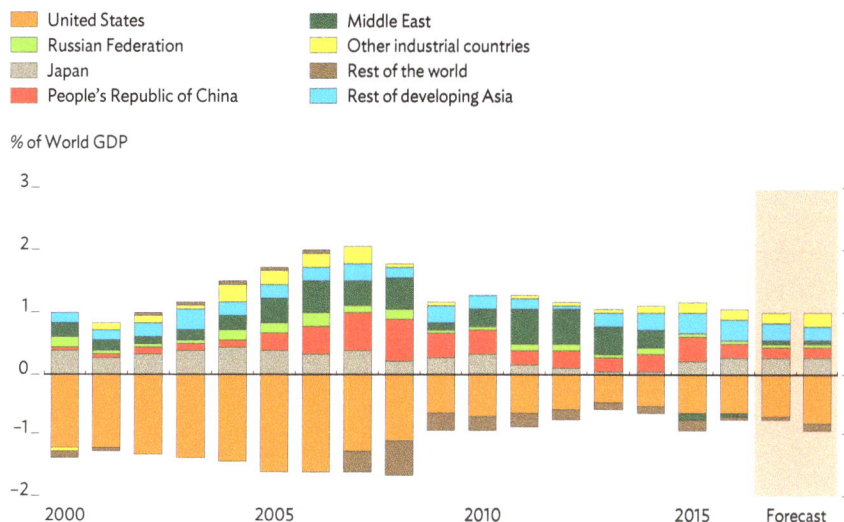

Source: Haver Analytics (accessed 28 August 2017).

East Asia's current account surplus this year is now revised down from the equivalent of 2.5% of GDP in *ADO 2017* to 2.0%, mainly reflecting a surge in imports of primary commodities into the PRC. The surplus in the PRC shrank from 2.1% of GDP in the first half of 2016 to 1.3% in the same period in 2017. In Mongolia, a 40% rebound in exports could not match a surge in imports that widened the current account deficit.

On net, the current account surplus of developing Asia with the rest of the world is expected to narrow as projected in *ADO 2017*. In 2017 and 2018, the surplus will be just below 0.5% of world GDP (Figure 1.1.23).

Risks to the outlook

Risks to the outlook have softened since April but remain tilted to the upside. With robust growth under way, developing Asia will easily counter the impact should any of these risks materialize. One risk highlighted in April was that oil prices could fall below baseline expectations. Indeed, oil prices came in lower than the baseline forecast in April but have fluctuated very little. If prices remain in the range of $50–$55/barrel, developing Asia will benefit in a balanced way. The incomes of oil exporters will receive a slight boost relative to 15 months ago, yet the costs to energy importers will not be high enough to affect investment plans. Futures prices for Brent crude indicate that large oil price fluctuations are unlikely to the outlook horizon.

An upside risk could come from sudden changes to US monetary policies. Unexpectedly high growth in import demand from the US could trigger faster inflation and cause the Fed to step on the brakes too hard for comfort in developing Asia. If export prices were to rise too quickly on exuberant export growth, the Fed would have to maneuver prudently toward an appropriately tight monetary policy to prevent large capital outflows from Asia. A US dollar that appreciated too quickly in the process could quell export demand. Changes to the Fed's asset holdings could also complicate capital flows from Asia. In March 2017, the Fed indicated that it would start to unwind the massive amounts of debt securities it had added to its balance sheet, which could trigger capital outflows from Asia. Sending clear signals about intentions should help investors adjust. The early announcement of its intention to start unwinding securities in October is a welcome step in this direction. Moreover, the impact on capital flows will be lessened if demand for Asian exports continues to grow at a healthy pace.

A second risk to the outlook, also discussed in *ADO 2017*, is unease stirred by the fear of possibly large and abrupt shifts in US fiscal and trade policies. Earlier in the year, the US administration indicated the possibility of a border tax, a tax on steel imports from the PRC, and fiscal policies that would favor US suppliers for higher public infrastructure spending. On the upside, infrastructure spending could boost demand for exports from developing Asia, particularly from the PRC. On the downside, protracted negotiations on other domestic issues in the US and the European Union has brought uncertainty forward, as few concrete decisions have been announced in these areas. Uncertainty could intensify in the coming months, with potential to make large investors in Asia's main export sectors increasingly nervous. This would threaten the sustainability of the renewed trade pickup. So far, concrete actions, to the extent that they are forthcoming, seem to favor the status quo, while business sentiment among the major trading nations seems to be optimistic.

Finally, possible economic disruption from a geopolitical or weather-related event in Asia is a very unlikely risk but one that should not be ignored. Some governments have already this year tested the resilience of alliances linking Asia and the West. Moreover, the frequency and size of various natural disasters in and around the Gulf of Mexico and the Caribbean in mid-2017 were timely reminders of the impact that climate change is having on weather patterns. Even when such storms occur outside of Asia, growing interlinkage of markets and suppliers means that a disruption in one region quickly affects others. Disruption could have a particularly strong effect on trade for high-tech manufacturers in developing Asia that are heavily enmeshed in global production chains.

The sustainability of the synchronized revival of global growth in the past few quarters is manifested in the strong trade pickup. If the Fed continues its gradual and predictable moves on interest rates, and if the unwinding of the Fed's debt holdings is predictable, this most likely scenario will bring balanced trade growth across developing Asia and the world to the outlook horizon. Most Asian economies are currently in an upswing part of their business cycle but growing more slowly than the average in past upswings.

Risks from unwinding quantitative easing

At its September 2017 meeting, the Federal Open Market Committee decided to start normalizing the US Federal Reserve's balance sheet the following month. The unwinding of the Fed's huge holdings of securities may unsettle global financial markets and challenge global financial stability. It is instructive to see how this situation came about and useful to explore its consequences for developing Asia.

To cope with the global financial crisis of 2008–2009 and its aftermath, the Fed unleashed unprecedented monetary expansion, injecting massive liquidity into financial markets to stabilize them and prop up economic growth. It rapidly lowered its benchmark Federal Funds rate from a peak of 5.25% in June 2007 to 0.25% in December 2008 to push down short-term interest rates. Once the Federal Funds rate hit the floor—effectively zero, the lowest rate possible—the Fed turned to unconventional monetary expansion in an attempt to operate beyond the limits of conventional monetary policy. To keep long-term interest rates low, it purchased large amounts of US government and agency securities in three rounds of quantitative easing (QE), in November 2008, November 2010, and September 2012. By the time the Fed ended its QE program in 2014, the size of its securities holdings had soared from less than $0.5 trillion to $4.2 trillion (Figure 1.2.1). Since then, the Fed has been maintaining its portfolio by reinvesting principal payments. Meanwhile, the US money supply increased by 61%, from $8.2 trillion to $13.2 trillion from December 2008 to December 2016.

The European Central Bank, Bank of England, and Bank of Japan pursued their own QE programs, contributing to abundant global liquidity, which contributed in turn to rapid credit growth, especially in emerging Asia (Figure 1.2.2). Aggregate money supply (M2) in 10 emerging Asian economies increased by 171%, from $10.8 trillion in December 2008 to $29.3 trillion in December 2016. Low interest rates and abundant money supply pushed up indebtedness in emerging Asia, exposing the region to risk in the event of a tightening of liquidity.

As economic growth regained momentum in the advanced economies, the Fed started to normalize its monetary policy. Since December 2015, it has raised policy rates four times by a total of 100 basis points, or 1 percentage point. After discussing since March 2017 its intention to normalize the Fed's asset holdings by reducing its reinvestment of principal payments, the

1.2.1 US Federal Reserve balance sheet and monetary policy

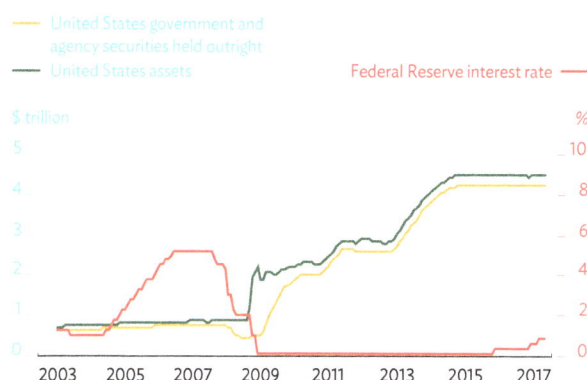

Source: Federal Reserve Bank of New York.

1.2.2 Aggregate money supply growth in the United States and emerging Asia

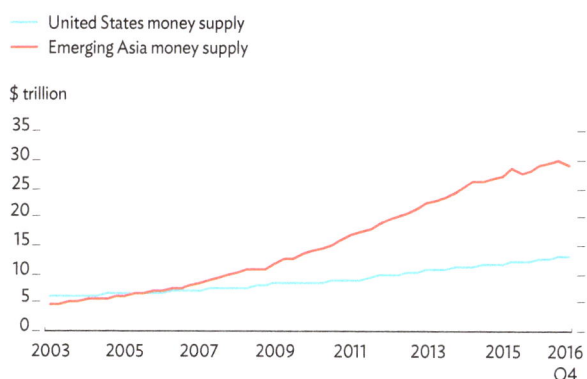

Q = quarter.

Note: The 10 emerging Asian economies are the People's Republic of China, India, Indonesia, the Republic of Korea, Malaysia, the Philippines, Singapore, Thailand, Taipei,China, and Hong Kong, China.

Source: Computation based on data from Haver Analytics.

Federal Open Market Committee revealed in its June meeting tentative plans to reduce portfolio holdings and, in its September meeting, formally announced the start of balance sheet normalization, to begin in October.

The normalization of the Fed's balance sheet may have a more direct impact on global financial and liquidity conditions than have its policy rate hikes. The rate hikes, which directly affect the price of money, push up market short-term interest rates. Balance sheet normalization, on the other hand, shrinks the quantity of money and, all other things being equal, lowers long-term bond prices, which can affect long-term interest rates. Historical trends suggest that the yield on the 1-year US Treasury bond closely tracks policy rate adjustments, but this is not necessarily true of the yield on the 10-year US Treasury bond (Figure 1.2.3). Moreover, the Fed's announcement back in May 2013 that it would begin tapering its asset purchases—the spark for the so-called "taper tantrum"—caused the 10-year government bond yield to surge but did not affect the 1-year Treasury bond yield. These patterns suggest that the Fed's asset purchasing plans would influence the long-term benchmark interest rate more than the short-term benchmark interest rate, as expected.

Global effects of the balance sheet normalization announcement

Unanticipated announcements of monetary policy normalization in the US can destabilize global financial markets. In tandem with 10-year US government bond yield, long-term interest rates in many emerging Asian economies were affected by the 2013 taper tantrum. From April to June 2013, 10-year government bond yields in selected emerging Asian economies rose by 57.6 basis points on average, with the largest increase, at 162.7 basis points, in Indonesia.

The Fed's announcement of balance sheet normalization did not trigger a repeat of the taper tantrum. The difference between the two episodes highlights the importance of communication between central banks and financial markets. Well before starting to normalize its monetary policy, the Fed released in 2014 a statement through its Federal Open Market Committee on "policy normalization principles and plans," which indicated that balance sheet normalization would come about as the Fed no longer reinvested principal payments, not through direct sales of securities on the market. This made the Fed operations more predictable. Since the March 2017 meeting of the committee, the Fed has gradually disclosed its normalization intentions, along with details about reducing its portfolio holdings later this year. This communication guided market expectations and helped minimize shocks to financial markets (Figure 1.2.4). From February to April 2017, markets for 10-year government bonds in selected emerging

1.2.3 Bond yield reactions to policy rate hikes and asset purchase tapering

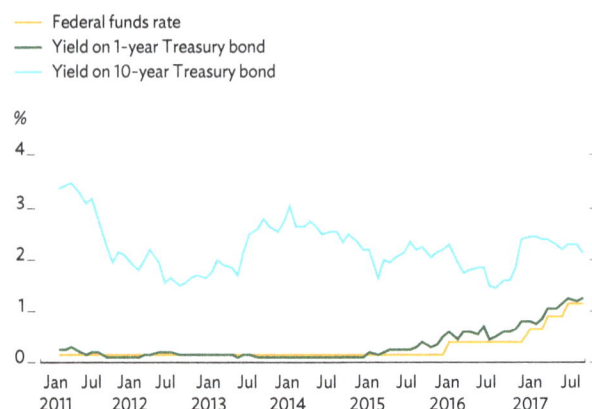

- Federal funds rate
- Yield on 1-year Treasury bond
- Yield on 10-year Treasury bond

Note: The policy rate and Treasury bond yield are recorded as of end of each month.
Source: Bloomberg (accessed 5 September 2017).

1.2.4 Changes in yields for 10-year government bonds in local currency

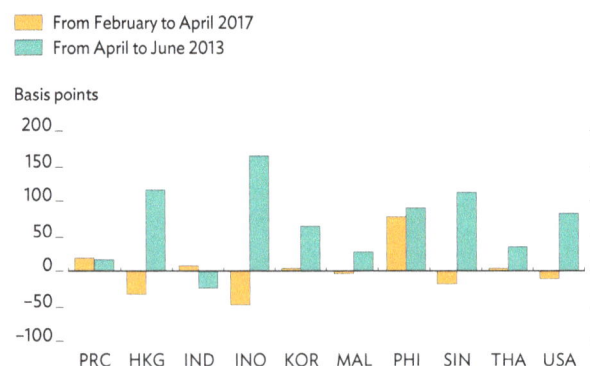

- From February to April 2017
- From April to June 2013

HKG = Hong Kong, China, IND = India, INO = Indonesia, KOR = Republic of Korea, MAL = Malaysia, PHI = Philippines, PRC = People's Republic of China, SIN = Singapore, THA = Thailand, USA = United States.
Source: Bloomberg (accessed 30 August 2017).

Asian economies remained calm. Many markets witnessed stable or decreasing bond yields (though bond yields rose in the PRC and the Philippines on factors specific to these economies). Indeed, during the taper tantrum, changes in US yields were systematically followed by bond yield changes in emerging Asia going the same direction. This time around, in contrast, market reactions to the Fed's recent signal on its balance sheet normalization plan have been much more muted.

The signal from the Fed clearly communicates cautious, gradual normalization, which should allow markets to price in the policy change calmly and rationally. This time, unlike in 2013, the signal did not come as an unanticipated shock able to trigger a world-wide market overreaction.

Beyond the effects of the announcement

Despite the muted short-term reaction to the balance sheet normalization announcement, a realized action by the Fed to normalize its balance sheet would have some practical implications for liquidity in the region. Changes to the Fed's balance sheet that reflect changes in either the conventional or the unconventional part of monetary policy action would alter the supply of liquidity in the US, which may spill over into global financial markets. A growing number of studies of unconventional monetary policy pursued by advanced economies and their spillover effects on emerging markets are drawn to a consensus that such policy does affect liquidity in emerging markets.

This section attempts to quantify the probable effects of changes in the Fed's balance sheet on capital flows in emerging Asia. To do this, a simple tri-variate VAR-X model is estimated to derive the likely dynamic responses of capital flows to changes in the Fed balance sheet (Box 1.2.1). In particular, the section focuses on three different measures of capital flow to the region: net capital flows to the region, net flows of capital excluding foreign direct investment (FDI), and aggregate net purchases of equity and debt by nonresidents.

Likely responses to the Fed's balance sheet shock

The Fed normalization plan entails reducing the assets on its balance sheet. This is a negative shock that would have a contractionary effect on aggregate liquidity in the economy. Figure 1.2.5 confirms this and shows that a negative shock to the Fed's balance sheet, all other things being equal, immediately reduces the amount of liquidity circulating in the US within the same quarter. This contraction in the US money supply implies an increase in the US interest rate and, because of how much the US dictates dynamics in global financial markets, is echoed by increases elsewhere. The increase in interest rates in emerging Asian markets is typically larger than in the US, perhaps partly reflecting policy makers' attempts to mitigate the destabilizing effects

1.2.5 Dynamic quarterly responses to a standard deviation fall in the Fed's balance sheet

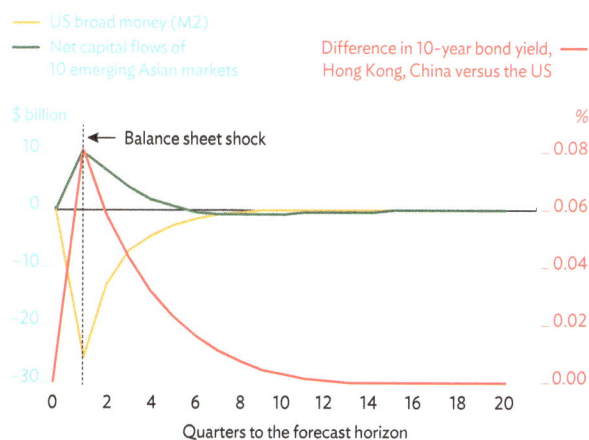

Note: The 10 emerging Asian economies are the People's Republic of China, India, Indonesia, the Republic of Korea, Malaysia, the Philippines, Singapore, Thailand, Taipei,China, and Hong Kong, China.
Source: ADB estimates.

1.2.1 Estimating the dynamic responses of the region's capital flows

The dynamic responses of the region's capital flows to a shock in the Fed's balance sheet is estimated by running a tri-variate vector autoregression with exogenous variables (VAR-X):

$$Y_t = A(L)Y_t + Fz_t$$

Y_t is a column vector with three endogenous variables: (i) a measure of changes in US aggregate liquidity (changes in US M2), (ii) a measure of the long-term interest rate spread between Asia and the US (represented by the difference in 10-year government bond yields in Hong Kong, China versus those in the US), and (iii) alternative measures of aggregate net capital flows to the region. Three alternative measures of aggregate net flows are considered: (i) net capital flows to 10 Asian economies,[1] consisting of FDI, portfolio investment, financial derivatives, and other investment; (ii) aggregate net capital flows excluding FDI to the 10 Asian economies; and (iii) aggregate net purchases of stocks and bonds by nonresidents in eight emerging Asian markets based on Institute of International Finance data.[2] Capital flows are measured in billions of US dollars.

z_t is a column vector of exogenous variables that represent possible shocks to Y_t. Specifically, it consists of the three residuals that represent exogenous shock to each of the endogenous elements of Y_t, and n additional exogenous variables that represent movements in the Fed's policy through changes in its balance sheet. Changes in the n measures of the Fed's balance sheet are considered exogenous because they represent discretionary monetary policy actions that appear to be shocks of interest in this exercise.

$A(L)$ and F are conformable 3×3 and $3x \ (3 + n)$ coefficient matrices that characterize the VAR-X system, which is estimated using quarterly data from the first quarter of 2003 to the second quarter of 2017.

The estimated results of the VAR-X provides a platform for analyzing the effects of the different shocks on each of the endogenous variables in the model. For the purposes of this section, the results are then used to derive the likely structural dynamic impulse responses of the region's capital flows to shocks emanating from negative changes in the Fed's balance sheet.

Notes:
[1]   The PRC, India, Indonesia, the Republic of Korea, Malaysia, the Philippines, Singapore, Thailand, Taipei,China, and Hong Kong, China.
[2]   Excluding Singapore and Hong Kong, China for lack of data from the Institute of International Finance.

of the shock. The interest rate gap between Asia and the US thus tends to widen. As a result, Asia tends to experience a short-term influx of capital in response to higher US rates, though the inflows reverse after about a year.

The effect on net capital flows to the region seems to be robust across different measures. Net capital flows excluding FDI seem to be the most responsive to a shock in the Fed's balance sheet. The response pattern of net capital flows to the region are similar if they include and exclude FDI. A one standard deviation decline (a negative shock) in the Fed's balance sheet will increase net inflows into emerging Asia by 12% of their standard deviation at impact if FDI is included and by 19% if FDI is excluded. This effect continues for up to a year following the shock, then is mildly corrected in the second year (Figure 1.2.6a–b). Nonresidents' net purchases of stocks and bonds have a shorter response to the Fed's balance sheet shock. These short-term flows jump by about 6% of their standard deviation at impact but immediately correct in the following quarters (Figure 1.2.6c). To illustrate the magnitude of responses, a reduction of the Fed's balance sheet by $1 billion increases aggregate net inflows to Asia by about $59 million at impact. Aggregate net inflows excluding FDI increase by about $87 million, while nonresidents' net purchases of stocks and bonds increase by about $4 million.

1.2.6 Effects of a negative shock to the Fed's balance sheet (% of standard deviation), contemporaneous and cumulative for 1 and 2 years

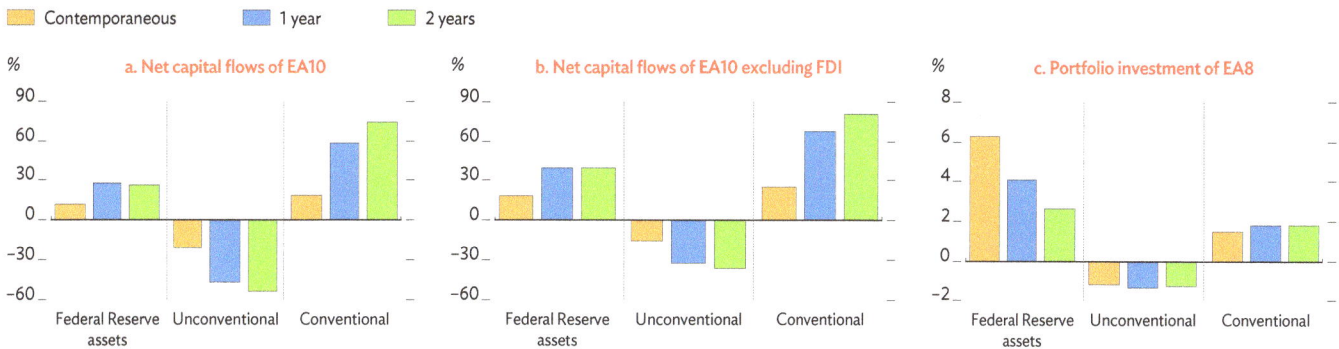

Contemporaneous   1 year   2 years

a. Net capital flows of EA10

b. Net capital flows of EA10 excluding FDI

c. Portfolio investment of EA8

EA = emerging Asia, FDI = foreign direct investment, unconventional = US government and agency securities held outright.

Note: The 10 emerging Asian economies are the People's Republic of China, India, Indonesia, the Republic of Korea, Malaysia, the Philippines, Singapore, Thailand, Taipei,China, and Hong Kong, China.

Source: ADB estimates.

Decomposing the Fed's balance sheet shocks

While the effects discussed above sound conceptually sensible, they are inconsistent with the capital inflows that many emerging markets, including in Asia, experienced following the Fed's QE. Intuitively, one would then expect outflows of capital from Asia when the Fed reverses its QE by normalizing its balance sheet.

To square the seemingly counterintuitive observation regarding the direction of capital flows above, the effect of changes in the Fed's balance sheet can be further decomposed into movements in conventional monetary policy to affect the short-term interest rate and movements in the unconventional policy effected through QE after the short-term interest rate hit the floor (Figure 1.2.1 above). Figure 1.2.7 shows the decomposition in terms of changes in the Fed's balance sheet. While conventional monetary policy was actively used before the target policy interest rate hit the floor toward the end of 2008, unconventional monetary policy then took over.

Now consider the impact of the two exogenous monetary policy shocks, conventional and unconventional, to the VAR-X system. The results are shown by the bars under conventional and unconventional US monetary policy in Figure 1.2.6. They suggest that conventional monetary policy actions by the US negatively relate to different measures of capital flow to Asia. That is, all other things being equal, monetary contraction conducted through conventional monetary policy instruments will increase capital flows into emerging Asia, and expansion will reduce those flows. However, the same policies conducted through unconventional policy instruments have the opposite effect on capital flows in the region. Therefore, the Fed's unconventional monetary policy operation during different QE episodes helps to explain the capital surges into the region. The additional liquidity that resulted from QE spilled over into other markets in search of better returns. This suggests that the Fed's unwinding of the unconventional parts of its balance sheet may cause some capital outflows from the region, or at least halt capital flows into it.

1.2.7 Changes in the Fed's balance sheet

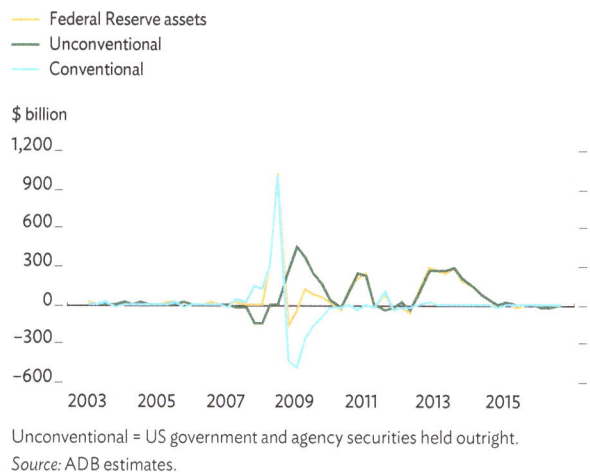

Federal Reserve assets
Unconventional
Conventional

Unconventional = US government and agency securities held outright.
Source: ADB estimates.

Normalization demands strengthened financial stability

While US balance sheet normalization will neither shock global financial markets nor immediately change accommodative global financial conditions, it signals a gradual tightening of global liquidity. It is thus opportune for emerging Asia to monitor and strengthen financial conditions to strengthen its resilience over the long term. A future change in global liquidity may influence emerging Asia in the following two ways.

First, a narrowing of return spreads may foster capital flows out of the region and challenge exchange rate stability. Reduction of the Fed's portfolio holdings and further policy rate hikes would jointly raise short- and long-term interest rates in the US. All other things being equal, higher US interest rates would strengthen the US dollar against other currencies, which would drain capital out of the region. Historical data show capital flows into emerging Asia negatively related to the US dollar index (Figure 1.2.8). Capital outflows would thus challenge the stability of Asian currencies, especially in countries with flexible exchange rate regimes.

Second, higher interest rates in the US could spill over into emerging Asia, raising interest rates in the region. Interest rates in emerging Asia correlate quite strongly with the US interest rate. The average correlation coefficient between policy rates of selected emerging Asian economies and the US is 0.64, while the corresponding figure for 10-year government bond yields is 0.60 (Figure 1.2.9). When US interest rates edge up, interest rates in many emerging Asian economies may follow suit.

The economic impact of rising interest rates in Asia could be twofold. First, the increase in the long-term benchmark interest rate would raise financing costs, affecting investment activity. Second, it would mean higher effective discount rates, which would lower asset valuation and weaken the balance sheets of financial institutions and corporations. During the recent era of low global interest rates, emerging Asia witnessed rapid credit expansion. A correction in asset prices triggered by tighter liquidity may harm highly leveraged institutions and thus challenge financial stability.

In sum, the gradual, transparent, and predictable nature of the Fed's balance sheet normalization seems to explain why its announcement had only limited impact on emerging Asia. However, the signal of a tightening global liquidity stance is getting louder and clearer. Further, economic recovery will spur monetary policy normalization in the euro area over the longer term. It is therefore high time for policy makers in emerging Asia to monitor possibly excessive leverage in regional economies and strengthen their financial positions toward preparing for the long-discussed return of more normal monetary conditions.

1.2.8 Capital flows into 10 emerging Asian markets and the US dollar index

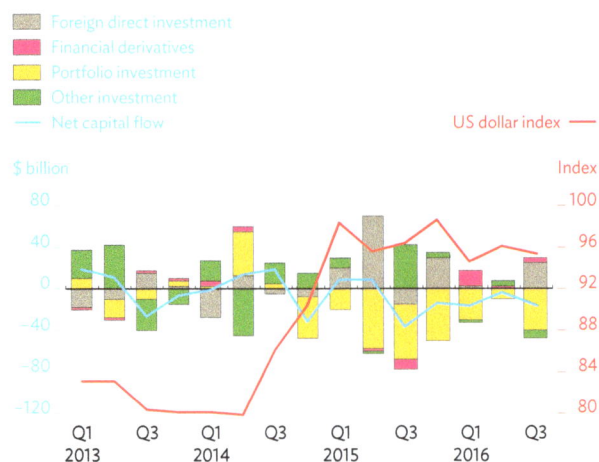

Q = quarter.
Note: The 10 emerging Asian economies are the People's Republic of China, India, Indonesia, the Republic of Korea, Malaysia, the Philippines, Singapore, Thailand, Taipei,China, and Hong Kong, China.
Sources: Bloomberg; Haver Analytics (both accessed 30 August 2017).

1.2.9 Emerging Asia's interest rates correlation with the US interest rate

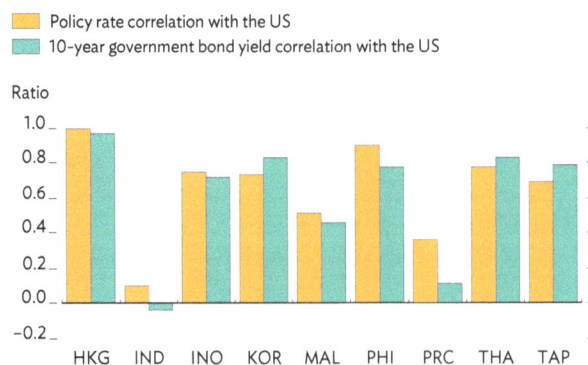

HKG = Hong Kong, China, IND = India, INO = Indonesia, KOR = Republic of Korea, MAL = Malaysia, PHI = Philippines, PRC = People's Republic of China, TAP = Taipei,China, THA = Thailand, US = United States.
Note: Correlation is estimated using month-end rates or yields during the sample period from July 2005 to June 2017.
Sources: Bloomberg; Haver Analytics (both accessed 5 September 2017).

Gauging Asia's business cycles

A decade after the global financial crisis of 2007–2008 erupted in the advanced economies and quickly spread around the world, what is the current state of the macro economy in developing Asia? The impact of the crisis was felt strongly in many Asian economies as GDP growth flagged. *Asian Development Outlook* noted in 2009 that the harsh global environment caused growth in developing Asia to slow by one-third from a peak of 10.2% in 2007 to 6.4% in 2008. Growth slowed further to 6.1% in 2009. Since then, economic activity has picked up in the region, supported extensively by domestic policy and benefitting from an eventual turnaround in global growth.

However, recovery has not been smooth, and frequent ups and downs muddle the view of present conditions for investors, consumers, and policy makers. The current state of the economy is typically identified by the cyclical state of macroeconomic indicators. Business cycles are recurring fluctuations in aggregate economic activity, defined as persisting for 8–32 quarters. Periods of accelerating growth, or upturns, alternate with periods of decelerating growth, or slowdowns.

Real GDP, the sum of macroeconomic activity in a national economy, is a popular series frequently used in business cycle analysis. It serves as a good reference, as cyclical fluctuations are manifested earlier or later in most other macroeconomic series, such as prices and employment. Characterizing the business cycle provides a picture of where the economy stands, to answer several questions. Is it in an upturn? What is the duration of the upturn, and how close is it to changing direction? How high is the upturn, and how does it compare to previous episodes? Knowing an economy's position on the cycle is important for assessing the outlook for future developments and thus can inform vital market and policy decisions.

Accelerating but at a slower pace

Using quarterly real GDP per capita from the first quarter of 1993 to the first quarter of 2017, Table 1.3.1 presents the chronology of turning points in the business cycles of 10 Asian economies and, for comparison, the US. The cyclical fluctuations are of the gap between current output and its long-run trend, the gap showing not only whether the economy is strengthening or slowing but also whether it is above or below the trend (Box 1.3.1). Blue squares indicate peak dates and orange squares troughs, in both cases turning points as the cycle changes direction. The shaded area between a peak and a trough is a slowdown period, and the area between a trough and a peak is an upturn.

A concurrent slowdown across economies in the region occurred during the Asian financial crisis of 1997–1998 and again during the global financial crisis in 2008–2009. Other cycles have been specific to individual economies, with some common periods of upturn and slowdown. Since the first quarter of 1993, Asian economies have experienced from two to six cycles of varying duration.

1.3.1 Chronology of business cycle turning points   *(continued...)*

Economy	1993	1994	1995	1996	1997	1998	1999	2000	2001	2002	2003	2004	2005	2006
Indonesia					P	T		P						T
Malaysia	T				P		T	P	T		P			T
Philippines	T				P		T	P	T P		T	P		T
Singapore		P		T	P		T	P			T			T
Thailand				P		T		P	T	P	T	P		T
Hong Kong, China		P		T	P		T		P		T			
Republic of Korea					P	T		P	T	P			T	
Taipei,China			P		T P		T	P		T		P		T
India[a]					T			P			T			
Japan		T		P			T	P			T	T	P T	
United States		P		T			P				T		P	T

Economy	2007	2008	2009	2010	2011	2012	2013	2014	2015	2016	2017
Indonesia		P	T	P					T		
Malaysia		P	T	P	T	P	T	P	T		
Philippines		P	T	P	T	P		T			
Singapore	P		T	P	T		T	P	T		
Thailand	P		T	P	T	P	T		T		
Hong Kong, China	P		T		P		T	P	T		
Republic of Korea	P		T	P			T	P	T		
Taipei,China	P		T	P			T	P	T		
India[a]	P				P						
Japan	P		T	P		T	P		T		
United States	P		T				P	T	P	T	

a Data started in the second quarter of 1996.

Source: ADB estimates.

Legend:
1997 Asian crisis
2008 Global financial crisis
P Peak
T Trough
P T Slowdown
T P Upturn

In the past decade, GDP has fluctuated around a positive underlying trend. The cycle gauges when the economy may be either overheating or underperforming. Currently, all the economies in this sample are in an upturn, with output exceeding the trend in most cases. In India, the upturn started from the second half of 2013. Indonesia, the Republic of Korea, and the Philippines started rising from the trough early in 2015. Malaysia, Singapore, Taipei,China, and Hong Kong, China began their upturns later that year. In some economies, the historical average length of an upturn is already surpassed. However, the pace of the upturn has been less than in the past average in most economies—an exception being the Philippines, where the current upturn seems to be on a par with those of the past.

Monetary policy actively used for stabilization

Production, consumption, trade, and employment typically rise during an upturn phase. As income increases, higher spending spurs demand for goods and services, pushing up prices and profits. Productive investment goes up further, and growth gathers momentum. But when an economy begins to heat up, inflationary pressures eventually start to build.

1.3.1 Dating the business cycle

Using GDP as a broad measure of economic activity, business cycle turning points are identified to establish phases of growth upturn and slowdown in Asian economies. An approach for extracting, dating, and measuring the cycle is adopted to establish the chronology of the growth cycle.

Preparing the data

Real GDP data for economies with multiple base years are linked based on growth rates to get a series from a common starting point in the first quarter of 1993 (1996 for India) (box table). Where official seasonally adjusted data are not available, the X-13-ARIMA procedure is applied to remove seasonality. Annual population data are interpolated to obtain a quarterly series. Finally, quarterly GDP per capita with seasonal adjustment removed is computed from the first quarter of 1993 to the first quarter of 2017 in 10 Asian economies and, for comparison, the US.

Extracting the business cycle

The business cycle is measured as deviation in output from its trend. A filter is needed to disaggregate the time series into the economy's long-term trend and cyclical deviations from the trend. The Christiano–Fitzgerald band pass filter is used to extract the cycle (Christiano and Fitzgerald 2003). Recognizing that a time series can have different frequency components, the filter eliminates the slow-moving trend components and the high-frequency noise while retaining intermediate business cycle fluctuations. A definition provided by the National Bureau of Economic Research in the US is used to specify the band, by which business cycle fluctuations persist for 8–32 quarters. For consistent comparison across economies, the cyclical component of GDP per capita is standardized by subtracting the mean and dividing by the standard deviation.

Determining turning points

A dating algorithm developed by Bry and Boschan (1971) and applied by Harding and Pagan (2002) to quarterly data is used to determine the chronology of business cycle turning points. The procedure identifies the dates at which the indicator reaches a peak or a trough. Other useful information can be obtained.

- An upturn is defined as the period from trough to peak, and a slowdown from peak to trough.
- The amplitude of an upturn or slowdown is the maximum difference between the trough and the peak.
- The cycle is the duration from peak to peak.

References

Bry, G. and C. Boschan. 1971. *Cyclical Analysis of Time Series: Selected Procedures and Computer Programs.* National Bureau of Economic Research. http://www.nber.org/chapters/c2145

Christiano, L. J. and T. J. Fitzgerald. 2003. The Band Pass Filter. *International Economic Review* 44(2).

Harding, D. and A. Pagan. 2002. *A Comparison of Two Business Cycle Dating Methods.* Melbourne Institute of Applied Economics and Social Research, University of Melbourne.

Data descriptions

Economy	Start	End	Base year (period)	Seasonal adjustment (SA)
Indonesia	1993 Q1	2017 Q1	1993 (1993 Q1–2003 Q4)	
			2000 (2000 Q1–2014 Q4)	
			2010 (2010 Q1–2017 Q1)	
Malaysia	1991 Q1	2017 Q1	1987 (1991 Q1–2006 Q4)	
			2000 (2000 Q1–2011 Q4)	
			2005 (2005 Q1–2014 Q4)	
			2010 (2010 Q1–2017 Q1)	
Philippines	1989 Q3	2017 Q1	1985 (1989 Q3–2010 Q4)	Official SA
			2000 (1998 Q1–2017 Q1)	Official SA
Singapore	1975 Q1	2017 Q1	2010 (1975 Q1–2017 Q1)	Official SA
Thailand	1993 Q1	2017 Q1	2002 (1993 Q1–2017 Q1)	Official SA
Hong Kong, China	1990 Q1	2017 Q1	2015 (1990 Q1–2017 Q1)	Official SA
Republic of Korea	1960 Q1	2017 Q1	2010 (1960 Q1–2017 Q1)	Official SA
Taipei,China	1982 Q1	2017 Q1	2011 (1982 Q1–2017 Q1)	Official SA
India	1996 Q2	2017 Q1	1999–00 (1996 Q2–2009 Q3)	
			2004–05 (2004 Q2–2014 Q3)	
			2011–12 (2011 Q2–2017 Q1)	
Japan	1980 Q1	2017 Q1	2000 (1980 Q1–2011 Q3)	Official SA
			2011 (1994 Q1–2017 Q1)	Official SA
US	1947 Q1	2017 Q1	2009 (1947 Q1–2017 Q1)	Official SA

Q = quarter.

Source: CEIC Data Company (accessed 24 July 2017).

The reverse process takes place during a slowdown; as growth decelerates, inflationary pressure eases. The authorities in Asia have actively used monetary policy to stabilize cyclical fluctuations in output and prices over the past decade, but seemingly in pursuit of varying policy targets depending on the situation (Figure 1.3.1).

In Indonesia, monetary policy responded primarily to price movements. Interest rates were lowered in 2011–2012 as inflation decelerated in line with a slowdown in the economy. Subsequently in 2013, interest rates were increased in response to inflationary pressures and the threat of currency depreciation. Recently, monetary policy has loosened as inflation eased. A similar objective is seen in the Republic of Korea and the Philippines, though to different degrees. A series of interest rate increases at the beginning of the decade responded to rising inflation. The rates were then brought down in tandem with slowing inflation since 2012. More recently, interest has been held to relatively low rates as inflationary pressure was still considered benign.

In India, Malaysia, and Thailand, monetary policy appears to respond to both inflation and output cycles. Interest rate increases in these economies at the beginning of the decade seem to have been driven mostly by decisions to cool the economy as expansion in output peaked. In India, monetary policy was then loosened as GDP slipped below trend, lowering interest rates to provide a boost. More recently, despite an upturn in output, interest rates were reduced as inflation continued slowing in tandem with lower oil prices. In Malaysia, interest rates were maintained once inflation started to decelerate, and were raised again when indications of heating up resurfaced in mid-2014. In Thailand, interest rates were brought down in 2012 as inflationary pressure eased. More recently, interest rates have been kept at rock bottom as inflation remained low.

In Taipei,China, policy mainly aimed to stabilize output. The policy rate was increased at the beginning of the decade in response to overheating. It was then kept slightly below 2% as a slowdown that started in 2011 was followed by only a brief and weak upturn in 2014 and 2015. When output dipped back below trend in 2015, the rate was lowered.

How much longer will the upturn last?

For policy makers who try to understand economic cycles, the financial crisis a decade ago came as an unexpected shock. A key takeaway from the experience is the need to develop the ability to predict the next turning point. A natural question now is how much longer Asia's economies are likely to maintain the current upturn. The short answer is that historical precedent shows some economies likely to continue their upturns and others already in the latter stages.

Starting in the first quarter of 1993, across all cycles, the average duration of upturn and slowdown is computed to indicate how many quarters pass before a turning point can be expected. Cycles are not uniform in duration, however, so a coefficient of variation is calculated to illuminate diversity in upturn and slowdown duration across cycles.

1.3.1 Interest, inflation, exchange rates, and the growth cycle in selected Asian economies

- Slowdown
- Interest rate
- Inflation rate
- Exchange rate
- Growth cycle

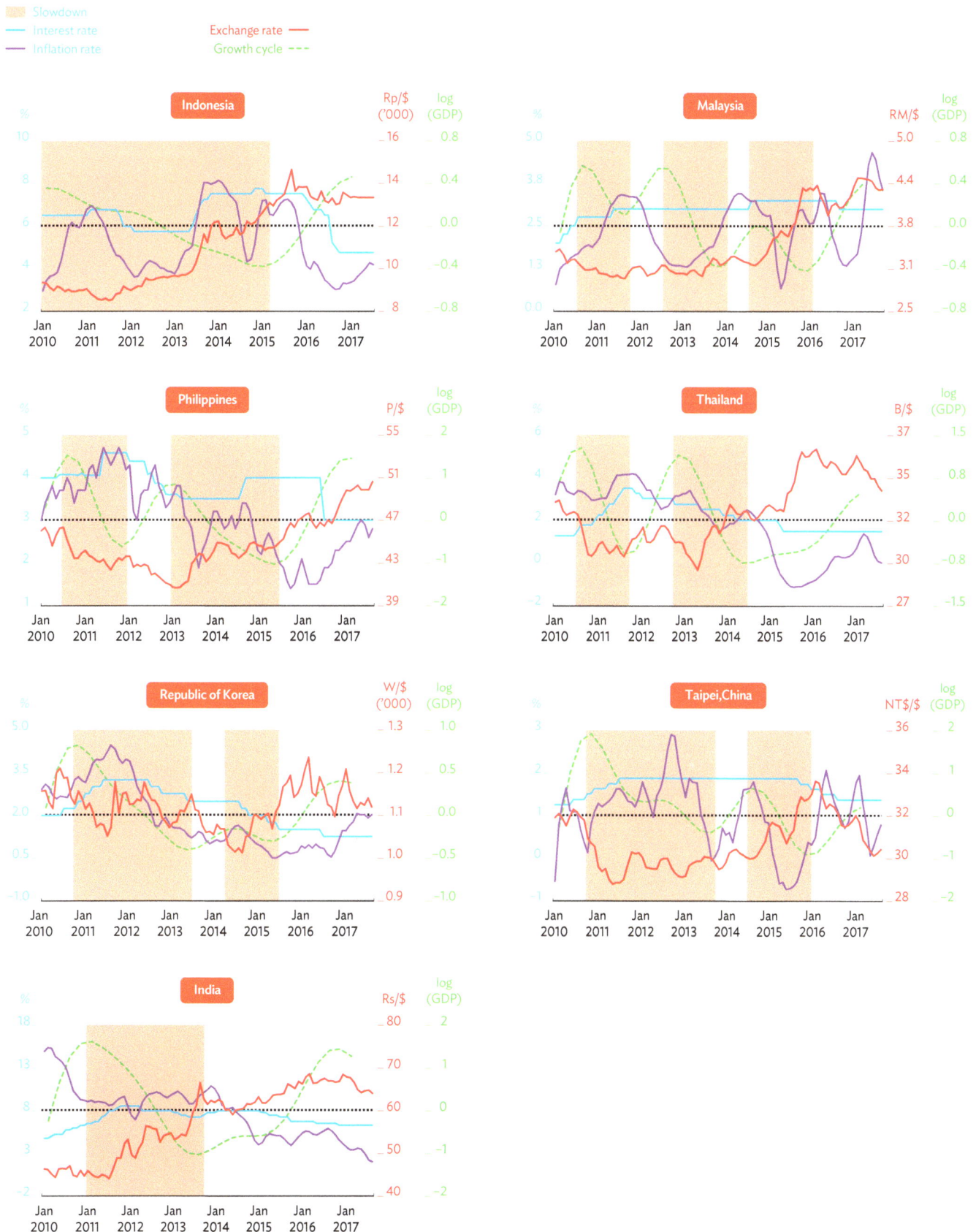

Note: The inflation rate is a 3-month moving average.

Sources: CEIC Data Company (accessed 4 September 2017); ADB estimates.

1.3.2 Summary statistics of the business cycle

Statistics	Hong Kong, China	Indonesia	India	Republic of Korea	Malaysia	Philippines	Singapore	Taipei,China	Thailand
Number of cycles	5	3	2	5	6	6	5	6	6
Average duration of cycle (quarters)	15.80	17.33	22.50	13.80	11.50	10.50	16.00	12.83	10.83
Average duration of downturn (quarters)	7.50	13.25	10.00	6.83	5.86	6.00	7.83	6.14	5.57
Average duration of upturn (quarters)	8.00	6.33	12.33	6.40	6.86	6.29	7.80	6.50	5.33
Maximum duration of upturn (quarters)	18	8	18	11	15	14	20	15	7
Duration of the current upturn (quarters)	5	8	14	7	5	7	5	5	11
Coefficient of variation of duration of downturn	0.31	0.70	0.30	0.44	0.40	0.30	0.25	0.40	0.40
Coefficient of variation of duration of upturn	0.73	0.33	0.45	0.42	0.59	0.59	0.89	0.67	0.23
Average amplitude of downturn	2.39	2.12	3.21	1.96	1.87	2.17	2.18	2.00	1.88
Average amplitude of upturn	2.62	1.75	3.23	1.88	1.96	2.20	2.42	2.09	1.65
Speed of downturn	0.32	0.16	0.32	0.29	0.32	0.36	0.28	0.33	0.34
Speed of upturn	0.33	0.28	0.26	0.29	0.29	0.35	0.31	0.32	0.31
Speed of the current upturn	0.14	0.10	0.16	0.10	0.16	0.35	0.11	0.22	0.11

Source: ADB estimates.

As there is variability around the average, the results presented here are indicative and can complement other analyses that inform policy decisions.

Table 1.3.2 shows the duration of the current upturn in comparison with the historical average for each economy. Malaysia, Singapore, Taipei,China, and Hong Kong, China have been in upturns for 5 quarters, all starting in the fourth quarter of 2015. History suggests that these economies are still several quarters away from the peak of their cycles.

In other economies, the current upturn has exceeded the average duration by more than a year, though there are some differences. From a trough in the second quarter of 2014, Thailand started experiencing an upturn that has continued for 11 quarters, well above its historical average of 5.3 quarters. In Indonesia as well, the current upturn has, at 8 quarters, lasted beyond the average of 6.3 and become the longest on record. Current upturns in India, the Republic of Korea, and the Philippines are protracted but not beyond precedent.

While these upturns are long, their generally weaker pace of growth means that average quarterly gains in output have been comparatively small. So have accumulated gains. In Thailand, seasonally adjusted real GDP increased by 9.1% in the 11 quarters of the current upturn, but the upturn that lasted the longest before this one, at 7 quarters from the third quarter of 1998 to the second quarter of 2000, yielded a real GDP gain of 10.5%. In economies with a cycle hovering near a likely tipping point, this observation has implications for policy decisions.

Additional support from accommodative policy would be welcome to spur activity and prolong the upturn phase. Some economies—Indonesia, Malaysia, Thailand, and Taipei,China—retain room for policy maneuver. Where inflation rates are falling and currencies are appreciating, maintaining easy monetary conditions is consistent with the objective of boosting growth. In the Republic of Korea, India, and the Philippines, however, the case for stimulus is less clear because the upturn has lasted longer than average and price pressures are building.

One way to strengthen and prolong economic upturns is to try to lift the output trend. This can be done by investing in sectors that address constraints on productivity growth, in particular the existing infrastructure gaps found in many developing economies in Asia. Government initiatives are necessary, but they can do only so much when they depend heavily, or even entirely, on public funds for investment into public infrastructure and the public services that depend on it. Governments need to encourage private sector involvement in infrastructure development by, among other avenues, establishing proper mechanisms to incentivize partnerships with the public sector.

References

ADB. 2017. *Key Indicators for Asia and the Pacific 2017*, Part III. Asian Development Bank.

IMF. 2016. Global Trade: What's Behind the Slowdown? *World Development Outlook,* Chapter 2. October. International Monetary Fund.

Manyika, J., M. Chui, P. Bisson, J. Woetzel, R. Dobbs, J. Bughin, and D. Aharon. 2015. The power of digitizing the physical world, *The Internet of Things: Mapping the Value Beyond the Hype.* McKinsey Global Institute. June, p. 17. http://www.mckinsey.com/business-functions/digital-mckinsey/our-insights/the-internet-of-things-the-value-of-digitizing-the-physical-world

North American Semiconductor Equipment Industry. 2017. $49.4 Billion Semiconductor Equipment Forecast—New Record, Korea at Top. July. http://www.semi.org/en/494-billion-semiconductor-equipment-forecast-new-record-korea-top

Annex: Solidifying global recovery

Growth in the major industrial economies of the United States, the euro area, and Japan is now seen to be stronger in aggregate than the rate anticipated in *Asian Development Outlook 2017* (*ADO 2017*). The forecasts for average growth rates are revised up from 1.9% to 2.0% in both 2017 and 2018 (Table A1.1). Brighter prospects in the euro area and Japan more than offset a somewhat muted recovery in the US. In the euro area, supportive fiscal and monetary policies, easing political uncertainty, and robust market confidence will shore up growth momentum. Upward revisions to the growth forecasts for Japan reflect growth better than expected and indications of resilient domestic demand. In the US, however, unexpectedly low growth in the first half of the year will drag on growth prospects for 2017.

The pickup in fuel and food prices was milder in the first half of 2017 than anticipated in *ADO 2017*. While the average price of Brent crude has climbed from its trough in 2016 and food prices continue to rise tentatively, international commodity prices are unlikely to generate inflationary pressures in the advanced economies. This will enable further extensions of loose monetary policy in the euro area and Japan and continued gradual monetary normalization in the US.

A1.1 Baseline assumptions on the international economy

	2015	2016	2017		2018	
	Actual		*ADO 2017*	*Update*	*ADO 2017*	*Update*
GDP growth (%)						
Major industrial economies[a]	2.3	1.5	1.9	2.0	1.9	2.0
United States	2.9	1.5	2.4	2.2	2.4	2.4
Euro area	1.9	1.7	1.6	2.0	1.6	1.8
Japan	1.1	1.0	1.0	1.5	0.9	1.1
Prices and inflation						
Brent crude spot prices (average, $/barrel)	52.4	44.0	56.0	52.0	58.0	54.0
Food index (2010 = 100, % change)	−15.4	2.0	3.0	0.3	2.0	2.0
Consumer price index inflation (major industrial economies' average, %)	0.2	0.6	1.7	1.7	1.8	1.8
Interest rates						
United States federal funds rate (average, %)	0.1	0.4	1.0	1.0	2.0	2.0
European Central Bank refinancing rate (average, %)	0.1	0.0	0.0	0.0	0.1	0.1
Bank of Japan overnight call rate (average, %)	0.1	0.0	−0.1	−0.1	−0.1	−0.1
$ Libor[b] (%)	0.2	0.5	1.0	1.0	2.0	2.0

ADO = Asian Development Outlook, GDP = gross domestic product.

[a] Average growth rates are weighted by gross national income, Atlas method.

[b] Average London interbank offered rate quotations on 1-month loans.

Sources: US Department of Commerce, Bureau of Economic Analysis, http://www.bea.gov; Eurostat, http://ec.europa.eu/eurostat; Economic and Social Research Institute of Japan, http://www.esri.cao.go.jp; Consensus Forecasts; Bloomberg; CEIC Data Company; Haver Analytics; and the World Bank, Global Commodity Markets, http://www.worldbank.org; ADB estimates.

Recent developments in the major industrial economies

United States

Growth in the US underperformed in the first half of 2017. After unusually warm weather caused disappointing expansion at a seasonally adjusted annualized rate (saar) of only 1.2% in the first quarter, the US economy accelerated to 3.0% saar in the second. The growth acceleration owed mainly to higher private consumption and private investment, both of which showed substantial improvement over the first quarter. Private consumption was the lead contributor to GDP growth in the second quarter, adding 2.3 percentage points, or 1.0 percentage point higher than in the first quarter. Private investment recovered from contraction in the first quarter to add 0.6 percentage points to GDP growth. Net exports contributed 0.2 percentage points, as in the first quarter, while government spending declined, subtracting 0.1 percentage points from growth (Figure A1.1).

Private consumption grew solidly at 3.3% saar, up from 1.9% in the first quarter on a March spike in the consumer confidence index (Figure A1.2). Confidence remained strong throughout the second quarter, despite some brief corrections, as the index averaged 114.3 (2007 = 100), a slight improvement from the average of 113.7 in the first quarter. The index rebounded quite sharply to 116.1 in July and 118.9 in August, auguring continued strength in private consumption going forward. Retail sales enjoyed steady improvement throughout the first half of 2017. All in all, the prospects for future growth in consumption, at least through this year and next, are positive on the basis of strong confidence and the trend in retail sales. Consumption should remain the pillar of growth.

Private investment registered growth at 3.6% saar in the second quarter after 1.2% contraction in the first. Fixed investment recorded strong growth at an average saar of 5.9% in the first half of 2017, up from 0.6% in the same period last year. Investment is projected to stay the course as both the industrial production index and the purchasing managers' index suggest US production continuing to expand at a moderate but steady pace.

The labor market remained robust at the beginning of the third quarter. The number of nonfarm jobs rose by more than 189,000 in July 2017 and 156,000 in August. Relatively strong job growth has been keeping the unemployment rate at a 16-year low of 4.3%–4.4% since April despite some gains in the size of the labor force. The average length of unemployment in the first 8 months of 2017 shortened to 25 weeks from 28 weeks in the same period last year. Average weekly earnings improved by 2.6% in

A1.1 Demand-side contributions to growth, United States

- Private expenditure
- Private investment
- Government expenditure and investment
- Net exports
- Gross domestic product

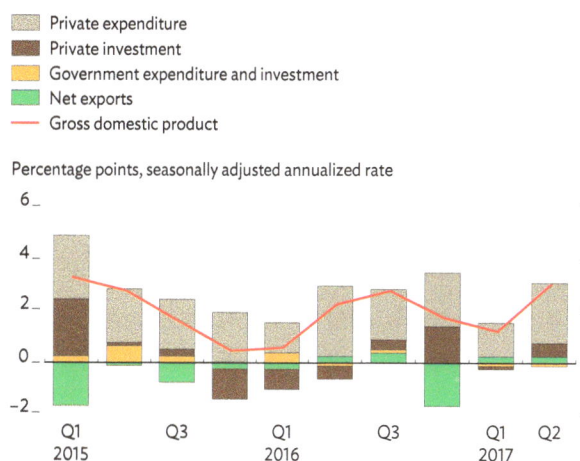

Percentage points, seasonally adjusted annualized rate

Q = quarter.
Sources: US Department of Commerce. Bureau of Economic Analysis. http://www.bea.gov; Haver Analytics (both accessed 4 September 2017).

A1.2 Business activity and consumer confidence indicators, United States

- Consumer confidence
- Industrial production
- Retail sales
- Purchasing managers' index

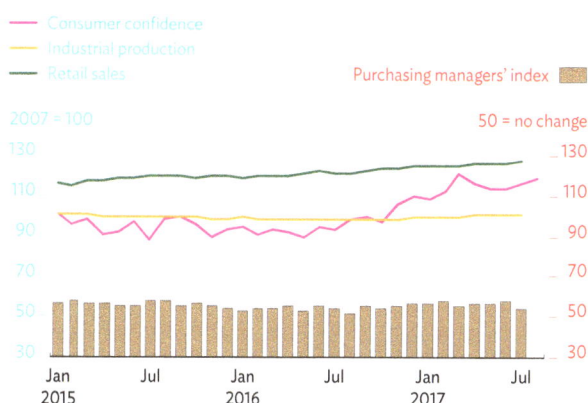

2007 = 100   50 = no change

Note: For the purchasing managers' index, a reading below 50 signals deterioration of activity, above 50 improvement. The index is compiled by the Institute for Supply Management.
Source: Haver Analytics (accessed 4 September 2017).

the first 8 months of 2017, slightly faster than the 2.3% pace in the same period last year. This should further support consumption.

Headline and core inflation continued to decelerate since March 2017. Headline inflation posting a rate of 1.6 in June 2017 and 1.7 in July, averaging 2.1% in the year to July (Figure A1.3). Core inflation, which excludes food and energy prices, fell back to stay below 2.0% since March 2017. In response to slower inflation, the Federal Reserve raised the federal funds rate only gradually, by 25 basis points in March to 0.85% and again in June to 1.10%. As the labor market continues to strengthen, the Fed is expected to continue its gradual normalization of monetary policy, probably by raising the policy rate by another 25 basis points toward the end of the second half.

With prospects for strong consumption growth and stable investment, the US economy is on track for further recovery and meaningful growth. However, unexpectedly slow growth in first half prompts to a downward revision to the 2017 forecast from 2.4% to 2.2%. The 2018 growth forecast is kept at 2.4%. Hurricanes that hit the US recently, Harvey and Irma, may slow growth a little in the third quarter. However, economic activity should rebound in the fourth quarter with reconstruction. In sum, this downward risk should not drag growth significantly below the current forecast.

Euro area

Momentum in the euro area continued in the second quarter of 2017 after a strong start to the year. The region grew by 2.6% saar, rising from 2.2% in the first quarter on broad improvements both at home and overseas. Household spending has strengthened, supported by accommodative policies and stable employment, while investment convincingly reversed its contraction in the previous quarter to grow by 2.4%. Net exports contributed to GDP growth for a second consecutive quarter after dragging on growth for most of 2016 (Figure A1.4).

As broad as expansion may be across demand categories, it is uneven across individual euro area economies. Dampened by net exports, second quarter growth in Germany, France, and Italy moderated from the first quarter. The Netherlands grew the fastest, more than doubling its first quarter pace on strong net exports and household spending. Spain saw its fastest growth in nearly 2 years, while Greece also improved on its first quarter performance.

Improving labor markets are lifting consumer confidence and spending. Retail sales resumed positive monthly growth in January, and the confidence indicator for the second quarter improved from the first quarter reading (Figure A1.5). Despite a fall in June, industrial production expanded by 0.3% in the second quarter after nearly stagnating in the first. Businesses appear more optimistic with new

A1.3 Inflation, United States

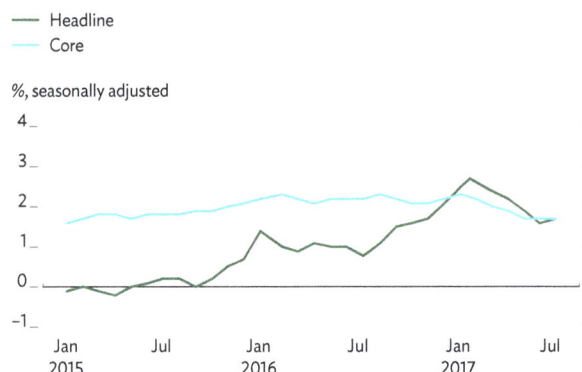

— Headline
— Core

%, seasonally adjusted

Source: Haver Analytics (accessed 4 September 2017).

A1.4 Demand-side contributions to growth, euro area

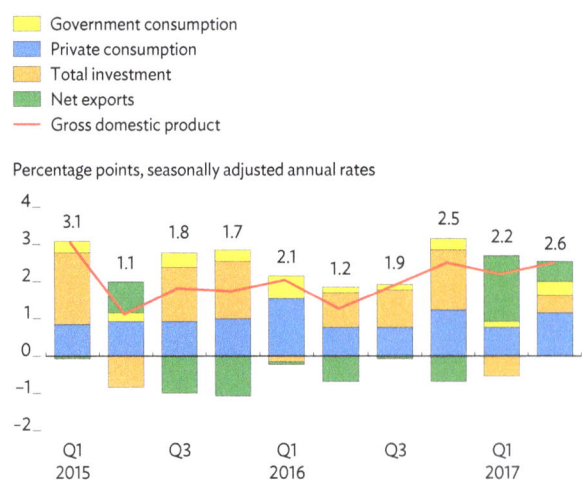

☐ Government consumption
☐ Private consumption
☐ Total investment
☐ Net exports
— Gross domestic product

Percentage points, seasonally adjusted annual rates

Q = quarter.
Source: Haver Analytics (accessed 8 September 2017).

orders up and robust increases in job numbers. The average composite purchasing managers' index for the second quarter improved to 56.6, a full point up from the previous quarter's average and well above the 50 point threshold between growth from decline. The economic sentiment index reached a near decade high in June at 111.1, with increases across all sectors of the economy.

The European Central Bank left its rates unchanged at its September meeting, thus keeping its ultra-accommodative monetary stance despite firmer economic activity. It also left intact its bond-buying program, which is intended to run until December 2017 at an average monthly pace of €60 billion. Inflation fell to 1.5% in August from 1.9% in April as price rises for energy, food, and services slowed beginning in the second quarter. Inflation stands at 1.6% year on year, still below the central bank's target of 2.0%, but recent upticks in core inflation suggest that price pressures may be resurfacing.

Early indicators for the third quarter suggest that expansion is likely to continue through the rest of the year. The seasonally adjusted unemployment rate fell to 9.1% in July, the lowest since March 2009, which is helping the recovery in retail sales. Business activity is still expanding, with the composite purchasing managers' index steady at 55.7 in July and August (Figure A1.6). The economic sentiment index further improved to 111.9 in August, and the manufacturing purchasing managers' index and industrial sentiment indicator anticipate healthy production growth in the short term.

With growth in the second half of the year likely to remain buoyant—given supportive fiscal and monetary policies, easing political uncertainty, and robust market confidence—the forecast for growth this year is revised up to 1.9% from 1.6% in *ADO 2017*. Consumer spending will continue to rise on steady employment gains and a more positive jobs outlook, and investment is likely to accelerate in the short term as businesses take advantage of low interest rates while they last. Investment is also boosted by improved political sentiment following elections (and fairly conventional results) earlier this year in the Netherlands and France that had caused firms to delay investment decisions. Net trade is likely to contribute to growth in 2017, reflecting favorable global trade dynamics and despite a steady rise of the euro against the US dollar.

Domestic demand should remain firm into 2018, supporting euro area growth at 1.8%. Household spending will soften somewhat. However, it will likely be more than offset by robust investment spending fostered by rising credit demand from firms, as indicated in recent bank lending surveys, and by upcoming projects under the European Commission's Investment Plan for Europe. External demand will be helped by favorable export conditions continuing into next year, as suggested by surveys of export orders.

A1.5 Selected economic indicators, euro area

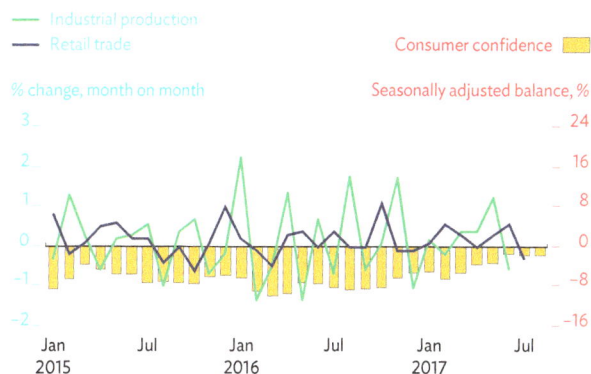

Source: Haver Analytics (accessed 8 September 2017).

A1.6 Economic sentiment and purchasing managers' indexes, euro area

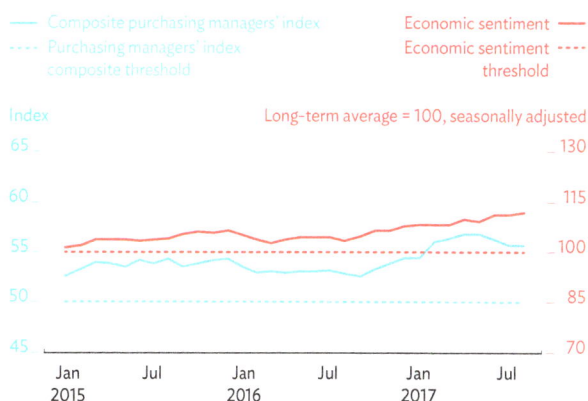

Sources: Bloomberg; Haver Analytics (both accessed 8 September 2017).

Risks have receded substantially since the *ADO 2017* assessment. Markets were appeased when the Government of Italy—having last year rescued Monte dei Paschi di Siena, one of Italy's largest banks—finally intervened in June with further cash and guarantees to rescue two struggling regional banks. Greece managed to place €3 billion in 5-year bonds in the market after coming to terms with its creditors in July. The French elections quelled political unease across the continent, though not uncertainty stemming from Brexit negotiations, which have shown little progress.

Japan

Economic growth in Japan is exceeding expectations, spurred first by recovery in external demand and more recently by strong domestic demand as business conditions and labor markets improve. Growth found support in accommodative monetary policy from the Bank of Japan, fiscal stimulus from the government, and an uptick in spending for the 2020 Tokyo Olympics. With the economy moving away from its past reliance on the external sector to generate growth, any recovery led necessarily by domestic demand can be derailed by core inflation near zero and tepid wage growth. The growth outlook is nonetheless positive to the forecast horizon.

With second quarter growth at 2.5% saar, Japan recorded its sixth consecutive quarter of growth—at its highest rate in 2 years. With growth at 1.2% in the first quarter, the first half came in moderately strong. Growth in the second quarter was fueled by robust private consumption that contributed 1.9 percentage points, and it was further supported by private investment that contributed 0.4 percentage points, signaling a pickup in domestic demand. Public investment added a significant 1.1 points to growth. These factors compensated for soft net exports, which dragged down growth by 1.2 percentage points, mainly reflecting a surge in imports. Net exports had been a key driver of economic recovery throughout 2016, buoyed by a pickup in global demand and a weak yen (Figure A1.7).

While a healthier external sector fed growth in domestic manufacturing, the recovery has been tentative. Production fell by 3.6% in May and rebounded by 2.1% in June only to fall again by 0.7% in July, at the start of the third quarter. Meanwhile, the purchasing managers' index remains above the threshold of 50, ticking up from 52.1 in July to 52.2 in August to indicate that manufacturing is expanding but at a weak pace (Figure A1.8). Core machinery orders, a leading indicator, declined in June, suggesting that capital spending may lose momentum going forward. On a positive note, in an environment of easier financing, Tankan surveys show business sentiment improving, possibly in response to higher corporate profits.

A1.7 Demand-side contributions to growth, Japan

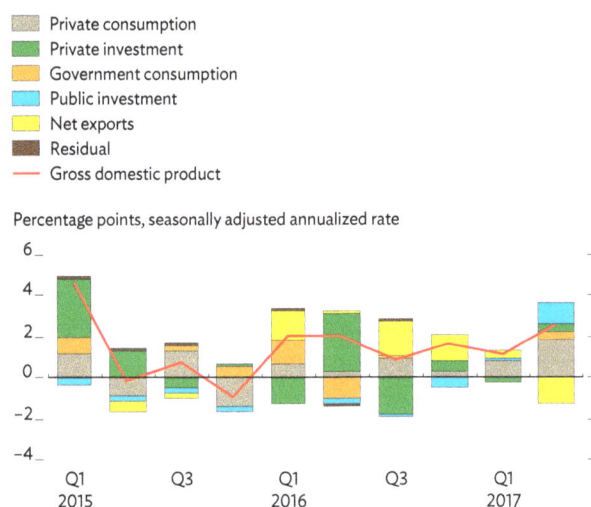

- Private consumption
- Private investment
- Government consumption
- Public investment
- Net exports
- Residual
- Gross domestic product

Percentage points, seasonally adjusted annualized rate

Q = quarter.

Source: Economics and Social Research Institute, Cabinet Office, Government of Japan, available: http://www.esri.cao.go.jp (accessed 8 September 2017).

A1.8 Business activity and consumer confidence indicators, Japan

- Industrial production
- Retail sales
- Manufacturing purchasing managers' index
- Consumer confidence

%, year on year   Index, >50 = better

Sources: Haver Analytics; Bloomberg (both accessed 8 September 2017).

An unexpected boost to growth came from consumption, which had struggled to gather steam since a sales tax hike in 2014. Latest data indicate that spending surged by 3.4% in the second quarter as consumers bought more durable goods. The consumption index of the Bank of Japan also strengthened in that quarter. Seasonally adjusted retail sales have increased since the start of the year, except for a downward blip in May, recovering in June by a slight 0.2% and then by a stronger 1.1% in July. Consumer confidence slipped by 0.4 points to 43.4 in August, but that is still high compared with the average of the past decade, implying that consumers are relatively upbeat about economic prospects. While low and declining unemployment, hovering at 2.8% in July, should encourage consumption, sluggish wage growth may prevent any sustained rise in spending.

With wage and price pressures slow to build, inflation remained resolutely low at 0.4% in July. In its last meeting, the Bank of Japan stuck to its expansionary monetary policy with the aim of achieving a stable consumer price index reading (for everything except fresh food) above 2% year on year (Figure A1.9). To this end, the short-term policy interest rate is –0.1%, and 10-year Japanese government bond yields are capped at around zero.

National accounts data showed exports of goods and services down by 1.9% in the second quarter, reversing an 8.0% increase in the previous quarter. Imports, on the other hand, increased by 5.7%. Monthly data had merchandise exports registering a 4.8% increase year on year in July, continuing their 14-month growth streak. The gradually improving outlook for global trade will continue to benefit Japan's exports, but their contribution to growth in Japan is diminishing.

On balance, the growth forecast for Japan in 2017 is revised up to 1.5% on output growth in the first half that exceeded expectations and on indications of strengthening domestic demand in the second half. The pace is expected to moderate, however, to 1.1% in 2018. Despite a significant upgrade and newly positive outlook for the economy, some risks remain. They include global trade winds that could turn and stall the export sector and, on the domestic front, lackluster wages and sluggish inflation that fall short of the economy's needs if it is to achieve a firmer growth trajectory.

Australia and New Zealand

The Australian economy expanded by 3.3% saar in the second quarter of 2017, improving on the 1.3% recorded in the first quarter (Figure A1.10). Consumption was the main driver of growth, contributing 2.5 percentage points, with fixed capital formation adding 1.5 percentage points and net exports 1.3 percentage points. Change in inventories subtracted 2.2 percentage points. Seasonally adjusted retail sales were stagnant in July 2017, falling to zero growth from 0.2% in the previous month. The consumer sentiment index

A1.9 Inflation, Japan

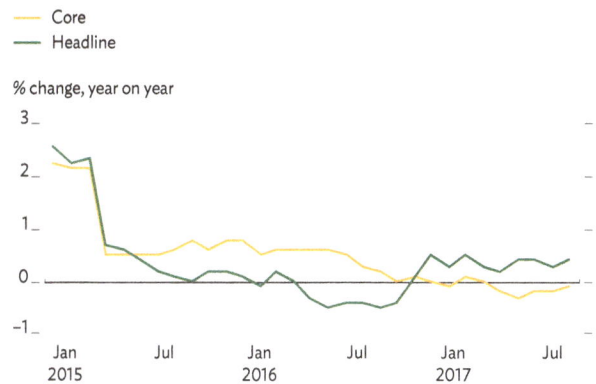

— Core
— Headline

% change, year on year

Source: Haver Analytics (accessed 8 September 2017).

A1.10 Demand-side contributions to growth, Australia

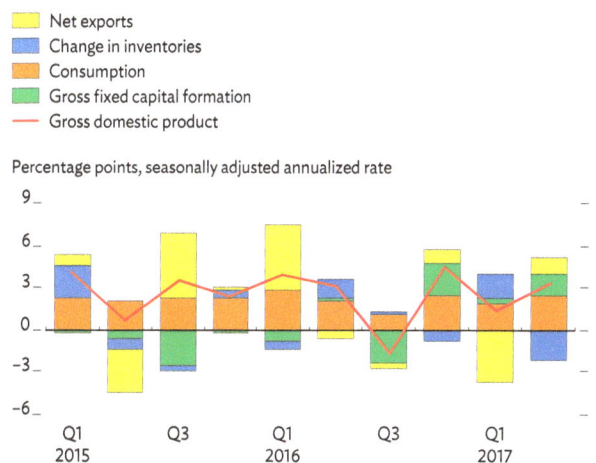

■ Net exports
■ Change in inventories
■ Consumption
■ Gross fixed capital formation
— Gross domestic product

Percentage points, seasonally adjusted annualized rate

Q = quarter.
Source: CEIC Data Company (accessed 8 September 2017).

marginally increased to 96.6 in July from 96.2 in June, still below the 100-point optimism threshold, while the seasonally adjusted unemployment rate held steady at 5.7%. The Australian Industry Group's performance of manufacturing index increased to 59.8 in August from 56.0 in the previous month, well above the threshold of 50 indicating expansion in manufacturing. Inflation dropped to 1.9% in the second quarter from 2.1% in the previous quarter, less than the Reserve Bank of Australia target of 2.0%–3.0%, prompting the central bank to retain its policy rate at 1.5%. Expecting mild economic activity this year because of continued weakness in the labor and real estate markets, panelists for the FocusEconomics Consensus Forecast predict GDP growth to slow to 2.3% in 2017 from 2.5% last year, but to accelerate to 2.7% in 2018.

New Zealand's economy grew by 0.9% saar in the first quarter of 2017, higher than the 0.4% growth recorded in the last quarter of 2016. Consumption was the biggest contributor to growth, adding 3.8 percentage points. Fixed capital formation contributed 1.2 percentage points, while change in inventories deducted 2.8 percentage points and net exports 2.2 percentage points (Figure A1.11). Retail sales expanded by 6.7% in the second quarter, as in the first. The seasonally adjusted performance manufacturing index declined slightly to 55.4 in July 2017 from 56.0 in June, still above the threshold of 50 indicating expansion. The business confidence index, which subtracts the percentage of pessimists from that of optimists, dropped to 18.3 in August from 19.4 in the previous month. Consumer confidence also remained positive, above the threshold of 100 and increasing by 1.5 points to 113.4 in the second quarter of 2017. Inflation slowed to 1.7% in the second quarter from 2.2% in the previous quarter, still within the Reserve Bank of New Zealand inflation target of 1.0%–3.0%. The seasonally adjusted unemployment rate improved marginally to 4.8% in the second quarter from 4.9% in the first—for its best showing since 2009. Considering robust domestic demand supported by accommodative monetary and fiscal policy, as well as strong net migration, the FocusEconomics Consensus Panel projects GDP to expand by 2.8% in 2017 and 2018.

Commodity prices

Favorable supply kept commodity prices broadly stable in the first 8 months of 2017. Oil prices increased some but remained low because of a supply glut, while food prices were steady.

Oil price movements and prospects

In the first 5 months of the year, the price of Brent crude oil hovered around $53/barrel (Figure A1.12). The Organization of the Petroleum Exporting Countries (OPEC) met on 25 May and decided to extend its voluntary production cuts, originally set to end in June 2017, through March 2018.

A1.11 Demand-side contributions to growth, New Zealand

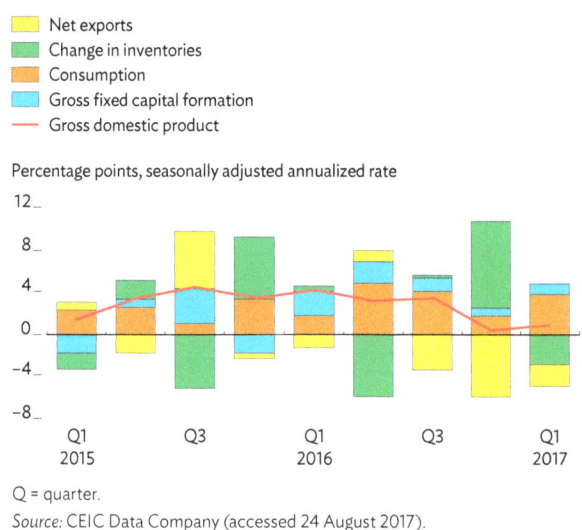

- Net exports
- Change in inventories
- Consumption
- Gross fixed capital formation
- Gross domestic product

Percentage points, seasonally adjusted annualized rate

Q = quarter.
Source: CEIC Data Company (accessed 24 August 2017).

A1.12 Price of Brent crude

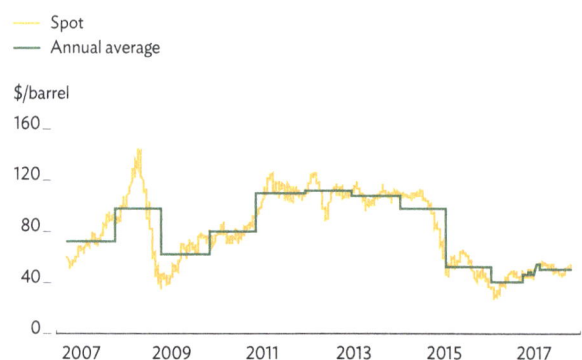

- Spot
- Annual average

$/barrel

Sources: Bloomberg; World Bank. Commodity Price Data (Pink Sheet). http://www.worldbank.org (both accessed 8 September 2017).

The extension was deemed necessary to stabilize the oil market, draw down a massive oil glut, and support prices.

However, oil prices failed to rebound following the OPEC decision because market participants had expected more aggressive measures such as deeper cuts of longer duration or the inclusion of more exporting countries in the deal. Brent crude prices then fell and averaged $46/barrel in June, the first month in 2017 in which Brent crude spot prices averaged below $50/barrel. Contributing to the lower prices was an additional 0.1 million barrels per day (mbd) of combined crude oil production in Libya and Nigeria (two OPEC members exempted from production quotas), as well as higher inventories in the US of crude oil and petroleum products, which exceeded their 5-year average in June. Oil prices rallied again in late July on news of strong demand from US refineries and Saudi Arabia's announcement that it would reduce its crude oil exports starting in August. Upward pressure on prices from production disruption in the US caused by severe storms, as well as from a weakening US dollar (in which prices are denominated), is being countered by increased production in Libya and Nigeria. The average price in the year to date was $51.6/barrel on 8 September 2017.

In its August 2017 report, the International Energy Agency reported global oil demand to have risen by 1.5 mbd in the first half of 2017 from a year earlier because of improving economic conditions. It forecasts global oil demand to increase by 1.5 mbd in 2017 and 1.4 mbd in 2018, driven mostly by growth in countries outside of the Organisation for Economic Co-operation and Development. Oil consumption outside of this wealthy group is projected to rise by 1.2 mbd in 2017 and 1.3 mbd in 2018. Global oil supplies were 0.5 mbd higher in the first half of 2017 than in the same period of 2016, with growth of 0.6 mbd in production outside of OPEC more than offsetting a 0.1 mbd decline from OPEC. The agreement to cut production has had only modest impact on global inventories because compliance has been incomplete and supply has risen from other producers, notably steady increases from US shale. According to the International Energy Agency, the 22 countries participating in the production cut are producing nearly 0.5 mbd in excess of their commitments. It forecasts supply from outside of OPEC to expand by 0.6 mbd in 2017 and 1.5 mbd in 2018.

Futures prices suggest Brent crude will trade near $53/barrel for the remainder of 2017 (Figure A1.13). Although increases in global oil demand and the extension of the oil production cut are putting upward pressure on crude oil prices, the forecast increases in global production and continued noncompliance by some oil producers are exerting downward pressure on prices and mitigating the potential for significant crude oil price increases through 2018. Forecasts for Brent crude are therefore lowered by $4 to $52/barrel in 2017 and $54/barrel in 2018.

A1.13 Brent crude futures and spot price

— Average spot price
- - - Futures price (8 Sep 2017)
- - - Futures price (8 Mar 2017)
- - - Futures price (8 Mar 2017)

Source: Bloomberg (accessed 8 September 2017).

Food price movements and prospects

The World Bank food price index averaged 89.5 points in August 2017, or 5.3% lower than a year earlier (Figure A1.14). This is the fifth consecutive month that the food price index fell year on year. The August decline reflected lower prices for edible oil and meal and the "other food" category, which more than compensated for increases in grain prices. The edible oil index declined by 7.7% in August, mainly on weaker soybean prices. Improved production prospects in the US weighed on market sentiment. Similarly, the "other food" index dropped by 6.9% as meat and sugar prices weakened. The decline in meat prices reflected increased supplies from Australia and the US, while favorable prospects for cane harvests in Brazil, Thailand, and India dampened sugar prices. By contrast, the grains index rose by 1.2% year on year largely on stronger wheat prices, with maize prices steady. Unfavorable weather in the US pushed wheat prices up. Meanwhile, upward pressure on maize prices from a more rapid pace of foreign purchases by the People's Republic of China was tempered by favorable crop prospects in the US. Conversely, benchmark rice prices fell by 5.3% year on year as import demand slowed. In the first 8 months of the year, food inflation averaged 0.8%.

In its August assessment, the US Department of Agriculture increased its forecast for global grain production in the 2017/2018 crop year to 2,540 million tons from 2,538 million tons in its July assessment. Although below record production in the previous crop year, the forecast is well above the 5-year production average. Global wheat production is expected to increase significantly because of excellent growing conditions in Kazakhstan, the Russian Federation, and Ukraine. Yield prospects are also good for maize as growing conditions remain favorable in Argentina, Brazil, India, Mexico, and the US. Forecast rice production is slightly lower than in the July assessment because of unexpectedly low yield in the US. The ratio of grains stocks to use will go down because of a projected increase in global grain consumption, but it will remain above its 5-year average.

Prospects for edible oil and oilseed are positive, as soybean and palm oil production are forecast to continue recovering from a decline caused by El Niño weather disturbances in 2015. Soybean production is projected to be higher by 11.0% than in 2016/2017, and palm oil 13.6% higher. The forecast for meat production in 2017 is raised from July as increases in commercial beef and broiler production more than offset declines in other meat. Upward pressure on sugar prices will remain as world consumption of sugar continues to exceed production, driving stocks down to their lowest since 2011/2012. With the latest production forecasts indicating higher global output than earlier anticipated, the forecasts for higher food prices are lowered to 0.3% for 2017 and kept at 2.0% for 2018.

A1.14 Food commodity price indexes

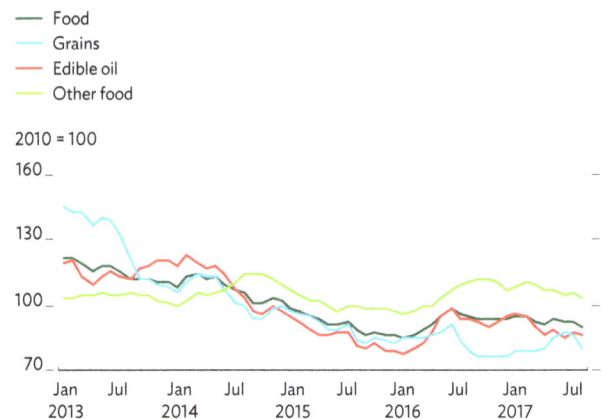

— Food
— Grains
— Edible oil
— Other food

Source: World Bank. Commodity Price Data (Pink Sheet). http://www.worldbank.org (accessed 8 September 2017).

External environment in sum

As growth in the major industrial economies becomes stronger, particularly in the euro area and Japan, developing Asia can anticipate higher external demand. Though the US got off to a slow start in the first half of the year, its recovery is expected to gather steam. The pickup in commodity prices is too mild to generate inflationary pressures in the region. Monetary policy remains accommodative in the euro area and Japan and is tightening only gradually in the US. Thus, monetary authorities in most of Asia's economies will therefore be inclined to leave their policy rates low, which should enhance the pace of economic expansion.

2

SUSTAINING DEVELOPMENT THROUGH PUBLIC–PRIVATE PARTNERSHIP

Sustaining development through public–private partnership

Despite rapid economic growth, developing Asia has large unmet infrastructure needs that leave many Asians without adequate basic services. The huge infrastructure gap results from both inadequate public resources and a dearth of effective mechanisms to channel private resources toward desired development outcomes. The private sector can be engaged to narrow or even close this gap.

Private enterprise has contributed substantially to the region's success, but sustaining Asia's future development requires it to take an expanded role. The private sector brings to the table innovation, superior technical and managerial skills, and financial resources. These strengths need to be directed toward a broader development agenda, with the primary focus on filling the infrastructure gap.

One mechanism to effectively channel private capital and funds toward a broader development agenda is to reinvent the relationship between the public and private sectors with the goal of sharing resources more efficiently. The public–private partnership (PPP) mechanism has evolved, especially over the past 3 decades, to more effectively address development issues. Benefits from PPP-based delivery arise from its unique structural and functional features: a lifecycle perspective on infrastructure provision and pricing, a focus on service delivery, and a sharing of risks between the public and private sectors. Instead of providing exclusively public assets and related services, governments have increasingly relied on the market for the direct provision of public goods and services. If appropriately deployed and managed, PPP facilitates the provision of adequate and efficient infrastructure services for users, profitable investment opportunities for the private sector, and a development mechanism that expands the capacity of the state.

Compared with other regions, developing Asia uses PPP for infrastructure development widely, though much of it happens in only a few economies (Figure 2.1.1). Benefits from PPP arise from its many incentives to innovate and its ability to improve the delivery of public infrastructure and services. This chapter identifies the major challenges the region must overcome to further promote PPP and suggests how PPP can be an effective catalyst for the region's sustainable development.

2.1.1 PPP committed investment by region, 1991–2015

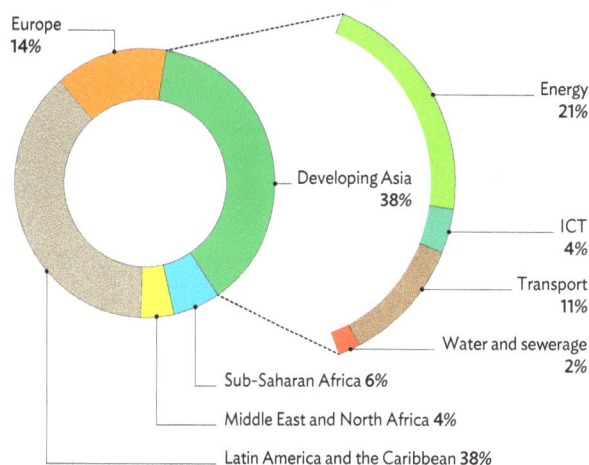

ICT = information and communication technology.

Note: Includes only low- and middle-income economies. Excludes full divestitures of state-owned assets (privatizations) and merchant projects that do not include government guarantees or that operate in a liberalized environment. Projects in the database must be at least 20% privately owned. State-owned enterprises are considered public. More information is available at http://ppi.worldbank.org/methodology/ppi-methodology

Source: World Bank Private Participation in Infrastructure database (accessed 25 May 2017).

This chapter was written by Minsoo Lee, Pilipinas Quising, Mai Lin Villaruel, and Xuehui Han of the Economic Research and Regional Cooperation Department and Vivek Rao of South Asia Regional Department, ADB, Manila; Akash Deep of Harvard Kennedy School of Government; Jungwook Kim of Korea Development Institute; and Raymond Gaspar and Emmanuel Alano, consultants, Economic Research and Regional Cooperation Department, ADB, Manila. It draws on the background papers listed at the end of the chapter.

Applying public–private partnership to Asia's infrastructure challenge

Developing Asia's impressive economic growth over the past 50 years comes in no small measure from its great strides in infrastructure development. Despite these efforts, the region still faces an infrastructure challenge. Access to infrastructure and associated services remains inadequate, particularly in poorer areas. Over 400 million Asians live without electricity, 300 million without safe drinking water, and 1.5 billion without basic sanitation. Even those with access to these services often find their quality inferior, in rural and urban areas alike. Notable problems are intermittent electric power supply, congested roads and ports, substandard water supply and sewerage, and poor quality schools and health facilities. The latest *Global Competitiveness Report* shows that many economies in developing Asia languish in the bottom half of the ranking on infrastructure (Figure 2.1.2).

Asia's infrastructure investment gap

Based on the assumption that economic growth will range from 3.1% to 6.5% across its subregions, developing Asia will need to invest an estimated $22.6 trillion (in 2015 prices) from 2016 to 2030 in transport, power, telecommunications, and urban water supply and sanitation. Factoring in climate mitigation and adaptation costs raises the investment requirement to $26.2 trillion, or $1.7 trillion annually, which is 5.9% of projected GDP of developing Asia in 2030 (ADB 2017).

The region annually invests $881 billion in infrastructure (estimated for 25 economies with adequate data, comprising 96% of the region's population). The infrastructure investment gap—the difference between investment needs and current investment—equals 2.4% of projected annual GDP in the 5-year period from 2016 to 2020, including the costs of climate change mitigation and adaptation. Excluding the People's Republic of China (PRC), the gap for the remaining economies doubles to 5% of their projected GDP. Without a significant boost to current efforts, infrastructure investment needs will continue to accumulate. The situation becomes more problematic when taking into account the aging and degradation of existing infrastructure.

Infrastructure development in the region has relied heavily on public sector funds, which account, on average, for 92% of the region's infrastructure investment, while continued support from multilateral development banks to public sector finance contributed 2.5% of developing Asia's infrastructure investment in 2015 (ADB 2017).

2.1.2 Infrastructure ranking of selected economies in developing Asia, 2016–2017

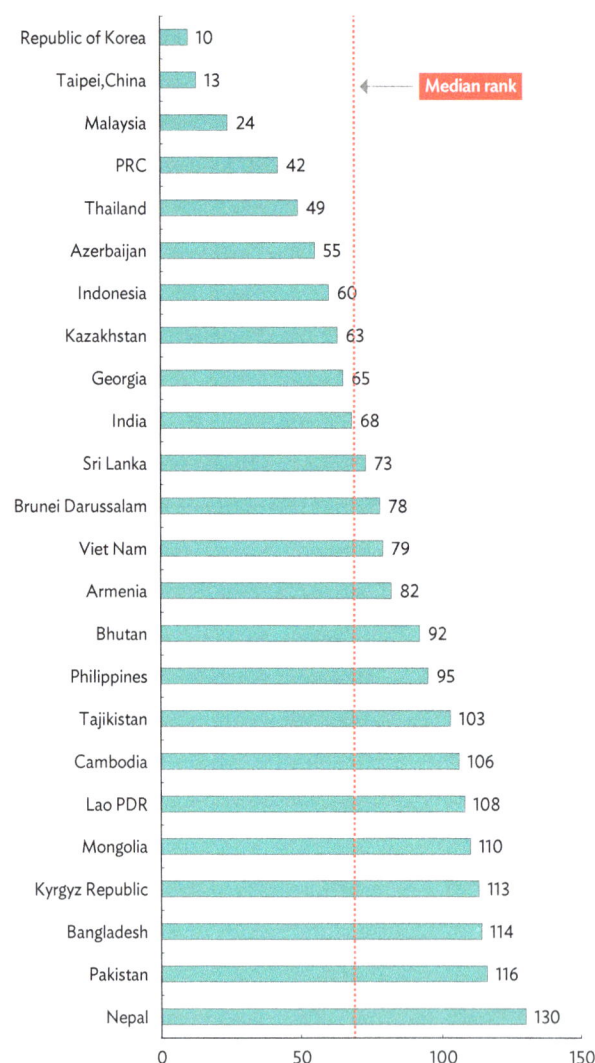

Lao PDR = Lao People's Democratic Republic, PRC = People's Republic of China.
Source: The Global Competitiveness Report, 2016–2017.

These traditional sources of financing for public infrastructure cannot meet the estimated investment needs. High fiscal deficits and deepening public debt inhibit the ability of most economies in the region to address the infrastructure challenge (Figure 2.1.3). Public finance reform could possibly raise additional revenues equal to 2% of GDP, but this would bridge only 40% of the infrastructure gap. If appropriate conditions were created, though, the private sector might eventually be able to fill the remaining 60% of the gap, or 3% of GDP. To do so, it would have to increase investments from $63 billion, as estimated for 2015, to as high as $250 billion per year over 2016–2020 (ADB 2017). An important source of private sector infrastructure investment is the estimated $100 trillion in global assets managed by pension funds, sovereign wealth funds, insurance companies, and other institutional investors (Arezki et al. 2016). The Organisation for Economic Co-operation and Development estimates that less than 1% of global pension fund assets are allocated directly to infrastructure investment (Kaminker and Stewart 2012). Approximately $17 trillion in private capital is available in Asia and the Pacific alone—the bulk of it in Japan and Australia but with sizable amounts in the PRC, the Republic of Korea, and India (World Bank 2015, WEF 2014, TheCityUK 2014, OECD 2016, Inderst 2016). These institutional investors have largely focused on infrastructure assets that are already operational and are averse to new infrastructure projects because they often experience regulatory challenges and other delays.

Filling the infrastructure gap through PPP

The role of the private sector in the provision of infrastructure should not be limited to addressing the financing gap. To tap its comparative advantages, the private sector should help improve operational efficiency, participate in granting incentivized finance, and share innovation capacity. The primary goal is to deploy all the resources and expertise of the private sector in the provision of infrastructure services.

PPP has been adopted by a number of national, state, and local governments to deliver public services, essential or otherwise. The fundamental idea behind PPP is not new. Private firms have been involved in delivering public services for centuries in a variety of different configurations. However, over the past 3 decades, PPP types have become better defined and acquired distinct characteristics as they have been used to deliver a broad range of public services: designing, building, financing, operating, and maintaining public infrastructure and facilities, or some combination of these tasks, to meet public needs.

But the use of PPP for infrastructure delivery, particularly in developing Asia, remains limited, despite the global surge in its use. Estimates show that up to one-third of infrastructure investment in selected economies in the region are procured through PPP where there are good frameworks and active PPP programs (Lee et al. forthcoming[a]).

Meanwhile, a separate policy and institutional framework for the promotion, execution, and management of PPPs has emerged in many countries. Indeed, PPP is becoming not only a widely available and attractive form of procurement but also a manifestation of a broader development in governance that has redrawn the boundary between the public and private sectors.

2.1.3 Public budget constraints

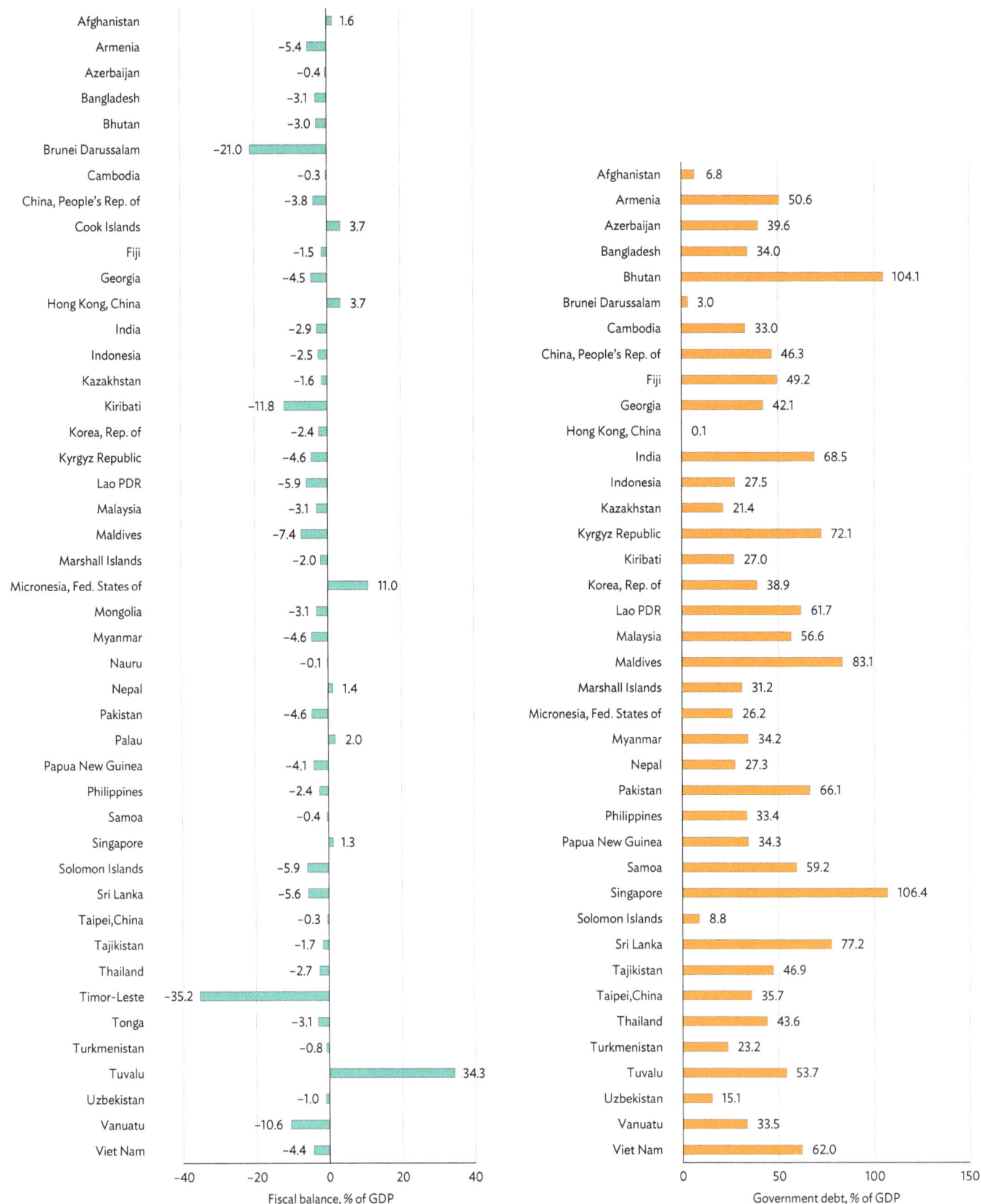

Country	Fiscal balance, % of GDP
Afghanistan	1.6
Armenia	-5.4
Azerbaijan	-0.4
Bangladesh	-3.1
Bhutan	-3.0
Brunei Darussalam	-21.0
Cambodia	-0.3
China, People's Rep. of	-3.8
Cook Islands	3.7
Fiji	-1.5
Georgia	-4.5
Hong Kong, China	3.7
India	-2.9
Indonesia	-2.5
Kazakhstan	-1.6
Kiribati	-11.8
Korea, Rep. of	-2.4
Kyrgyz Republic	-4.6
Lao PDR	-5.9
Malaysia	-3.1
Maldives	-7.4
Marshall Islands	-2.0
Micronesia, Fed. States of	11.0
Mongolia	-3.1
Myanmar	-4.6
Nauru	-0.1
Nepal	1.4
Pakistan	-4.6
Palau	2.0
Papua New Guinea	-4.1
Philippines	-2.4
Samoa	-0.4
Singapore	1.3
Solomon Islands	-5.9
Sri Lanka	-5.6
Taipei,China	-0.3
Tajikistan	-1.7
Thailand	-2.7
Timor-Leste	-35.2
Tonga	-3.1
Turkmenistan	-0.8
Tuvalu	34.3
Uzbekistan	-1.0
Vanuatu	-10.6
Viet Nam	-4.4

Country	Government debt, % of GDP
Afghanistan	6.8
Armenia	50.6
Azerbaijan	39.6
Bangladesh	34.0
Bhutan	104.1
Brunei Darussalam	3.0
Cambodia	33.0
China, People's Rep. of	46.3
Fiji	49.2
Georgia	42.1
Hong Kong, China	0.1
India	68.5
Indonesia	27.5
Kazakhstan	21.4
Kyrgyz Republic	72.1
Kiribati	27.0
Korea, Rep. of	38.9
Lao PDR	61.7
Malaysia	56.6
Maldives	83.1
Marshall Islands	31.2
Micronesia, Fed. States of	26.2
Myanmar	34.2
Nepal	27.3
Pakistan	66.1
Philippines	33.4
Papua New Guinea	34.3
Samoa	59.2
Singapore	106.4
Solomon Islands	8.8
Sri Lanka	77.2
Tajikistan	46.9
Taipei,China	35.7
Thailand	43.6
Turkmenistan	23.2
Tuvalu	53.7
Uzbekistan	15.1
Vanuatu	33.5
Viet Nam	62.0

Lao PDR = Lao People's Democratic Republic.

Sources: Asian Development Outlook 2017; Government Finance, World Economic Outlook online database (accessed 8 August 2017).

PPP has no unique or precise definition. As the approach evolved, countries and developmental institutions adopted different definitions of PPP in accordance with their own practices and criteria. To find common ground, the World Bank, Asian Development Bank (ADB), and Inter-American Development Bank broadly defined PPP as "a long-term contract between a private party and a government entity, for providing a public asset or service, in which the private party bears significant risk and management responsibility, and remuneration is linked to performance" (World Bank 2017). PPP is the framework for the asset over a large part of its useful life, addressing not only construction but also financing, operation, and maintenance.

Traditional public procurement versus PPP

Perhaps one of the main reasons why a precise and comprehensive definition has remained elusive is that PPPs do not really constitute a single form of organization. Instead, they occupy a continuum of structures and activities between the purely private and the purely public. Public procurement is the manner in which most countries have provided infrastructure to their citizens for much of history. It is therefore useful to define what public procurement is and then examine how PPP is different.

This approach is useful not only to distinguish PPP from public procurement but also because any government that is considering PPP for delivering public services must do so using a system of administrative institutions and procedures that was set up for public procurement. As public procurement is often the alternative to PPP, it provides a benchmark by which the value that comes with PPP might be measured and evaluated.

In traditional public procurement, the government—either national, state, or local, or one or more government agencies—occupies the center of the structure, the node through which flow all the activities required to provide services. Under this system, the government or a designated public authority first selects a private or public firm to design the infrastructure asset and another one to build it. The government finances the project through a combination of public and private funds. Finally, it manages and operates the facilities or selects a private operator to perform the task.

Under a PPP system, the whole process is bundled together and handed over to a single entity that is organized as a "special purpose vehicle" (Figure 2.1.4). It is this entity that occupies the center of the structure—designing, building, financing, operating, and maintaining the infrastructure asset in a way that delivers services to the public in accordance with the PPP contract. The government is still engaged, regulating the activities through the contract, and paying the special purpose vehicle directly, or authorizing it to collect user fees. Finally, the government takes over responsibility for the asset from the vehicle at the end of the contract period.

2.1.4 Typical PPP structure

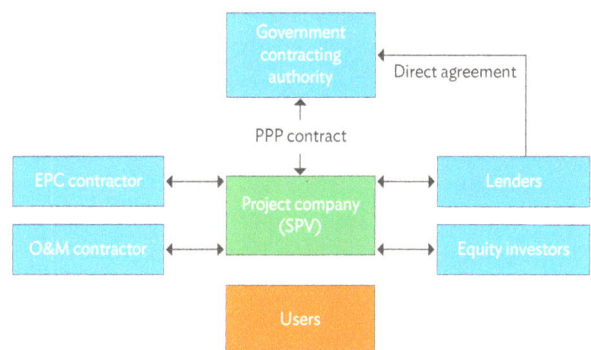

EPC = engineering, procurement, and construction, O&M = operation and maintenance, SPV = special purpose vehicle.
Source: World Bank 2017.

Well-structured PPPs manage risks by allocating them across the public and private sectors in a manner that optimizes their cost and aligns incentives for performance. Typically, responsibilities for design, construction, and operating risks are passed to the private partner, which is able to optimize the design of the facility in view of its lifecycle costs and potential to meet performance obligations stipulated under the contract. These same risks are usually present in traditionally procured projects, but risks are not transferred to the private party, at least not in full, and not beyond a limited project life. Full transfer of risks motivates the construction company to complete the project on time and on budget, and to deliver services that meet the key performance indicators of the contract.

The decision to use a PPP structure for a given infrastructure investment hinges on whether it offers better value for money than public procurement. The value-for-money approach factors in all pertinent project characteristics—target quality, performance standards, risk exposure, costs, and possibly other measures of social benefit such as environmental impact—to determine if PPP would be more desirable than public procurement. An important point is that the value-for-money approach goes beyond questions of cost differences to take into account risk transfer, which is a key argument in favor of PPP.

A PPP contract for a public service project may be monopolistic, as is often the case with public infrastructure projects. Such a contract must ensure that public concerns of affordability, safety, and reliability are respected. At the same time, the contract must provide enough latitude to the private owner and manager to control and bear the risks inherent in the project. The government role is therefore instrumental, and the government must remain actively involved in PPP projects throughout their lifecycles.

PPP options differ in how the services are paid for. It is common for PPPs to charge users directly, such as collecting fees from drivers that use toll roads. However, direct user charges are not necessarily the only revenue source, or necessarily levied at all. The PPP contract may promise payments directly from the government as long as performance targets are met. These payments may be linked to usage, as are so-called shadow tolls, or independent of usage, as are availability payments. The different forms of payment have important implications for risk allocation, incentives, budgetary impact, and public access to the services provided by the PPP.

The range of PPP arrangements

The primary defining characteristics of different forms of PPP, upon which payment arrangements are made, are as follows:
1.   What are the functions performed by the private party?
    a.   Designing the infrastructure?
    b.   Building, upgrading, or renovating the infrastructure?
    c.   Financing the capital investment?
    d.   Operating the infrastructure?
    e.   Maintaining the infrastructure?
2.   Who will pay the private party, users of the infrastructure or the government?

2.1.1 Summary of key features of the basic forms of public–private partnership

	Service contracts	Management contracts	Lease contracts	Concessions	BOT
Scope	Multiple contracts for a variety of support services such as meter reading, billing, etc.	Management of entire operation or a major component	Responsibility for management, operations, and specific renewals	Responsibility for all operations and for the financing and execution of specific investments	Investment in and operation of a specific major component, such as a treatment plant
Asset ownership	Public	Public	Public	Public/Private	Public/Private
Duration	1–3 years	2–5 years	10–15 years	25–30 years	Varies
O&M responsibility	Public	Private	Private	Private	Private
Capital investment	Public	Public	Public	Private	Private
Commercial risk	Public	Public	Shared	Private	Private
Overall level of risk assumed by private sector	Minimal	Minimal/Moderate	Moderate	High	High
Compensation terms	Unit prices	Fixed fee, preferably with performance incentives	Portion of tariff revenues	All or part of tariff revenues	Mostly fixed, partly variable, depending on production parameters
Competition	Intense and ongoing	One time only; contracts not usually renewed	Initial contract only; subsequent contracts usually negotiated	Initial contract only; subsequent contracts usually negotiated	One time only; often negotiated without direct competition
Special features	Useful as part of a strategy for improving the efficiency of public company Promotes local private sector development	Interim solution during preparation for more intense private participation	Improves operational and commercial efficiency Develops local staff	Improves operational and commercial efficiency Mobilizes investment finance Develops local staff	Mobilizes investment finance Develops local staff
Problems and challenges	Requires ability to administer multiple contracts and strong enforcement of contract laws	Management may not have adequate control over key elements, such as budgetary resources, staff policy, etc.	Potential conflicts between public body, which is responsible for investments, and the private operator	How to compensate investments and ensure good maintenance during last 5–10 years of contract	Does not necessarily improve efficiency of ongoing operations May require guarantees

BOT = build–operate–transfer, O&M = operation and maintenance.
Source: Table 3 of ADB (2008).

The functions performed by the private sector and the different payment mechanisms can be combined in a variety of ways to produce many different forms of infrastructure provision, some of which fall within the PPP concept described above. A variety of different names are given to the various forms of PPP. Table 2.1.1 presents a summary of these basic forms and their characteristics. While all of them are PPPs, their differences are significant. Thus, it is not enough just to decide that PPP is the preferred mode of procurement for a project because, within the PPP model, a range of designs may be feasible. One of the determining factors is the ultimate objective of the procuring authority and the outputs that are expected from the private partner. Figure 2.1.5 shows the range of PPP arrangements, the extent to which ownership and capital investment responsibility sits with each party, and the relative risk borne by each party.

2.1.5 Public–private partnership spectrum

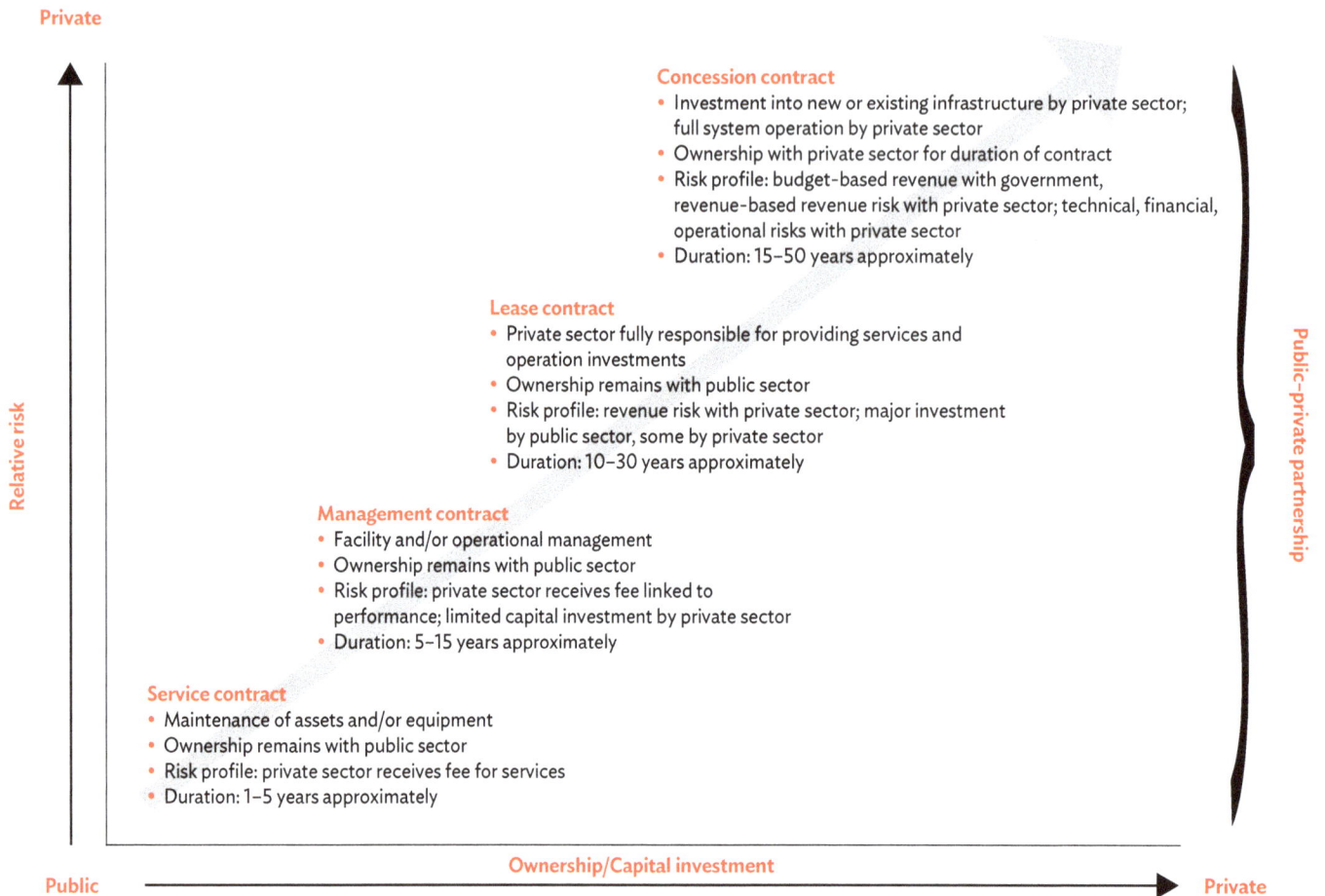

Private

Relative risk

Public–private partnership

Concession contract
- Investment into new or existing infrastructure by private sector; full system operation by private sector
- Ownership with private sector for duration of contract
- Risk profile: budget-based revenue with government, revenue-based revenue risk with private sector; technical, financial, operational risks with private sector
- Duration: 15–50 years approximately

Lease contract
- Private sector fully responsible for providing services and operation investments
- Ownership remains with public sector
- Risk profile: revenue risk with private sector; major investment by public sector, some by private sector
- Duration: 10–30 years approximately

Management contract
- Facility and/or operational management
- Ownership remains with public sector
- Risk profile: private sector receives fee linked to performance; limited capital investment by private sector
- Duration: 5–15 years approximately

Service contract
- Maintenance of assets and/or equipment
- Ownership remains with public sector
- Risk profile: private sector receives fee for services
- Duration: 1–5 years approximately

Public

Ownership/Capital investment   **Private**

Source: ADB 2012a.

The specific design selected for a project may be influenced by the nature of the assets and legal jurisdictions involved. More often, actual design is a conscious choice made by the government based on the sort of arrangement that is deemed to be contractually optimal, legally enforceable, politically implementable, and financially affordable. For example, water projects in many countries are structured as management contracts with little private involvement because citizens are highly sensitive to the political risks of handing over to a private firm a role in water supply at the distribution level. PPPs are thus more common in bulk water supply, not retail, and in wastewater management.

Motivations to engage in PPP

A wave of interest in PPP sometimes generates explicit declarations to "do PPPs," as if it were a policy objective on a par with more substantive goals to promote, such as economic well-being, commerce, reliable infrastructure, or high-quality education and health care.

Policy makers and advocates alike ought to consider PPP as just one procurement option to deliver public services. However, strong theoretical rationales exist, as does mounting empirical evidence, that support the belief that PPP can deliver better outcomes when deployed appropriately, structured correctly, and managed effectively.

Enhanced efficiency and fiscal flexibility

The increased use of PPP as a procurement method in many countries and across various sectors has been spurred by the expectation that it will yield better results than traditional public procurement. This expectation is generally based on an examination of how PPP differs from public procurement structurally and functionally toward delivering efficiency gains.

Lee and Kim (forthcoming) described one of the primary theoretical underpinnings for the attraction of PPP. The optimal structure of procurement contracts between the public and private sector is studied by comparing PPP with traditional public procurement. A principal–agent model based on Hart (2003) and Iossa and Martimort (2015) focuses on how bundling affects procurement and shows the advantages PPP has over traditional public procurement in this regard.

Under contract theory, PPP is seen as a new type of contract that counters the inefficiency that can arise from asymmetrical access to information enjoyed by the government and the private party. When setting up a large public investment project, uncertainties at each stage of the process leave substantial information asymmetry between the two parties, usually favoring the private partner (Kim forthcoming).

Contract theory suggests that efficiency can be attributed to the long-term nature of PPP contracts and careful monitoring by providers of private funding. Long-term contracts can motivate the operator to manage the facility with a full lifecycle perspective and plan. Engel, Fischer, and Galetovic (2014) emphasized that the third crucial feature of PPP is the degree of control that the private partner of a PPP enjoys through ownership rights, as well as its autonomy in the management of infrastructure assets.

In practice, better results are realized when the emphasis of PPP is on service delivery—that is, when a PPP delivers a service rather than a physical asset. Yet traditional public procurement is concerned first with the creation and financing of an asset, and only later with its operation. The primary focus on service delivery makes the special purpose vehicle assume responsibility for the provision of services over a relatively long period and their delivery at a standard that is satisfactory, along with other criteria.

Bundling the different responsibilities for designing, building, financing, and operating an asset over its full life creates in PPP a lifecycle perspective. It is easy to see that a company responsible for constructing and maintaining a building over its useful life will make some construction choices differently than would a company that has no responsibility for maintenance. These choices may be more expensive up front but are still chosen because they will reduce maintenance costs or provide better service over the life of the project.

Benefits can arise from competitive bidding across consortia. Not only does it facilitate the search for and pulling together of a strong team of individual firms spanning the full range of required competencies, it also ensures that pricing is attractive as each consortium seeks to strengthen its bid by exerting pressure on its members to be as efficient as they can be. In the process, the bidding consortia are expected to develop the necessary coordination required to work together and take collective responsibility to deliver the contracted services. In public procurement, by contrast, the government is the interface for all the interactions between different entities as they perform their functions. It therefore bears the lion's share of transactional costs, endures the friction that sometimes arises, and risks possible failure if peripheral entities fail to coordinate effectively.

Payment or compensation to the provider of services in a PPP is usually contingent on achieving specified performance targets. These targets relate not only to price and volume of usage but also to a variety of indicators of quality and reliability. Performance-based compensation and penalties are powerful shapers of incentives that help focus attention on final outcomes and standards, and thus improve accountability.

PPP facilitates a better match between the timing of usage and costs from the perspective of public finance. Unlike a public procurement project in which a large amount of capital has to be raised up front, payment for a PPP is more evenly spread out and may even be linked to the volume of usage (Figure 2.1.6). Early lump sum financing is usually provided by sponsors, as well as by banks and financial market investors, thus enhancing fiscal flexibility for the public agency. This sidesteps the heavy fiscal burden that large projects can impose at the outset if the full cost of construction must be borne by the public purse. It also allows a larger number of projects to be undertaken where government access to long-term capital markets is limited.

2.1.6 Payment mechanism of PPP and traditional public procurement

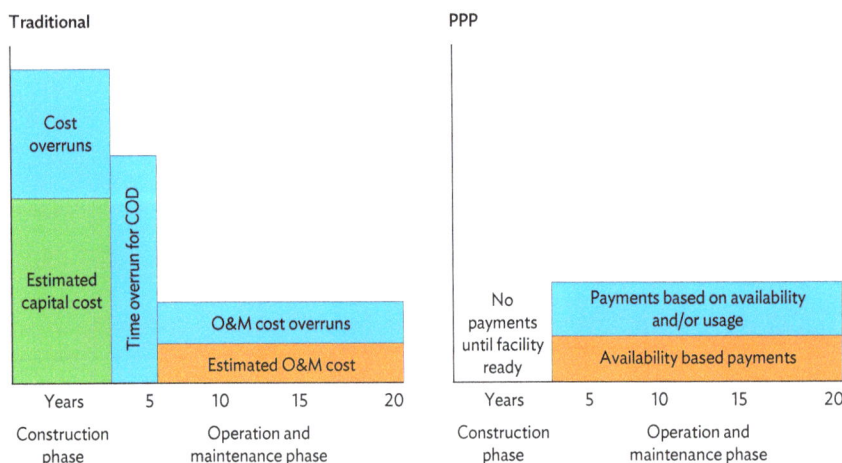

Traditional

Cost overruns

Estimated capital cost

Time overrun for COD

O&M cost overruns

Estimated O&M cost

Years   5   10   15   20

Construction phase   Operation and maintenance phase

PPP

No payments until facility ready

Payments based on availability and/or usage

Availability based payments

Years   5   10   15   20

Construction phase   Operation and maintenance phase

COD = commercial operations data, O&M = operation and maintenance, PPP = public–private partnership.
Source: Sampath 2006.

A related benefit of PPP, though it does not show up in traditional forms of budgeting, is the transfer of risk from the public to the private sector. Such risk transfer not only reduces the vulnerability of the public budget to large unexpected costs that would be present under traditional public procurement, it also ensures that risks are borne by private entities that are better equipped to handle them, either by heading off problems before they materialize or by coping with them effectively once they occur.

An emphasis on service delivery creates a procurement process that, while strict on performance standards, allows greater flexibility on how the standards are achieved. Traditional public procurement rules are more rigid. Flexibility allows greater scope and capacity for innovation from private sector bidders able to arrive at solutions that meet the public service imperative or improve on it, and do so more efficiently.

Because functional incentives are embedded in the design of a PPP, it is not surprising that they are associated with greater innovation and the delivery of projects on time and within budget much more often than is true with public procurement. The timely delivery of infrastructure demonstratively provides public welfare benefits. Using 14 PPP road projects in operation since 2006 in the Republic of Korea, Kim et al. (2011) estimated that benefits arising from their advanced completion and operation were worth as much as W2.5 trillion (Table 2.1.2). Similarly, build–operate–transfer tunnel projects in Hong Kong, China provide clear examples of how PPP facilitates the timely delivery of infrastructure and their services, as the tunnels were completed ahead of their target completion dates (Table 2.1.3).

2.1.2 Welfare loss from delayed delivery of PPP road projects (W billion)

	1-year service delay	2-year service delay	3-year service delay
Start service in 2006	623.3	1,455.1	2,471.9

Note: The study computed the net monetary benefits of the 14 selected PPP road projects over 30 years following the presumed opening year in 2006, while setting succeeding years as delayed opening years.

Source: Kim et al. 2011.

2.1.3 Delivery of BOT tunnel projects in Hong Kong, China

Project	Construction date	Target completion (months)	Actual completion (months)	Operation date
Cross Harbour Tunnel	September 1969	47	36	August 1972
Eastern Harbour Crossing	August 1986	42	38	September 1989
Tate's Cairn Tunnel	July 1988	37	34	June 1991
Western Cross Harbour	August 1993	48	44	April 1997
Route 3 (Country Park Section)	May 1995	38	36	May 1998

BOT = build–operate–transfer.
Source: Mak and Mo 2005.

The quick delivery of the Eastern Harbour Crossing was made possible by the private partner's technological and innovative capability (Mak and Mo 2005). A Japanese construction company applied novel construction techniques such as an innovative watertight sealing system to join tube sections (Levy 1996). Meanwhile, Downer and Porter (1992) believed that competitive tendering in the PPP approach incentivized bidders for the Tate's Cairn Tunnel project to come up with creative design proposals. An alternative design accepted by the government helped reduce the costs of tunnel construction without compromising on specifications. Heavy traffic volume and substantial savings in time allowed quicker repayment of initial construction costs.

This does not mean, however, that PPP is always more efficient than traditional procurement. PPP may or may not be a more efficient method depending on the characteristics of the project and the system. In some cases, PPP can be less efficient than the traditional procurement system, in which the government itself finances the project and places orders. Only if the contracting and practice of PPP are designed appropriately can PPP enhance efficiency.

Positive macroeconomic impacts

Building appropriate infrastructure is widely acknowledged to bolster and sustain economic activity. Infrastructure helps emerging economies avoid unnecessary bottlenecks as they pursue productive activities. Economies at all levels of development need infrastructure to improve connectivity and linkages, toward pursuing a broader agenda for economic development.

The few macroeconomic evaluations of PPPs provide mixed views. Trujillo et al. (2002) found that private sector involvement in transport infrastructure investment as a policy reform, including through PPP, has a positive effect on per capita income. Kim et al. (2011) showed that an increase in capital expenditure arising from PPP investment on social overhead capital would have expanded the Republic of Korea economy by as much as 0.2% in 2008. Meanwhile, Rhee and Lee (2007) found a negative but statistically insignificant coefficient on PPP investment.

In an event analysis, Lee et al. (forthcoming[a]) observed higher real per capita GDP growth after a PPP investment boom (Figure 2.1.7). A PPP investment boom occurs when PPP investment, measured as a percentage of GDP, grows at accelerating rates for 3 consecutive years. The positive relationship between PPP investment and economic growth can be attributed to the huge capital outlays involved in PPP projects. Shediac et al. (2008) noted that these large undertakings generate short- and long-term employment and attract private investment, thereby creating a sustainable model for economic growth.

The direction of macroeconomic impact from PPP can be gleaned from micro-level case studies, analyses of value for money, and quasi-experimental studies of various PPP projects. Drawing from micro-level analyses as well as the theoretical literature, several direct and indirect channels are identified through which PPP can bring macroeconomic benefit (Figure 2.1.8). The direct channel stems from the ability of a PPP to attract private resources, including expertise and know-how, into infrastructure investment. Using monthly data on the value of construction investment in the Republic of Korea, Rhee and Lee (2007) observed a brief increase in private investment associated with an increase in PPP investment.

2.1.7 **Real per capita GDP growth before and after the PPP investment boom**

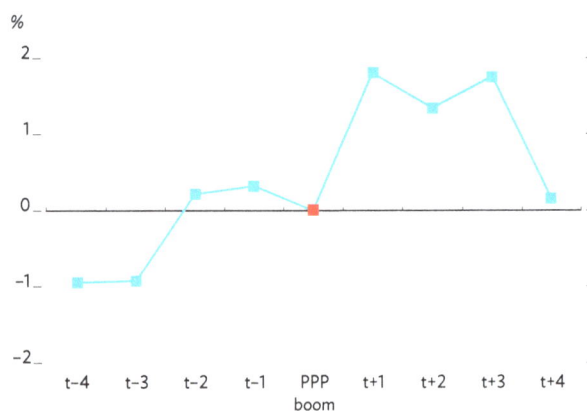

PPP = public–private partnership.
Source: Lee et al. forthcoming[a].

2.1.8 Macroeconomic benefits from PPP project delivery mechanism

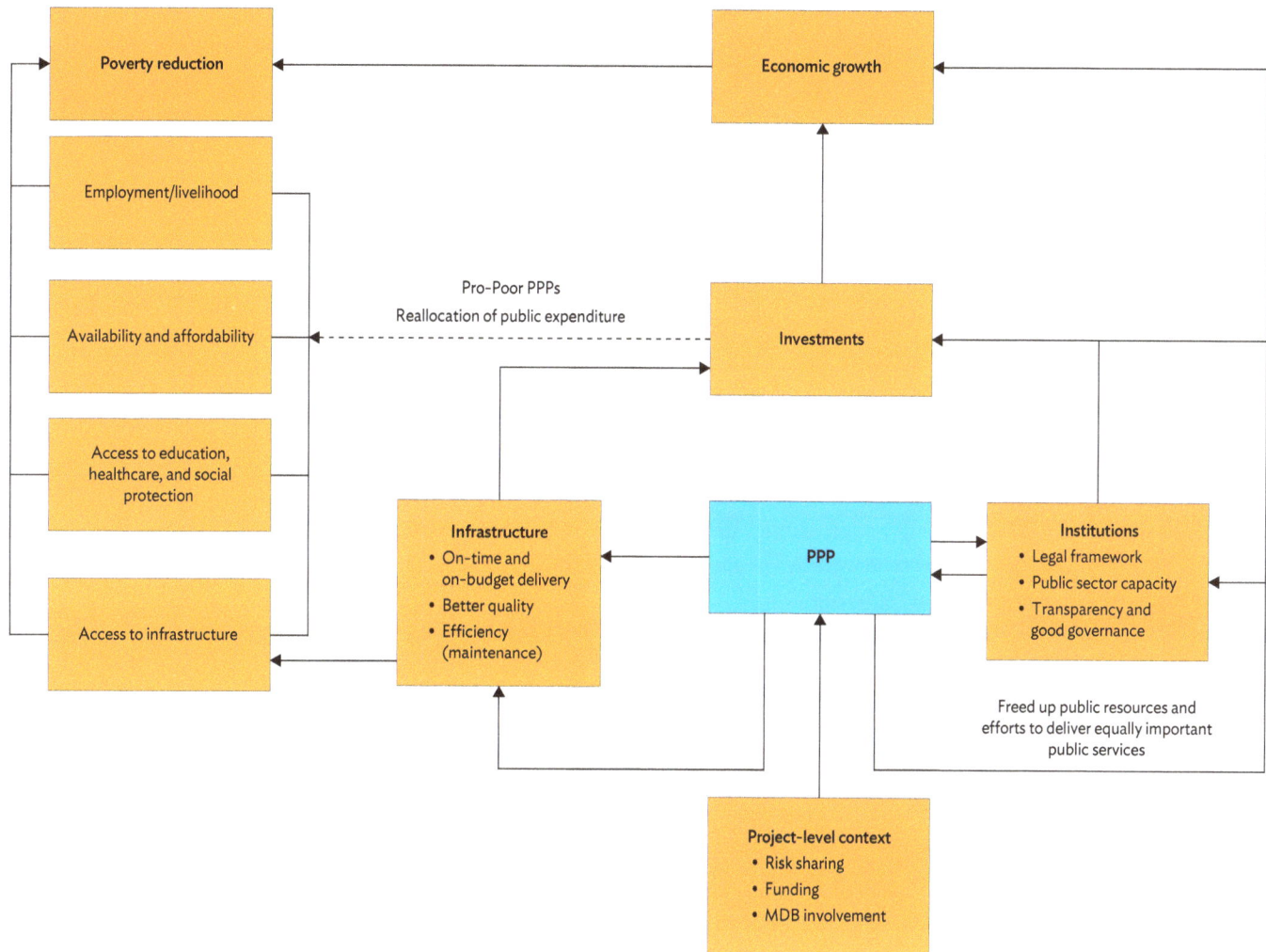

Poverty reduction	**Economic growth**
Employment/livelihood	
Availability and affordability	Pro-Poor PPPs Reallocation of public expenditure → **Investments**
Access to education, healthcare, and social protection	
Access to infrastructure	**Infrastructure** • On-time and on-budget delivery • Better quality • Efficiency (maintenance)

Infrastructure
• On-time and on-budget delivery
• Better quality
• Efficiency (maintenance)

PPP

Institutions
• Legal framework
• Public sector capacity
• Transparency and good governance

Freed up public resources and efforts to deliver equally important public services

Project-level context
• Risk sharing
• Funding
• MDB involvement

MDB = multilateral development bank, PPP = public–private partnership.
Source: Lee et al. forthcoming[a].

Without the promotion of PPP, infrastructure investment in the Republic of Korea would have fallen substantially, particularly during the Asian financial crisis of 1997–1998. Rising unemployment and swelling financial restructuring costs severely squeezed financial resources for infrastructure investment. Against this backdrop, the government worked out a policy package for reinvigorating private investment through PPP and so maintaining investment in infrastructure (Kim 2011).

The following empirical estimates of potential macroeconomic benefits from PPP are conditional on a range of qualifications (Lee et al. forthcoming[a]). The impact of PPP may differ from country to country, and may depend heavily on institutional factors such as the quality of governance, the degree of transparency, and public sector capacity.

Lee et al. (forthcoming[a]) found PPP associated with better access to necessary infrastructure services in developing Asia, including in rural areas. Doubling current PPP investment, from the equivalent of

2.1.4 PPP, economic growth, and infrastructure services in developing Asia

Variables	PPP ratio from 0.5% to 1.0%	PPP ratio from 0.5% to 2.0%	PPP ratio from 0.5% to 3.0%
Increase in per capita GDP growth (percentage points)	0.1	0.3	0.4
Reduction in the number of people without electricity (million)	14	41	69
Reduction in the number of people without proper sanitation (million)	16	47	78
Reduction in the number of people without safe drinking water (million)	12	36	60

Note: The study used data from the World Bank Private Participation in Infrastructure database and World Development Indicators. Following the ADB, World Bank, and Inter-American Development Bank definition of PPP, it excludes full divestiture and merchant projects. Values reflect the marginal effect of increasing the regional average PPP share of GDP at 0.5%.

Source: Lee et al. forthcoming[a].

0.5% of GDP to 1.0%, could deliver safe drinking water to 12 million of the 300 million Asians who currently lack it and provide electricity to 14 million of the 400 million now without supply (Table 2.1.4). In addition, a higher PPP ratio is associated with higher quality of infrastructure and services, reflecting the innovation and efficiency found in PPP. These access and quality improvements can translate into higher economic performance through raised productivity and competitiveness. Doubling the PPP ratio would add an estimated 0.1 percentage points to regional per capita GDP growth, all other factors being constant.

Facilitating poverty reduction

The underlying rationale for PPP is to widen access to infrastructure and improve its quality, either of which can boost economic growth. The benefits eventually reach the poor through expanded wage employment and other livelihood opportunities.

PPPs affect employment redistribution across industries and potentially provide jobs not only during construction but over the long economic life of the infrastructure asset. PPP investment helps reduce poverty by moving agricultural labor into more productive and remunerative industry. Indeed, flows of labor from low-productivity and low-earning activities like agriculture into high-productivity and high-earning sectors have been key to development in Asia (McMillan and Rodrik 2011).

Pro-poor PPP (called 5P by the United Nations Economic and Social Commission for Asia and the Pacific) can be viable in developing Asia. To reduce poverty, PPP projects should be accessible to the poor, affordable, reliable, efficient, and able to generate jobs and other livelihood opportunities (Zen forthcoming, ADB 2008). Several social projects are better at reducing poverty and providing to the poor such welfare services as basic health care and lower and middle education, as well as housing. The application of the PPP modality in social infrastructure is, however, limited in Asia. From 2000 to 2016, the region accounted for only 5% of all PPP projects in education, health care, housing, and other social sectors, compared with 90% in the advanced economies of the Organisation for Economic Co-operation and Development (Figure 2.1.9).

Though PPP projects in social infrastructure are relatively new to Asia, there is potential for expansion. Social support tends to be high, and issues complicating land acquisition are minimal, improving the odds that a PPP project in line with pro-poor programs will be able to go ahead (Zen forthcoming).

Pro-poor PPP is also possible in economic infrastructure. For instance, community initiatives in resource-rich areas take advantage of untapped energy sources and turn them into utilities through public and private investment. Such initiatives leverage the strengths of government, the technical and financial resources of the private sector, and the development interests of communities (UNESCAP 2014a). An example is a mini-hydroelectric power plant jointly owned in Indonesia by the local community at Cinta Mekar, with financial support from the United Nations Economic and Social Commission for Asia and the Pacific, and a private company that has been sustainably operating since 2004, providing income and livelihoods to the community. This demonstrates the successful use of private sector participation to reform public utilities and improve services in underserved areas (Box 2.1.1).

Catalyzing public sector reform

The complexity of PPP requires improvements to local technical and institutional capacity. The successful practice of PPP necessitates improved transparency and good governance.

2.1.9 Social infrastructure public–private partnerships, 2000–2016

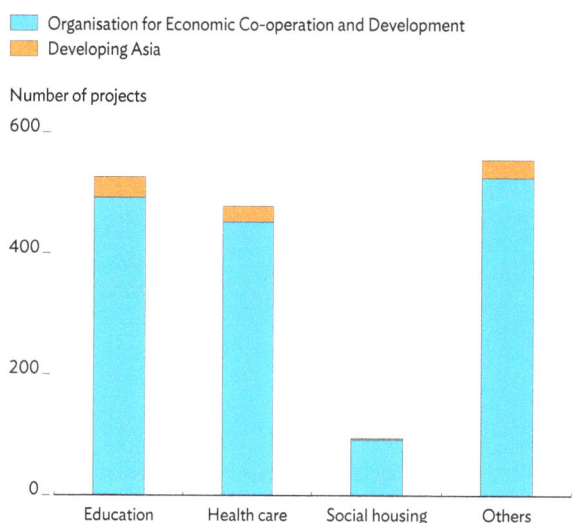

Notes: Developing Asia includes Bhutan, India, Kazakhstan, the Republic of Korea, Malaysia, Pakistan, the Philippines, Singapore, and Taipei,China. Others include projects on waste treatment, leisure, trial law courts, distribution utilities, training centers, fire and rescue services, and municipal buildings.
Source: IJGlobal (accessed 28 July 2017).

2.1.1 Pro-poor PPP in developing Asia

Basic services have been improved in Asia through community participation and ownership in PPP projects. At Halgahakumbura in Sri Lanka, 600 poor families used to receive water through public stand posts notable for their poor quality and waste of water. The national water agency partnered with a local nongovernmental organization for consultation and awarded a 5-year concession to a private company to install pipe networks. This provided safe drinking water and revenue for both the government and the private provider, as well as reducing waste. A similar scheme using easy payment terms and nongovernmental participation is implemented through the Water for the Community Program by a water concessionaire in the Philippines.

Similarly, alternative energy sources have expanded rural populations' access to electricity in the region. From 2002 to 2007, more than 400,000 solar power systems for homes were distributed in rural areas, including to nomadic herders in the People's Republic of China under the Renewable Energy Development Project, supported by the World Bank and the Global Environment Facility. Participating companies were required to comply with quality standards and provide innovative technology to reduce costs. Evaluations showed positive effects on household income. In India, a multisector initiative including a nonprofit nongovernmental organization, the State Bank of Mysore, microenterprise groups, and a private company rent solar lanterns to street vendors. Monitors report increased business activity and expansion into other areas.

Sources:

Ludeña, M. 2009. Towards a New Model of PPPs: Can Public Private Partnerships Deliver Basic Services to the Poor? *UNESCAP Working Paper* WP/09/01.

Sovacool, B. 2013. Expanding Renewable Energy Access with Pro-poor Public Private Partnerships in the Developing World. *Energy Strategy Reviews* 1.

The implementation of PPPs provides opportunities to re-examine regulatory and policy arrangements, thereby enabling improvement in governance and public sector capacity. Learning from its first experience with a very large PPP project for a high-speed rail system, Taipei,China promulgated in 2000 legislation to promote private participation in infrastructure projects, which became the institutional framework for PPP in that economy.

With the required institutional improvements to carry out PPP and derive hoped-for benefits, PPP can improve governance and leverage better incentives, among other improvements to the investment environment, that can have ripple effects into other private endeavor and the general economy.

Emerging patterns in Asian PPP

Public service delivery has evolved considerably in recent years in developing Asia. The government is no longer the sole provider of essential public assets and related services. Although investment in infrastructure is still dominated by the public sector, the private sector has recently begun to play a larger and increasingly critical role in building, developing, and improving public goods and services. PPP is now a popular mechanism to build vital public infrastructure and deliver public services.

Geographical distribution

The use of PPP in developing Asia has become increasingly widespread, especially in the Republic of Korea, where it is well established, and with varying regularity and success in the PRC, India, Indonesia, Malaysia, the Philippines, and Singapore.

Infrascope 2014 reported significant improvements in developing Asia in governments' handling of PPP projects, based on its evaluation of regulatory and institutional frameworks, the investment climate in individual economies, and the availability of finance. Figure 2.1.10 shows the scores of selected economies in Asia and the Pacific in terms of their readiness and capacity for PPP projects. Of the 20 economies reviewed, four in the region were considered "developed," the second highest categorization in the ranking system: the Republic of Korea, Japan, India, and the Philippines, in order of their scores. Other economies are "emerging" in terms of capacity to select, design, deliver, and manage projects, and to develop local finance facilities. The PRC leads the emerging PPP market group in the region. Others in the emerging group are Indonesia, Thailand, Bangladesh, Kazakhstan, Pakistan, Mongolia, Armenia, Papua New Guinea, and Viet Nam. Economies classified as "nascent," or yet to have developed the institutional and technical capacity required to deliver complex PPP projects, are the Kyrgyz Republic, Tajikistan, and Georgia.

The number of PPP projects in the region that reached financial closure grew from 1991 to 2015 by a compounded annual rate of 11%. In Figure 2.1.11, the panel on the left shows that developing Asia accounts for half of PPP activities in 139 low- and middle-income

2.1.10 PPP readiness score of selected economies in Asia and the Pacific

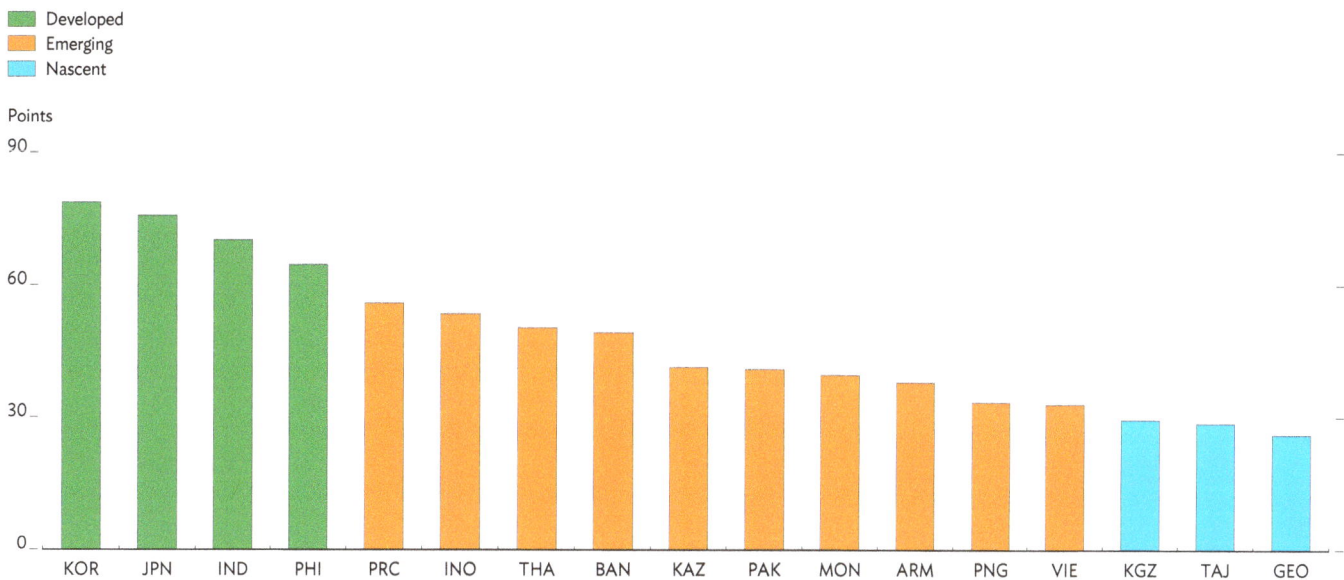

ARM = Armenia, BAN = Bangladesh, GEO = Georgia, IND = India, INO = Indonesia, JPN = Japan, KAZ = Kazakhstan, KGZ = Kyrgyz Republic, KOR = Republic of Korea, MON = Mongolia, PAK = Pakistan, PHI = Philippines, PNG = Papua New Guinea, PPP = public–private partnership, PRC = People's Republic of China, TAJ = Tajikistan, THA = Thailand, VIE = Viet Nam.
Note: Developed PPP market group (60.0–79.9 points), emerging PPP market group (30.0–59.9 points), and nascent PPP market group (0.0 to 29.9 points).
Source: Economist Intelligence Unit 2015.

economies worldwide, followed by Latin America and the Caribbean with almost a third. The panel on the right shows that the value of PPP investments is relatively high but has declined in recent years.

Within developing Asia, the extent of PPP activity varies by subregion. PPP transactions are observed mainly in East and South Asia, which together accounted for more than 70% of all projects in 1991–2015 (Figure 2.1.12). Some 90% of that portion are in the PRC and India. Both governments have proactively promoted and improved PPP. In particular, the PRC promotes PPP to develop infrastructure and drive investment in fixed assets in its Thirteenth Five-Year Plan, 2016–2020. By the end of 2016, there were more than 11,000 projects with total investment of CNY13.5 trillion at various stages in the PPP pipeline from identification to implementation. In the first half of 2017, the number of projects increased to more than 13,000, with accumulated investment of CNY16.3 trillion. State-owned enterprises (SOEs), many in construction, are the main capital contributors to PPP infrastructure projects in the PRC. Returns on PPP are, at 5%–8%, not appealing to many private investors but sufficient for SOEs because they enjoy lower financing costs. In addition, local governments and banks in the PRC tend to view SOEs as stable, long-term partners. However, in PPPs for purposes other than infrastructure development, such as health care, elderly care, and environmental protections, the private sector is more active.

Meanwhile, India accounts for almost half of PPP transport projects in developing Asia, the sector having grown in India at a compounded rate of 34% from 1991 to 2015. Private sector participation in road development recently improved with reform that included the

2.1.11 PPP by region, 1991–2015

- 🟩 Developing Asia
- 🟧 Europe
- 🟦 Latin America and the Caribbean
- 🟨 Middle East and North Africa
- ⬜ Sub-Saharan Africa

Number of projects

$ billion

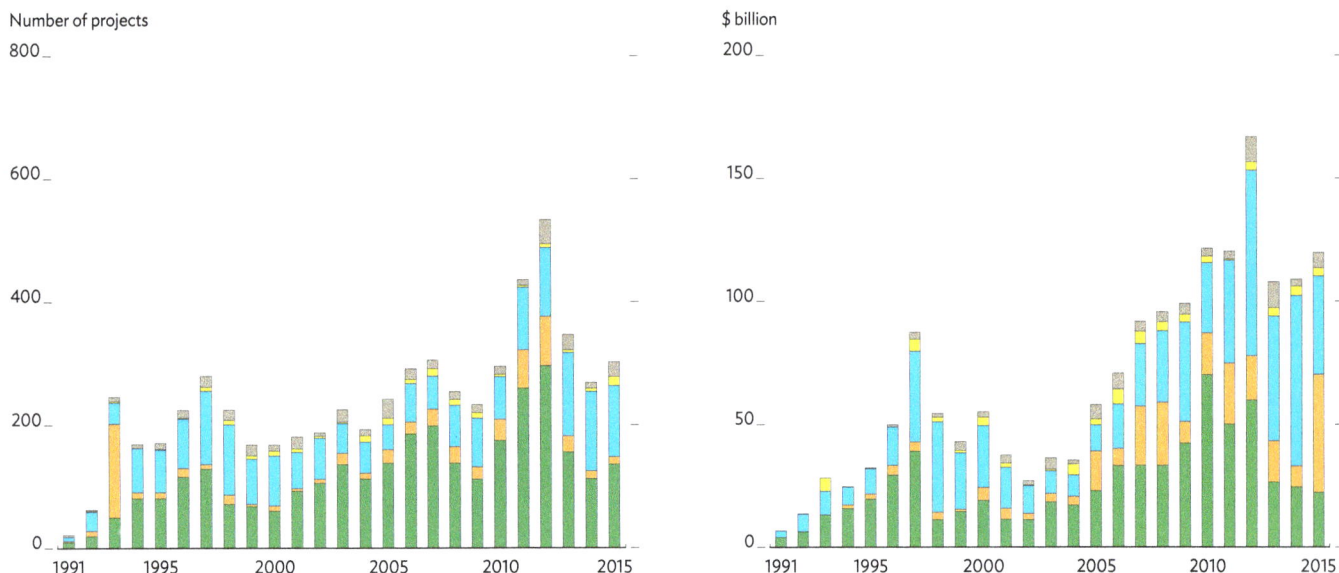

PPP = public–private partnership.

Note: Includes only low- and middle-income economies. Excludes full divestitures of state-owned assets (privatizations) and merchant projects that do not include government guarantees or that operate in a liberalized environment. Projects in the database must be at least 20% privately owned. State-owned enterprises are considered public. More information is available at http://ppi.worldbank.org/methodology/ppi-methodology

Source: World Bank Private Participation in Infrastructure database (accessed 25 May 2017).

2.1.12 PPP in developing Asia by subregion, 1991–2015

- 🟩 Central Asia
- 🟦 East Asia
- ⬜ South Asia
- 🟧 Southeast Asia
- 🟫 The Pacific

Number of projects

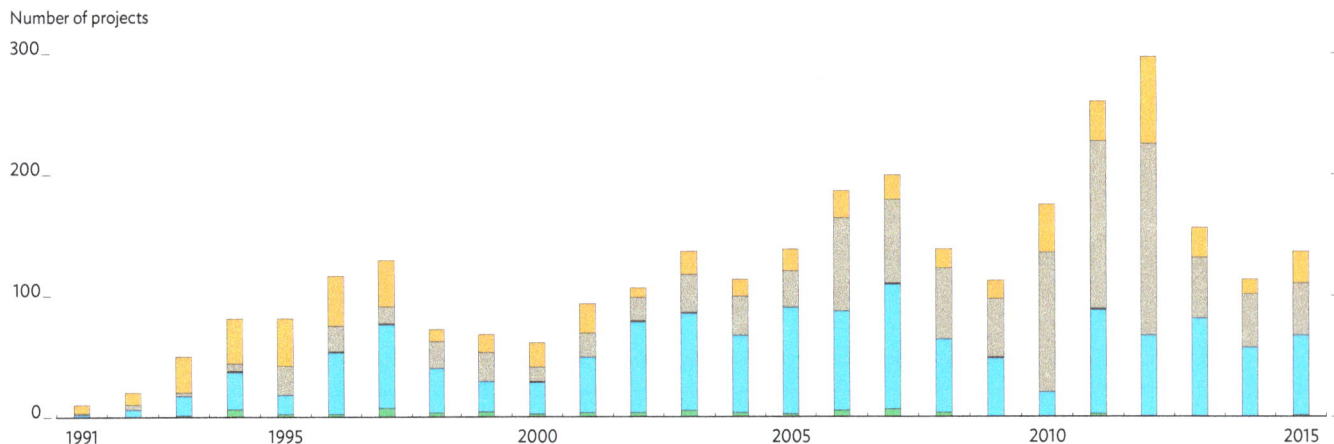

PPP = public–private partnership.

Note: Includes only low- and middle-income economies. Excludes full divestitures of state-owned assets (privatizations) and merchant projects that do not include government guarantees or that operate in a liberalized environment. Projects in the database must be at least 20% privately owned. State-owned enterprises are considered public. More information is available at http://ppi.worldbank.org/methodology/ppi-methodology

Source: World Bank Private Participation in Infrastructure database (accessed 25 May 2017).

government's launch in 2015 of its Hybrid Annuity Model to speed up the process by which projects are awarded. The primary aim of the model is to safeguard developers and lenders from the risks and challenges posed by conventional models, such as design–build–finance–operate–transfer and built–operate–transfer. The National Highways Authority of India approved the model in 2016, and from January to May of that year started preparing some 16 such projects.

PPP is gaining ground in Southeast Asia, particularly in Cambodia, Indonesia, Malaysia, the Philippines, and Thailand (Figure 2.1.13). This trend may be attributed to recent reform in these countries of the legal and regulatory framework of PPP. Central Asia and the Pacific have lagged behind, accounting for only 2% of PPP projects.

Sectoral distribution

By sector, most PPP investment in developing economies went into the energy and transportation sectors (Figure 2.1.14). A similar situation held in developing Asia. In recent years, PPP investment in energy has declined as energy projects matured and the sector no longer needed as much support, and investment has shifted into transportation (Figure 2.1.15).

2.1.13 PPP in developing Asia by economy, 1991–2015

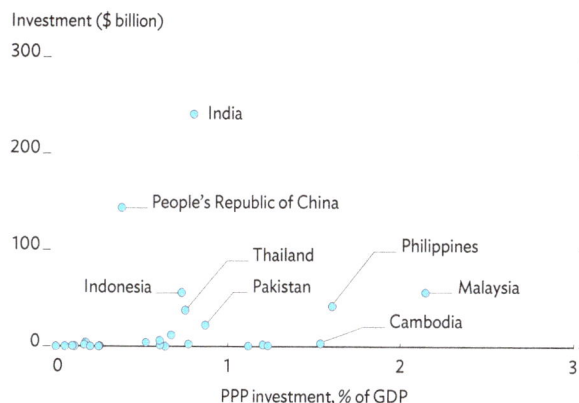

PPP = public–private partnership.

Note: Includes only low- and middle-income economies. Excludes full divestitures of state-owned assets (privatizations) and merchant projects that do not include government guarantees or that operate in a liberalized environment. Projects in the database must be at least 20% privately owned. State-owned enterprises are considered public. More information is available at http://ppi.worldbank.org/methodology/ppi-methodology

Sources: World Bank Private Participation in Infrastructure database (accessed 25 May 2017); World Development Indicators.

2.1.14 PPP in developing economies by sector, 1991–2015

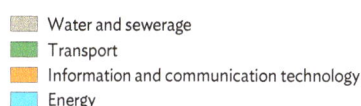

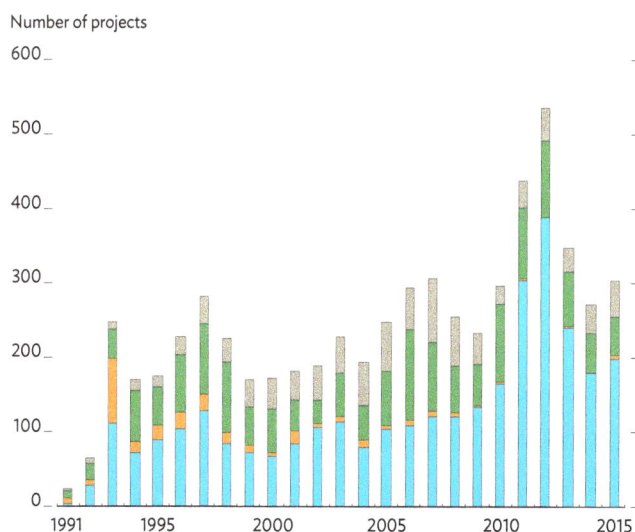

- Water and sewerage
- Transport
- Information and communication technology
- Energy

PPP = public–private partnership.

Note: Includes only low- and middle-income economies. Excludes full divestitures of state-owned assets (privatizations) and merchant projects that do not include government guarantees or that operate in a liberalized environment. Projects in the database must be at least 20% privately owned. State-owned enterprises are considered public. More information is available at http://ppi.worldbank.org/methodology/ppi-methodology

Source: World Bank Private Participation in Infrastructure database (accessed 28 March 2017).

2.1.15 PPP in developing Asia by sector, 1991–2015

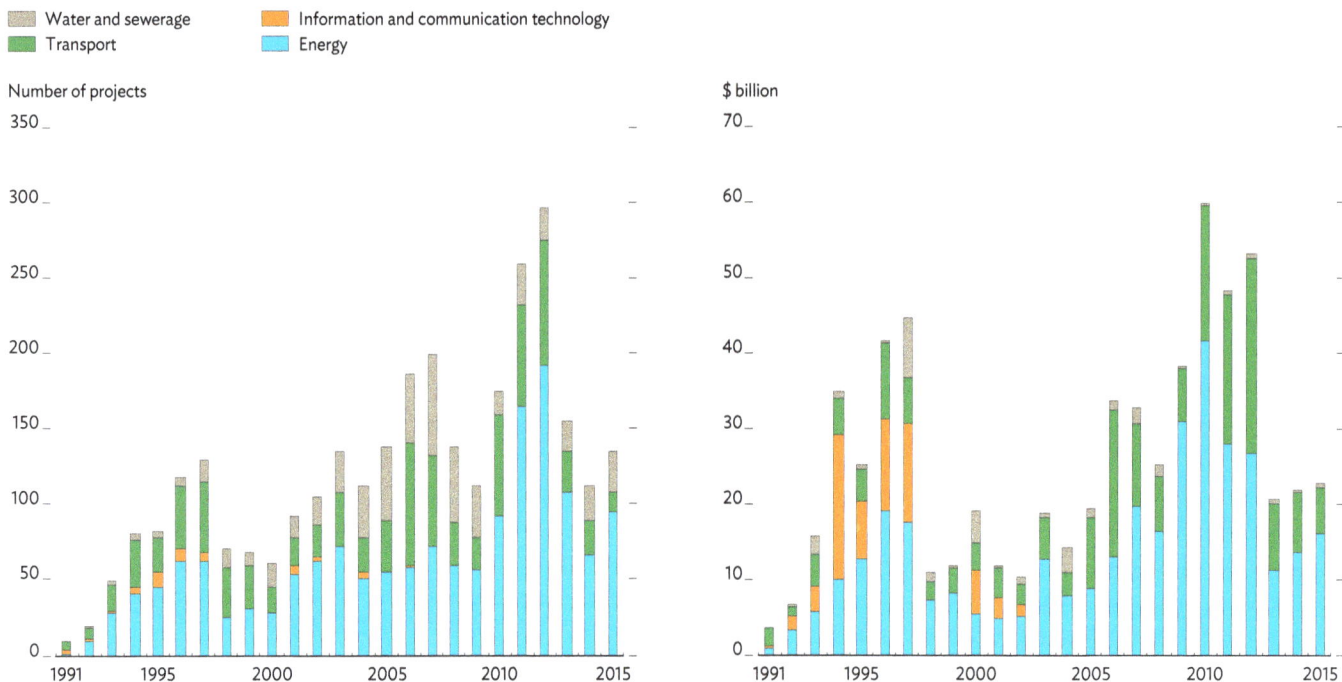

- ▨ Water and sewerage
- ▩ Transport
- ▨ Information and communication technology
- ▨ Energy

Number of projects

$ billion

PPP = public–private partnership.

Note: Includes only low- and middle-income economies. Excludes full divestitures of state-owned assets (privatizations) and merchant projects that do not include government guarantees or that operate in a liberalized environment. Projects in the database must be at least 20% privately owned. State-owned enterprises are considered public. More information is available at http://ppi.worldbank.org/methodology/ppi-methodology

Source: World Bank Private Participation in Infrastructure database (accessed 25 May 2017).

Types and modalities

The public and private sectors collaborate to deliver public goods or services using several possible arrangements. PPP modalities vary in terms of how much risk is transferred to the private sector, how much each party invests, and who owns and controls the resulting assets during and after the concession period (PPIAF 2009). Figure 2.1.16 shows that competing PPP modalities enjoy similar frequency of use around the world and within developing Asia. The most common modality is build–operate–transfer, especially in developing Asia.

In developing Asia, greenfield infrastructure projects, starting from scratch, are the most common in terms of project numbers and committed investment (Figure 2.1.17). Greenfield projects are usually built and operated by private firms, which take on the commercial risk. Political and exchange rate risks can sometimes be shared with the public sector. Greenfield sites allow maximum design flexibility, the better to meet project requirements and reduce maintenance costs. However, they are also the most susceptible to renegotiation because of their complexity.

2.1.16 PPP modality by region, 1991–2015
(% to total PPP projects)

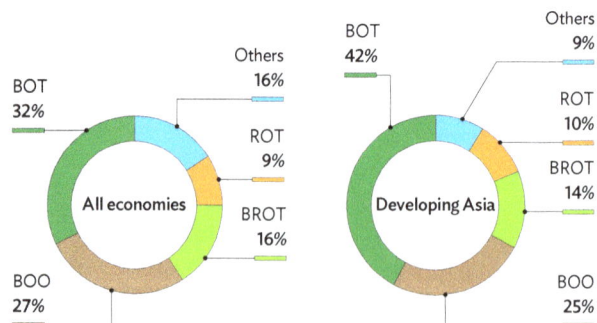

All economies: BOT 32%, Others 16%, ROT 9%, BROT 16%, BOO 27%

Developing Asia: BOT 42%, Others 9%, ROT 10%, BROT 14%, BOO 25%

BOO = build–own–operate, BOT = build–own–transfer, BROT = build–rehabilitate–operate–transfer, PPP = public–private partnership, ROT = rehabilitate–operate–transfer.

Note: Includes only low- and middle-income economies. Excludes full divestitures of state-owned assets (privatizations) and merchant projects that do not include government guarantees or that operate in a liberalized environment. Projects in the database must be at least 20% privately owned. State-owned enterprises are considered public. More information is available at http://ppi.worldbank.org/methodology/ppi-methodology

Source: World Bank Private Participation in Infrastructure database (accessed 25 May 2017).

2.1.17 PPP in developing Asia by type, 1991–2015

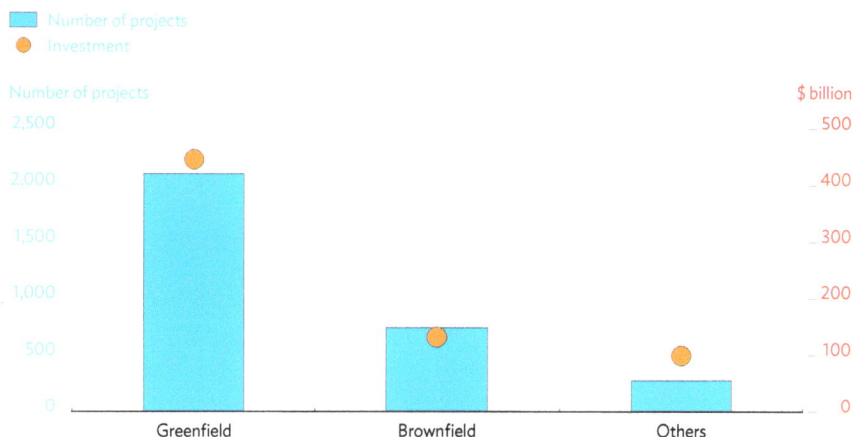

PPP = public–private partnership.

Notes: "Others" includes management and contract lease, and partial divestiture. Excluded are full divestitures of state-owned assets (privatizations) and merchant projects that do not include government guarantees or that operate in a liberalized environment. Projects in the database must be at least 20% privately owned. State-owned enterprises are considered public. More information is available at http://ppi.worldbank.org/methodology/ppi-methodology

Source: World Bank Private Participation in Infrastructure database (accessed 25 May 2017).

Despite the high risk in investment on new projects, developing economies prefer greenfield projects to brownfield projects, which involve investing in existing infrastructure. Greenfield projects are the most prevalent sort in most sectors, with the important exception of transportation, for which brownfield projects are still preferred (Figure 2.1.18).

2.1.18 Type of PPP project by sector in developing Asia, 1991–2015

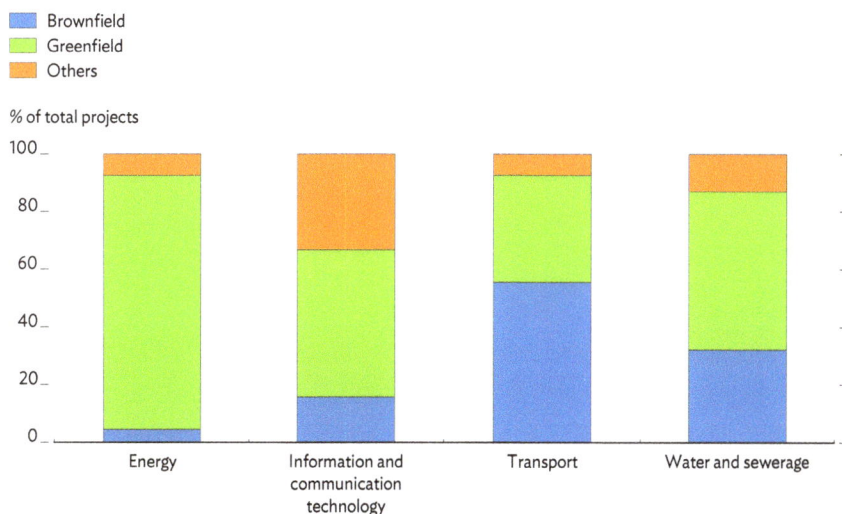

PPP = public–private partnership.

Notes: "Others" includes management and contract lease, and partial divestiture. Excluded are full divestitures of state-owned assets (privatizations) and merchant projects that do not include government guarantees or that operate in a liberalized environment. Projects in the database must be at least 20% privately owned. State-owned enterprises are considered public. More information is available at http://ppi.worldbank.org/methodology/ppi-methodology

Source: World Bank Private Participation in Infrastructure database (accessed 25 May 2017).

Unfortunately, the World Bank Private Participation in Infrastructure database includes data only for low- and middle-income economies. For a sense of the state of PPP in other regions and Asian economies, the Project Finance & Infrastructure Journal (IJGlobal) dataset contains information on over 12,000 infrastructure transactions and 10,000 projects in all economies, as well as a broad range of information relating to the type of project or transaction and its contractual structure, value, ratio of debt to equity, sponsors, and creditors. However, it contains far less descriptive information than the World Bank dataset and uses a different classification scheme.

2.1.19 PPP investment in OECD and developing Asia by sector

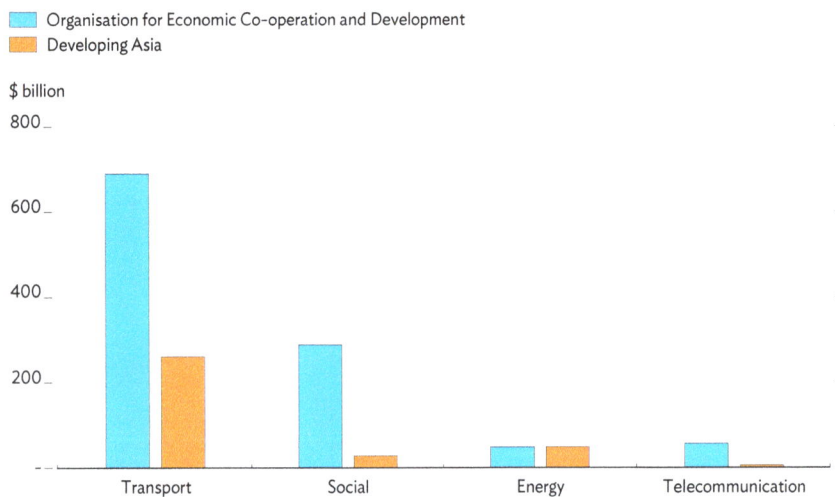

OECD = Organisation for Economic Co-operation and Development, PPP = public–private partnership.
Note: "Social" includes waste treatment, leisure, trial law courts, distribution utilities, training centers, fire and rescue services, and municipal buildings.
Source: IJGlobal (accessed 28 July 2017).

Unlike in developing economies, most PPP investments in developed economies are in transport and social infrastructure (Figure 2.1.19). However, as in developing Asia, developed economies use mostly the greenfield modality, the common form of which is design–build–finance–maintain–operate (Figure 2.1.20).

Augmenting the information derived from the World Bank database, the focus of this survey now turns to PPP projects in Asia's newly industrialized economies (NIEs): the Republic of Korea, Singapore, Taipei,China, and Hong Kong, China. PPPs in these four economies account for 3.2% of all PPPs worldwide and almost 20% of PPPs in developing Asia, as listed in the IJGlobal database. Asian NIEs have been implementing the PPP model since the 1990s for infrastructure development. The Republic of Korea is regarded as the most mature PPP market in the region. PPP was first introduced there with the enactment of a law in 1994 (Kim et al. 2011). In Hong Kong, China, PPP was introduced when the government accumulated an unsustainable budget deficit following the Asian financial crisis of 1997–1998 and needed to explore ways to cut expenditure while still delivering needed infrastructure. Singapore and Taipei,China introduced PPP in the 2000s.

2.1.20 PPP investment by modality

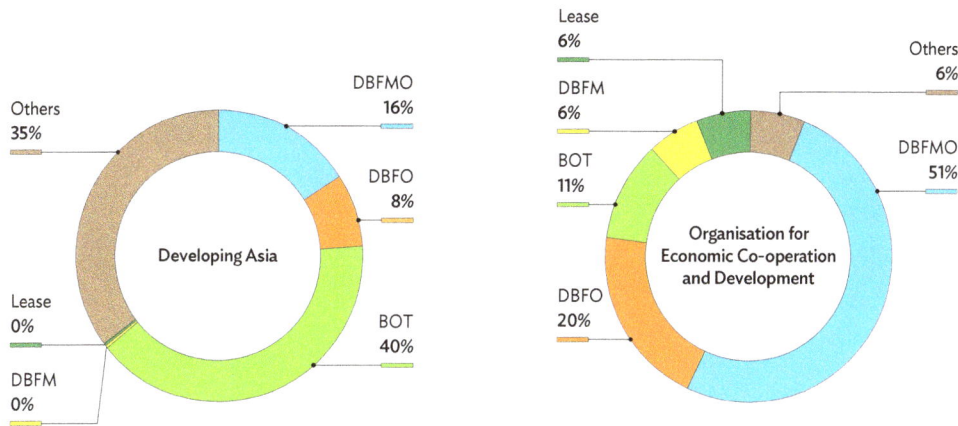

BOT = build–operate–transfer, DBFM = design–build–finance–maintain, DBFMO = design–build–finance–maintain–operate, DBFO = design–build–finance–operate, PPP = public–private partnership.

Note: "Others" include build–transfer–operate, design–build–finance, design–build–finance–operate–transfer, and design–build–own–operate.

Source: IJGlobal (accessed 28 July 2017).

Transportation is the dominant sector for PPP projects in the Asian NIEs. Unlike in other economies in developing Asia, demand for energy PPP investment is low in the NIEs, but social infrastructure has grown to occupy almost a 30% share of PPPs (Figure 2.1.21). Singapore is the first Southeast Asian economy to adopt PPP models for social infrastructure development. NIEs usually invest in new infrastructure projects. The most common type of PPP is a variation on design–build–finance–manage–operate or build–operate–transfer (Figure 2.1.22).

From accessing needs to filling them

Governments in developing Asia have made significant efforts to facilitate PPP investments. Indeed, if successfully pursued, PPP offers a triple-win solution, bringing public and private resources into alignment with community priorities through active collaboration. It is important to go beyond the public and private sector participants to perceive PPP as "People PPP," in which the community is an equal stakeholder. Despite differences in motives, all stakeholders in PPPs can expect to receive their fair share of benefits: adequate and efficient infrastructure and services for users, profitable investment opportunities for the private sector, and for the state a development mechanism that expands its capacity. The following section will discuss the challenges in achieving this triple win.

2.1.21 NIE PPP projects by sector, 2000–2017

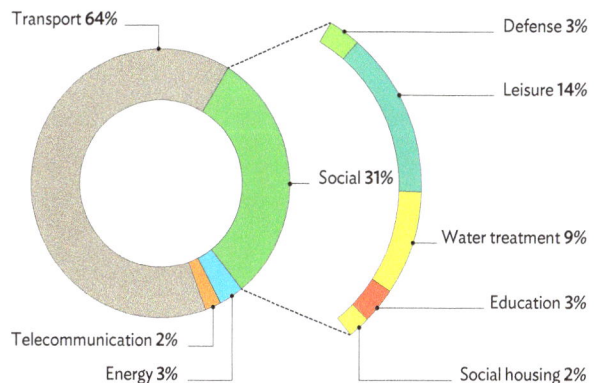

NIE = newly industrialized economy, PPP = public–private partnership.
Source: IJGlobal (accessed 28 July 2017).

2.1.22 NIE PPP projects by modality, 2000–2017

BLT = build–lease–transfer, BOT = build–operate–transfer, BTO = build–transfer–operate, DBFMO = design–build–finance–maintain–operate, DBFO = design–build–finance–operate, NIE = newly industrialized economy, PPP = public–private partnership.

Note: "Others" include build–own–operate, design–build–own–operate, and lease.

Source: IJGlobal (accessed 28 July 2017).

Hurdles to public–private partnership

Considering the potential benefits of PPP over other approaches to addressing the infrastructure gap in developing Asia, it is puzzling how this approach has played only a limited role to the region's infrastructure development. PPP investment in five major economies in the region—Indonesia, Malaysia, the Philippines, Thailand, and Viet Nam—is less than 1% of GDP in recent years (Figure 2.2.1). Adding to this is the persistent problem of project cancellations. This section examines these shortcomings and their causes.

2.2.1 PPP share to GDP in selected economies, 2005–2015

— Philippines
— Viet Nam
— Thailand
— Malaysia
— Indonesia

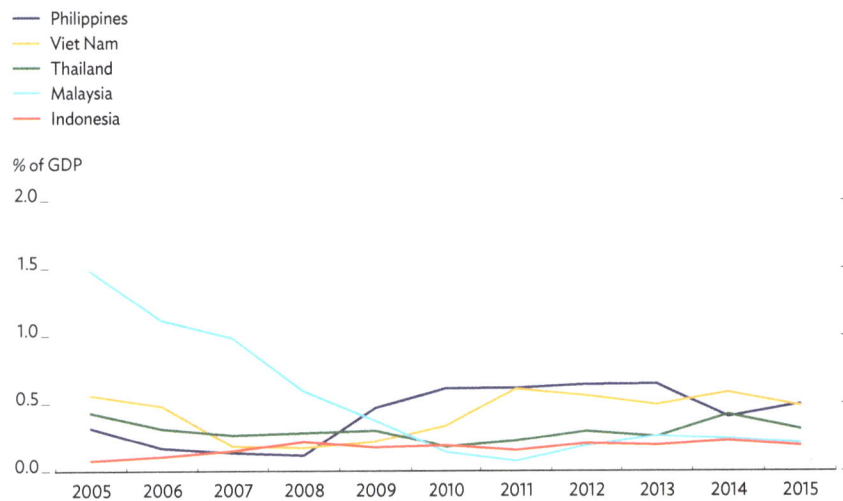

Source: IMF. 2017. Investment and Capital Stock Dataset 1960–2015. http://www.imf.org/external/np/fad/publicinvestment/

Risk of project cancellation

PPP projects are often at heightened risk of becoming distressed or eventually cancelled owing to the many different stakeholders involved and the long-term nature of contracts. Following the World Bank Private Participation in Infrastructure definition, PPP projects are cancelled when the private sector has exited by selling or transferring its economic interest back to the government before the end of the agreed contract period. Cancellations also occur when the removal of all management and personnel forces the cessation of operation, service provision, or construction for 15% or more of the contract term following the revocation or repudiation of the contract. The cancellation of PPP projects has raised great concern, especially in developing countries under stringent fiscal constraints. It can impose large efficiency losses, discourage private investment, and disrupt the provision of public infrastructure and services.

The amount invested in all cancelled PPP projects from 1991 to 2015 was $76.4 billion, or 4.4% of total committed investment in 139 developing countries. The value of cancelled PPP projects in developing Asia amounted to $41.6 billion, which was 54.5% of the value of all cancelled PPP projects (Figure 2.2.2). Transport had the highest number of cancelled projects in the region. The sector accounted for almost 45% of all cancelled PPP projects in the region, followed by energy at 28%. Cancelled brownfield projects had more committed investment than cancelled greenfield projects (Figure 2.2.3).

Project cancellations in developing Asia occur 5 years after financial closure, on average, which typically places cancellation during the final stage of the project construction (Figure 2.2.4). Bureaucratic changes and delays with permits are the top reasons cited to explain why PPPs are at risk during construction (Bain 2007).

Lee et al. (2017b) used survival analysis to estimate how different factors affect the hazard rate for the cancellation of PPP projects. Table 2.2.1 lists the identified factors: (i) project-related factors (type of PPP, contract award method, proposal mode, government support, involvement of multilateral development banks [MDBs], and public partner), (ii) macroeconomic factors (growth, debt level, and occurrence of natural disaster), and (iii) institutional factors (law and order issues and degree of corruption).

Empirical results suggest that appropriate design makes PPP projects more likely to survive. Greenfield PPP projects are at lower risk of cancellation than are brownfield projects because greenfield agreements allow governments to divest themselves of design, construction, and market risks (Shediac et al. 2008). However, the World Bank (2016a) found that greenfield projects are more susceptible to renegotiation, largely because of their complexity and riskiness but also because of improper selection criteria and procurement procedures. Meanwhile, solicited PPP projects (those identified by the public sector) are intuitively less likely to be cancelled than unsolicited projects (those emanating from the private sector). Solicited projects are identified in accordance with government development plans and investment priorities. To reduce the likelihood of cancellation and the corresponding burden to government, unsolicited proposals should be regulated and put up for competitive bidding.

Adequate government support for projects and the involvement of MDBs significantly reduce the hazard of project cancellation. Indirect government support such as payment, revenue, or debt guarantees can make projects more financially viable. MDBs play important roles not only by narrowing funding gaps but also by significantly mitigating the risk of project cancellation.

2.2.2 Cancelled PPP projects (amount of investment), 1991–2015

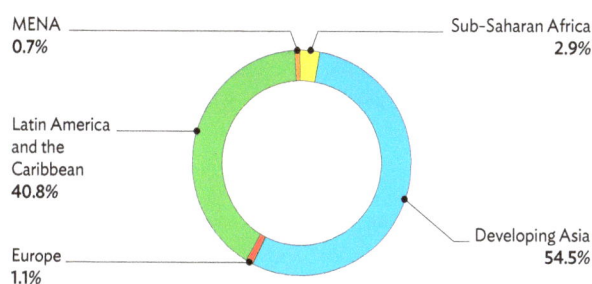

MENA = Middle East and North Africa, PPP = public–private partnership.
Note: Includes only low- and middle-income countries in the region. Excludes full divestitures of state-owned assets (privatizations) and merchant projects that do not include government guarantees or that operate in a liberalized environment. Projects in the database must be at least 20% privately owned. State-owned enterprises are considered public. More information is available at http://ppi.worldbank.org/methodology/ppi-methodology
Source: World Bank Private Participation in Infrastructure database (accessed 25 May 2017).

2.2.3 Cancelled PPP by sector and project type (amount of investment), 1991–2015

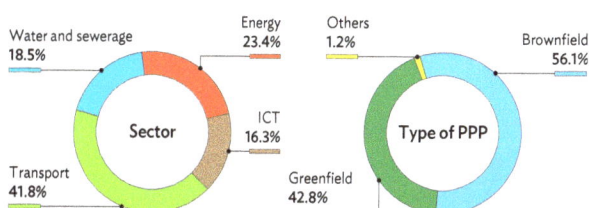

ICT = information and communication technology, PPP = public–private partnership.
Note: Other types of PPP include management and lease contract and partial divestiture. Excludes full divestitures of state-owned assets (privatizations) and merchant projects that do not include government guarantees or that operate in a liberalized environment. Projects in the database must be at least 20% privately owned. State-owned enterprises are considered public. More information is available at http://ppi.worldbank.org/methodology/ppi-methodology
Source: World Bank Private Participation in Infrastructure database (accessed 25 May 2017).

2.2.4 Mean duration of project cancelled

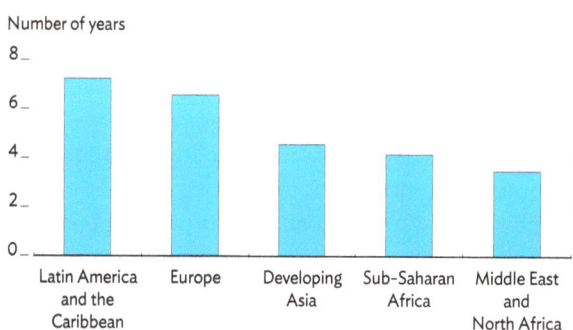

Note: Duration is measured as the difference from the financial closure year (i.e., the year in which private sponsors legally entered an agreement to invest funds or provide services) through the year in which the project was cancelled. Includes only the low- and middle-income countries in each region.
Sources: World Bank Private Participation in Infrastructure database (accessed 28 March 2017); ADB estimates.

2.2.1 Direction of coefficients of the survival analysis results

Variables	Direction of impact to hazard rate
Project-based factors	
Unsolicited proposal that undergone competitive bidding***	–
Solicited proposal***	–
Greenfield***	–
Local government as public partner***	–
Provision of indirect government support***	–
Multilateral development bank involvement**	–
Macroeconomic factors	
Natural disaster occurrence ratio***	+
Ratio of debt to GDP***	–
GDP per capita compounded growth rate**	–
Political and institutional factors	
Dedicated PPP unit**	–
Law and order***	–
Degree of corruption***	–

PPP = public–private partnership.

Note: *** $p < 0.01$, ** $p < 0.05$, * $p < 0.1$. Higher score for political and institutional factors reflect better quality.

Source: Lee et al. forthcoming[b].

Of equal importance to the likelihood of project success are the macroeconomic and institutional environments. Robust macroeconomic performance, measured by average growth of real GDP per capita, improves investor confidence and encourages brisk economic activity. To further ensure project success, economies in developing Asia should provide a more transparent, less corrupt business environment with strong, impartial legal systems. A dedicated PPP unit plays a significant role in project survival.

As shown above, many factors affect the likelihood of project success during implementation. However, addressing factors that make failure more likely should start with project selection and continue through contract preparation all the way to actual project implementation. The discussion below addresses the challenges involved in conceptualizing and implementing PPP projects.

Shortcomings in governance

Factors that can make PPP less attractive to prospective private partners are inefficient government bureaucracy, corruption, and political and government instability. Schomaker (2014) found higher private participation in public service provision, including through PPP, with better institutional quality, as measured by government effectiveness. This has implications for developing Asia's efforts to promote PPP because most economies in the region have relatively low scores for the quality of the legal and institutional environment (Figure 2.2.5).

2.2.5 Scores in selected global competitiveness indicators (1–7 [best]), 2016

— Developing Asia
— Organisation for Economic Co-operation and Development

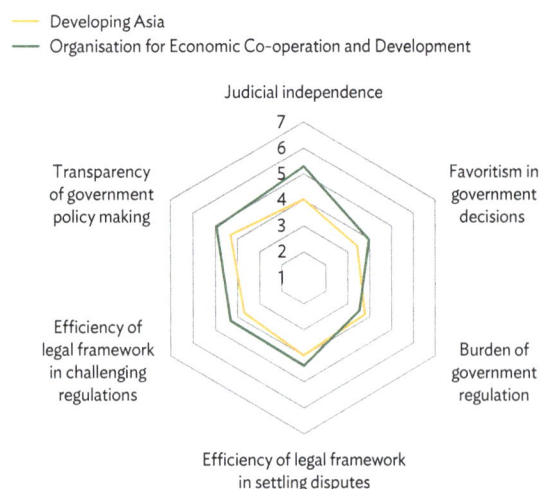

Source: World Economic Forum. The Global Competitiveness Index Historical Dataset. http://reports.weforum.org/global-competitiveness-index/downloads/

In one example, a tollway project in Thailand failed because the government was unable to perform critical obligations under the concession agreement. During the operational phase in the early 1990s, the government did not remove a local road competing for traffic, though it was obligated to do so. This caused traffic volume and revenue to fall short of expectations, leaving the project unable to service its debt only 6 years after operation began. The government had to authorize a substantial toll increase and take over some of the project's loans (Cuttaree 2008, Charoenngam and Kurniawan 2015). Thus, government's implicit commitment to the success of a PPP project may be a hidden contingent liability for the government.

PPP transactions can be put at risk by untoward political developments such as political violence, project nationalization, new restrictions on currency convertibility and transfer, changes to other laws, or adverse government actions including breach of contract. A special study on ADB assistance to PPPs showed that political risk had constrained the development of PPP in Indonesia, Nepal, and Sri Lanka (ADB 2009).

Insufficient institutional capacity

Insufficient institutional and public sector capacity and experience are other key challenges to PPP in developing Asia. PPP contracts are complex and require appropriate skills and institutional support throughout the project cycle (Kim et al. forthcoming).

Absence of a dedicated PPP unit

A dedicated PPP unit plays an important role in a country's PPP program. A dedicated PPP unit is an office for coordination, quality control, accountability, and information on PPP for one or more sectors (ADB 2008). These units are created as a new agency or within a government division such as the finance ministry, which is seen to be at arm's length from the government offices that use PPP to deliver services. A dedicated PPP unit enables public partners to disseminate information and provides specialized management advice on the procurement process to put the public partner on an equal footing with the private partner in PPP negotiations (Trebilcock and Rosenstock 2015). It enhances private sector confidence by signaling transparency, consistency, and the government's commitment to provide a programmed approach to PPP development (Istrate and Puentes 2011).

The World Bank (2007) reported that PPP unit efficiency is highly correlated with the success of a country's PPP program. For example, the Republic of Korea established a PPP unit in 1998, and the rate of private participation as a percentage of total social overhead capital—in effect, central government infrastructure investment—increased by fourfold in the decade to 2008 (OECD 2010). Similarly, readiness in the Philippines for PPP improved dramatically when its PPP Center was reorganized and strengthened. The Philippines further demonstrates how useful it is to adopt a programmatic approach to developing PPPs.

2.2.6 PPP institutional arrangement

- No dedicated PPP unit
- With one PPP unit
- With more than one PPP unit

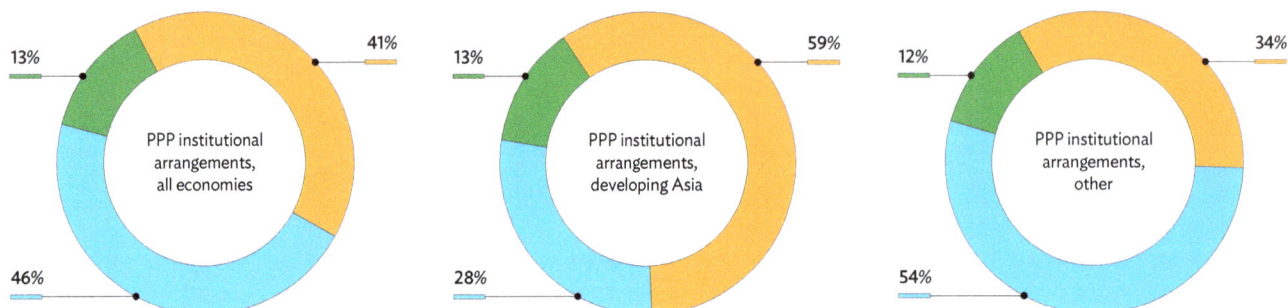

PPP institutional arrangements, all economies

13%   41%   46%

PPP institutional arrangements, developing Asia

13%   59%   28%

PPP institutional arrangements, other

12%   34%   54%

PPP = public–private partnership.

Notes: A total of 160 economies were surveyed. Developing Asia includes Afghanistan, Armenia, Azerbaijan, Bangladesh, Bhutan, Brunei Darussalam, Cambodia, the People's Republic of China, the Cook Islands, Fiji, Georgia, India, Indonesia, Kazakhstan, Kiribati, the Republic of Korea, the Kyrgyz Republic, the Lao People's Democratic Republic, Malaysia, Maldives, the Republic of the Marshall Islands, the Federated States of Micronesia, Mongolia, Myanmar, Nauru, Nepal, Pakistan, Palau, Papua New Guinea, the Philippines, Samoa, Singapore, Solomon Islands, Sri Lanka, Tajikistan, Thailand, Timor-Leste, Tonga, Turkmenistan, Tuvalu, Uzbekistan, Vanuatu, Viet Nam, Taipei,China, and Hong Kong, China. "Other" includes Albania, Algeria, Angola, Argentina, Austria, Australia, Belarus, Belgium, Benin, Bosnia and Herzegovina, Botswana, Brazil, Bulgaria, Burkina Faso, Cameroon, Canada, Chile, Colombia, Costa Rica, Croatia, Czech Republic, the Democratic Republic of the Congo, the Republic of the Congo, Cote d'Ivoire, Denmark, Dominican Republic, Ecuador, Egypt, El Salvador, Estonia, France, Finland, Gabon, Germany, Ghana, Granada, Greece, Guatemala, Guinea-Bissau, Honduras, Hungary, Iceland, Iran, Iraq, Ireland, Israel, Italy, Jamaica, Japan, Jordan, Kenya, Kosovo, Kuwait, Latvia, Lebanon, Liberia, Lithuania, Luxembourg, Macedonia, Madagascar, Malawi, Mali, Malta, Mauritania, Mauritius, Mexico, Moldova, Montenegro, Morocco, Mozambique, the Netherlands, New Zealand, Nicaragua, Nigeria, Norway, Panama, Paraguay, Peru, Poland, Puerto Rico, Romania, the Russian Federation, Rwanda, Saint Lucia, Saudi Arabia, Serbia, Seychelles, Senegal, Sierra Leone, the Slovak Republic, Slovenia, Somalia, South Africa, Spain, Swaziland, Sweden, Switzerland, Syria, Tanzania, Togo, Trinidad and Tobago, Tunisia, Ukraine, Turkey, Uganda, the United Arab Emirates, the United Kingdom, the United States of America, Uruguay, Venezuela, Yemen, Zambia, and Zimbabwe.

Sources: World Bank PPP Knowledge Lab; World Bank 2016b; UNESCAP 2017; various government websites; ADB estimates.

The Philippine PPP program started in 2010, when the PPP Center became the central coordinating and monitoring agency for all PPP projects. Its key functions include the provision of advisory and facilitation services, technical assistance, training and capacity development in project preparation and development, and managing the Project Development and Monitoring Facility, a dedicated facility that prepares PPP projects. Further, it advocates reform to policy governing PPP. The PPP Center was put under the National Economic and Development Authority, the country's premier socioeconomic planning and policy coordinating body, as one of its attached agencies.

As important as PPP units are to PPP success, such units are lacking in more than 40% of the countries examined worldwide (Figure 2.2.6). The situation is worse in developing Asia, where the majority of countries still lack dedicated PPP units. This shortfall is particularly pronounced in Central Asia and the Pacific (Figure 2.2.7).

In practice, the functions of PPP units vary widely, as do their location within the government structure. This reflects variation in priorities and the constraints facing PPP programs. Table 2.2.2 sketches the various roles played by these units in selected economies in developing Asia. PPP units are usually under the ministry of finance in recognition of the budget implications of PPP projects. Some countries, such as Bangladesh and Indonesia, have more than one central PPP unit,

2.2.7 Institutional arrangement in developing Asia

- No dedicated unit
- With at least one PPP unit

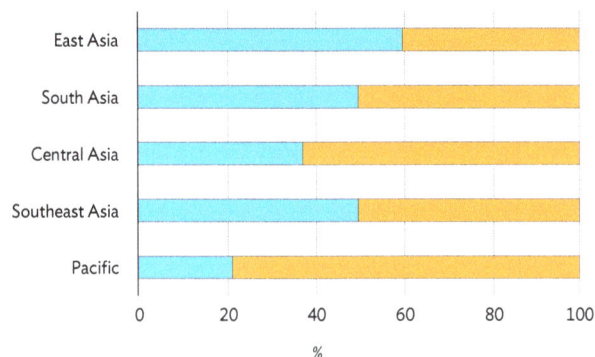

East Asia
South Asia
Central Asia
Southeast Asia
Pacific

0   20   40   60   80   100
%

Sources: World Bank PPP Knowledge Lab; World Bank 2016b; UNESCAP 2017; various government websites; ADB estimates.

2.2.2 PPP units in selected economies in developing Asia

Countries	PPP unit	Location	PPP regulation	Policy guidance and capacity building	Promotion	Technical support in implementing PPP projects	Approval of PPP projects	Procurement of PPPs	Oversight of PPP implementation
Afghanistan	Central Partnership Authority	Ministry of Finance	x	x	x				x
Bangladesh	Public–Private Partnership Authority	Prime Minister's Office; Ministry of Finance	x	x	x	x	x	x	x
Bhutan	PPP Agency	Ministry of Finance		x	x	x			
PRC	China PPP Center	Ministry of Finance	x	x	x	x			x
Fiji	PPP Unit	Ministry of Public Service, Public Enterprises, and Public Sector Reforms							
India	PPP Cell, Department of Economic Affairs	Department of Economic Affairs	x	x	x	x	x		x
Indonesia	Directorate of Development for Public–Private Partnerships; Directorate of Government Support Management and Infrastructure Financing	Ministry of National Development Planning; Ministry of Finance	x	x	x	x	x		x
Kazakhstan	Kazakhstan Public–Private Partnerships Center	Independent	x	x	x	x			
Korea, Rep. of	Public and Private Infrastructure Investment Management Center	Independent	x	x	x	x	x	x	x
Kyrgyz Rep.	PPP Unit of the Investment Promotion Agency of the Kyrgyz Republic; Fiscal Risk Management Unit	Ministry of Economy; Ministry of Finance	x	x	x	x	x		x
Malaysia	Public–Private Partnership Unit	Prime Minister's Department	x	x	x	x	x		x
Mongolia	PPP and Concession Division	Ministry of Economic Development	x	x	x	x		x	x
Pakistan	Infrastructure Project Development Facility	Ministry of Finance		x	x	x	x		x
Philippines	Public–Private Partnership Center	National Economic and Development Authority	x	x	x	x			x
Tajikistan	State Enterprise on Implementation of PPP Projects	State Committee on Investments and State Property Management	x	x	x	x	x		x
Thailand	State Enterprise Policy Office	Ministry of Finance	x	x	x	x	x		
Timor-Leste	Public–Private Partnership Unit	Ministry of Finance		x	x	x			x
Viet Nam	The State Steering Committee for PPP	Ministry of Planning and Investment	x	x	x				x

PPP = public–private partnership, PRC = People's Republic of China.

Sources: World Bank. 2016. *Benchmarking Public–Private Partnership Procurement 2017*; Akintola, A., M. Beck, and M. Kumaraswamy. 2016. *Public–Private Partnerships: A Global Review.* Routledge; UNESCAP. 2017. *PPP Policy, Legal and Institutional Frameworks in Asia and the Pacific*; various government websites.

each performing a specific role. In Bangladesh, the PPP Authority under the Prime Minister's Office provides advice and oversees PPP projects, while a PPP unit in the Ministry of Finance assesses the financial viability of the projects and determines the amount of government support to extend. The PPP unit in the Indonesian Ministry of National Development Planning coordinates the PPP program, gives guidance, and disseminates information, while the Committee for Acceleration of Priority Infrastructure Delivery acts as the project management office for priority projects. The PPP unit in the Indonesian Ministry of Finance oversees quality control, supports project preparation using the Project Development Fund, and assesses the eligibility of proposed projects to receive government assistance. While their functions differ, there is obvious overlap, and coordination problems may arise with multiple PPP centers if responsibilities are not clearly defined.

In some cases, PPP units are established at both the national and the subnational level. In Pakistan, the Infrastructure Project Development Facility under the Ministry of Finance acts as the central PPP unit, but PPP units are also set up in the province of Sindh under the provincial Finance Department and in Punjab in the Planning Department. Provincial PPP units exist as well in the PRC. After the establishment of the PPP Center at the end of 2014 within the Ministry of Finance, the provincial governments of Hainan and Jiangsu set up separate centers responsible for policy and research, technical support, the collection of statistics, and regional communication on PPP projects (Werneck and Saadi 2016). All provinces have since established PPP centers. Policy makers should remember, however, that a PPP unit is not a miracle pill that will instantly cure governmental ineffectiveness.

Inadequate PPP preparation

Capacity to handle activities necessary to PPP preparation is crucial to successful PPP implementation. PPP is a very complex arrangement and usually extends over a long period of time, with some contracts running for 30–40 years. Further, contracts are very detailed, specifying the full range of required service standards, the payments and penalties that apply, and the manner in which any disputes may be resolved.

Putting together such an arrangement requires significant capacity on the part of the government as well as the private sector. It is usually both time-consuming and expensive. Procuring authorities therefore need to keep in mind transaction costs when structuring and procuring PPPs, as well as how they can be held to a reasonable level. Interaction between the public and private sectors during project preparation and tendering can be beneficial to both parties, and to the project itself. Indeed, some governments have sought to orchestrate a joint process of developing project details, allowing potential bidders to contribute to the project even in its conceptual stage while ensuring that the government does not prescribe project parameters that would leave little room for private innovation.

Developing Asia needs to redouble its efforts to gain parity with mature PPP markets in its ability to prepare PPPs. A World Bank report *Benchmarking PPP Procurement 2017* assessed the performance of

2.2.8 PPP procurement performance, score by region

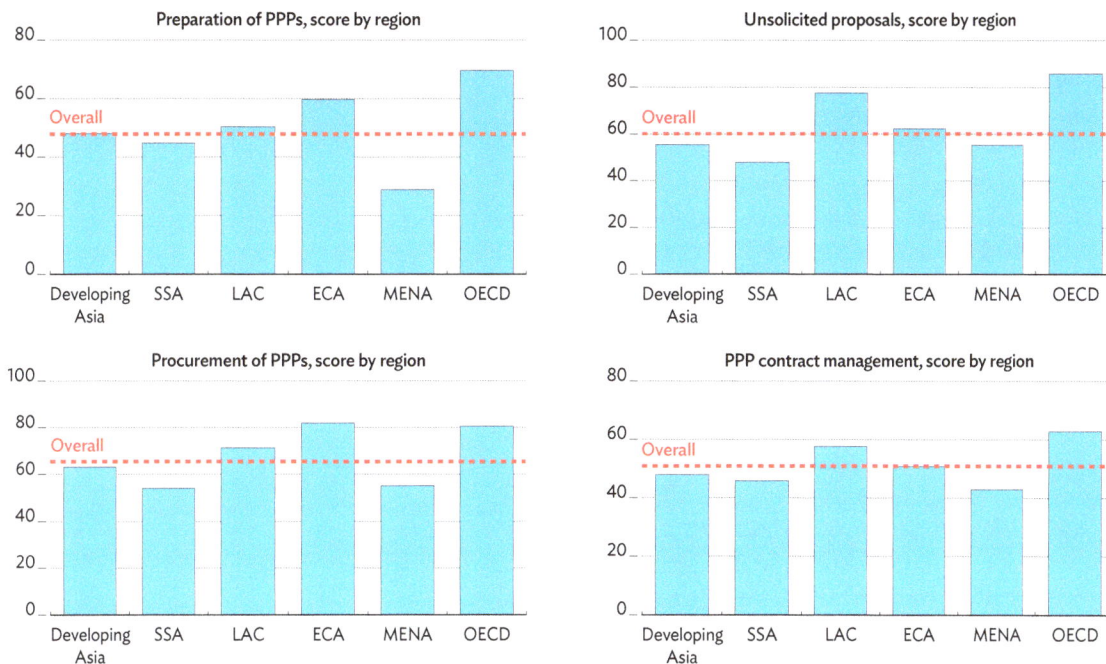

Preparation of PPPs, score by region

Unsolicited proposals, score by region

Procurement of PPPs, score by region

PPP contract management, score by region

ECA = Europe and Central Asia, LAC = Latin America and the Caribbean, MENA = Middle East and North Africa, PPP = public–private partnership, OECD = Organisation for Economic Co-operation and Development, SSA = Sub-Saharan Africa.

Notes: A total of 82 economies were surveyed. Data pertain to average scores of economies per region. For unsolicited proposals, the chart is limited to the 56 economies that explicitly regulate unsolicited proposals. Developing Asia includes Afghanistan, Armenia, Bangladesh, Cambodia, the People's Republic of China, India, Indonesia, Kazakhstan, the Republic of Korea, the Kyrgyz Republic, Malaysia, Mongolia, Myanmar, Nepal, Pakistan, Papua New Guinea, the Philippines, Singapore, Sri Lanka, Tajikistan, Thailand, Timor-Leste, and Viet Nam. ECA includes Albania, Bosnia and Herzegovina, Bulgaria, Lithuania, Moldova, Romania, the Russian Federation, and Ukraine. LAC includes Argentina, Brazil, Chile, Colombia, Costa Rica, Dominican Republic, Ecuador, Guatemala, Honduras, Jamaica, Mexico, Nicaragua, Panama, Peru, and Uruguay. MENA includes Algeria, Egypt, Iraq, Jordan, Lebanon, Morocco, and Tunisia. OECD includes Australia, Canada, France, Italy, Poland, Portugal, Turkey, the United Kingdom, and the United States. SSA includes Angola, Benin, Cameroon, the Democratic Republic of the Congo, the Republic of the Congo, Cote d'Ivoire, Gabon, Ghana, Kenya, Madagascar, Malawi, Mauritius, Mozambique, Nigeria, Senegal, South Africa, Tanzania, Togo, Uganda, and Zambia.

Source: World Bank. 2016. *Benchmarking Public–Private Partnerships Procurement 2017.*

82 economies in four thematic areas of the PPP process: preparation, procurement, contract management, and unsolicited proposals. It found Asia and the Pacific close to the average score (Figure 2.2.8).

The absence of detailed procedures for identifying and prioritizing PPPs is observed in the majority of economies in developing Asia. The report reveals that only 13% of economies in the region have a detailed procedure to ensure the alignment of PPPs with public investment priorities (Figure 2.2.9). The Philippines is one. It requires procuring authorities to identify specific priority projects through an infrastructure plan or a development program; ensure that the priority list aligns with the Philippine Development Plan, the Provincial Development Plan, and the Physical Framework Plan; and submit the list for approval from the National Economic and Development Authority or the Investment Coordination Committee.

It is generally accepted that the Ministry of Finance plays a definitive role in approving PPPs (World Bank 2017).

2.2.9 Consistency between prioritization of PPP projects and public investment priorities, developing Asia

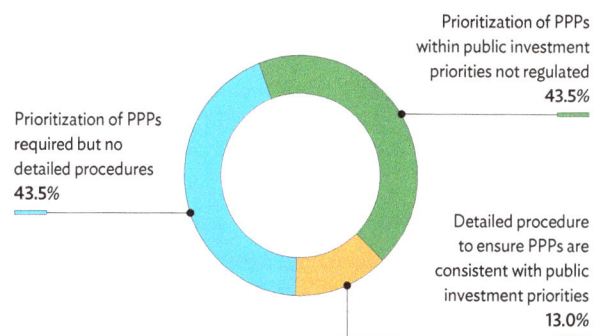

Prioritization of PPPs within public investment priorities not regulated
43.5%

Prioritization of PPPs required but no detailed procedures
43.5%

Detailed procedure to ensure PPPs are consistent with public investment priorities
13.0%

PPP = public–private partnership.

Note: Developing Asia includes Afghanistan, Armenia, Bangladesh, Cambodia, the People's Republic of China, India, Indonesia, Kazakhstan, the Republic of Korea, the Kyrgyz Republic, Malaysia, Mongolia, Myanmar, Nepal, Pakistan, Papua New Guinea, the Philippines, Singapore, Sri Lanka, Tajikistan, Thailand, Timor-Leste, and Viet Nam.

Source: Adapted from Figure 6 of World Bank. 2016. *Benchmarking Public–Private Partnerships Procurement 2017.* http://bpp.worldbank.org/data/exploreeconomies/uruguay/2018#bpp_ppp

Finance ministry involvement helps ensure that the PPP program focuses on achieving value for money and that fiscal risks are managed. *Benchmarking PPP Procurement 2017* reports that 79% of the economies surveyed in developing Asia require the finance ministry or the central budgetary authority to approve PPP projects.

Many countries recognize the crucial role of conducting assessments as part of the PPP process. Lithuania, the Philippines, South Africa, and Viet Nam legally require and enact specific methodologies to conduct such assessments. A PPP project must be assessed in terms of its affordability, risk allocation, commercial viability, and value for money. The same is true in developing Asia, where more than 90% of countries surveyed conduct socioeconomic impact analysis; 83% check fiscal affordability; 78% identify and allocate risks, determine bankability, and conduct comparative assessment with traditional procurement procedure; and 56% conduct market assessment.

For risk assessments, the Philippines uses the generic preferred risk allocation matrix, which indicates the type of risks, proposed allocation and rationales, possible risk mitigation efforts, and suggested contract provisions. Market assessment is the least commonly required appraisal among all the surveyed economies and in developing Asia. This creates a risk that the government will structure the project in a way that will not attract a competitive bidding field. In Singapore, government procurement entities sound out the market on their proposed PPP approach to gather private sector feedback for 3–6 months before the issue of the PPP tender.

Uncompetitive PPP procurement

Countries tend to favor competitive bidding for PPP contracts. The share of PPP projects awarded through competitive bidding has been on the rise across all regions, though the share in developing Asia is lower than in Latin America and the Caribbean (Figure 2.2.10).

The complexity of PPP contracts and their long-term nature may limit participation in tenders, thus favoring anti-competitive agreements. In some cases, only one bidder submits a proposal. Technically, there should be no problem with this as long as due diligence ensures that no steps were omitted and that the bidder is qualified and fully compliant. However, a tender that attracts only one bid raises concerns about the suitability of the project and whether the bidder is really qualified, so the PPP regulatory framework must pay close attention to single-bidder cases. Moreover, it is always beneficial to the procuring authority to keep the market competitive. Competition is undermined when there is only one bidder for a project.

However, despite the importance of competitive bidding, half of the economies surveyed in *Benchmarking PPP Procurement 2017* do not address the single-bidder issue at all. In developing Asia, only 14 of 23 surveyed economies have procedures that kick in when only one bid is received. Among the economies that address this issue, the Kyrgyz Republic and Tajikistan require retendering.

Meanwhile, one of the biggest constraints on bringing PPP projects to the market is a lack of planning and capacity to properly structure and

2.2.10 Competitive bidding by region

- 2011–2015
- 2006–2010
- 2001–2005
- 1996–2000
- 1991–1995

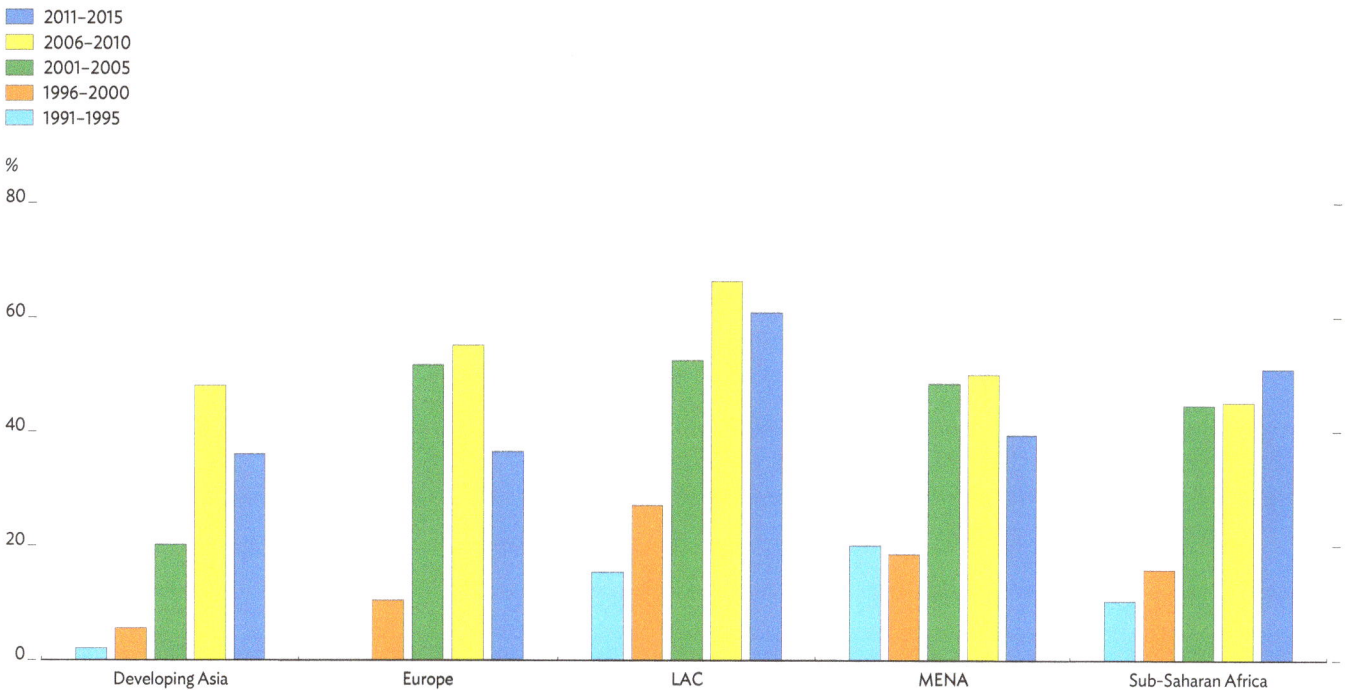

LAC = Latin America and the Caribbean, MENA = Middle East and North Africa.

Note: Includes only low- and middle-income countries in the region. Excludes full divestitures of state-owned assets (privatizations) and merchant projects that do not include government guarantees or that operate in a liberalized environment. Projects in the database must be at least 20% privately owned. State-owned enterprises are considered public. More information is available at http://ppi.worldbank.org/methodology/ppi-methodology

Source: World Bank Private Participation in Infrastructure database (accessed 25 May 2017).

prepare projects. Most developed countries with strong PPP programs can prepare a set of projects that attract private investors without relying on unsolicited proposals. While proposals initiated by a private party may offer some advantages by, for example, bringing innovation to the sector, many cases deviate from a competitive process of procurement, which then raises project costs. Entering into a sole-source process can save the government time and money and may alert it to an unrealized opportunity for PPP. However, sole sourcing can encourage corruption through lack of transparency, and it forfeits the benefits of competitive bidding (ADB 2008). Zou, Wang, and Fang (2008) identified a lack of competition as an important reason for project failure.

Unsolicited proposals may not align with government development plans because they did not emerge from the government planning process. Also, as is true of many solicited projects, unsolicited proposals may seek some form of government undertaking such as assuming financial obligations. Unsolicited proposals must therefore be properly evaluated, with at least some market testing, to ensure that they align with the investment needs of the country and, if they require government support, make good use of public resources.

Of the 56 economies surveyed that regulate unsolicited proposals, including 15 in developing Asia, all but Cameroon evaluate unsolicited proposals. However, regulatory provisions do not always require that they be consistent with government priorities. Such is the case in 18 of the economies, including Kazakhstan, Pakistan, and Papua New Guinea. Among the economies that regulate unsolicited proposals, only Kenya and Viet Nam do not require a competitive procurement procedure.

Further, procedures must allow sufficient time for bidders other than the proponent of the unsolicited proposal to submit their proposals. The literature suggests that the allowance should be at least 60 days, so that enough high-quality proposals can be received. Only the Republic of Korea, Mongolia, the Philippines, and Sri Lanka indicated a legally required period of 60 days or longer.

State-owned enterprises as partners

The fundamental functional feature of a successful PPP is credible risk transfer that shapes the incentives that draw out efficiency gains. In light of this, should a state-owned enterprise (SOE) be allowed to bid as a private partner for a PPP?

Traditionally, SOEs are backed by an explicit or implicit guarantee from the state, so any risks that may be transferred contractually to them eventually end up back with the state. If the risk effectively remains with the public sector, the arrangement fails to engender the incentives for performance that are the hallmark of successful PPP. Sometimes, however, an SOE embraces mechanisms for corporatization and improving governance and transparency, such that SOE management makes it functionally similar to a private entity. In this case, the SOE can indeed partner with the public sector to form a successful PPP.

Assigning SOEs to develop infrastructure projects has both advantages and disadvantages. It brings some benefits: fast realization, support from SOE financial leverage, and expected returns from the use of public funds. At the same time, it has limitations, crowding out private sector participation and limiting the funds available for infrastructure investment. SOEs depend heavily on public capital placement because of their relatively low capacity to issue bonds or find new equity sponsors. In the absence of market discipline, care is required when assessing the real returns of SOEs to avoid overly optimistic readings that can create future liabilities. In line with this, a classic problem with government-owned institutions is the soft budget constraint, as SOE executives may be subject to moral hazard because they feel safe from strict penalties for poor performance.

In the PRC, reliance on SOEs as PPP partners may skew the access enjoyed by SOEs versus that of private investors. In recent years, private participation in the PRC has been generally limited as SOEs played a more prominent role. This may not only increase existing SOE debt but also call into question the sustainability of growing government liabilities. According to an August 2017 quarterly report on the project database of the National PPP Integrated Information Platform, the PRC had 785 signed social capital partners, of which 247 were wholly owned by the state and 189 were state controlled (Figure 2.2.11).

2.2.11   Classification and proportion of 785 social capital partners in the People's Republic of China

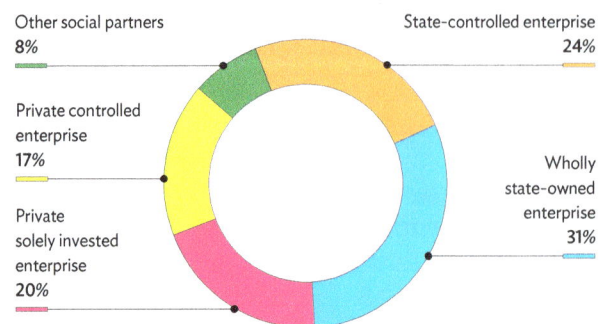

Other social partners 8%

State-controlled enterprise 24%

Private controlled enterprise 17%

Wholly state-owned enterprise 31%

Private solely invested enterprise 20%

Note: Other social partners include enterprises registered overseas and in Hong Kong, China; Macao, China; and Taipei,China.

Source: www.cpppc.org

Meanwhile, regional or local governments usually retain from 10% to 30% equity ownership in PPP projects.

The dominance of SOEs in PPP infrastructure projects may undermine the very essence of PPP—the effective leveraging of private capital—yet local governments and banks in the PRC often choose to partner with SOEs. A pressing issue is that transactions too often have not been at arm's length. Further, although local government payments to PPP projects have been included in their medium-term budgets since September 2016, some provinces may still use PPP to find ways around Ministry of Finance restrictions on local deficits. A result is projects that offer poor value for money and effectively transfer no risk to the private sector.

Lack of capacity to manage contracts

While a robust contract may help a PPP reach financial closure, it is also essential to adhere to its terms and adjust it when necessary. PPP thus imposes a significant monitoring and regulatory burden on the government. Indeed, the role of government becomes even more challenging in a PPP than in public procurement because it requires a careful balance to safeguard the public interest without constraining the innovative capacity of the private sector.

Unregulated contract renegotiation or modification

Even the most complex and detailed PPP contract cannot possibly cover every possible contingency to arise over its long life. PPP contracts may need to undergo renegotiation. Renegotiation should occur with the mutual consent of the parties involved. Cases arise, however, when renegotiation may encourage opportunistic and rent-seeking behavior from one party or another to capture as much as it can of the surplus created by the PPP project. It is thus critical for countries to ensure that possible renegotiations are well regulated.

Of the 82 economies surveyed, more than 75% regulate renegotiation, with Algeria, Lebanon, Malawi, and Myanmar among those silent on the question. Regarding provisions that regulate renegotiation, 27% of economies require approval from beyond the procuring authority, 33% impose restrictions on the scope of changes, and 21% restrict how risk allocation can be changed.

Absence of clear dispute settlement

An effective way to prevent contract renegotiation or termination is to have a good mechanism for settling disputes. The World Bank classifies forms of legal redress available to the parties as judicial and non-judicial. Non-judicial systems include both domestic and international arbitration and such alternative mechanisms as high-level negotiation, mediation, and determination by independent experts. PPP contracts that provide for international arbitration in a neutral jurisdiction give investors, contractors, and lenders confidence that disputes will be resolved fairly and efficiently. As shown in Figure 2.2.12,

2.2.12 Dispute resolution mechanisms for PPPs in selected economies in developing Asia

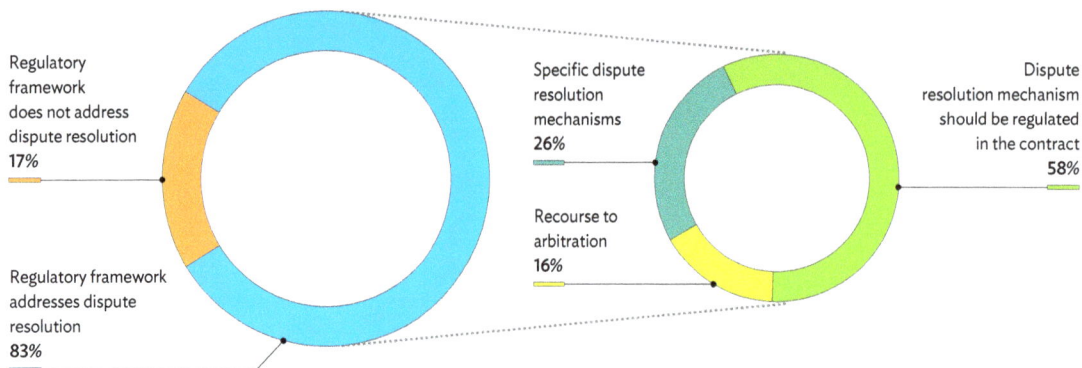

Regulatory framework does not address dispute resolution
17%

Regulatory framework addresses dispute resolution
83%

Specific dispute resolution mechanisms
26%

Recourse to arbitration
16%

Dispute resolution mechanism should be regulated in the contract
58%

PPP = public–private partnership.

Note: Developing Asia includes Afghanistan, Armenia, Bangladesh, Cambodia, the People's Republic of China, India, Indonesia, Kazakhstan, the Republic of Korea, the Kyrgyz Republic, Malaysia, Mongolia, Myanmar, Nepal, Pakistan, Papua New Guinea, the Philippines, Singapore, Sri Lanka, Tajikistan, Thailand, Timor-Leste, and Viet Nam.

Source: Adapted from Figure 6 of World Bank. 2016. *Benchmarking Public–Private Partnerships Procurement 2017.*

fewer than 20% of the economies surveyed in developing Asia fail to refer to dispute resolution mechanisms in their regulatory frameworks. Among the economies that do refer to them, close to half make only a general statement that dispute resolution will be regulated in the contract. The remaining economies turn to arbitration or provide for another dispute mechanism.

Inadequate PPP laws and policies

A policy framework provides the rationale and process for entering into PPP. A legal framework ensures that PPP contracts are effective, binding, and enforceable, and a regulatory framework provides the technical, safety, and economic safeguards necessary to enforce a PPP contract. In economies where regulations change unpredictably or where there is not enough guidance, investors may find themselves in a serious financial mess, with high sunk costs, when the government changes the rules of the game without good reason. Albalate, Bel, and Gedes (2015) found that favorable PPP-enabling laws facilitate private participation in infrastructure.

Public procurement laws are the most common way of handling PPP in developing Asia, especially in the Pacific, though the promulgation of a PPP law or act comes a close second (Figures 2.2.13 and 2.2.14). Even if an economy has only general procurement laws, this does not prevent it from implementing PPP projects.

The group of economies with PPP laws displays some heterogeneity. The Philippines adopted a build–operate–transfer law. Viet Nam issued executive decrees rather than enact PPP laws, and Indonesia has regulations governing PPP transactions. Finally, 20% of the economies in developing Asia regulate PPP through guidelines, policies, or similar instruments: Bhutan, Brunei Darussalam, the PRC, India, Malaysia, Pakistan, Singapore, Sri Lanka, and Hong Kong, China. Not surprisingly, most of these economies operate are under a common law system.

2.2.13 PPP legal framework

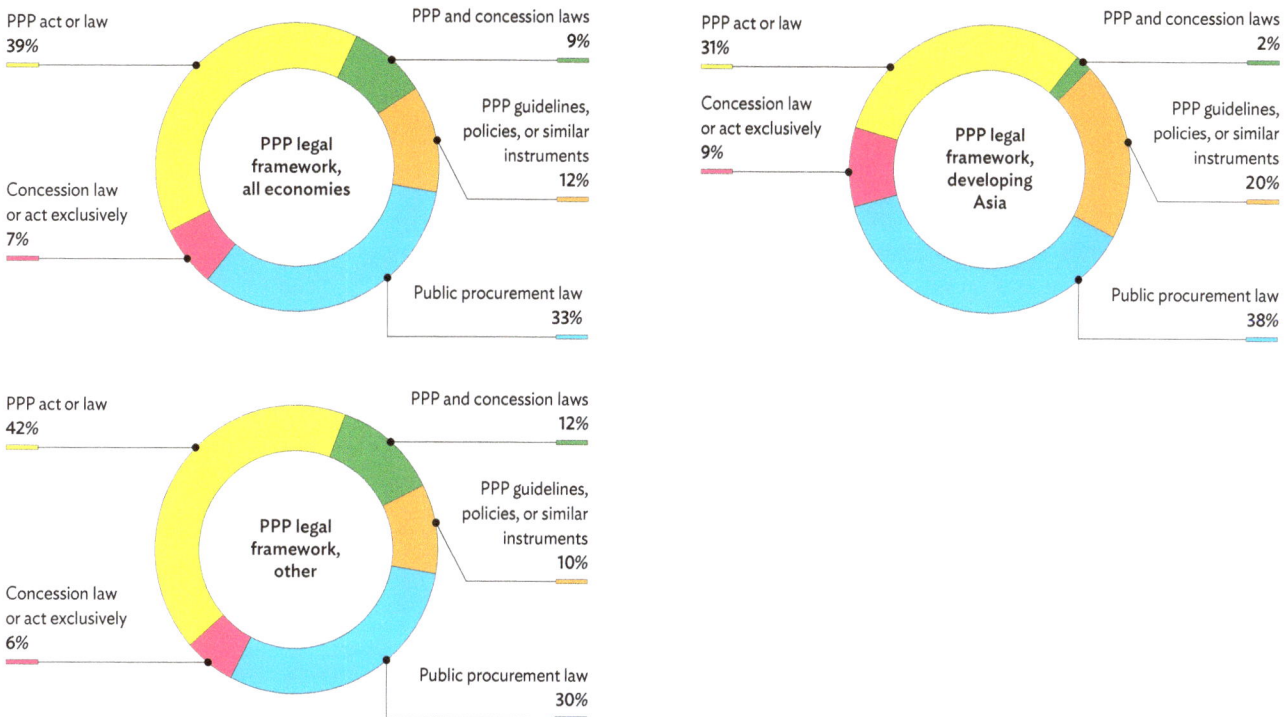

PPP act or law
39%

PPP and concession laws
9%

PPP guidelines,
policies, or similar
instruments
12%

PPP legal
framework,
all economies

Concession law
or act exclusively
7%

Public procurement law
33%

PPP act or law
31%

PPP and concession laws
2%

Concession law
or act exclusively
9%

PPP guidelines,
policies, or similar
instruments
20%

PPP legal
framework,
developing
Asia

Public procurement law
38%

PPP act or law
42%

PPP and concession laws
12%

PPP legal
framework,
other

PPP guidelines,
policies, or similar
instruments
10%

Concession law
or act exclusively
6%

Public procurement law
30%

PPP = public–private partnership.

Notes: A total of 160 economies were surveyed. Developing Asia includes all 45 Asian Development Bank developing member countries: Afghanistan, Armenia, Azerbaijan, Bangladesh, Bhutan, Brunei Darussalam, Cambodia, the People's Republic of China, Cook Islands, Fiji, Georgia, India, Indonesia, Kazakhstan, Kiribati, the Republic of Korea, the Kyrgyz Republic, the Lao People's Democratic Republic, Malaysia, Maldives, Marshall Islands, the Federated States of Micronesia, Mongolia, Myanmar, Nauru, Nepal, Pakistan, Palau, Papua New Guinea, the Philippines, Samoa, Singapore, Solomon Islands, Sri Lanka, Tajikistan, Thailand, Timor-Leste, Tonga, Turkmenistan, Tuvalu, Uzbekistan, Vanuatu, Viet Nam, Taipei,China, and Hong Kong, China. Others include Albania, Algeria, Angola, Argentina, Austria, Australia, Belarus, Belgium, Benin, Bosnia and Herzegovina, Botswana, Brazil, Bulgaria, Burkina Faso, Cameroon, Canada, Chile, Colombia, the Democratic Republic of the Congo, the Republic of the Congo, Costa Rica, Côte d'Ivoire, Croatia, the Czech Republic, Denmark, the Dominican Republic, Ecuador, Egypt, El Salvador, Estonia, France, Finland, Gabon, Gambia, Germany, Ghana, Greece, Grenada, Guatemala, Guinea-Bissau, Honduras, Hungary, Iceland, Iran, Iraq, Ireland, Israel, Italy, Jamaica, Japan, Jordan, Kenya, Kosovo, Kuwait, Latvia, Lebanon, Liberia, Lithuania, Luxembourg, Macedonia, Madagascar, Malawi, Mali, Malta, Mauritania, Mauritius, Mexico, Moldova, Montenegro, Morocco, Mozambique, the Netherlands, New Zealand, Nicaragua, Nigeria, Norway, Panama, Paraguay, Peru, Poland, Portugal, Puerto Rico, Romania, the Russian Federation, Rwanda, Saint Lucia, Saudi Arabia, Serbia, Seychelles, Senegal, Sierra Leone, the Slovak Republic, Slovenia, Somalia, South Africa, Spain, Swaziland, Sweden, Switzerland, Syria, Tanzania, Togo, Trinidad and Tobago, Tunisia, Turkey, Uganda, Ukraine, the United Arab Emirates, the United Kingdom, the United States of America, Uruguay, Venezuela, Yemen, Zambia, and Zimbabwe.

Sources: ADB resident missions; World Bank PPP Knowledge Lab; World Bank 2016b; UNESCAP 2017; various government websites.

2.2.14 PPP legal framework in developing Asia

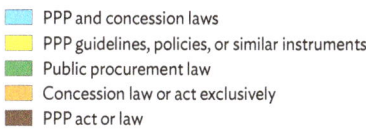

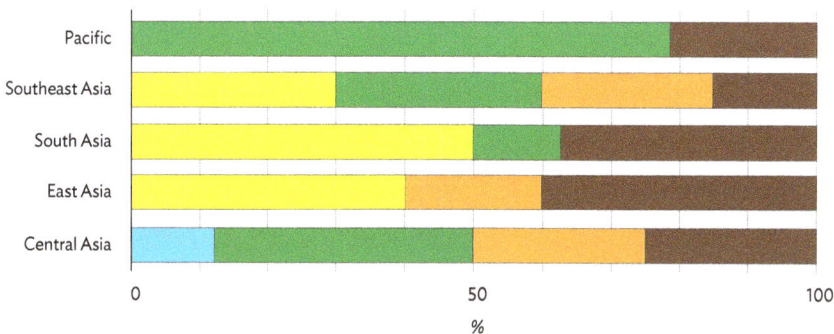

- ■ PPP and concession laws
- ■ PPP guidelines, policies, or similar instruments
- ■ Public procurement law
- ■ Concession law or act exclusively
- ■ PPP act or law

PPP = public–private partnership.

Sources: ADB resident missions; World Bank PPP Knowledge Lab; World Bank 2016b; UNESCAP 2017; various government websites.

Indeed, the design of the legal framework for PPP varies across countries and depends largely on the type of the legal system in the country. Incoherent policies, changing or discriminatory regulations, and redundant processes confuse and discourage investors, create additional burdens, and prolong legal processes. Overarching privatization legislation had been an issue in the water sector of the PRC. Its build–operate–transfer projects and other PPP reform strategies are governed by a series of government policy papers. Developing a wastewater build–operate–transfer project is complicated, requiring consideration of a range of issues: land use, water company management, investment mechanisms, taxation, accounting systems, and the credit policies of multilateral development banks. In 2004, over half of projects for wastewater treatment in the PRC could not be implemented because of conflict with land-use policies (ADB 2008).

One legal barrier that hinders the implementation of PPP in developing economies is land acquisition. Compulsory acquisition is the power of government to acquire private land for a public purpose without the willing consent of its owner or occupant (Keith et al. 2008). As resolving such cases can take great deal of time, especially if many claimants are involved, land acquisition is one of the biggest challenges for PPP projects. The implementation of several projects in the region has been delayed by compulsory acquisition, one example being right-of-way required for an expressway in the Philippines (Rickards and Hermelin 2015). Related issues include the relocation of squatters and sometimes poor coordination in governments when opposed by landowners and environmental groups (Safitri 2015).

Yet, despite being a core and necessary governmental power, compulsory acquisition is always controversial because of the human costs in terms of disrupted community cohesion, livelihood patterns, and ways of life, which may not be fully mitigated by standard compensation packages, however generous they may be (Lindsay 2012). These costs are compounded when coupled with poor design and implementation, which leaves tenure insecure, land markets weak, investment incentives undermined, and communities and livelihoods destroyed even as it creates opportunities for corruption.

In sum, different forms of PPP require different sets of prerequisites to succeed (ADB 2008). More complex forms of PPP, those that transfer greater risk to the private sector, require a more sophisticated legal and regulatory framework, more political support, and more skilled staffing to implement and monitor the project (Table 2.2.3).

2.2.3 Prerequisites of public–private partnership options

Options	Political commitment	Cost recovery tariffs	Regulatory framework	Information base	Government capacity for contracting, management, and analysis
Service contract	Low	Low	Low	Low	Moderate
Management contract	Moderate	Moderate	Moderate	Low	Moderate
Lease	Moderate	High	High	High	High
Concession	High	High	High	High	High
Build-operate-transfer	High	Variable	High	High	High

Source: ADB 2008.

Issues not directly related to projects

Apart from the challenges discussed above, PPP can face other risks not directly related to the project. The discussion below is by no means exhaustive or comprehensive, but recognizing these challenges can help address potential limits to PPP.

Macroeconomic instability

PPP projects are vulnerable to financial and other implications of sharp changes in macroeconomic variables. Macroeconomic shocks affect the availability and cost of credit, slow economic growth, and cause exchange rate volatility. Such shocks can increase the cost of project financing through either exchange rate movements, if financing is in a foreign currency, or higher domestic interest rates (Burger et al. 2009). This shifts cost burdens among the parties involved, rendering PPP less attractive.

Many theoretical and empirical studies have confirmed how macroeconomic factors determine the success or failure of PPP projects by affecting either operations or profitability. For example, Galilea and Medda (2010) confirmed that in the transport sector GDP growth and the current account balance, measured as a percentage of GDP, affect PPP success. Meanwhile, Hyun, Park, and Tian (forthcoming) found the macroeconomic factors economic growth and inflation the most influential determinants of PPP investments. Lee et al. (forthcoming[b]) observed that a stable macroeconomy significantly reduced the hazard of a PPP project facing cancellation. An example is an elevated railway project in Thailand that faced severe financial problems from overly optimistic demand projections and a lack of appropriate mitigation for exchange rate risk. In accordance with the contract, the revenue stream for the private partner came completely from fares, without any funds from the government. Initial ridership was lower than forecast because of high fares and a gap in infrastructure integration that undermined accessibility. Revenue was collected in local currency, but the debt was in US dollars (UNESCAP 2014b, Allport et al. 2008).

Climate risks

Infrastructure is subject to climate risks, whether it is delivered through public procurement or PPP. Because the region is particularly exposed to climate risks, and because of the long-term nature of PPP projects and the effect of investment decisions on the lifecycle of the infrastructure assets, the management of climate risks in infrastructure PPPs is becoming more important as they become more prevalent (Sundararajan and Suriyagoda 2016).

The exposure of infrastructure assets to climate risk is rising as extreme weather events such as storms, floods, landslides, heat waves, and droughts become more frequent and intense. Lee, Villaruel, and Gaspar (2016) found that, along with agriculture and industry, investment endeavors potentially become channels through which higher temperatures significantly affect economic productivity. Research showed that, in the business-as-usual scenario, global warming that reached 3.9°C above pre-industrial levels by 2100 could cause economic losses in developing Asia equal to more than 10% of regional GDP.

2.2.4 The long-term climate risk index: the 10 countries most affected from 1996 to 2015 (annual averages)

Rank	Country	Climate risk index score	Death toll	Death per 100,000 inhabitants	Total losses ($ million PPP)	Losses per unit of GDP in %	Number of events (1996–2015)
1	Honduras	11.3	302	4.36	568.0	2.100	61
2	Myanmar	14.2	7,146	14.71	1,300.7	0.737	41
3	Haiti	18.2	253	2.71	221.9	1.486	63
4	Nicaragua	19.2	163	2.94	234.8	1.197	44
5	Philippines	21.3	862	1.00	2,761.5	0.628	283
6	Bangladesh	25.0	679	0.48	2,283.4	0.732	185
7	Pakistan	30.5	505	0.32	3,823.2	0.647	133
8	Viet Nam	31.3	340	0.41	2,119.4	0.621	206
9	Guatemala	33.8	97	0.75	401.5	0.467	75
10	Thailand	34.8	140	0.22	7,574.6	1.004	136

PPP = purchasing power parity.

Source: Germanwatch. 2017. *The Global Climate Risk Index 2017.* https://germanwatch.org/en/download/16411.pdf

ADO 2016 Update described developing Asia as particularly vulnerable to climate risks. The 2017 Global Climate Risk Index ranked six developing economies in Asia among the top 10 countries most affected by climate change in 1996–2015 in terms of the frequency of disruption, death tolls, and economic losses (Table 2.2.4). Average losses in these six countries during the period amounted to $3.3 billion.

Similarly, Lee et al. (forthcoming[b]) found that natural disasters can interrupt the implementation of PPP projects, delaying construction, or else disrupt their operation, losing revenue. Excessive insurance and compensation demands and reliance on the government for disaster bailouts are not sustainable, particularly as risk allocation among project partners should be appropriately apportioned. In many instances, the magnitude of damage overwhelmed the ability of insurers to cover recovery and replacement costs (Baxter 2017).

However, climate risks are rarely allocated explicitly, though often contracts implicitly allocate risks of various consequences of climate change. For example, in a typical road PPP, if climate change brings higher temperatures and rainfall that accelerate pavement degradation, requiring more frequent repairs and resurfacing to keep the road open to traffic and meet contractual performance indicators, this risk is implicitly allocated to the private sector, which consequently faces higher maintenance costs.

Risk sharing and the need to build climate-resilient infrastructure together give rise to several challenges affecting PPP. Admittedly, few innovative solutions exists to manage climate risks, for lack of expertise and because climate risks are not explicitly identified or allocated. Where standard PPP contracts address climate risks they do so only indirectly. Table 2.2.5 identifies some of the gaps in current PPP contract terms regarding climate risks. Further, existing provisions in standard PPP contracts address climate risks after the fact, which produces inferior outcomes. There is thus a pressing need for PPP climate risk management to be more flexible.

2.2.5 Gaps in PPP measures to address climate risks

Measure	Gap
Relief and compensation	As there is no comprehensive list of climate risks to PPP assets, events such as storms or hail damage cannot be claimed for relief or compensation.
Force majeure	The lack of any standard treatment of force majeure provisions across jurisdictions creates investment uncertainty.
	The lack of standard catch-all provisions or itemized lists that fully capture all climate risks under force majeure limits the extent of coverage.
	What were rare climate events in the past may become more frequent in the future, making current force majeure provisions inappropriate.
Insurance	Lack of access in developing countries to commercial insurance markets exposes PPP assets to long-term climate risks.
	Limited access to affordable insurance increases risk in PPP projects and dissuades investors from investing in risky PPPs.
Uninsurability	Uninsurability provisions can remove incentives for the private sector to develop climate-resilient infrastructure or proactively manage climate risks.
	When the public sector assumes insurance risk under uninsurability provisions, it does not have the same ability and capacity of a commercial insurer to enforce a disciplined approach to risk management.

PPP = public–private partnership.

Source: Sundararajan and Suriyagoda 2016.

Country risks

Jett (forthcoming) reported that a recent survey found infrastructure investors in Asia concerned about the ability of government entities to fulfill their contractual obligations. This threatens either explicit breach of contract or state entities' failure to pay.

There is a strong correlation between country risk and the closure of PPP projects in developing economies. Araya, Schwartz, and Andrés (2013) found improvement by one standard deviation in a country's sovereign risk score associated with 27% higher private participation in infrastructure and 41% more investment. As PPPs are assessed project by project, this does not mean that PPPs are not generally viable, but it does indicate that PPPs have a lower probability of being implemented when country risk is high.

An assessment of country risk in terms of payment to participants, the financial situation, and the economic situation found that a worse rating translated into a higher interest rate and consequently less financial viability for PPP (OECD 2017). More importantly, many banks simply will not lend to projects in the bottom categories, or they may restrict eligibility to PPPs that pledge hard currency revenues, such as oil wells or international airports. In developing Asia, 41% of economies are rated in the bottom categories (6 or 7 for the highest country risk), and another 31% are unrated. The Standard & Poor's measure of sovereign risk, meanwhile, refers to the creditworthiness of the sovereign to meet its payment obligations. This rating does not put as strong an emphasis on payment history or political risk. With 26% of developing Asia below investment grade at BBB–, and a further 59% unrated, only 15% are investment grade and therefore acceptable to international lenders (Figure 2.2.15).

2.2.15 Survey of 39 developing member countries that borrow from ADB

- Category 1–5
- Category 6 or 7 (highest risk)
- Unrated (considered risky)
- At or above investment grade
- Below investment grade (BBB–)
- Unrated (considered below investment grade)

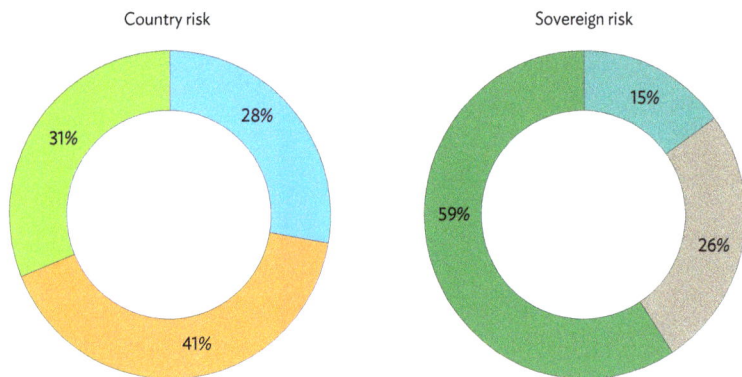

Country risk

28%
41%
31%

Sovereign risk

15%
26%
59%

ADB = Asian Development Bank.
Source: OECD ECA Country Risk Classifications and Standard & Poor's Foreign Currency.

In Asia, country and sovereign risks are thus strong impediments to financing for PPP. One way to overcome country risk is to require further credit-enhancement guarantees from the government. The next section deals with this concern along with the general issue of generating financing for PPP.

Financing public–private partnership

The large infrastructure gap exists in developing Asia alongside substantial private savings that can be mobilized if risks associated with infrastructure investment are properly addressed and mitigated. A PPP makes the delivery of public infrastructure and services a good business opportunity by allocating risks to the parties that can best manage them.

The ability to mobilize financing from private sources for public infrastructure is considered the most attractive benefit of PPP. *Sources of Financing for Public–Private Partnership Investments in 2015* (World Bank 2015) showed that 83% of PPP committed investment in East and Southeast Asia and the Pacific was from private sources in the form of debt or equity, 13% from public sources, and 4% from multilateral development banks (MDBs).

A significant amount of the accumulated savings is managed by institutional investors. Mobilizing these savings to finance infrastructure projects requires a concerted and coordinated effort by the government, private investors, and development institutions. This is the principal challenge policy makers face in attracting private capital to long-term infrastructure contracts like the PPP. This section deals with the main sources of private finance for PPP projects. Understanding the nature of these sources enables the selection of the most appropriate financing structure. When evaluating each source, important criteria are not only its ability to bring private financing at a reasonable price but also its ability to share risks and control in the manner that promises the efficient delivery of infrastructure and its dependent services over its full lifecycle.

Obtaining capital from appropriate sources at reasonable cost may require policy interventions to offset some of the risks involved. If left unaddressed, these risks could impede the mobilization of financing for PPP. In other words, the infrastructure gap in developing Asia is more of a risk gap than a financing gap.

In light of this, the role of financial innovation is analyzed here along with the role of MDBs, which are not only sources of financing but also catalysts for bridging the risk gap that is holding up Asia's infrastructure development.

Project finance and optimal risk sharing

The organizational structure of most PPPs is a special purpose vehicle (SPV) established using a financial structuring process called "project finance." It involves creating a distinct legal and economic entity to act as the counterparty to various contracts and to obtain the financial resources required to develop and manage a project. Setting up a SPV is the necessary first step for the private sector to deliver infrastructure through a PPP.

The SPV is financed with both debt and equity provided by different partners. The main distinction between project finance and conventional corporate or public financial structures is that debt and equity providers depend solely on the capacity of the project to generate cash flows to repay their investments. Typically, providers have only limited recourse to the government or project sponsors. Hence, project finance is sometimes described as limited-recourse financing or off-balance-sheet financing. Figure 2.3.1 shows the contractual structure of a typical project financed by a variety of participants.

2.3.1 Project finance

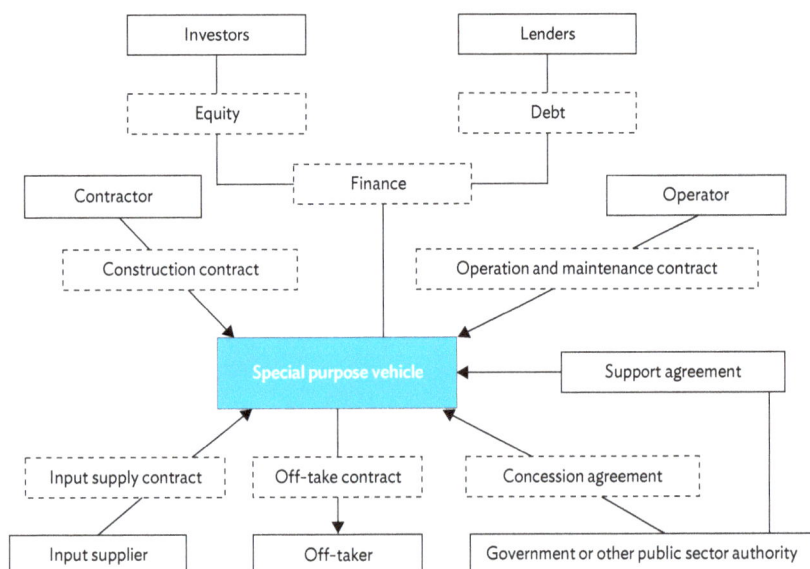

Source: Yescombe 2013.

Limited-recourse project finance ensures that returns to financial investors closely reflect project performance. If the SPV defaults under the loan agreement, the lenders will enforce their security and recover all outstanding principal and interest. Further, they may step in when either the SPV or the contractors have defaulted or there is reasonable belief that they will default in the near future. In the event of a termination, the lenders are expected to first receive all of their unpaid debt. Any residual goes to equity investors. If the lenders cannot fully recover, they suffer a loss and equity investors will not receive anything.

Instead of project finance, sometimes a PPP is structured as a pure corporate finance transaction, wherein the project appears on the balance sheet of a private entity. Or it may be structured with a full financial guarantee from the government to some or all of the private financiers. However, as a successful PPP requires risk sharing and incentive alignment, its financing requires not just private capital but capital that is subject to risk related to project performance. In other words, successful PPP requires "risk capital" to create incentives for financial investors to exert oversight as necessary on SPV participants to deliver the expected outcomes.

Project finance is an effective structure not only for financing but also for corporate governance. Kleimeier and Versteeg (2010) argued that the contractual structure unique to project finance engenders better investment management. Their empirical results showed that project finance compensates for lack of domestic financial development, particularly in less-developed economies where governance mechanisms are weak. Loan covenants compensate for deficient laws on investor protection and insider information. As such, project finance fosters economic growth. In another empirical study, Hainz and Kleimeier (2012) showed that project finance loans are more likely to be used if political risk is higher. This encourages the participation of MDBs in the syndicate.

The sound and transparent corporate governance structure of project finance enables risk management to be more effective. Brealey, Cooper, and Habib (1996) argued that the contractual arrangements found in project finance can be used to address agency problems that can render large private and public organizations inefficient. Contracts connecting multiple parties in project finance can be viewed as devices designed to shift a variety of project risks to those parties best able to appraise and control them. Corieli, Gatti, and Steffanoni (2010) confirmed that lenders in project finance use the deal's network of nonfinancial contracts as a mechanism to control agency costs and project risks.

Because of the many risks present in large PPP transactions, project finance is structured to match risks and their corresponding returns to the parties best able to manage them successfully. By facilitating the equitable and rational distribution of risk, it creates an environment in which investors can work together easily. The ring-fenced nature of project finance ensures that the risk to equity investors in the SPV is limited to the amount invested, such that project failure does not threaten to sink investors' larger businesses, at least not if they are healthy. Project finance also allows the leveraging of long-term debt, which is necessary to finance high capital expenses. A longer-term loan may reduce the risk of default during a PPP project's early years of operation by reducing the portion of cash flow earmarked for debt service, thereby giving the project more time to find its footing (Yescombe 2007).

Sources of project finance

The choice of financing method depends on the project's requirements and risks, the amount of capital available for direct investment in equity, and the quality of the financing consortium.

Equity finance

In all financing structures, equity financiers own the asset, exercise control over all decisions related to it, and receive any profits it generates. As residual claimants to the asset's cash flows, or the last to be paid, equity investors have the strongest incentive to draw out of other PPP players their best performance. One of the most important features of a good financing structure for PPP is therefore securing funding for the long term. As substantial leverage is the hallmark of project finance, each dollar of equity can channel $5 or more of investment into infrastructure. The proportion of debt to equity is ultimately determined by the project's contractual and capital structures, and how various risks are mitigated.

With limited recourse, project finance provides powerful incentive to equity investors at the bottom of the cash flow waterfall. All risks that have not already been transferred away through contractual and hedging mechanisms to different parties affect equity returns. Equity investors must therefore possess the necessary skills and degree of control over the project to manage the project effectively and efficiently to earn the necessary returns for its shareholders. At the same time, public regulation must ensure that profit extraction aligns with the public interest, particularly in the event of any refinancing gains during the life of the concession.

Traditionally, industrial sponsors—corporate entities that play a significant role in equipment provision, construction, or project operation—have provided equity for PPP projects. The result has often been a governance structure in which the three different responsibilities—the provision of engineering and technical expertise, delivery of equity dividends from profits, and management of the infrastructure asset—are bundled together and provided by the industrial sponsors. But even with substantial leverage, Asia's infrastructure requires a large amount of equity capital. And the lifecycle perspective on PPPs requires this equity capital to be in place for a long time. Because industrial partners have only limited capacity to provide large quantities of equity capital for long periods, PPPs have to tap other sources of equity such as institutional investors.

The advent of infrastructure funds was a significant innovation in the provision of equity for PPP. It marks the arrival of outside equity investors in infrastructure as "financial sponsors," which have taken center stage in the consortia that structure, build, own, operate, and manage infrastructure projects. Such funds have emerged over the past 2 decades as a distinct and significant funding source for infrastructure projects in many developed and developing countries.

The first infrastructure funds were considered a subclass of private equity funds (Box 2.3.1). Like private equity funds, they were organized as limited partnerships. The general partner would set up the fund and invest capital raised from a number of limited partners, usually institutional investors. The general partner would also manage the funds in exchange for a fee based upon the volume of assets under management and receive a share of the returns from the investments after a minimum performance threshold had been met. The general partner enjoyed significant discretion to decide investment and control questions related to the fund, subject to some broad guidelines. Over time, and responding to the unique needs of infrastructure investments, infrastructure funds started to adopt features that made them quite distinct from traditional private equity funds: their investment horizons lengthened, their management fees became lower, and, most significantly, some infrastructure funds listed on exchanges and could be traded (though this trend has reversed to some extent). Thus, infrastructure funds gave rise to a project governance structure in which the three different responsibilities—the provision of technical expertise, provision of funding, and management of the infrastructure asset—could be split across three different parties.

Infrastructure funds have played a smaller role in developing countries, including in Asia, than in more developed markets. However, this is changing. Preqin (2016) reported that 108 Asia-focused unlisted infrastructure funds reached final closure (that is, fulfillment of financing conditions) in the decade from 2006, accumulating $39 billion in institutional capital commitments. Fundraising reached a peak in 2013, a year in which 18 funds closed, having raised an aggregate amount of $6.3 billion. Further, 90% of these infrastructure funds invested in equity only, though some of them used debt or mezzanine investments as part of their approach (page 108). Seventy-eight percent of the closed funds targeted greenfield assets. The majority of Asia-focused infrastructure funds in the past decade were managed by firms based in Asia. Preqin (2015) predicted that economic expansion and rising demand for infrastructure across Asia would ensure further growth in the asset class in the region, and that the privatization of assets in Asia had created further opportunities, with fund managers likely to continue viewing Asian infrastructure as an important component in their portfolios.

Debt finance

Debt finance constitutes the largest component of financing for PPP projects. Debt instruments for infrastructure projects can be structured to have long-term maturities relying on the cash flow and the security that extend over the life of long-term assets. Debt financing can be provided through multiple instruments and may take the form of direct loans held on the balance sheets of financial institutions. Debt financing can also be structured for resale to investors or distribution to private markets as private-placement debt or to public markets through registered project, corporate, or government bonds. Unlike public debt financing, such as that provided by the government through either budgetary allocation or the issuance of government-backed debt, private debt finance earns returns only through the proceeds of project bonds. Financiers of infrastructure projects can tailor products to fit the preferences of certain investors such as pension funds and insurance companies.

Bank loans

Banks have been the largest providers of debt finance for infrastructure projects, both in Asia and around the world. Bank loans have several advantages over bonds and other structured instruments because (i) banks play an important monitoring role, (ii) bank lending has the flexibility required to meet infrastructure projects' need for

2.3.1 Infrastructure funds are not new to Asia

What is believed to be one of the first private equity funds dedicated entirely to infrastructure was set up in 1994. The $1.08 billion AIG Asian Infrastructure Fund was established by Emerging Markets Partnership, a global private equity fund. The fund made 24 investments in a wide variety of sectors, including fixed line and mobile telecommunications, toll roads, container terminals, electric power, and water supply in the People's Republic of China, India, the Republic of Korea, the Philippines, Thailand, and Taipei,China.

Other examples of infrastructure funds are the ASEAN Infrastructure Fund of the Association of Southeast Asian Nations, the Leading Asia's Private Sector Infrastructure Fund, and the IFC Global Infrastructure Fund of the International Finance Corporation.

Source: Quint, M. 1994. New Fund Raises $1 Billion for Investment Plan in Asia. *New York Times*. 2 June.

funds to be gradually disbursed, and (iii) infrastructure projects often require, because of unforeseen circumstances over their long lives, debt restructuring that banks can quickly negotiate among themselves (Esty and Megginson 2003). Further, bank financing can provide earlier and greater pricing certainty through the relatively structured tender process of a well-designed PPP.

Debt data from 413 projects in India, Indonesia, the Republic of Korea, Malaysia, the Philippines, Thailand, and Viet Nam from 2011 to 2016 provide a snapshot of syndicated bank lending in Asia. The average project cost exceeds $300 million. Debt constitutes almost 87% of the original capital structure, and the average maturity of the loans is 13 years. Only 10% of the projects involve bilateral or multilateral lenders, such as MDBs. On average, 85% of the banks in each syndicate are headquartered in the country where the project is located. Finally, 75% of projects have debt finance denominated entirely in local currency. Rao (2017) sought to explain the factors influencing bank lending for infrastructure financing in Asia, with an emphasis on project finance for PPP projects.

The Asian evidence seems to suggest that the volume of debt financing in Asia is driven more by the country's macroeconomic variables, such as GDP per capita and the ratio of gross debt to GDP, than by other macro variables related to institutional quality or microeconomic variables related to project characteristics. This contrasts with findings in similar studies in developed countries with advanced PPP markets, where project characteristics are more significant.

Thus, banks seem to prefer lending in countries that have reached minimum acceptable conditions in terms of economic growth and a reasonable risk profile in terms of the ratio of debt to GDP. From a policy perspective, these results imply that attracting bank debt for infrastructure PPP projects through project finance depends on having policies to sustain economic growth.

However, banks' ability to provide debt financing for Asia's vast infrastructure needs is limited. Some limits derive from recent changes in bank regulation and capital requirements. Put together in the aftermath of the global financial crisis of 2008–2009, bank capital requirements under Basel III have tightened requirements for project finance lending by commercial banks. Ma (2016) predicted that restrictions will raise costs for project finance debt by 60–110 basis points, shorten tenor, and constrict the provision of letters of credit and revolving credit facilities.

Bonds

Bonds have several advantages over bank lending toward providing financing well suited for long-term PPP contracts. First, bond financing is normally cheaper than bank financing because bond investors can lend at fixed rates, eliminating the need for interest rate swaps and associated costs. Even fully insured bonds have been seen to have a lower all-in cost than bank loans. Second, bond financing can be drawn from investors with natural long-term liabilities, compared with banks' relatively short-term funding sources. Thus, bond investors can offer tenors that are better matched to the term of underlying concessions, allowing projects to avoid refinancing risk.

As bond holders are typicaly averse to construction and the initial ramp up risk, they are hesitant to invest in greenfield infrastructure projects. Bond financing is rarely used in the construction phase mainly because infrastructure bonds are interesting mostly to long-term investors, who are typically less willing or able to invest in high-risk debt securities, and also because debt restructuring during the construction phase could trigger selective bond defaults (Ehlers 2014). In the operational phase, however, bond finance is preferable to bank finance. This makes the refinancing of brownfield projects with proven track records a better fit for bond financing.

Indeed, bond buyers—prominently long-term institutional investors such as pension funds and insurers—should naturally be attracted to infrastructure PPP assets because of their favorable investment characteristics such as low competition and predictable and stable cash flows over the long term, which enables liability matching and inflation hedging. According to OECD (2016), global private pension funds had accumulated assets worth $38 trillion as of 2015. Attracting such funds into infrastructure investment could be an effective way to bridge the infrastructure gap.

In spite of the attractive features of bond financing, Rao (2017) documented empirical evidence that bonds are used only minimally for infrastructure and PPP in Asia and offered some explanations. Distinguishing between infrastructure bonds and project bonds provides a useful starting point.

The term "infrastructure bond" has a variety of meanings. First, a few sovereign and sub-sovereign bonds may be dedicated to infrastructure. Municipal bonds are a major source of infrastructure financing, especially in the US. Second, utility and infrastructure companies issue corporate bonds that may be included in corporate bond indexes. Third, project bonds are prominent in project finance, especially for PPPs. These bonds are serviced entirely from project-specific cash flows, especially as project finance limits the liability of the project sponsor to the equity invested in the project SPV. Project bonds in this narrow sense constituted about 10% of global project debt from 1994 to 2012. Several Asian countries, including the Republic of Korea, Malaysia, and Thailand, have developed domestic capital markets and were early users of infrastructure bonds, corporate bonds, and listed equities.

For one project in the Republic of Korea, infrastructure bonds underwritten by the Korea Development Bank were structured such that they were issued at different times in line with the completion schedule. This indicates that the success of a bond issue may depend on the underwriting ability of a financial institution (Kim et al. 2011). To widen investment opportunities for Korean investors, infrastructure bonds should be encouraged to help Republic of Korea companies enhance their financing capability in the Asian infrastructure market (Hyun 2017). Data from *AsianBondsOnline* show as of June 2017 infrastructure-related bond issuances account for less than a fifth of the issuances of the top 30 local currency corporate bond issuers. Infrastructure bonds in the Republic of Korea came to $3.0 trillion from 2012 to 2017, most of them in the transport sector (Table 2.3.1).

2.3.1 Issues of infrastructure bond in the Republic of Korea, 2012–2017

	Sectors				
	Logistics	Railway	Road	Others	Grand Total
Amount of bond issuance (W billion)	92.4	1,129.4	1,765.0	43.0	**3,029.8**
Total project cost (W billion)	164.0	4,279.0	9,425.0	103.0	**13,971.0**
Amount of issuance/total project cost (%)	56.3	26.4	18.7	41.7	**21.7**

Note: "Others" include enviromental and sports center infrastructure.
Source: Korea Credit Guarantee Fund.

In some countries such as Malaysia, *sukuk* (Islamic) bonds are used to raise funds. In 2016, Malaysia dominated the *sukuk* market with 46.4% of total new issuances, followed by Indonesia with 9.9% and the United Arab Emirates with 9.0%. For infrastructure projects, $73.1 billion in infrastructure *sukuk* bonds were issued by more than 10 countries from 2002 to the third quarter of 2015 (Figure 2.3.2). Malaysia dominated this market with a 61% share of issuances, followed by Saudi Arabia with 30% and the United Arab Emirates with 7% (Musa 2015).

In November 2010, the Trans Thai–Malaysia *sukuk* bond was successfully issued for RM600 million. This was the first project finance bond transaction in Malaysia since the 2008 financial crisis. Notably, it achieved a financing tenor longer than typical US dollar-denominated project financing in Thailand or Malaysia. This bond issuance further highlighted the importance of capital market strength in infrastructure financing (HSBC Amanah 2012).

In Asia and the Pacific, infrastructure bonds accounted for 20% of global issues from 2000 to 2013, compared with 41% in North America, 21% in Europe (including 4% in emerging Europe), and 15% in Latin America (Deutsche Bank 2016). Most infrastructure bonds are issued in local currency. The PRC had $439 billion in outstanding infrastructure bonds as of November 2015. The Republic of Korea issuers were the second most active in the region, backed by their country's strong sovereign rating and deep domestic capital market. Other advanced economies in developing Asia with established capital markets, such as Singapore and Hong Kong, China, have seen active issuance by government-linked companies. In the PRC and India, where banking sectors are constrained by domestic factors such as deleveraging policies or legacy nonperforming loans, many companies or state entities have increasingly turned to issuing bonds.

In a more recent study, Hyun (2017) showed that economies in Europe had relatively developed infrastructure bond markets with average issuance equal to 11.4% of GDP, while economies in developing Asia had comparatively small issuance at 6.8% of GDP (Table 2.3.2). As Eichengreen and Luengnaruemitchai (2006) speculated, economy size positively relates to bond market development because the small and fragmented economies in Asia may lack the critical mass needed for deep and liquid bond markets. The study further noted Asia's small aggregate economic size and varying stages of economic

2.3.2 Infrastructure *sukuk* bonds issued by domicile of issuer (2012–3Q 2015)

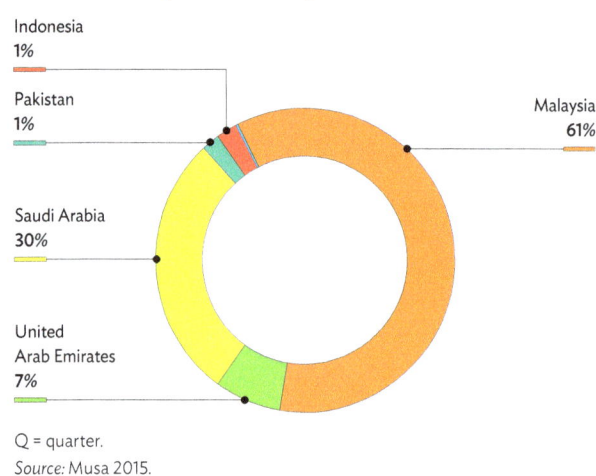

Indonesia 1%
Pakistan 1%
Saudi Arabia 30%
United Arab Emirates 7%
Malaysia 61%

Q = quarter.
Source: Musa 2015.

2.3.2 Descriptive statistics related to infrastructure bond markets in Asia and Europe

	ASEAN +3			Europe		
	Mean	Standard deviation	Observations	Mean	Standard deviation	Observations
Amount of infrastructure bonds (% of GDP)	6.845	−8.75	143	11.370	−21.33	221
Log of GDP	26.487	−1.84	143	26.857	−1.33	221
Log of GDP per capita	9.567	−0.97	143	10.608	−0.27	221
General government balance (% of GDP)	−0.963	−3.74	143	−2.756	−4.10	221
Inflation (GDP deflator, %)	3.888	−4.71	143	1.656	−1.43	221
Exchange rate volatility	1.271	−0.70	117	0.724	−0.50	221
Domestic credit by banks (% of GDP)	94.188	−48.03	138	118.837	−43.48	221
Average institutional factors	48.031	−24.28	143	78.289	−12.13	221
Property index	48.636	−28.10	143	81.425	−13.43	221
Corruption index	46.577	−24.54	143	75.095	−15.62	221
Investment freedom index	48.881	−22.90	143	78.348	−12.23	221

ASEAN = Association of Southeast Asian Nations.

Note: ASEAN +3 includes Brunei Darussalam, Cambodia, the People's Republic of China, the Republic of Korea, Japan, the Lao People's Democratic Republic, Malaysia, Myanmar, the Philippines, Singapore, Thailand, and Viet Nam.

Source: Hyun 2017.

development, as reflected in the region's small means and large standard deviations in economic variables relative to Europe. These factors may impede the further development of infrastructure bond markets with adequate liquidity and depth. For variables measuring institutional factors—such as the corruption index, property index, and investment freedom index—the means for Europe are higher than for Asia, which indicates a more favorable environment for infrastructure financing in Europe. As discussed in the previous section, these factors are critical barriers to financing infrastructure projects through bond markets in Asia.

Project bonds in emerging Asia are rare and limited to a few economies such as Malaysia, indicating relative underdevelopment in the market. A major reason that project bonds are not used more often is that, whereas bankers know how to assess risk in project finance transactions, the portfolio managers of pension funds and other institutional investors usually demand a minimum level for credit ratings but may not have the time, inclination, or expertise to assess the creditworthiness of individual infrastructure assets in Asia. Issuances of Asian project bonds recorded in the Thomson Reuters and Project Finance International databases ranged from $1 billion to $3 billion in recent years (Kitano 2015). Despite the complexity of project bonds, developing this market is essential for financing PPP projects because it would allow for the transfer of financing risk from banks to the capital market after the project is completed. In addition to enabling institutional investors to invest in infrastructure, project bonds can alleviate the risk of mismatch between bank assets and liability by allowing banks to exit the financing structure earlier and recycle their capital for new projects (Figure 2.3.3). This is especially important since the implementation of Basel III standards in May 2016.

2.3.3 Project finance in selected economies in developing Asia, 2009–2014

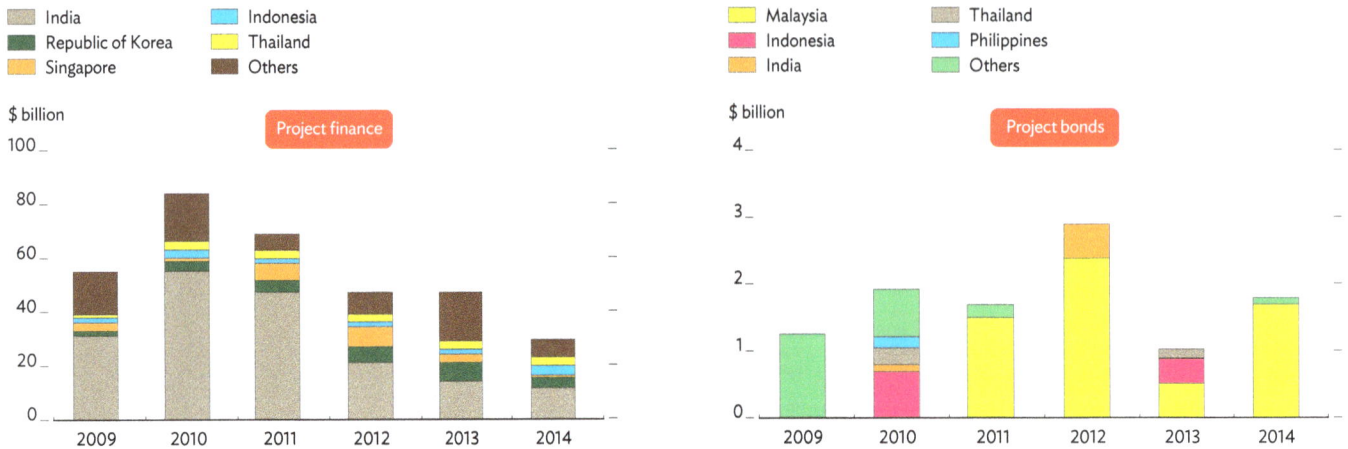

- India
- Republic of Korea
- Singapore
- Indonesia
- Thailand
- Others

- Malaysia
- Indonesia
- India
- Thailand
- Philippines
- Others

$ billion

Project finance

$ billion

Project bonds

Notes: "Others" include countries in Central Asia and the Pacific (excluding Australia). Data includes financing of some non-infrastructure projects.
Source: Kitano 2015.

In light of the relative weakness of Asian capital markets and of the challenges encountered in placing and pricing project bonds, most infrastructure bonds in the region are issued by infrastructure companies for general corporate purposes. A survey of corporate bonds outstanding in Indonesia, Malaysia, the Philippines, Singapore, Thailand, and Viet Nam found 18.5% of them to be infrastructure bonds, virtually all of them issued by infrastructure companies (ADB 2015). Malaysia accounted for 40% of the corporate bonds and half of the infrastructure bonds.

Drawbacks in Asian capital markets

The general weakness of capital markets in Asia makes it more difficult for PPP projects to tap debt finance without concerted efforts from market participants, governments, and MDBs. Failure to do so continues to strain bank balance sheets and limit the availability of long-term finance. A diagnosis of the primary reasons underlying weakness in Asian project bond markets provides valuable indicators of the required course of action.

Limited demand for higher risk bonds

One reason why project bonds are rare in emerging Asia is that corporate bond markets in the region largely frown on diversity in credit quality. Table 2.3.3 shows the distribution of local-currency corporate bonds issued in selected economies from 2010 to the third quarter of 2015 according to their credit rating. For the most part, issuers and investors do not take full advantage of the wide range of credit risks as indicated by credit ratings. In the PRC and the Philippines, essentially all local-currency corporate bond issues are rated either AAA or AA by the main local rating agency. In Indonesia, the Republic of Korea, and Malaysia, the share in the AAA or AA category ranges from two-thirds to nine-tenths, with the bulk of the remainder of issues rated A. Only in Thailand does the distribution of ratings span the entire spectrum of investment-grade ratings, with A-rated and BBB-rated issues at more than fourth-fifths (three-fifths of which are rated A). At the same time, however, even Thailand has less than 1% with ratings below investment grade, and the Republic of Korea ranks first in terms of the proportion of issues below investment grade, at 2%. This is a key factor behind the scarcity of project bonds in emerging Asia, as they typically have ratings at the lower end of investment grade or below.

2.3.3 Credit ratings by local rating agencies for local-currency corporate bonds as a percentage of local-currency corporate bonds issued, 2010–Q3 2015

| Countries | Rating | | | | |
	AAA–AA	A	BBB	Below BBB	Unrated/ Withdrawn
People's Republic of China	99.9	0.0	0.0	0.1	0.0
Indonesia	65.8	28.8	3.9	0.8	0.8
Republic of Korea	80.9	13.0	2.9	2.1	1.0
Malaysia	88.9	8.9	1.0	0.8	0.3
Philippines	100.0	0.0	0.0	0.0	0.0
Thailand	16.7	62.9	18.2	0.9	1.3
India	82.3	10.6	2.9	3.4	0.3
Other markets					
Russian Federation	31.8	13.6	9.1	45.5	0.0
South Africa	42.1	57.9	0.0	0.0	0.0
Advanced economies					
Japan	59.0	34.1	6.8	0.1	0.0
United States (Q1 2015)	4.7	16.1	23.5	55.7	N/A
Europe (Q1 2015)	6.9	26.8	24.3	42.0	N/A

N/A = not available, Q = quarter.

Sources: Bloomberg; Standard & Poor's and Bank of International Settlement 2016.

Limited liquidity

Liquidity in secondary markets is an equally important aspect of bond market development, especially for project bonds, which are less liquid than general obligation corporate bonds. Liquidity affects the cost and timeliness of corporate fundraising and the degree to which market prices reflect credit risk across securities in a stable and consistent fashion. Bid–ask spreads are a commonly used metric of bond market liquidity. Recent estimates of the range for bid–ask spreads for corporate bonds in the region suggest that, not only do they remain well above those of government bonds in the same jurisdiction, in most jurisdictions they have not declined in a decade (BIS 2016) (Table 2.3.4).

Deficient project preparation

Poor project preparation is the single biggest reason for the short supply of bankable projects. Assembling this structure requires highly specialized skills on the part of the sponsors, and similar skills are required of potential investors. However, once a sufficient pipeline of bankable projects is developed, institutional investors will have incentive to develop the specialized skills required.

2.3.4 Bid–ask spreads in select Asian bond markets (basis points)

Country	Government	Corporate	
	2014	2005	2015
People's Republic of China	2–3	5–20	5–10
Hong Kong, China	10.00	10–30	10–15
Indonesia	5–15	50–200 cents[a]	
Republic of Korea	0.5–1	2–4	2–5
Malaysia	2.4	5–10	5–10
Philippines	5–15	17	
Singapore	3	15–25	10–15
Thailand	1–6	5–10	5–10

[a] Quoted in price.

Sources: AsianBondsOnline; HSBC Amanah 2012; Gyntelberg, Ma, and Remolona 2005; Bank for International Settlements.

While SPVs will be incentivized to explore capital market instruments with Basel III norms kicking in, several studies, including Gatti, Gaffeo, and Gallegati (2010) and Subramanian and Tung (2016), observed that project finance is a nexus of contracts, and contract quality has implications on volumes and pricing in project finance deals.

In a project finance transaction, the quality of contracts and the optimality of risk allocation achieved through them are determining factors for attracting investors into project-specific capital market instruments, especially as bond investors are far removed from projects and cannot directly monitor projects. Creating a pipeline of bankable projects based on a network of viable and credible contracts requires a coherent and trusted legal framework. The economic viability of infrastructure projects often depends on government decisions about pricing, environmental regulations, or transportation and energy policy. In some countries, reliable frameworks do not exist.

Corporate insolvency

One of the most important provisions in a debt contract relates to when and how a lender can collect on any collateral or effect a secured claim. This is often through the process of insolvency, winding up, and liquidation. The current regime for corporate insolvency in many Asian countries is far from efficient. The World Bank ranks economies on their ease of doing business and on insolvency procedures, which provides insight on how much project security is available. In weak jurisdictions, the enforcement of contracts through insolvency encounters significant delays, such that company liquidation can take up to 10 years.

In a PPP, the government typically grants step-in rights to the financiers, allowing them to rectify defaults by the SPV under the PPP contract. Step-in rights provide an important mechanism that enables financiers to avoid contract termination and formal insolvency proceedings when the project is distressed but can still be rescued. Despite their importance, these rights are rarely addressed by national regulatory frameworks. Of the 23 developing economies in Asia sampled in *Benchmarking PPP Procurement 2017* (World Bank 2016b), only 5 expressly regulated step-in rights.

Rating agency limitations

Rating agencies have a critical role to play if project bond financing is to become more prevalent. In successful project bond issuances, especially when credit enhancement measures have been required, the rating agency provides a standalone rating for the bond, advises how much first-loss guarantee cover is required to enhance ratings enough to attract investors, and certifies the credit-enhanced rating. Table 2.3.5 illustrates the limited capacity of rating agencies to rate project bonds in selected Asian economies.

2.3.5 Overview of capacity of rating agencies in select economies in developing Asia

Country	Name of agency	Ability to rate project bonds and/or credit enhancement
Malaysia	RAM Rating Services Berhad	Has ratings on 95% of banks in Malaysia, and 80% of all project bonds issued in the country
Indonesia	PT Pemeringkat Efek Indonesia (PEFINDO)	Rated 86% of listed bond issues. However, will not rate structured finance products such as credit enhanced project bonds via partial credit enhancement products.
Republic of Korea	Korea Ratings Corporation	Rating coverage of companies in the Republic of Korea: 65% (as of the end of 2015). Credit rating service for securities including bond, asset-backed securities and commercial paper, project finance, etc.
India	CRISIL	Rated India's first commercial mortgage-backed securities. Rated ADB-supported project bond issuances and provided guidance on credit enhancement structures.
Thailand	TRIS Rating	Has provided credit rating services to over 400 clients. It also provides credit rating services for structured finance transactions and hybrid instruments.
Philippines	Philippine Rating Services	Provided 48 issue and issuer credit ratings (as of the end of 2015) for an 88% market share. Offers rating of asset-backed securities and structured finance transactions.

ADB = Asian Development Bank.

Source: ADB compilation.

Untapped private and institutional investors

Private savings in pension funds, insurance companies, mutual funds, sovereign wealth funds, and other institutional investments can finance the infrastructure gap in developing Asia by redirecting these resources to infrastructure projects through PPP. PPP infrastructure projects offer the long-term index-linked return on investments normally sought by institutional investors.

Estimates of assets under management by institutional investors in 2013 range from $70 trillion to $100 trillion (World Economic Forum 2014, World Bank 2015, Arezki et al. 2016). However, only about 1% is invested in infrastructure (OECD 2013, Inderst 2013), which the World Bank estimates to be $1 trillion. The World Economic Forum (2014) reckons that about $700 billion is directly invested in illiquid assets such as private equity, real estate, and infrastructure.

Approximately $17 trillion in private capital is available in Asia and the Pacific. The bulk of this is in Japan and Australia, with sizable portions in the PRC, India, and the Republic of Korea. About 40% of the $7 trillion in sovereign wealth funds is based in Asia, 29% of which is invested in infrastructure (Figure 2.3.4 and Table 2.3.6).

2.3.4 Estimated available private funds: institutional investors' assets under management, end of 2013

- Global
- Asia and the Pacific

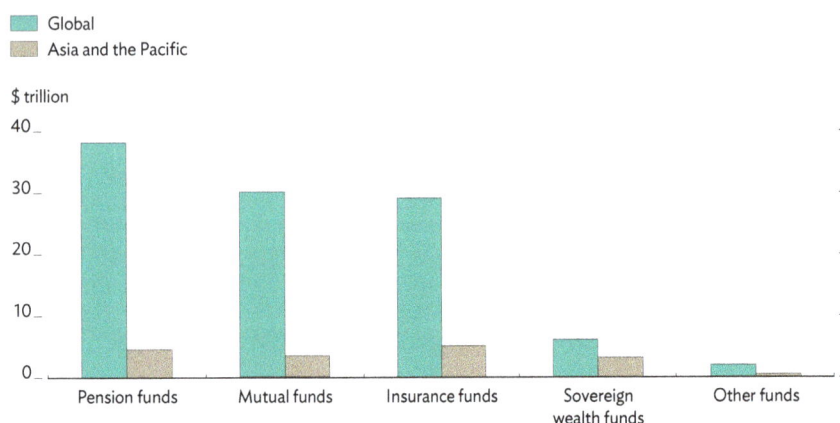

Note: Other funds include family offices, foundation, endowments, and other institutions.
Source: ADB estimates based on OECD 2016, TheCityUK 2014, World Bank 2014, 2015, World Economic Forum 2014, and Inderst 2016.

2.3.6 Select Asian economies by number of PPP investors

Headquarters	Number of investors	Funds under management ($ billion)
Republic of Korea	37	2,797
People's Republic of China	31	6,779
India	27	1,504
Japan	24	7,301
Philippines	9	167
Hong Kong, China	6	222
Singapore	6	1,183
Taipei,China	5	182
Malaysia	4	208
Indonesia	3	21
Thailand	3	105
Viet Nam	2	2

Note: Includes all investors of any type that are currently investing and considering investing in PPP projects in all sectors.
Source: Preqin database (accessed 19 September 2017).

Despite the potential for investment from large private funds, they remain largely untapped, especially in developing economies. This is for various reasons, notably investment risks, aversion in many institutional investors to foreign exchange risks, and slow integration into global financial markets. Another reason is that project debt typically cannot be rated higher than the sovereign rating, and the sovereign rating of many developing countries is below the threshold set by offshore institutional investors. Recent innovative partnerships have been initiated by MDBs and international financial institutions to match institutional investors with infrastructure investments in developing countries. The various types of financing are analyzed below to determine how each can be designed to attract more institutional investors.

Bridging the risk gap through credit enhancement

Analysis of the various sources of private finance indicates that the infrastructure financing gap in developing Asia is more of a risk gap than a gap in available funds.

"Credit enhancement" refers to a range of interventions that seek to improve the risk rating of projects, often measured using its credit rating. Some interventions are effective tools for policy makers in governments and MDBs. Others seek to use innovative market instruments such as mezzanine finance (page 108). The goal in all cases is to ameliorate project risk enough to attract private investors, particularly institutional investors, from domestic and international markets.

Partial risk (or credit) guarantees

Insurance available in the private marketplace is not necessarily well-suited to mitigating sovereign risk. One reason is that the tenor of insurance available is often much shorter than required. Further, private insurers often apply high fees in developing economies based on the country risk, which may render the project less financially viable.

One tool that MDBs can use to address this country risk is the sovereign partial risk guarantee, which should not be confused with political risk insurance (Box 2.3.2). Below is an illustration of the triggering mechanism for a sovereign partial risk guarantee with a letter of credit. The major steps are as follows:

1. A default in the payment obligation of the government or state-owned enterprise is flagged.
2. The bank issuing the letter of credit pays the letter of credit to the project company.
3. The bank issuing the letter of credit then seeks reimbursement from the Ministry of Finance or the state-owned enterprise that is the off-taker. If reimbursement is paid, then the MDB guarantee will not be triggered.
4. If reimbursement is not paid within the specified period, then the guarantee is called and the MDB pays the bank that issued the letter of credit.
5. The counterindemnity is triggered if reimbursement fails to occur within a specified period, triggering a second payment from the government to the MDB.

This mechanism has several advantages over traditional insurance. The first is price, as the sovereign counterindemnity and guarantee agreement ensures that the project can be priced at an interest rate similar to sovereign loans offered by the MDB.

The second advantage is timing. With traditional political risk insurance, the sponsor needs to have an arbitral award to receive payment. The sovereign partial risk guarantee has the advantage of paying out automatically based on pre-established triggers that are defined in the PPP contract. These triggers should be linked to contractual provisions

2.3.2 Political risk insurance

Political risk insurance or guarantees cover losses caused by specified political risks. They can be called political risk guarantees or political risk insurance (PRI) depending on the provider. PRI insures equity investors or lenders against default by a sovereign or corporate entity but only if the reason for the loss is political. Coverage is generally limited to less than 100% of the investment or loan. Providers of investment insurance include export credit agencies, investment insurers, private political risk insurers, and multilateral insurers. PRI includes relatively standardized risk coverage offered by the insurance industry for traditional political risks, which include losses arising from inability to convert local currency into foreign exchange or to transfer funds outside the host country; actions taken by the host government that may reduce or eliminate ownership of the insured investment, or control or rights pertaining to it; and damage to, or the destruction or disappearance of, tangible assets caused by politically motivated acts of war or civil disturbance in the host country. Relatively newer political risks covered include losses arising from the host government's breach or repudiation of a contract and from the government's refusal to pay when a binding decision cannot be enforced.

Source: Matsukawa, T. and O. Habeck. 2014. Review of Risk Mitigation Instruments for Infrastructure Financing and Recent Trends and Developments. *Trends and Policy Options* No. 4.

specifying how the payment is to be calculated and providing for the payment to be verified by an independent party with appropriate expertise. Likewise, the verification of the independent party should be legally binding on both the government and private sector parties of the PPP contract.

One example of credit enhancement is the partial credit guarantee applied to local-currency bonds for a geothermal project in the Philippines (ASIFMA–ICMA 2016). The project was initially financed on an all-equity basis because the operating company was unable to secure project financing from commercial banks. To refinance its capital, operational, and maintenance expenditures, as well as transform its capital structure to a mix of debt and equity, the company entered into a loan agreement with an MDB and issued project bonds that were partly guaranteed. This financing was noteworthy as a watershed use of project bonds in the region (excluding Malaysia) since the Asian financial crisis of 1997–1998, as the first local-currency project bond in the Philippine power sector, and as the first project bond in the Philippines credit-enhanced by an MDB (ASIFMA-ICMA 2016).

The financing was highly negotiated, marrying the need for international standards for the project bond that would accelerate the development of the private sector bond market in the Philippines with the expectations of the company as an experienced owner and operator of a high-quality brownfield asset. The project bond model is an exciting opportunity for issuers in developing Asia to access domestic debt capital markets for projects that would not otherwise qualify for financing and for a broader range of investors to gain exposure to emerging market infrastructure. The deal for this geothermal plant shows that the model can work in developing Asia.

Another example of credit enhancement using a partial credit guarantee is in India. A government-owned financial institution there partnered with an MDB on a facility to enhance the credit ratings of project bonds issued by the SPVs of completed infrastructure projects to a rating of AA or to the minimum rating required by investors (ADB 2012b). The funds raised are then used to prepay existing bank loans, thus allowing banks to recycle capital for new projects. The credit-wrapped project bond is a win for all parties: as the issuer gets long-term, fixed-rate financing that offers savings over bank loans, investors gain access to a highly rated instrument that offers a better return than government securities with minimal additional risk, and banks recycle capital for new projects.

Bond guarantees

Bond financing allows the issuer to borrow directly from individuals and institutions. Rating agencies will assess the riskiness of the project and assign a credit rating to the bonds, signaling to bond purchasers the attractiveness of the investment and its appropriate price. If the credit rating is sufficiently strong, bond financing provides lower borrowing costs than loans. Problems arise when the private partners cannot get high enough credit ratings. Addressing this problem requires credit-enhancement mechanisms for bonds, like bond guarantees.

This instrument functions as a credit-enhancement mechanism by providing guarantees to long-term bond issuances by infrastructure entities with credit ratings below AA. A bond guarantee fund charges guarantee fees based on the market spread and the reduced interest cost because of the guarantee upgrade (Rao 2015). The gains from the lower interest rates are then shared with the issuer, though most of them go to the bond guarantee fund to cover its risks. If the spreads available in the market are insufficient to cover the cost of capital, the guarantee will not succeed.

The Bond Guarantee Fund of India, for example, can be established to provide a guarantee for long-term bond issuances by infrastructure entities with credit ratings below AA (ADB 2015). The guarantee will help their bond issues achieve a structured rating of AA or above, enabling them to attract bond market investors and raise money to prepay existing banks loans. This helps recycle bank capital for new lending.

The guarantee products target instruments rated BBB– and above and with a maximum tenor of 15 years. Market analysis indicated that issuers could potentially enjoy cost savings to the tune of 50–100 basis points through the guarantee fund. The facility is expected to free up bank funds in the amount of $15 billion. More importantly, by releasing insurance and pension funds for investment, the guarantee fund can support the development of the bond market. Indeed, the fund's value proposition to shareholders will be not so much through its financial returns but through its opening of the bond market to a new class of issuers and paving the way for market acceptance of guarantee products.

Project completion risk guarantees

Delays in implementing infrastructure PPP projects can be caused by risk factors beyond the control of the project sponsor, such as delays in the issuance of land and environmental permits, licenses, and clearances; failure to issue tariff adjustments as specified in the concession agreement; changes in regulations; law and order problems; and the unavailability of materials. Additional factors include legal changes, failure to fulfill preconditions, and parties' failure to comply with contractual obligations.

To protect investors from such risks, a project completion risk guarantee facility can be established. The facility guarantees servicing interest to banks during periods of delay that are beyond the control of the project. An example of such a facility is the one proposed for India (Rao 2017). The facility houses a mechanism to protect projects and lenders exposed to completion delays (Figure 2.3.5). The proposed mechanism would make good cash flows such as interest obligations that accumulate during a construction delay (beyond what was capitalized in the original project cost at financial closure). A guarantee fee would be charged to the project and the amount of any claim triggered by project delays would be converted into a subordinated loan to the SPV with a significant grace period. Typically, the project would apply for the guarantee before financial closure and negotiate a reduction in bank charges that would compensate for the guarantee fee.

2.3.5 Project completion risk guarantee facility framework

Business model: flow of payments by and repayments to project completion risk guarantee facility

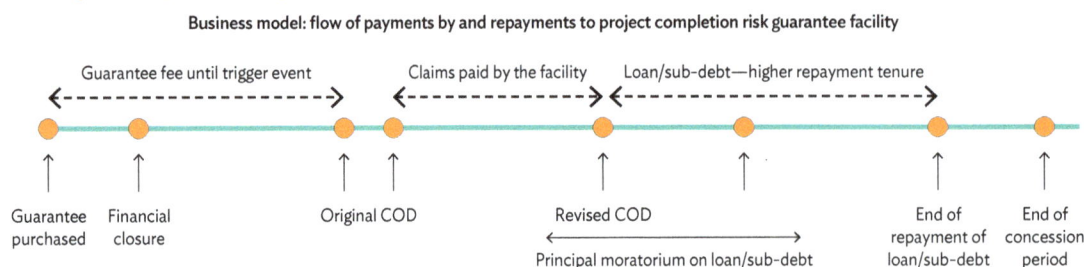

COD = commercial operation date.
Source: ADB.

The proposed mechanism addresses several issues. First, the facility would secure the interest obligations of project SPVs arising from delays and reduce the incremental equity potentially needed to fund cost escalation. Second, banks would expand financing for guaranteed projects as the risk profile improves. Next, the incidence of nonperforming assets and restructuring would fall as interest before construction is serviced. The facility would also expedite financial closure and shortens any delays caused by the need to negotiate bank lending to stressed projects.

A somewhat similar mechanism is provided through Indonesia's Infrastructure Guarantee Fund, which provides guarantees to the private sector for risks emanating from government action or inaction that cause project losses, including delays in processing permits and licenses, changes to rules and regulations, and breach of contract.

Mezzanine and subordinated debt instruments

Innovative market instruments can be devised to tap into the greater risk appetite of some investors and so alleviate the risks faced by more cautious investors. Mezzanine finance seeks to do just that.

In this arrangement, mezzanine creditors take a subordinate role among creditors, so when the project fails or debt payments to senior creditors cannot be processed, the mezzanine debt can be converted into equity. In return, the mezzanine creditors are compensated with higher interest rates (Ehlers 2014).

Infrastructure borrowers indicate that flexibility in capital supply and the inherent value proposition of the instrument make mezzanine capital an important part of infrastructure financing.

Mezzanine finance is useful when project sponsors want to avoid selling assets to raise liquidity and to maintain the leveraging ratio. Mezzanine capital is also sought when there is an added risk element in the project. Several emerging markets are subject to periodic dislocations from a host of exogenous factors, which can cause capital from high-yield bonds, B loans, and leveraged loan markets to exit projects. This creates an entry point for mezzanine instruments, which can move more quickly than banks as they can have more streamlined processes. Table 2.3.7 provides an indication of mezzanine financing with a focus on Asian investments.

2.3.7 Sample infrastructure debt funds targeting mezzanine financing

Name	Location	Fund vintage	Fund length (years)	Investment status	Current size ($ million)	Target size ($ million)	Target net IRR (%)	Asset location
AMP Capital Infrastructure Debt Fund I	Australia	2011	10	Fully invested	424.75	530.94	6	North America, Europe, Asia
AMP Capital Infrastructure Debt Fund II	Australia	2013	10	Investing	1,100.00	1,000.00	6	North America, Europe, Asia
AMP Capital Infrastructure Debt Fund III	Australia	2016	10	Fund raising	1,000.00	2,000.00		North America, Europe, Asia
Brookfield Infrastructure Debt Fund	Canada	2016		Fund raising		1,000.00		North America, Europe, Asia
Global Infrastructure Partners Capital Solutions Fund	United States	2014	10	Investing	1,123.00	2,500.00	9–11	North America, Middle East, Latin America, Europe, Asia
International Infrastructure Finance Company Fund II	United States	2016		Fund raising		500.00	11–14	North America, Europe, Asia
North American Infrastructure Debt Fund	United States			Pre-launch, Fund raising		500.00		North America

IRR = internal rate of return.

Source: Lee, J. 2017. Mezzanine Financing look for home in infrastructure. *InfraAmericas.* April. www.infra-americas.com

Role of multilateral development banks

The international and regional development banks play a crucial role as catalysts to attract private sector investment into infrastructure assets. As MDBs bring vast expertise to the negotiating table, and in many cases insurance against political risks, their loan commitments are in some cases a precondition for private lenders to make their funding available (Ehlers 2014). Despite this, the involvement of multilateral institutions in PPP in low- and middle-income economies is minimal, particularly in developing Asia. Of all PPP projects in the region from 1991 to 2015, only 7.3% received support of any kind from MDBs. In contrast, 20% of the PPP projects in other regions have engaged MDBs (Figure 2.3.6).

Catalyzing PPP in developing economies with higher risk ratings often requires sovereign risk mitigation. In Asia, sovereign risk and country risk are often high. Reducing these risks through credit enhancement provided by MDBs is only one solution. A variety of solutions exist, such as private insurance and letters of credit (Jett 2017).

Apart from credit enhancement, the involvement of multilateral agencies can offer PPP transactions specific advice, technical assistance, and program lending. Further, their involvement heightens the confidence of private parties (Hofman 2010). Nose (2014) deemed the involvement of multilateral agencies to have potential to curb the risk of breached contracts as governments try to maintain their reputation with the international community. Yehoue (2013) noted that engaging multilateral institutions has improved standards of transparency and accountability in PPP development.

2.3.6 Multilateral development banks' involvement in PPP by region across years

- Developing Asia
- Europe
- Latin America and the Caribbean
- Middle East and North Africa
- Sub-Saharan Africa

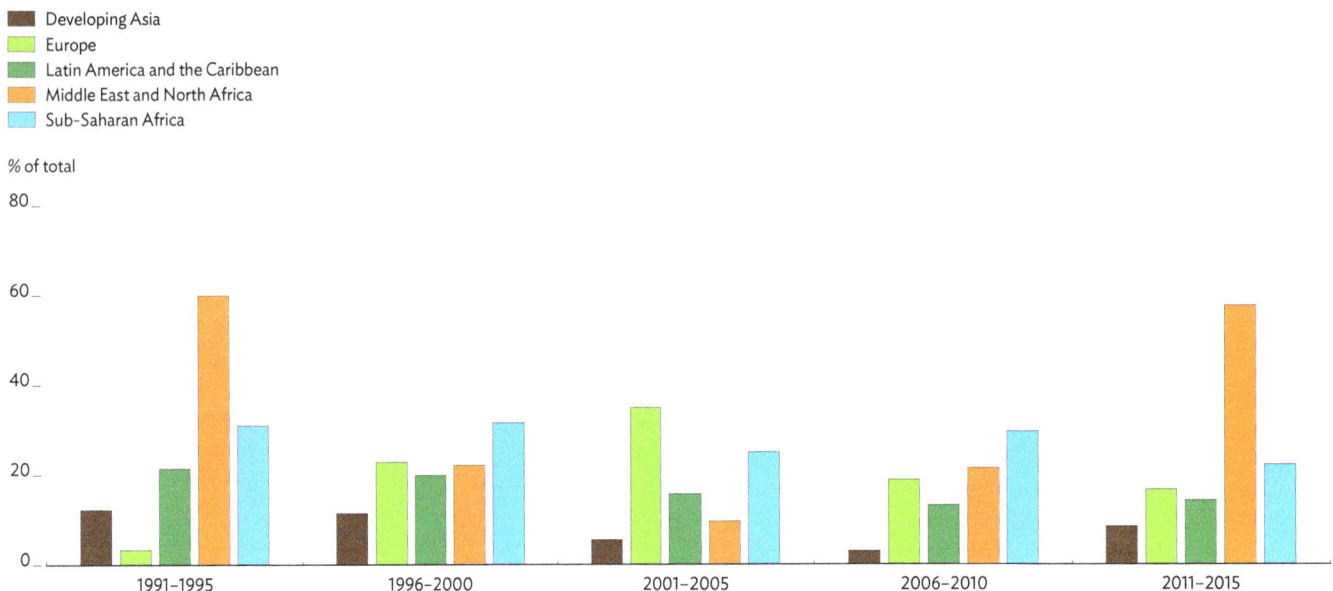

Includes only low- and middle-income economies. Excludes full divestitures of state-owned assets (privatizations) and merchant projects that do not include government guarantees or that operate in a liberalized environment. Projects in the database must be at least 20% privately owned. State-owned enterprises are considered public. More information is available at http://ppi.worldbank.org/methodology/ppi-methodology

Source: World Bank Private Participation in Infrastructure database (accessed 25 May 2017).

MDBs can assist in promoting financial sector development and supporting capital markets by enhancing senior debt to the level that can successfully attract institutional investors. Ehlers, Packer, and Remolona (2014) found that infrastructure bonds are typically issued in local currencies to minimize potential currency mismatches. Hence, local and regional capital markets need to be deeper and broader to channel Asia's large savings to infrastructure investment. MDB assistance is also essential to strengthen the expertise of local banks in project finance.

Further, MDBs can expand their risk-mitigation products, to target climate risks in particular. Currently, the Green Climate Fund, Climate Investment Funds, and Green Bonds can provide financing for climate-resilient infrastructure. A recent example is the Coastal Climate-Resilient Infrastructure Project in Bangladesh. The proposed investments will improve coastal embankments, rural connectivity, and water supply and sanitation, as well as promote public–private financing and capacity building to mainstream climate resilience and knowledge management.

Toward better-performing partnership

This theme chapter examines how the role of PPP in providing infrastructure and related services can be enhanced. When designed and implemented appropriately, PPP can deliver enormous benefits. On the other hand, there are cases of cancelled and distressed projects generating significant administrative, procedural, and financial burdens. Any successful infrastructure development strategy must use PPP judiciously and selectively. Not all infrastructure gaps can be addressed using PPP. Evidence shows that even in countries where PPP is widely used, the PPP share of public infrastructure investment is low, at around 10% in the United Kingdom, for example, and 5% in Australia. In most advanced economies, the share is less than 5% (OECD 2014). However, given the vast infrastructure needs in many developing economies, it may be possible to procure up to a third of infrastructure assets using PPP, if conditions are right.

The success of the PPP approach is, like public procurement, predicated on a list of prerequisites. A systematic evaluation of a project's feasibility is necessary to determine whether features required for PPP are present or can be produced with reasonable effort. These features include the technical, legal, and institutional constraints the project has to address, its financial requirements, market interest in the project, and specific sectoral requirements. A subsequent step is determining the optimality of PPP relative to other procurement methods.

This section outlines a systematic approach to evaluating whether an infrastructure project is suitable to be procured as a PPP. Even when the project has these features, government and private entities may not have the requisite capacity to form a partnership. And, even if a project is suitable for PPP with qualified stakeholders, the right process has to be carried out and risks appropriately managed and allocated to generate the benefits. Projects considered for selection must stand to benefit from the features of PPP, be pursued by partners possessing complementary abilities, and adhere to a process that reinforces strengths and mitigates risks, toward ensuring that all stakeholders enjoy their intended benefits. In other words, there are three Ps in every well-designed and competently implemented PPP: Project, Partner, and Process.

Suitable projects

Not all projects can be implemented through PPP, nor are all projects best implemented through PPP. A project is suitable for PPP if it (i) promises net social benefit for all stakeholders, (ii) generates sufficient private sector interest, (iii) offers scope for innovation and real efficiency gains in service delivery, and (iv) submits to observable and verifiable performance-based indicators.

Net social benefit for all stakeholders. This condition comes first and foremost, as it is the reason for doing the project in the first place. Impact on social welfare must be positive after factoring in all positive and negative externalities. Many countries require a formal cost–benefit analysis before a project can be considered for PPP procurement. If the net social benefit from the project is large but the project lacks enough commercial viability to elicit private sector interest, the government can consider providing subsidies, viability gap financing, or tax breaks to strike a balance between public welfare and private sector returns. Further, a project should be subjected to distributional analysis across all stakeholders to identify where it has support and where it faces resistance. If a socially viable project falls short of a minimum threshold to make it financeable with private capital, governments may consider providing viability gap financing. A project that does not bring net social benefit, both in aggregate and also across a large cross-section of stakeholders, is less likely to be a successful PPP.

Sufficient private sector interest. For private sector participants, the first requirement for any type of involvement is the potential to derive sufficient cash flow from the project to repay debt and get a reasonable profit. Similarly, before committing its own capital in the development of projects, it will require clear legal and regulatory structures, and will want to see the potential for future economic growth, together with reasonable levels of political support and stability.

Scope for innovation and real efficiency gains. This condition is important during both construction and operation. It enables private participation to provide greater value than what would be achieved through public procurement.

Observable and verifiable performance-based indicators. Such indicators are necessary to ensure transparent incentives and contract terms. Indicators can be easily identified and measured if project performance is based on volume of usage or other quantitative criteria. If project performance depends on clear quality thresholds, as is the case for most service-delivery projects, these thresholds should be clearly spelled out in contracts to facilitate their verification and to document that the PPP adheres to the agreement.

Qualified partners

PPP is not a mechanism by which the government controls private finance and expertise to meet public goals in a manner that only it sees as appropriate. Nor is a PPP an attempt to infuse the private sector with zeal to perform public service without adequate return and protection. A successful partnership requires public and private partners to bring to the project complementary skills and motivations.

Challenges for private sector participants

PPP requires private sector agents that possess the innovative capacity and expertise to bring about real efficiency gains. The required expertise includes not only traditional skills in construction, operations, and technology, but also higher skills in contracting, finance, and governance. Bids from private consortia are required to offer all the skills required to build, operate, manage, and finance the infrastructure asset over its lifecycle.

Because the PPP approach is predicated on the optimal allocation of risk, prospective private partners should be adequately skilled, experienced, innovative, and reputable to bear risk credibly and reliably. Governments have often enlisted PPP to promote private activity in their countries. While this objective may be served in the long run, it is important that the playing field for potential bidders in PPP projects be as wide as possible to orchestrate the maximum possible competition and the highest possible efficiency gains.

One factor that deters private partners is the lack of a level playing field. In many countries, infrastructure has traditionally been provided by state-owned entities that have become potential competitors to private bidders for PPP projects. The experience, size, and access to resources that these state-owned agencies enjoy threatens to restrict competition and crowd out players in the private sector. To avoid this, tighter restrictions can be placed on noncompetitive procurement to ensure that open, competitive bidding is the norm. This helps to level the playing field for private firms and give them confidence to bid for PPP contracts against state-owned enterprises. Moreover, competition helps ensure that the winning bidder provides the best value for money over the entire asset life.

To further widen competition and attract strong bids from viable partners, a well-structured process for sounding out the market must be established to communicate the aims and status of the project to the private sector, allow interested companies to start preparing their tenders, and gauge interest among potential partners. Market sounding provides an opportunity for a structured dialogue between the private and public sectors at early stages of the PPP process. This can be an opportunity to test project assumptions with the market, obtain feedback on how aspects of the project should be defined to ensure private sector participation, and foster competition. Having a venue to discuss all issues pertaining to the project—whether technical, financial, or legal—allows the parties to come up with the balanced and mutually acceptable risk-allocation framework that is critical to the success of long-term projects.

Finally, private partners must have access to private finance through banks and capital markets. In some countries, private finance may be limited or inaccessible to many bidders. In others, it may be available but only through state-owned banks, limiting the incentives that private lenders bring to a PPP.

A critical role for multilateral development banks

The private sector and development finance institutions can work together toward bridging the financing gap. Disparity in access to private finance is, as mentioned above, significantly a function of financial development in each country. While project bonds are widely used in Malaysia, for example, project financing in lower-income countries is provided largely by banks.

Aside from being an important source of infrastructure financing, multilateral development banks (MDBs) add value to the private financing of infrastructure projects by developing local capital markets, participating in bond issues, providing guarantees and credit enhancement, and supporting private equity infrastructure funds to attract a broader array of private investors, including institutional investors. By spearheading the application of innovative means of financing, MDBs can continue their catalytic role of enhancing private finance geared toward infrastructure development.

MDBs can leverage private sector finance by supplementing their downstream financing activities with upstream activities such as conducting economic analysis, ensuring political viability, and building regulatory capacity (Box 2.4.1). Regulatory reform analysis must be followed up with detailed implementation plans and appropriate institutional arrangements, along with financial, capacity building, and consulting support.

Knowledge generation and sharing, and in particular knowledge brokering, should continue to be an MDB activity. A recent effort in line with this is SOURCE, designed by MDBs, and the Sustainable Infrastructure Foundation to help develop infrastructure projects that are investment-ready. SOURCE is an online project preparation platform that uses templates to ensure that government officials provide the necessary technical and preparatory information that financiers need to assess public and private projects.

MDBs can also facilitate regional cooperation for the provision of regional public goods, such as sharing services and resources among neighboring countries through cross-border collective action and coordination. An example is the ongoing gas pipeline project connecting Afghanistan, India, Pakistan, and Turkmenistan, which enlists an MDB to act as its secretariat, transaction advisor, and facilitator of shareholder and investment agreements.

Right process

For the benefits of PPPs to be fully realized, they must be designed and implemented through an objective, competitive, and transparent process. Even if a project is suitable for PPP with qualified stakeholders, the right process must be carried out to generate the benefits and hold vulnerabilities in check.

An enabling legal and regulatory framework

A policy framework provides the rationale for using PPP and the process for entering into such arrangements. A legal framework ensures that PPP contracts are effective, binding, and enforceable, and a regulatory framework provides the necessary technical, safety, and economic safeguards for PPP contract enforcement. In countries where regulations change unpredictably or where there is not enough guidance,

2.4.1 Project preparation supported by multilateral agencies

One factor that holds back infrastructure investment is a lack of properly designed investable projects. To address this, organizations involved in PPP have established project preparation facilities (PPFs) that aim to enhance the quality of projects at entry and make them more attractive to alternative sources of capital, in particular private investors.

PPFs may be country-specific, regional, or global. They can be funded and/or managed by MDBs, bilateral aid agencies, and other financing institutions supported by development partners, either nongovernment organizations or states. Most PPFs in Asia are involved in the core activities of concept development, feasibility studies, and project delivery planning, and some others are involved in upstream activities that improve national conditions and enabling environments for PPPs by, for example, implementing sector reform and building up institutions to manage the PPP process.

Some of the PPFs in Asia are as follows:
- Asia–Pacific Project Preparation Facility (managed by the Asian Development Bank),
- Infrastructure Project Preparation Facility (European Bank for Reconstruction and Development),
- Project Development and Monitoring Facility (PPP Center, Philippines),
- PDCOR Limited (Rajasthan state, India),
- Cities Development Initiative for Asia (various),
- Global Infrastructure Facility (World Bank), and
- Public–Private Infrastructure Advisory Facility (World Bank)

Because filling Asia's infrastructure gap can only benefit from having more well-designed infrastructure projects that potential financiers can invest in, the scale of project preparation support needs to be ramped up. The Group of Twenty realizes this, and the international forum has included in its Infrastructure Action Plan improving the effectiveness of project preparation funds.

Sources:
G20. 2011. Infrastructure Action Plan. http://www.g20india.gov.in/pdfs/B-2011-MDBs_Infrastructure_Action_Plan.pdf

——. 2014. Assessment of the Effectiveness of Project Preparation Facilities in Asia. http://www.g20australia.org/sites/default/files/g20_resources/library/assessment-effectiveness-ppfs-in-asia-15092014.pdf

investors and other project participants will view any project as very risky and fear that laws and contracts may be disregarded and unenforced.

Because the legal systems of countries differ, so does the way PPP is regulated. If a legal framework provides an enabling environment for a PPP, it may not matter much whether the country has a separate PPP law, on the one hand, or, on the other, addresses PPP matters with measures embedded in other laws. The critical point is to have coherent investment and PPP-related policies to avoid and eliminate inefficiencies.

As it can take a great deal of time to resolve issues with multiple parties, land acquisition needs close attention. Governments should acquire land before embarking on a PPP project, or else assume all risk connected with land acquisition. Streamlining land acquisition for PPP implementation is strongly recommended. Land acquisition laws should provide a process, a definite timeline and financing, and a formula for compensating landowners. Changes in land acquisition regulations to reduce the time and cost required may be desirable, but such changes require consensus agreement from politicians and citizens.

A competitive process

Most governments have rules requiring some form of competitive bidding for procuring any private sector goods or services. In addition, most international lending institutions and assistance organizations require competitive bidding procedures as a condition of any associated financing or technical assistance. Competition makes the process more transparent, helps avoid corruption, and enables the selection of the proposal that offers the best value based on a pre-defined set of criteria.

Disclosure and transparency

Transparency is key to any public procurement process. The private sector is interested in PPP programs only if the procurement rules provide for and protect transparency and fairness in selection. Potential bidders often spend significant amount of capital preparing for bids and need access to meaningful information and studies on projects to enable them to assess the opportunity effectively and efficiently and prepare a competitive bid.

During the tendering process, transparency is achieved by supplying as much information about the process as possible, and by drawing up procedures that explicitly ensure that all parties are treated equally. This gives bidders confidence that the outcome will be appropriate and not influenced by extraneous factors.

Making information about the PPP program publicly available enables the media to report on the program and allows the public to develop informed opinions on the government's performance in implementing PPPs. International standards require the disclosure of financial commitments to PPPs in national accounts. Disclosure requirements may advisedly extend to entire PPP contracts or at least key contract clauses.

Active monitoring and management

After a PPP project reaches financial closure, there comes the arduous task of implementing and monitoring it. Given the long-term nature of PPP projects, adequate preparation and procurement alone do not guarantee project success. Well-established contract management systems are needed to ensure the smooth and unimpeded implementation of the project. Vigilant monitoring though credible public agencies is required to ensure that performance targets are met and risk transfer is enforced.

Appropriate public sector capacity to deliver PPP

The private sector often considers the main country risks to be weak public sector capacity and a lack of appropriate institutions. One important aspect of the PPP institutional setting is that the roles of different government agencies in PPP project procurement are clearly defined and distinguished in laws and regulations. In some countries, multiple organizations and agencies play substantial roles in implementing PPP projects, often without apparent coordination among them.

As potential investors in the private sector prefer a consistent approach to PPP and a single point of contact for regulatory and administrative issues, setting up a dedicated PPP unit in the public sector is recommended. The creation of a dedicated PPP unit with experienced staff within the government helps to ensure for the administration an equal footing with the private partner during negotiations. Further, it signals to the private sector the government's dedication and commitment to the PPP process and serves as an internal government regulator competent to monitor and oversee PPP projects (Trebilcock and Rosenstock 2015).

However, one must remember that PPP units are no panacea. Governments that are ineffective tend to have ineffective PPP units. Where government agencies are not well coordinated, it is difficult for a PPP unit to escape the same fate. Further, PPP-related operations typically involve multiple ministries in the government, some of which may view a PPP unit as a threat to traditional public procurement. It is therefore important to coordinate the different units of government. Where PPP units have been successful, they have enjoyed able and effective leadership and strong support from PPP champions in the government, often holding very senior positions.

Most economies in developing Asia have experienced difficulties in PPP preparation and implementation because their public sector lacks capacity. Much of the bureaucracy's expertise still lies in traditional public procurement. Preparing and managing PPP projects requires different skills and greater capacity because the contracts that need to be put together are much more complex, as are contract negotiations.

Institutional capacity can be enhanced through workshops, training, and conferences. PPP units in countries with significant experience offer regular courses. For example, in the Republic of Korea, the Public and Private Infrastructure Investment Management Center provides several PPP training programs every year. Meetings of the Asia Public–Private

Partnership Practitioners' Network serve as forums for PPP practitioners, to connect and share their knowledge. One can even enroll online in e-courses, for example the UNESCAP E-Learning Series on PPPs and the APMG Public–Private Partnerships Certification Program, a joint project of MDBs.

However, even governments with extensive PPP experience may not have all the in-house expertise needed to develop PPP projects. Governments should engage external experts and advisors to help them make informed decisions even as they institutionalize capacity development. Over time, responsible government teams should be able to acquire technical skills from external experts. It is also important that the government, while working with external experts, oversees their work and makes decisions on its own.

Flexible mechanisms

The private sector initiates refinancing to allow the early realization of profits from the change in financing structure. The public sector must therefore exercise prudence to ensure that refinancing does not destabilize a project and compromise its social benefits. The government should set clear standards and principles for refinancing. Well-structured concession documents specify the mechanism by which the grantor and the concessionaire will share any refinancing gains during the concession period.

Though it is desirable to maintain contract terms to reduce uncertainty and risk, renegotiation may be inevitable for some PPP projects. Substantial contract changes may be required to ensure the continuous operation of the project and that contract terms remain optimal for all parties. Therefore, the agreement should include the details of conditions on renegotiation to ensure flexibility over the long haul.

Adjusting the terms of the agreement to retain private investment is undoubtedly preferable to terminating a project. Voluntary measures such as negotiation, mediation, and arbitration should be pursued in an orderly manner along with compulsory measures of court adjudication. However, termination must remain an option. If the private sector knows that government will always renegotiate and never terminate, this knowledge may render the PPP contract worthless.

Government support

Concrete government support is often necessary to ensure private sector participation and profitability, and it can enhance the optimal sharing of risks between the private and the public sectors. Capital and revenue subsidies and guarantees are often necessary to attract investors to new markets or new sectors within those markets by providing, for example, right-of-way acquisition, viability gap financing, and national support for subnational projects.

Although PPP projects can accelerate the building of social infrastructure by addressing the problem of limited financial resources in the government, it is neither possible nor desirable to increase the amount of PPP investment without limits. Building infrastructure through PPP investment means that the government borrows from future funding needs. In effect, it is a loan that needs to be paid off in the medium- to long-term.

PPP should not be pursued as a way to procure infrastructure off budget. The motivation should be increased efficiency, not a desire to meet fiscal targets. The increasing number of PPP projects has made it critical to establish fiscal rules for PPP projects and so maintain sound and stable fiscal management. To this end, some of targets that need to be considered are (i) setting a government subsidy between the competent authorities and the private concessionaire, (ii) contracting future payment obligations for 20 years or longer, (iii) determining whether or not the PPP assets are recognized in the government's balance sheet, and (iv) forecasting future expected or contingent government revenues (Kim et al. 2011).

Conventionally, PPP investment has been treated separately from publicly financed investment, not coming under direct regulation as government expenditure. Because large parts of future government obligations connected with PPPs are long-term commitments, it is important to examine from a fiscal perspective whether a government can maintain fiscal adequacy and stability while promoting PPP projects.

There should be clear rules for budgeting and accounting. No comprehensive accounting standards exist for PPP in national budgets or international statistics, such as national accounts. Adding to the complexity, the various kinds of PPP arrangements have no precise, agreed definition or delimitation. Steps have been taken in the accounting profession to offer guidance on this issue but with little progress so far. The notable exception is the Eurostat manual on government deficits and debt for the implementation of the European System of Accounts 2010, released in 2016. It states that the assets involved in a PPP can be considered nongovernment assets in national accounts only if there is strong evidence that the private partner involved in that partnership bears most of the risks and earns most of the rewards attached to them, either directly or through their use. Therefore, analysis of the allocation of risk and rewards between government and the nongovernment partner must be considered the core issue. Here, the notion of risk refers to the impact on revenue or on profit of explicit actions by one party related to construction, maintenance, and the provision of services for which it has been given responsibility, and/or the consequences of the behavior of other economic agents for which the activity is carried out, such as a change in the demand for the service from a government unit or an end user.

Those who bear risks demand entitlement to act in order to forestall risks or to mitigate their impact if they are unavoidable. In general, the absence of standards makes it possible to avoid normal spending controls and use PPP to circumvent spending ceilings and fiscal rules. It may also create incentives to move investment that would otherwise be considered public off the government's balance sheets. Taxpayers bear the risk of future costs. It is therefore important that robust measures close any loopholes that enables PPP to be used to bypass expenditure controls, or to move public investment off budget and debt off the government's balance sheet.

Another need is for governments to incorporate national procedures in their budgeting systems to deal with arrangements such as PPP contracts. Governments should regularly update their national budgeting procedures and systems to ensure a focus on affordability, value for money, and long-term fiscal sustainability. It is important to develop internationally accepted accounting and reporting standards for PPP to promote transparency in regard to the government balance sheet and to provide a suitable assessment of the fiscal consequences of individual PPPs (IMF 2004). As PPP gains more prominence, and as a better appreciation of the fiscal risks involved with PPP is developed, the emphasis should be on countries comprehensively disclosing the known and future costs of commitments under PPPs and their contingent liabilities. One way to address this would be to incorporate PPP-related costs into a debt-sustainability analysis within a medium- to long-term budget framework.

Government leadership

Putting together successful PPPs requires significant political will on the part of the government (Kim et al. forthcoming). Because PPPs often require direct payment for user charges, they may suffer backlash from users, especially if users have become accustomed to receiving those services for free. Political leaders need to prepare potential users through a robust consultation and communications strategy before every project, but even more so at the start of a long-term PPP program.

Multilateral partners' involvement in contracts provides insurance against the risk of disputes. While MDBs can support infrastructure development and play a critical role in mitigating risks in infrastructure PPP projects in Asia, the public sector should take leadership in driving the process. The lack of government commitment to honor the terms of contracts has significantly raised transaction costs in countries with weak institutions. Failure to honor contracts is the main regulatory risk, affecting the amount of investment that can be attracted, the cost of capital, and tariffs because additional premiums are required to cover that risk. Credible and stable regulation and transparent rules reduce the risk.

Political changes and powerful vested interests can hinder PPP. The government must set out the case for PPP in a convincing and transparent process that highlights the goal of improving services at reasonable cost. Only then can broader support for PPP be marshalled against short-term political pressures.

Experiment and learn

Despite developing Asia's great strides in infrastructure development, a hefty $1.7 trillion annual investment through 2030 is still needed to address its current infrastructure woes. This cost must be paid to maintain the region's growth momentum and thereby enable further poverty reduction and fund an effective response to climate change. Private enterprise has contributed substantially to the region's success, but sustaining Asia's future development requires that it assume an expanded role.

Bridging the infrastructure gap demands improved infrastructure delivery. Because PPP effectively marshals the private sector's most valued strengths, it can be an effective tool to deliver infrastructure and related services. It is not automatically the right scheme to venture into, as its success is predicated on a list of prerequisites. But if appropriately implemented and successfully pursued, PPP facilitates the provision of adequate and efficient infrastructure and services for users, profitable investment opportunities for the private sector, and a development mechanism that expands the capacity of the state.

Yet, despite the advantages that PPP offers relative to other avenues for addressing the regional infrastructure gap, and notwithstanding the progress many countries around the world have made so far in implementing PPP, some major challenges must be tackled to further promote PPP. They include technical, legal, and institutional constraints on PPP projects, as well as the financial requirements that persist as stumbling blocks interfering with the region's ability to tap long-term finance from an ample regional supply of long-term savings.

Indeed, finance is the main challenge to policy makers and PPP practitioners. Currently, financing infrastructure is done mostly through a combination of direct equity investment and bank loans. But this is not sustainable. The pool of potential investors must be expanded, and the vast financial resources of the capital markets must be tapped. To this end, MDBs play a key role.

Many of the recommendations above may appear all too obvious. However, experience with PPP over the years shows that the obvious still needs to be made explicit and repeated. Although PPP is not automatically the right mode or the default procurement option, it may be good to keep in mind what Ferroni and Castle (2011) wrote: "Every PPP is an experiment—a new mixture of partners, needs, technologies, goals, and intended beneficiaries. Open-mindedness and a willingness to learn are therefore always essential."

PPP can be an innovative tool to meet Asia's infrastructure needs. Leaders in developing Asia have recognized this and are stepping up efforts to facilitate the execution of PPP projects. Although designing and implementing a PPP can be complex and challenging, if a suitable project is pursued with qualified private partners and overseen through transparent and competitive processes, this is the surest route to the efficient and effective delivery of public infrastructure and the services it enables.

Background Papers

Hyun, S., D. Park, and S. Tian. Forthcoming. *Determinants of Public–Private Partnerships in Infrastructure in Asia: Implications for Capital Market Development.* Asian Development Bank.

Jett, A. Forthcoming. *Risk Mitigation and Sovereign Guarantees for PPPs in Developing Economies.* Asian Development Bank.

Kim, J. Forthcoming. *Rationale and Institution for Public–Private Partnerships.* Asian Development Bank.

Kim, K., J. Kim, Y. Koh, M. Jung, and M. Park. Forthcoming. *Public–Private Partnership System in the Republic of Korea, the Philippines, and Indonesia.* Asian Development Bank.

Lee, H. and K. Kim. Forthcoming. *Traditional Procurement (TP) vs. Public Private Partnership (PPP): Comparison of Procurement Modalities Focusing on Bundling Contract Effects.* Asian Development Bank.

Lee, M., X. Han, R. Gaspar, and E. Alano. Forthcoming[a]. *Deriving Macroeconomic Benefits from Public–Private Partnerships.* Asian Development Bank.

Lee, M., X. Han, P. Quising, and M. Villaruel. Forthcoming[b]. *Hazard Analysis of Public–Private Partnership Projects.* Asian Development Bank.

Rao, V. Forthcoming. *An Empirical Analysis of Factors Influencing Project Financing by Banks of Infrastructure PPP Projects in Select Asian Economies.* Asian Development Bank.

Zen, F. Forthcoming. *Public–Private Partnership Development in Southeast Asia.* Economic Research Institute for the Association of Southeast Asian Nations and East Asia.

References

Albalate, D., G. Bel, and R. R. Geddes. 2015. *Do Public–Private Partnership Enabling Laws Increase Private Investment in Infrastructure?* http://www.econ.pitt.edu/sites/default/files/Geddes.PPPlaws.pdf

Allport, R., R. Brown, S. Glaister, and T. Travers. 2010. *Success and Failure in Urban Transport Infrastructure Projects.* KPMG Infrastructure Spotlight Report. KPMG International.

Araya, G., J. Z. Schwartz, and L. A. Andrés. 2013. The Effects of Country Risk and Conflict on Infrastructure PPPs. *World Bank Policy Research Working Paper* No. 6569. World Bank.

Arezki, R., P. Bolton, S. Peters, F. Samama, and J. Stiglitz. 2016. From Global Savings Glut to Financing Infrastructure: The Advent of Investment Platforms. *Working Paper*/16/18. International Monetary Fund.

ADB. 2008. *Public–Private Partnership Handbook.* Asian Development Bank.

_____. 2009. *Special Evaluation Study on ADB Assistance for Public–Private Partnerships in Infrastructure Development—Potential for More Success.* Asian Development Bank.

_____. 2012a. *Public–Private Partnership Operational Plan 2012–2020.* Asian Development Bank. https://www.adb.org/sites/default/files/institutional-document/33671/ppp-operational-plan-2012-2020.pdf

_____. 2012b. *Report and Recommendation of the President to the Board of Directors on India Partial Credit Guarantee Facility of Credit Enhancement of Project Bonds.* Asian Development Bank.

_____. 2015. *Asia Bond Monitor.* Asian Development Bank.

_____. 2017. *Meeting Asia's Infrastructure Needs*. Asian Development Bank.

ASIFMA–ICMA. 2016. *Guide to Infrastructure Financing in Asia*. Asia Securities Industry and Financial Markets Association and International Capital Market Association.

Bain, R. 2007. *PPP Construction Risk: International Evidence from the Roads Sector*. Institute for Transport Studies of University of Leeds.

Baxter, D. 2017. *How Resilient Are Your PPP Projects to Adverse Natural Events?* Linkedin. https://www.linkedin.com/pulse/how-resilient-your-ppp-projects-adverse-natural-events-david-baxter

BIS. 2016. A Spare Tire for Capital Markets: Fostering Corporate Bond Markets in Asia. *BIS Papers* 85. Bank for International Settlements.

Brealey, R., I. Cooper, and M. Habib. 1996. Using Project Finance to Fund Infrastructure Investments. *Journal of Applied Corporate Finance 9*.

Burger, P., J. Tyson, I. Karpowicz, and M. D. Coelho. 2009. The Effects of the Financial Crisis on Public–Private Partnerships. *IMF Working Paper* 09(144). International Monetary Fund.

Charoenngam, C. C. and F. Kurniawan. 2015. Concession Contract in the Public Private Partnership: Case Study of Don Muang Tollway and Second Stage Expressway in Thailand. *Proceedings of Narotama International Conference on Civil Engineering*. Narotama University.

Corieli, F., S. Gatti, and A. Steffanoni. 2010. Risk Shifting through Nonfinancial Contracts: Effects on Loan Spreads and Capital Structure of Project Finance Deals. *Journal of Money, Credit and Banking* 42(7).

Cuttaree, V. 2008. *Successes and Failures of PPP Projects*. World Bank.

Deutsche Bank. 2016. *Annual Report 2016*. https://annualreport.deutsche-bank.com/2016/ar/deutsche-bank-group/deutsche-bank-share-and-bonds.html

Downer J. and J. Porter. 1992. Tate's Cairn Tunnel, Hong Kong: South East Asia's Longest Road Tunnel. In *Proceedings of the 16th Australian Road Research Board Conference* 7: 153–165. Perth.

Economist Intelligence Unit. 2015. Evaluating the Environment for Public–Private Partnerships in Asia-Pacific: The 2014 Infrascope.

Ehlers, T. 2014. Understanding the Challenges for Infrastructure Finance. *BIS Working Papers* 454. Bank for International Settlements.

Ehlers, T., F. Packer, and E. Remolona. 2014. Infrastructure and Corporate Bond Markets in Asia. In *Financial Flows and Infrastructure Financing: Proceedings of a Conference*. 20–21 March. Sydney. https://www.rba.gov.au/publications/confs/2014/pdf/conf-vol-2014.pdf

Eichengreen, B. and P. Luengnaruemitchai. 2006. Why Doesn't Asia Have Bigger Bond Markets? *BIS Papers* No. 30. Bank for International Settlements.

Engel, E., R. Fischer, and A. Galetovic. 2014. *The Economics of Public–Private Partnerships*. Cambridge University Press.

Esty, B. and W. Megginson. 2003. Creditor Rights, Enforcement, and Debt Ownership Structure: Evidence from the Global Syndicated Loan Market. *The Journal of Financial and Quantitative Analysis* 38(1).

Ferroni, M. and P. Castle. 2011. Public–Private Partnerships and Sustainable Agricultural Development. *Sustainability* 3. Syngenta Foundation for Sustainable Agriculture.

Galilea, P. and F. Medda. 2010. Does the Political and Economic Context Influence the Success of a Transport Project? An Analysis of Transport Public–Private Partnerships. *Research in Transportation Economics* 30. Elsevier.

Gatti, D., E. Gaffeo, and M. Gallegati. 2010. Complex Agent-Based Macroeconomics: A Manifesto for a New Paradigm. *Journal of Economic Interaction and Coordination* 5(2).

Gyntelberg, J., G. Ma, and E. Remolona. 2005. Corporate Bond Markets in Asia. *BIS Quarterly Review*. Bank for International Settlements.

Hainz, C. and S. Kleimeier. 2012. Political Risk, Project Finance, and the Participation of Development Banks in Syndicated Lending. *Journal of Financial Intermediation* 21(2).

Hart, O. 2003. Incomplete Contract and Public Ownershop: Remarks and an Application to Public–Private Partnerships. *The Economic Journal* 113(486).

Hofman, B. 2010. *Infrastructure Philippines 2010: Investing and Financing in Public–Private Partnership Projects*. World Bank. http://www.worldbank.org/en/news/speech/2010/11/18/multilateral-bilateral-roles-infrastructure-development-philippines

HSBC Amanah. 2012. Global *Sukuk* Market: Current Status and Growth Potential. http://siteresources.worldbank.org/FINANCIALSECTOR/Resources/Haneef_Global_Sukuk_Market_HSBC.pdf

Hyun, S. 2017. The Importance of Infrastructure Bond Market Development in Asia. *Nomura Journal of Asian Capital Markets* 1(2).

IMF. 2004. Public–Private Partnerships. International Monetary Fund. https://www.imf.org/external/np/fad/2004/pifp/eng/031204.pdf

Inderst, G. 2013. Private Infrastructure Finance and Investment in Europe. *EIB Working Papers* 2013/02. European Investment Bank.

———. 2016. Infrastructure Investment, Private Finance, and Institutional Investors: Asia from a Global Perspective. *ADBI Working Paper* 555. Asian Development Bank Institute.

Inderst, G. and F. Stewart. 2014. Institutional Investment in Infrastructure in Developing Countries: Introduction to Potential Models. *Policy Research Working Paper* 6780. World Bank.

Iossa, E. and D. Martimort. 2015. The Simple Microeconomics of Public–Private Partnerships. *Journal of Public Economic Theory* 17(1).

Istrate, E. and R. Puentes. 2011. *Moving Forward on Public–Private Partnerships: US and International Experience with PPP Units*. Brookings-Rockefeller Project on State and Metropolitan Innovation.

Kaminker, C. and F. Stewart. 2012. The Role of Institutional Investors in Financing Clean Energy. *OECD Working Papers on Finance, Insurance, and Private Pensions* 23. Organisation for Economic Co-operation and Development.

Keith, S., P. McAuslan, R. Knight, J. Lindsay, P. Munro-Faure, and D. Palmer. 2008. Compulsory Acquisition of Land and Compensation. *FAO Land Tenure Studies* 10. Food and Agriculture Organization.

Kitano, Y. 2015. Infrastructure Financing in Asia. Current Situation and Future Outlook. *Nomura Journal of Capital Markets* 6(4).

Kim, J. H. 2011. *Performance Evaluation and Best Practice of Public–Private Partnerships*. Korea Development Institute.

Kim, J. H., J. Kim, S. Shin, and S. Y. Lee. 2011. *Public–Private Partnership Infrastructure Projects: Case Studies from the Republic of Korea: Volume 1: Institutional Arrangements and Performance*. Asian Development Bank.

Kleimeier, S. and R. J. Versteeg. 2010. Project Finance as a Driver of Economic Growth in Low-Income Countries. *Review of Financial Economics* 19(2).

Lee, M., M. L. Villaruel, and R. Gaspar. 2016. Effects of Temperature Shocks on Economic Growth and Welfare in Asia. *ADB Economics Working Paper Series* 501. Asian Development Bank.

Levy, S. 1996. The Eastern Harbour Crossing. In S. Levy, ed. *Build, Operate, and Transfer—Paving the Way for Tomorrow's Infrastructure*. Wiley.

Lindsay, J. M. 2012. Compulsory Acquisition of Land and Compensation in Infrastructure Projects. *PPP Insights* 1(3).

Ma, T. 2016. Basel III and the Future of Project Finance Funding. *Michigan Business & Entrepreneurial Law Review* 6(1).

Mak, C. K. and S. Mo. 2005. Some Aspects of the PPP Approach to Transport Infrastructure Development in Hong Kong. http://www.civil.hku.hk/cicid/3_events/32/papers/8.pdf

McMillan, M. and D. Rodrik. 2011. Globalization, Structural Change, and Productivity Growth. *NBER Working Paper* 17143. National Bureau of Economic Research.

Musa, N. M. D. N. 2015. *Role of Islamic Finance in Infrastructure Financing*. Central Bank of Malaysia.

Nose, M. 2014. Triggers of Contract Breach: Contract Design, Shocks, or Institutions? *Policy Research Working Paper Series* 6738. World Bank.

OECD. 2010. *Dedicated Public–Private Partnership Units: A Survey of Institutional and Governance Structures*. Organisation for Economic Co-operation and Development. http://www.oecd.org/gov/budgeting/dedicatedPublic-Privatepartnershipunitsasurveyofinstitutionalandgovernancestructures.htm

———. 2013. *Annual Survey of Large Pension Funds and Public Pension Reserve Funds*. Organisation for Economic Co-operation and Development. http://www.oecd.org/daf/fin/private-pensions/LargestPensionFunds2012Survey.pdf

———. 2014. *Pooling of Institutional Investors Capital—Selected Case Studies in Unlisted Equity Infrastructure*. Organisation for Economic Co-operation and Development.

———. 2016. Pension Markets in Focus. Organisation for Economic Co-operation and Development. http://www.oecd.org/daf/fin/private-pensions/Pension-Markets-in-Focus-2016.pdf

———. 2017. Country Risk Classification. Organisation for Economic Co-operation and Development. http://www.oecd.org/trade/xcred/crc.htm

Preqin. 2015. *Preqin Special Report: Asian Infrastructure*. https://www.preqin.com/docs/reports/Preqin-Special-Report-Asian-Infrastructure-June-2015.pdf

———. 2016. A Decade of Asia-Focused Infrastructure Fundraising. https://www.preqin.com/blog/0/14146/decade-of-asian-infrastructure

PPIAF. 2009. PPP Modalities. Public–Private Infrastructure Advisory Facility. https://ppiaf.org/sites/ppiaf.org/files/documents/toolkits/highwaystoolkit/6/pdf-version/5-36.pdf

Rao, V. 2015. Developing the Financial Sector and Expanding Market Instruments to Support a Post-2015 Development Agenda in Asia and the Pacific. *ADB Sustainable Development Working Paper Series* 36.

Rhee, C. Y. and H. Lee. 2007. Public–Private Partnerships in Infrastructure and Macroeconomy: The Experience of Korea. In Kim, J. H. ed. *Performance Evaluation and Best Practice of Public Private Partnerships*. Korea Development Institute.

Rickards, M. and A. Hermelin. 2015. Philippines PPP: Prospects and Challenges. *InfraRead* 6.

Safitri, H. 2015. Commoditization of Energy: A Case of PPP Scheme Implementation in Central Java Power Plant/CJPP Project. In *Land Grabbing: Perspectives from East and Southeast Asia Conference*.

Sampath, S. 2006. PPPs for Infrastructure Development and Service Delivery: Defining the Nature and Scope. Presentation at the "Need to Know" Knowledge and Skills Training Workshop for the Government of Fiji's PPP Network. 11 September. Nadi, Fiji.

Schomaker, R. 2014. Institutional Quality and Private Sector Participation: Theory and Empirical Finding. *European Journal of Government and Economics* 3(2).

Shediac, R., R. Abouchakra, M. Hammam, and M. R. Najjar. 2008. *Public–Private Partnerships—A New Catalyst for Economic Growth*. http://www.pppcouncil.ca/web/P3_Knowledge_Centre/Research/Public-Private_Partnerships__A_new_Catalyst_for_Economic_Growth.aspx?WebsiteKey=712ad751-6689-4d4a-aa17-e9f993740a89#sthash.AIu83A8M.dpuf

Subramanian, K. V. and F. Tung. 2016. Law and Project Finance. *Journal of Financial Intermediation* 25. Elsevier.

Sundararajan, S. and N. Suriyagoda. 2016. Climate Risks and Resilience in Infrastructure PPPs: Issues to Be Considered. *Public–Private Infrastructure Advisory Facility Issue Brief*.

TheCityUK. 2014. *UK Fund Management 2014 An Attractive Proposition for International Funds*.

Trebilcock, M. and M. Rosenstock. 2015. Infrastructure Public–Private Partnerships in the Developing World: Lessons from Recent Experience. *The Journal of Development Studies* 51(4).

Trujillo, L., N. Martin, A. Estache, and J. Campos. 2002. Macroeconomic Effects of Private Sector Participation in Latin America's Infrastructure. *Policy Research Working Paper Series* 2906. World Bank.

UNESCAP. 2014a. *About the 5P Approach*. United Nations Economic and Social Commission for Asia and the Pacific. http://www.unescap.org/5p/about

———. 2014b. *Public–Private Partnerships Case Study #1: Traffic Demand Risk: The Case of Bangkok's Skytrain (BTS)*. United Nations Economic and Social Commission for Asia and the Pacific.

———. 2017. *PPP Policy, Legal and Institutional Frameworks in Asia and the Pacific*. United Nations Economic and Social Commission for Asia and the Pacific.

Werneck, B. and M. Saadi. 2016. The Public–Private Partnership Law Review. *Law Business Research*.

World Bank. 2007. *Public–Private Partnership Units: Lessons for their Design and Use in Infrastructure*.

_____. 2014. *Mutual Funds in Developing Markets: Addressing Challenges to Growth*.

_____. 2015. Institutional Investors: The Unfulfilled $100 Trillion Promise. http://www.worldbank.org/en/news/feature/2015/06/18/ institutional-investors-the-unfulfilled-100-trillion-promise

_____. 2016a. *The State of PPPs: Infrastructure Public–Private Partnerships in Emerging Markets and Developing Economies 1991–2015*.

_____. 2016b. *Benchmarking PPP Procurement 2017*.

_____. 2017. Public–Private Partnerships: Reference Guide, Version 3.0. https://openknowledge.worldbank.org/handle/10986/20118

World Economic Forum. 2014. *Direct Investing by Institutional Investors: Implications for Investors and Policy-Makers*.

Yehoue, E. 2013. Financial and Sovereign Debt Crises and PPP Market Structure. In P. de Vries and E. Yehoue, eds. *The Routledge Companion to Public–Private Partnerships*. Routledge.

Yescombe, E. R. 2007. *Public–Private Partnerships Principles of Policy and Finance*. Elsevier.

Zou, P., S. Wang, and D. Fang. 2008. A Life-Cycle Risk Management Framework for PPP Infrastructure Projects. *Journal of Financial Management of Property and Construction* 13(2).

3

ECONOMIC TRENDS AND PROSPECTS IN DEVELOPING ASIA

Central Asia

The outlook for the subregion has brightened thanks to stable oil prices, improving prospects for the Russian Federation, and rising remittances. Growth is now projected at 3.3% in 2017 and 3.9% in 2018, up from earlier forecasts of 3.1% and 3.5%, with improvement for Kazakhstan. Forecast inflation is raised to 8.9% in 2017 and 7.8% in 2018, mostly on higher inflation in Azerbaijan and Uzbekistan. The current account deficit is now expected at 3.4% in 2017 and 2.0% in 2018, wider than earlier projected mostly because of deterioration in Azerbaijan and Kazakhstan.

Subregional assessment and prospects

This *Update* raises subregional growth forecasts to 3.3% in 2017 and 3.9% in 2018 (Figure 3.1.1). These upgrades from 3.1% and 3.5% projected in *Asian Development Outlook 2017* (*ADO 2017*) reflect a strong first half this year and improved outlooks for Kazakhstan and the four remittance-receiving countries in the subregion—Armenia, Georgia, the Kyrgyz Republic, and Tajikistan—a group in which growth remains highly variable.

In Armenia, stronger remittances and external demand accelerated growth in the first half of 2017. Georgia benefitted from higher infrastructure spending that is expected to continue through 2018, as well as from strong exports, higher remittances and tourism earnings, and increased foreign direct investment. In the Kyrgyz Republic, higher gold production and improved remittances spurred expansion. Faster growth in industry raises Tajikistan's growth prospects somewhat.

Growth picked up in Kazakhstan, the subregion's largest economy, in the first half of 2017. Expansion came mainly from extractive industries and manufacturing, as well as from trade, and is likely to continue thanks to countercyclical programs and broadly stable commodity prices. While recovery remains fragile, this *Update* revises up the growth forecast for Kazakhstan in 2017 to 2.7% from 2.4% in *ADO 2017* and in 2018 to 3.0% from 2.2%.

The subregion's other hydrocarbon exporters—Azerbaijan, Turkmenistan, and Uzbekistan—still feel the effects of low oil prices since the end of 2014. Azerbaijan continues to see its gross domestic product (GDP) shrink, all the more so with a 9% decline in oil production in the first half of 2017 from the same period last year, reflecting negotiated commitments to cut production and probably

3.1.1 GDP growth, Central Asia

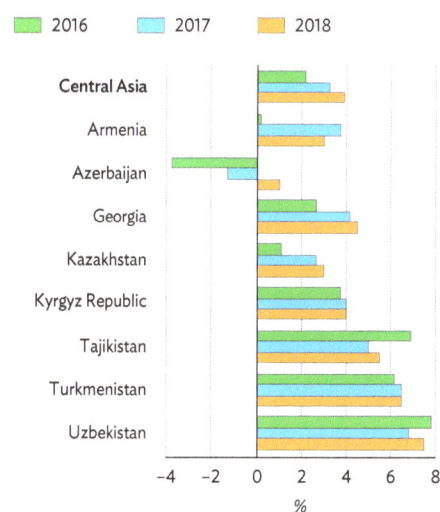

Legend: 2016, 2017, 2018

Categories: Central Asia, Armenia, Azerbaijan, Georgia, Kazakhstan, Kyrgyz Republic, Tajikistan, Turkmenistan, Uzbekistan

%

Source: Asian Development Outlook database.

The subregional assessment and prospects were written by Dominik Peschel. The section on Kazakhstan was written by Zhanat Murzakulova and the part on other economies by Muhammadi Boboev, Iskandar Gulamov, Grigor Gyurjyan, Jennet Hojanazarova, George Luarsabishvili, Gulkayr Tentieva, and Nail Valiyev. All authors are in the Central and West Asia Department of ADB.

diminished capacity in its oil fields. Growth there is now expected to contract slightly more in 2017 than forecast in *ADO 2017* before finally resuming in 2018. In Turkmenistan, continued adjustment to lower natural gas prices will likely slow growth in 2018. In Uzbekistan, growth is now expected to be slightly weaker in 2017 as the economy adjusts to a currency devaluation and a loosening of the legal requirements for access to foreign exchange, both of which occurred in early September 2017 and will likely spur growth in 2018.

Inflation in Central Asia arises mainly from factors specific to individual economies, with the subregional average skewed by high inflation in Azerbaijan and Uzbekistan. Inflation forecasts are raised for Georgia in 2017, Tajikistan and the Kyrgyz Republic in 2018, and Azerbaijan and Uzbekistan in both years. Average inflation in the subregion is now projected to reach 8.9% in 2017 and 7.8% in 2018, up from 7.8% and 7.3% forecast in *ADO 2017* (Figure 3.1.2).

Tighter foreign exchange restrictions and expectations of further domestic currency depreciation stoked inflation in Azerbaijan, where the average in the first 8 months of 2017 reached 14.0% and will likely remain this year. In Uzbekistan, currency devaluation argues for higher inflation forecasts for this year and next. In Kazakhstan, inflation averaged 7.5% in the first 8 months of 2017 and will likely rise somewhat above that rate. In Turkmenistan, slightly lower inflation forecasts in this *Update* recognize government efforts to contain inflation through administrative price controls and higher domestic production of consumer and industrial goods.

In Georgia, inflation has exceeded expectations, averaging 5.8% in the first 8 months of 2017, but is expected to moderate in 2018 as the effects of recent tax reform wane. In the Kyrgyz Republic, a modest recovery in domestic demand and higher commodity prices are expected to spur inflation from 0.4% in 2016 to 3.5% this year, though less than forecast in *ADO 2017*. With Kyrgyz import tariffs projected to rise toward prevailing rates in the Eurasian Economic Union, the inflation forecast for 2018 is raised. The 2018 inflation forecast for Tajikistan is raised slightly, reflecting further increases in electricity tariffs.

The forecast subregional current account deficit is widened to 3.4% of GDP from 3.0% for 2017 and to 2.0% from 1.7% for 2018, as projected deterioration in Armenia, Azerbaijan, and Kazakhstan more than offsets anticipated improvement in Turkmenistan (Figure 3.1.3). In Uzbekistan, currency devaluation narrows the current account surplus projected for 2017 but widens it for 2018. In Kazakhstan, stronger recovery and higher imports justify a wider projection for the current account deficit, while in Azerbaijan the unexpected decline in oil production is likely to narrow the trade surplus despite a slowdown in imports. In Armenia, a trade deficit above expectations slightly widens the current account deficit projected for the year. In Turkmenistan, higher gas exports to the People's Republic of China are now projected to narrow the current account deficit more than forecast in April.

3.1.2 Inflation, Central Asia

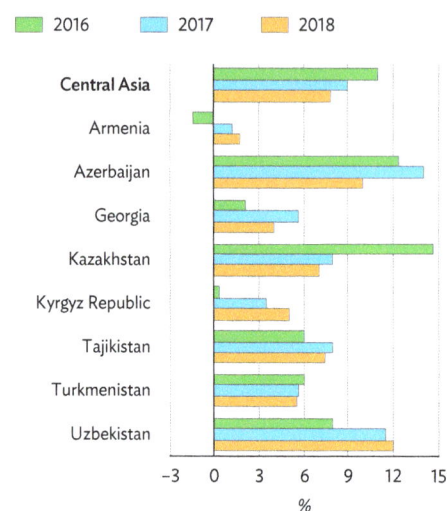

Source: *Asian Development Outlook* database.

3.1.3 Current account balance, Central Asia

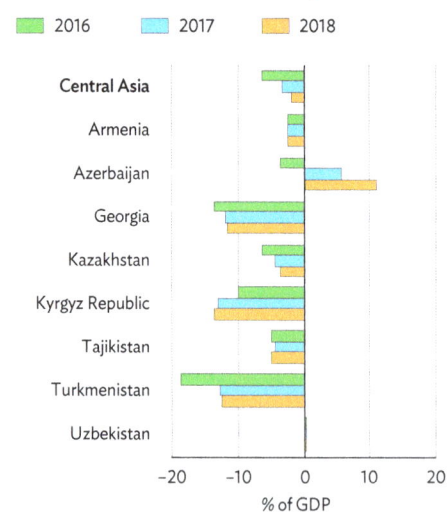

Source: *Asian Development Outlook* database.

Kazakhstan

Growth in the first half of 2017 rose to 4.2% on expansion in extractive industries and higher oil and metal prices. Inflation slowed to 7.7%. With a stable external environment and recovering oil production, growth forecasts are raised to 2.7% for 2017 and 3.0% for 2018, while inflation forecasts are maintained at 8.0% and 7.0%. Projected current account deficits are widened to 4.5% for 2017 and 3.5% for 2018 as higher private consumption raises forecasts for imports.

Updated assessment

Growth averaged 4.2% year on year in the first half of 2017 as industrial output improved (Figure 3.1.4). Higher oil prices and a low base for 2016 contributed to an unexpectedly strong performance in the first quarter, though preliminary data indicate slower growth in the second. In the first half, industry expanded by 7.8%, reflecting gains of 9.4% in mining and 6.5% in manufacturing. Crude oil production, representing nearly 40% of output, grew by 9.7%, while metallurgy expanded by 7.9%. Higher livestock production contributed to a 3.1% rise in agriculture. Construction expanded by 5.9%, slightly below the 6.6% recorded in the same period of 2016. Services grew by 2.3%, reflecting gains of 2.4% in trade, 3.9% in transportation, and 2.5% in information and computer technology.

Demand-side data are available for only the first quarter of 2017 (Figure 3.1.5). In this period, consumption grew by 1.7% as private consumption rose by 2.6% and public consumption contracted by 1.5%. Investment expanded by 2.5%, mainly from a 3.0% rise in fixed investment. Net exports rose substantially in nominal terms to equal 10.8% of GDP in the first quarter, up from 6.9% in the same period of 2016. Exports in the first quarter were 4.8% lower than in the same period of 2016, when they contracted by 9.2% year on year. Meanwhile, imports fell by 9.8%, more than doubling the year-earlier decline of 4.5%.

Average inflation in January–August 2017 was reported at 7.5%, less than half the 16.4% rate in the same period of 2016. The biggest contributor was food, rising by 9.2% mainly because meat and vegetables remained in short supply despite the beginning of the summer harvest. Prices for other goods climbed by 8.2%, while prices for services rose by 4.8% (Figure 3.1.6).

Fiscal policy remained expansionary, with oil-income transfers from the National Fund of the Republic of Kazakhstan (NFRK) to the state budget in the first half of 2017 higher by 50.9% than in the same period of 2016. Total revenue rose by 21.2%, with taxes up by 14.1%. Higher tax receipts reflected mainly increases in corporate taxes from mining companies and financial institutions, value-added tax on imports, extraction taxes, and export duties on crude oil. Expenditure rose by only 8.0% as program administrators postponed drawing down allotments to help limit the budget deficit (Figure 3.1.7).

On the monetary front, the National Bank of Kazakhstan, the central bank, lowered in August 2017 its policy rate to 10.25% from 10.50% in response to slower inflation, signs of economic recovery, and continued de-dollarization, which saw the value of deposits

3.1.4 Supply-side contributions to growth

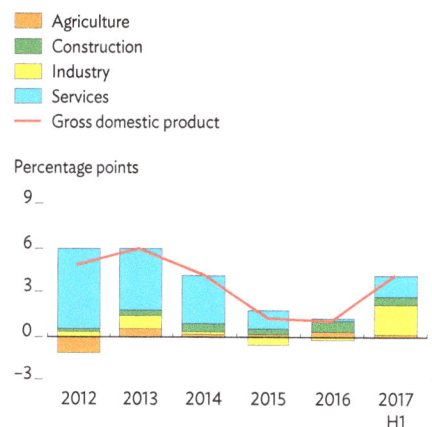

- Agriculture
- Construction
- Industry
- Services
- Gross domestic product

Percentage points

H = half.

Sources: Republic of Kazakhstan. Ministry of National Economy. Committee on Statistics; ADB estimates.

3.1.5 Demand-side contributions to growth

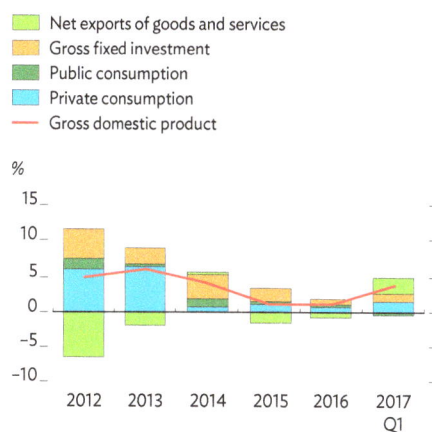

- Net exports of goods and services
- Gross fixed investment
- Public consumption
- Private consumption
- Gross domestic product

%

Q = quarter.

Source: Republic of Kazakhstan. Ministry of National Economy. Committee on Statistics.

denominated in foreign currency fall to 49.5% of all deposits at the end of June from 54.6% in December 2016 (Figure 3.1.8). Bank lending remained constrained, with new loans only 4.8% higher in the first half of 2017 than a year earlier. Total credit showed little change in the first half. While bank credit remains sluggish, the central bank continues to absorb excess liquidity in the money market by issuing short-term notes. The dip in oil prices around midyear affected the local currency market. To meet higher demand for US dollars and support the Kazakh tenge, the central bank injected $101 million into the market in June and $70 million in August. These were the first injections since September 2016.

The current account recorded a deficit of 4.0% of GDP in the first half of 2017, down from 6.8% during the same period in 2016. The trade surplus improved significantly, reaching 13.1% of GDP, up from 8.1% in the first half of 2016, as exports jumped by 36.2%, more than double the 16.9% rise in imports. However, the deficit in services expanded by 7.4%, and larger profit outflows on foreign direct investment raised the income deficit to 13.7% of GDP from 11.2%. By the end of August 2017, international reserves totaled $32.9 billion, equivalent to 10.0 months of imports of goods and services, while the NFRK held $57.9 billion in assets.

Prospects

Although economic recovery remains fragile and dependent on potentially volatile external developments, strong growth in the first half of the year justifies revising projected growth up to 2.7% in 2017 and 3.0% in 2018. Moreover, increased trade flows are likely in light of improving economic conditions in the euro area, modest recovery in the Russian Federation, and growth in the People's Republic of China that remains sturdy even as it slows. Low oil prices still limit the prospects for significantly faster growth, highlighting the need to diversify the economy.

On the supply side, gains in extractive industries will continue to propel growth as oil prices hover around $50/barrel. Oil production is projected to grow with expanded operations at the Kashagan oil field. Oil output may exceed 81 million tons in 2017, and the government aims for output to reach 86 million tons in 2018. On the demand side, higher private consumption will bolster growth as slowing inflation raises real incomes—and in the wake of consumer loans having risen by 4.9% in the first half of 2017. Growth prospects for consumer lending will depend on the dynamics of interest rates for individuals, which currently average a high 20% per year.

Monetary policy aims to avoid large swings in the exchange rate, and inflationary expectations should dampen under supportive external conditions that include low inflation in major trading partners and stable global commodity markets for food. Inflation forecasts are therefore maintained at 8.0% for 2017 and 7.0% for 2018. No dramatic change in food prices is expected by the end of the third quarter, considering the expected seasonal increase in food supply, and this should restrain the average annual inflation rate. However, higher private consumption will slow the deceleration of price hikes for goods other than food.

3.1.6 Monthly inflation

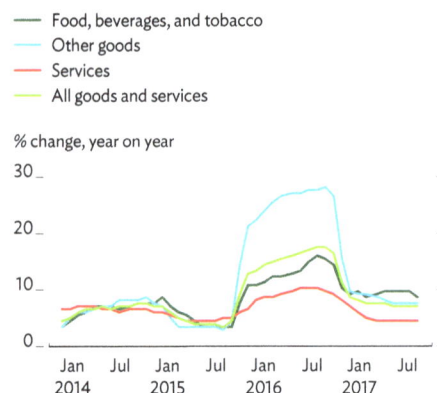

— Food, beverages, and tobacco
— Other goods
— Services
— All goods and services

% change, year on year

Source: Republic of Kazakhstan. Ministry of National Economy. Committee on Statistics.

3.1.7 Fiscal indicators

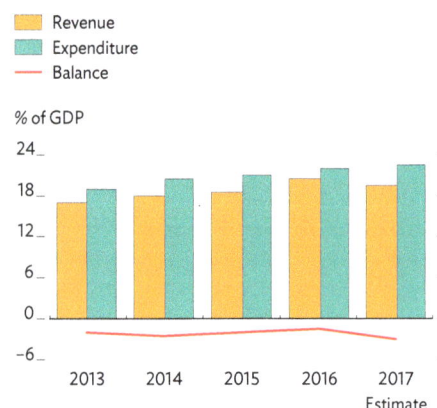

■ Revenue
■ Expenditure
— Balance

% of GDP

Sources: Ministry of Finance of the Republic of Kazakhstan; ADB estimates.

3.1.8 Dollarization in the banking system

■ Share of loans
■ Share of deposits

%

Source: National Bank of the Republic of Kazakhstan.

As inflationary pressures ease, no major changes in monetary policy are expected this year. Continued economic recovery in 2018 may encourage monetary tightening at that point, however, if needed to keep inflation within the central bank target range of 5%–7% for the year.

Fiscal policy is expected to remain expansionary, with continuing large (and initially unplanned) transfers from the NFRK. The budget deficit is now planned to equal 3.1% of GDP in 2017, not 1.2% as previously envisioned. Total revenue is anticipated at 19.4% of GDP in 2017, with transfers from the NFRK providing 45.8% and taxes 49.7%. Expenditure is planned at 22.5% of GDP. The fragile banking sector has already absorbed most of the rise in budget expenditure, and any additional support will be off budget or through the central bank. The impact of state intervention in the banking sector remains to be seen, as Halyk Bank's acquisition of Kazkommertsbank was settled only in early July 2017, following the purchase by the government's Problem Loans Fund of its bad loans, equal to nearly 4.0% of GDP. Other areas receiving higher public financial support include agriculture (envisioned as a new driver of economic development), transportation, energy, and construction. The government aims to accelerate growth by implementing several state programs under its third modernization plan. It has indicated that fiscal policy will be less expansionary in 2018, with plans to limit the budget deficit to 1.0% of GDP and to control external borrowing.

Kazakhstan's banking system remains troubled, even after the Problem Loans Fund's assumption of Kazkommertsbank liabilities. Outside observers estimate the nonperforming loan rate to be 25%–30%. The central bank has announced plans to provide further support by creating a special subsidiary with T500 billion to recapitalize banks through a quasi-fiscal operation. Banks will be eligible to receive support if their shareholders' contribute at least 50% of what the new central bank subsidiary provides. The central bank announced that the program will start in the third quarter of this year.

The current account deficit is now forecast to equal 4.5% of GDP in 2017, higher than the 3.4% forecast in *ADO 2017*, and 3.5% in 2018, up from 3.0% (Figure 3.1.9). Exports are projected to increase by 15% this year on higher oil production, with oil prices expected to average $52/barrel. However, imports are expected to grow by 21%, reflecting higher consumption and investment and a less variable exchange rate. The deficit in services is projected to rise by 5%, and that of income by more than 1%, while net outward transfers in the form of remittances and grants should decline by 8%. In 2018, exports are projected to rise by 14%, and imports by 4%.

3.1.1 Selected economic indicators, Kazakhstan (%)

	2017		2018	
	ADO 2017	*Update 2017*	*ADO 2017*	*Update 2017*
GDP growth	2.4	2.7	2.2	3.0
Inflation	8.0	8.0	7.0	7.0
Current acct. bal. (share of GDP)	–3.4	–4.5	–3.0	–3.5

Source: ADB estimates.

3.1.9 Current account balance

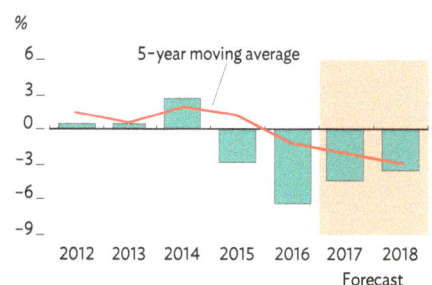

Source: *Asian Development Outlook* database.

Other economies

Armenia

Growth accelerated to 6.0% in the first half of 2017 from 3.6% in the same period in 2016 and 0.2% in all of 2016. On the supply side, strong gains in industry and services offset declines in agriculture and construction. Industry excluding construction expanded by 7.6%, reflecting expansion in all subsectors. Services grew by 8.2% as trade, transport, finance, and other services benefited from reviving demand, both domestic and external. Bad weather caused agriculture to contract by 4.0%, and reduced public investment slashed construction by 12.0%.

On the demand side, both consumption and investment strengthened, offsetting drag from net external demand as imports of goods and services expanded. In the first half of 2017, private consumption grew by an estimated 6.0% year on year, reflecting recovery in remittances. However, growth in public consumption eased to 2.0% as the government contained public sector wages and pensions. Total investment rose by an estimated 7.0%, propelled by significant inventory restocking, and despite a decline in gross fixed capital formation in line with lower government capital spending.

Because domestic demand was stronger than anticipated in the first half, projections for growth are raised for both 2017 and 2018. While plans for medium-term fiscal consolidation limit the ability of fiscal policy to support growth, the government's efforts to promote the private sector and improve the business climate should promote expansion, as should continued growth in remittances.

Monetary policy remained accommodative in the first 8 months of 2017. To support growth, the Central Bank of Armenia reduced its policy rate by 25 basis points to 6.0% in February 2017. Solid domestic demand and higher food prices lifted average inflation to 0.6% in the first 8 months of 2017, reversing 1.6% deflation in the same period of 2016. Inflation stood at 0.9% month on month in August 2017, well below the central bank's target band of 2.5%–5.5%. Forecasts for inflation this year and next are unchanged, with inflation expected to remain moderate in 2017 and rise slightly in 2018 in response to both domestic and external factors.

The current account deficit narrowed to equal 3.4% of GDP in the first quarter of 2017 from 6.3% a year earlier thanks to improved balances for services, investment income, and personal transfers, as well as higher employee earnings abroad. Exports expanded vigorously at 17.8% but were outpaced by imports, which reversed a 9.8% slump in the first quarter of 2016 to grow by 19.9%, widening the merchandise trade deficit to the equivalent of 9.9% of GDP from 9.6% a year earlier. The services account remained in surplus as receipts from tourism, information technology, and construction services continued to grow. After 3 consecutive years of declines, remittances, measured as the net inflow of private noncommercial transfers through banks, rose by 8.5% to $372.4 million in first 7 months of 2017, with remittances from the Russian Federation surging by 21.9%. In view of the trade deficit expanding faster than anticipated, the forecasts for the current account deficit are revised up marginally for both 2017 and 2018.

3.1.2 Selected economic indicators, Armenia (%)

	2017		2018	
	ADO 2017	Update 2017	ADO 2017	Update 2017
GDP growth	2.2	3.8	2.5	3.0
Inflation	1.2	1.2	1.8	1.8
Current acct. bal. (share of GDP)	−2.3	−2.5	−2.0	−2.3

Source: ADB estimates.

Azerbaijan

In the first half of 2017, the economy contracted by 1.3% but nevertheless improved on a 3.4% decline in the first half of 2016. Industry shrank by 5.8%, reflecting decreases of 6.6% in mining and 2.0% in refineries. Oil production fell by 9.0%, far exceeding the 0.4% slide in the same period of 2016. Meanwhile, public sector capital outlays held the decline in construction to 3.6%, much better than the 33.6% plunge a year earlier. Growth in services, at 2.3%, reflected increases of 6.7% in transportation, 1.8% in retail trade, and 2.1% in tourism and recreation. Agriculture expanded by 2.2% with the help of higher state support for cotton and horticulture production.

On the demand side, private consumption was weak and will likely remain so for the rest of 2017, given continuing banking sector problems and anticipated further tightening of monetary policy. Net exports contributed 17.3% of GDP in the first half of 2017, up from 10.1% in the same period in 2016, mostly reflecting a price-induced 20.3% rise in oil exports. Weak oil production, though, prompts this *Update* to downgrade the growth forecasts for both 2017 and 2018, with that for 2017 remaining negative.

Consumer price inflation accelerated to 14.3% year on year in August 2017. Prices surged by 18.5% for food and rose by 13.3% for other goods and 10.1% for services. Average annual inflation stood at 14.0% in the first 8 months of 2017. Price increases were mainly spillover from a 16% rise in electricity tariffs. A 28% jump in fuel prices in June 2017 is expected to push inflation still higher in the second half. With inflation rising, the central bank maintained its policy rate at 15% in the first half of 2017. Inflation is expected to slow in 2018 with a more stable currency and in the absence of utility tariff increases. This *Update* therefore raises the inflation forecast for 2017 substantially, and less so for 2018.

Falling production and low oil prices will likely put pressure on the exchange rate, which may trigger central bank intervention in the foreign exchange market and a higher policy interest rate. However, the banking sector stabilized after creditors restructured $3.3 billion in foreign obligations of the International Bank of Azerbaijan in return for government bonds. Budget outlays rose by 20.1% in the first half of 2017 as the government continued stimulus measures, and the budget is projected to record a deficit for the year equal to 1.3% of GDP.

The trade surplus nearly doubled to $3.2 billion in the first half from $1.7 billion in the same period of 2016. Though oil production fell, merchandise exports grew by 21.1%. This stemmed partly from some oil price recovery but also from a 19.8% rise in other exports with the implementation of a program promoting them. Imports declined by 15.4%, reflecting mainly lower imports of machinery, automobiles, and raw metals. Because declining oil production may narrow the trade surplus, this *Update* trims the *ADO 2017* projection for the current account surplus in both 2017 and 2018.

Georgia

Growth accelerated to 5.1% in the first quarter of 2017 from 2.7% in the whole of 2016. The strong performance reflected gains of 21.6% in construction, 11.5% in communication, and 8.7% in hotels and restaurants. On the demand side, growth drew support from increased government

3.1.3 Selected economic indicators, Azerbaijan (%)

	2017		2018	
	ADO 2017	*Update*	ADO 2017	*Update*
GDP growth	−1.1	−1.3	1.2	1.0
Inflation	9.0	14.0	8.0	10.0
Current acct. bal. (share of GDP)	5.9	5.6	11.4	11.0

Source: ADB estimates.

outlays and expanded private consumption enabled by higher remittances and accommodative monetary policy during 2016. Net exports contributed to growth for the first time since 2013. Also contributing were larger tourism receipts and improved business activity from higher lending to enterprises. Preliminary official estimates put growth at 4.5% in the first half of the year.

Given the strong expansion and a better outlook for key trading partners, as well as continued infrastructure spending and higher investment, this *Update* modestly raises the growth forecast for 2017. It retains the *ADO 2017* projection for 2018 in light of the higher base now anticipated in 2017 and expected monetary tightening later this year.

Consumer prices rose by 5.7% in August 2017 from a year earlier, well above the 4.0% annual target, as prices increased by 17.5% for tobacco and alcoholic beverages, 11.6% for transport, and 6.2% for food. The increases reflected unexpectedly robust economic activity, higher excise taxes and imported inflation, and an expansion in credit growth to 17.9% in the first half of the year. Average annual inflation stood at 5.8% in the first 8 months of 2017. The policy rate, currently at 7.0%, or 50 basis points above the rate at the end of 2016, is expected to be adjusted to a more neutral stance in 2018. In view of higher food prices and a rise in the excise tax on fuel, the inflation forecast is raised for 2017. The inflation forecast for 2018 is reduced as the impact of recent one-time price increases will dissipate, and inflationary expectations and supply-side pressures should ease.

Some tightening of current expenditure is expected in 2017 with a new policy framework to reduce contingent liabilities and contain fiscal risks. Greater stimulus is anticipated in 2018. A flexible exchange rate has helped the economy adjust to external shocks, and full compliance with Basel III requirements, including stricter capital adequacy rules, promises to strengthen the financial sector in this highly dollarized economy.

The current account deficit narrowed to an estimated 11.8% of GDP in the first quarter of 2017 from 13.5% in 2016 because of higher remittances and a larger surplus in services, and foreign direct investment rose by 3.4% on increased inflows in construction and finance. In the first half of the year, merchandise exports increased by 30.1% year on year. Meanwhile, imports rose by 8.8% as growth quickened and remittances surged by 19.7% year on year. Higher tourism receipts strongly boosted service exports. Ongoing reform to make shipping and logistical services more competitive and to diversify exports are likely to enhance service exports, bolster foreign investment, and narrow the current account deficit in both 2017 and 2018, the projections for which remain unchanged from *ADO 2017*.

Kyrgyz Republic

Economic expansion reached 6.0% in the first 8 months of 2017, up from no growth in the same period of 2016. Growth outside of the important gold sector was 3.6%. Industry expanded by 26.4%, also reversing contraction in the same period of last year, by 8.3%, and reflecting hefty gains of 91.2% in gold mining, 24.0% in manufacturing, and 12.2% in electricity generation. Construction expanded by 5.6%, supported by a 4.1% rise in investment. Agriculture increased by 1.1%

3.1.4 Selected economic indicators, Georgia (%)

	2017		2018	
	ADO 2017	Update	ADO 2017	Update
GDP growth	3.8	4.2	4.5	4.5
Inflation	4.2	5.7	4.5	4.0
Current acct. bal. (share of GDP)	–12.0	–12.0	–11.5	–11.5

Source: ADB estimates.

on gains in animal husbandry. On the demand side, private consumption is estimated to have grown slightly as higher retail sales, largely from much higher remittances, boosted trade by 3.9%. In view of unexpectedly strong economic performance in the first 8 months, this *Update* raises the growth projection for 2017 and, with the improved outlook for Kazakhstan and the Russian Federation, for 2018 as well.

Average annual inflation stood at 3.0% from January to August 2017, reflecting price increases of 1.3% for food and 6.0% for services, as well as a 0.5% price decline for goods other than food. This *Update* cuts the projection for inflation in 2017 by 1.5 percentage points. Inflation could be higher, though, if further depreciation of the Kazakhstan and Russian Federation currencies drags down the Kyrgyz som, which depreciated by only 0.6% in the first half of the year. With import tariffs projected to rise in 2018 toward rates prevailing in the Eurasian Economic Union, the inflation forecast for 2018 is raised by 1.0 percentage point.

The fiscal deficit is projected to narrow to the equivalent of 3.0% of GDP in 2017 and 2.5% in 2018 as the government strives to restrain expenditure despite a presidential election in October 2017. Raising tax revenues, reducing the wage bill, and streamlining less-essential spending remain high government priorities. External debt, all of it public or publicly guaranteed, declined slightly to 59% of GDP at the end of 2016, but it could rise above 63% in 2017 or 2018 if the som depreciates significantly.

In the first 7 months of 2017, trade expanded by 13.4%, with gains in gold and agricultural products raising exports by 27.1%, while higher imports of oil products, construction materials, and consumer goods lifted imports by 8.7%. The trade deficit reached $1.44 billion, while remittances recovered to $1.09 billion, 28.8% higher than in the first 7 months of 2016. On balance, projected current account deficits for 2017 and 2018 are retained from *ADO 2017*, though weak demand in the Eurasian Economic Union, especially as Kyrgyz products struggle to comply with union veterinary and agricultural standards, could worsen the outlook for trade and the current account balance.

Tajikistan

Growth slowed to 6.0% in the first half of 2017 from 6.5% in the same period of 2016. Industry expanded by 21.3%, up from 12.1% a year earlier on gains of 26.3% in mining, 20.9% in manufacturing, and 16.2% in electricity generation. Primary aluminum output fell by nearly a third because of unstable global prices and damage to several production facilities from a power outage in October 2016, but gold and silver extraction jumped by 70%. Retail trade and services recovered by 3.6% despite low remittances because of earlier recession in the Russian Federation. Favorable weather maintained expansion in agriculture at 6.4%. Meanwhile, capital investment fell by 17.2%, reflecting a 12.6% drop in private sector credit in the first half of 2017 caused by weak demand and continued financial sector problems.

Growth in retail trade and services is projected to remain modest in the second half of the year because of low household income and uncertain remittances. Despite this, expansion in the first half of 2017 motivates this *Update* to raise the growth forecast for 2017 marginally, while retaining the *ADO 2017* forecast for 2018.

3.1.5 Selected economic indicators, Kyrgyz Republic (%)

	2017		2018	
	ADO 2017	*Update 2017*	*ADO 2017*	*Update 2017*
GDP growth	3.0	4.0	3.5	4.0
Inflation	5.0	3.5	4.0	5.0
Current acct. bal. (share of GDP)	–13.0	–13.0	–13.5	–13.5

Source: ADB estimates.

3.1.6 Selected economic indicators, Tajikistan (%)

	2017		2018	
	ADO 2017	*Update 2017*	*ADO 2017*	*Update 2017*
GDP growth	4.8	5.0	5.5	5.5
Inflation	8.0	8.0	7.0	7.5
Current acct. bal. (share of GDP)	–5.5	–5.5	–6.0	–6.0

Source: ADB estimates.

In the first 8 months of 2017, average annual inflation accelerated to 7.7% mainly because the recapitalization of troubled banks helped expand broad money by 17.8%. Consumer prices rose cumulatively by 5.9% in the first half of 2017, up from 3.1% a year earlier, reflecting price increases of 8.3% for food, 1.3% for other goods, and 4.9% for services. To curb inflation, the National Bank of Tajikistan, the central bank, raised the refinancing rate by 5 percentage points in two steps, from 11.0% to 12.5% in February 2017 and to 16.0% in March, and more than doubled open market sales of securities and Treasury bills to rein in liquidity. Despite these measures, the Tajik somoni depreciated by 11.9% against the US dollar in the first half of 2017, mainly because the official exchange rate became realigned with the market rate. This *Update* retains the *ADO 2017* inflation forecast for 2017 and raises it by half a percentage point for 2018, reflecting further increases in electricity tariffs.

State budget expenditures are currently projected to equal 32.9% of GDP in 2017 and 32.8% in 2018. Deficits excluding public investment program loans financed by development partners are now forecast at 4.3% of GDP in 2017 and 3.8% in 2018. However, expected large infrastructure outlays financed by $500 million in proceeds from Tajikistan's first international bond, issued in early September 2017, are likely to widen the deficit. In addition, ongoing asset quality reviews of large banks may reveal further need for government bailouts.

Uncertain remittances contributed to a 15.0% decline in imports in the first half of 2017, while higher industrial production contributed to a 73.4% rise in exports. Expected further currency depreciation and uncertainty about remittances leave the forecasts for the current account deficit unchanged in both 2017 and 2018.

Turkmenistan

Despite low global energy prices and stagnation in Turkmenistan's trading partners, the government reported growth as broadly stable in the first half of 2017 at 6.5%, up from 6.1% in the same period last year. On the supply side, expansion came mainly from outside the hydrocarbon sector, with services rising by 9.0% on gains of 10.9% in transport, 9.4% in trade, 4.1% in construction services, and 10.3% in other services. Agriculture expanded by 3.8%, and industry by 3.2%. On the demand side, public and foreign direct investment supported growth. Gross investment is expected to remain sizable, equal to 42% of GDP, but less than last year, estimated at 47%. This *Update* maintains the *ADO 2017* growth projection for 2017 but reduces the projection for 2018 by half a percentage point.

As the government has slowed investment spending and started to phase out subsidies, the fiscal deficit is projected to nearly halve from the equivalent of 1.3% of GDP in 2016 to 0.7% in 2017 and move to a fiscal surplus of 0.2% in 2018. To consolidate the budget, the authorities have curtailed some public investment projects and gradually reduced subsidies, while protecting social programs. To boost import substitution and promote exports, the government continues to support the private sector outside of the hydrocarbon economy. It reported having already nearly attained the goal of expanding private activity to provide 70% of the non-hydrocarbon economy by 2020.

3.1.7 Selected economic indicators, Turkmenistan (%)

	2017		2018	
	ADO 2017	Update	ADO 2017	Update
GDP growth	6.5	6.5	7.0	6.5
Inflation	6.0	5.7	6.0	5.5
Current acct. bal. (share of GDP)	–15.0	–12.8	–13.0	–12.4

Source: ADB estimates.

To contain inflation, the Central Bank of Turkmenistan aims to slow credit growth and reduce directed lending at concessional rates for large public projects, while maintaining private sector credit. Growth in credit to the economy is expected to slow to 18% this year from 24% in 2016. The central bank further limits cash in circulation by rationing foreign exchange conversion and promoting the use of noncash payments. Broad money growth is projected to slow to 7% in 2017 from 10% last year. The government aims to keep inflation within projections with lower public spending, administrative price controls, and higher domestic production of consumer and industrial goods. In view of these developments, this *Update* reduces *ADO 2017* inflation projections for 2017 and 2018.

Exports are expected to expand with higher gas exports to the People's Republic of China. Although shrinking slightly, imports of high-tech services and machinery will remain substantial to supply large hydrocarbon investments. The current account deficit is now projected to be narrower than forecast in *ADO 2017* for both years. Strong foreign direct investment, estimated to equal 6% of GDP in 2017, will continue to support the development of hydrocarbon infrastructure. External debt is projected to remain sustainable at the equivalent of 21.9% of GDP in 2017 and 23.6% in 2018.

Uzbekistan

According to government sources, GDP grew by 7.0% in the first half of 2017, less than the 7.8% recorded in the same period of 2016. On the supply side, industry excluding construction was the main driver at 7.6%, up from 4.7% a year earlier. Within manufacturing, which is 80% of the industry sector, machinery and equipment production rose by 33.0% as external demand for passenger vehicles increased, particularly in the Russian Federation, lifting machinery exports by 81%. Meanwhile, growth in construction and services was less than in the same period of 2016 as import costs rose on faster depreciation of the Uzbek sum and associated inflation. The resulting slowdown in consumer demand almost halved growth in trade to 7.7% from 14.1% a year earlier. Agriculture expanded by 5.8%, slightly below the 6.8% rate in the same period of 2016, presumably reflecting slower growth in grain and livestock production.

On the demand side, public consumption and investment were the main sources of growth in the first half. Outlays for social security and urban infrastructure rose, while gross fixed capital investment increased by 8.3%, less than the 11.8% recorded a year earlier. As the sum depreciated by 20.3% against the US dollar from January to June 2017, gross fixed capital investment, mainly to import equipment and other capital goods, declined in dollar terms from $7.7 billion in the first half of 2016 to $7.4 billion in the same period of 2017. Mining and manufacturing received the most investment, for continued industrial modernization and public infrastructure development programs. At the same time, the government reported a notable increase in foreign investment, by 13.8% year on year, primarily for hydrocarbons and telecommunications. The main drivers of foreign investment were a recent investment agreement with the Russian Federation energy giant Gazprom, which

3.1.8 Selected economic indicators, Uzbekistan (%)

	2017		2018	
	ADO 2017	Update 2017	ADO 2017	Update 2017
GDP growth	7.0	6.8	7.3	7.5
Inflation	9.5	11.5	10.0	12.0
Current acct. bal. (share of GDP)	0.2	0.1	0.4	0.5

Source: ADB estimates.

expanded regional investment cooperation in Central Asia, and investors' anticipation of upcoming exchange rate reform.

Early September 2017 saw a key reform that liberalized access to foreign exchange and unified the official and parallel foreign exchange markets (Box 3.1.1). As a consequence, the sum was devalued by 92.4% against the US dollar. With the devaluation expected to reduce private consumption and slow expansion in services in the near term, this *Update* trims the projection for growth in 2017. However, because reform is expected to improve the business environment and spur foreign investment over time, the projection for 2018 is upgraded.

The government reported average monthly inflation at 0.9% in the first half of 2017, more than double the 0.4% observed a year earlier. Year on year, inflation is projected at 11.5%, or double the lower end of the monetary authority's target range of 5.7%–6.7%. Inflation resulted from accelerated sum depreciation and a corresponding 5.9% rise in food prices in the first half of 2017. To stem inflation, the central bank raised its policy rate from 9.0% to 14.0% in June 2017, but foreign exchange reform still requires higher inflation projections for 2017 and 2018. The central bank revised its 2017 inflation target on 14 September from 11% to 12% and has indicated that inflation will remain above 10% in 2018.

While expanding public investment, the government maintained a positive fiscal balance, reporting a small surplus equal to 0.1% of GDP. While no data are available on the operations of the sovereign wealth fund, the augmented budget that includes it is expected to have posted a deficit because the fund substantially expanded its domestic investments in 2017 against the backdrop of stalling revenues.

The fiscal authorities offset the rise in public investment and social expenditures with savings from restructuring the public administration system beginning early in 2017. Accordingly, the government reported central budget expenditures in the first half of the year edging down from the equivalent of 22.7% of GDP in 2016 to 21.8%, as central budget revenues declined from 22.8% to 21.9%. This presumably reflected stagnant global prices for key export commodities and higher tax preferences for small and medium-sized enterprises.

Exports of goods and services were reported to have risen by 13.1% in dollar terms in the first half of 2017. Growth came mainly from expansion by 5.5% in services (27.9% of the total), 20.3% in metals, and 81.0% for machinery. Contributing to higher exports were faster sum depreciation and the government's efforts to diversify export markets and promote the export of manufactures. Imports of goods and services grew by 9.2%, reflecting sum depreciation, higher import costs, and continued demand for machinery and metals to supply industrial modernization and public infrastructure development programs. The overall trade balance posted a deficit of $0.1 billion in the first half of the year. However, remittances increased thanks to gradually improving external demand, with remittances from the Russian Federation, the main source, rising to $1.2 billion in the first half of 2017 from $0.9 billion in the same period of 2016. With foreign exchange reform, the revised projections for the current account surplus are slightly narrower for 2017, as higher imports are anticipated, but slightly wider for 2018, as the end of the mandated surrender of foreign exchange is expected to boost exports.

3.1.1 Foreign exchange reform in Uzbekistan

On 2 September 2017, the government initiated comprehensive exchange rate reform to address long-standing difficulties associated with limited access to foreign exchange and requirements to surrender foreign exchange, which brought parallel exchange markets and economic distortions. Repeated business surveys revealed that the lack of access to foreign exchange was for years a key deterrent to foreign investment and private sector development. The September reform thus aimed to promote foreign investment, private sector development, and exports. It gave private firms access to foreign currency at market rates and allowed banks more flexibility in negotiating loans and setting commissions for foreign exchange transactions.

In the months before implementing the reform, the government undertook a series of actions to minimize the impact of the inevitable currency devaluation. To make the banking sector more resilient, in June the government injected $500 million in additional capital into several large state-owned commercial banks. To limit the effect of devaluation on inflation, it introduced a system to monitor prices and tariffs for socially important goods and services, established a fund to stabilize prices for critical foods, and abolished the excise tax on imports of meat and flour products beginning in September.

East Asia

Economic developments were remarkably similar across East Asia in the first half of 2017. Subregional growth accelerated on higher exports and rising business sentiment that lifted investment and consumption. Inflation paused, and the current account weakened. In 2017 and 2018, East Asia's growth rate will be higher than previously forecast as demand strengthens at home and abroad. Inflation will be lower on moderating food price increases, and the current account surplus will narrow further as surging imports outpace rising exports.

Subregional assessment and prospects

Growth in East Asia was higher in the first half of 2017 than previously expected. Expansion accelerated in all economies in the subregion on strengthening exports and regional trade, with knock-on benefits for business sentiment and domestic demand. GDP growth in the People's Republic of China (PRC) rose to 6.9% on favorable external demand, even as investment growth weakened despite continued strong government support for infrastructure. Growth fed on restored political calm in the Republic of Korea, rising coal production in Mongolia, and strong labor markets in Taipei,China and Hong Kong, China.

Inflation remained tame throughout the subregion in the first half of 2017. It moderated in the PRC as pork and vegetable prices plummeted from oversupply, and as administered energy prices were cut. Inflation halved in Hong Kong, China on electricity tariff reductions and slower increases for rent, food, and transport. In the Republic of Korea, rising food prices pushed headline inflation marginally above the central bank target. Mirroring a trend in food prices, inflation returned in Taipei,China. It rose less rapidly in Mongolia than expected on the limited pass-through of the excise tax hike on fuel so far.

East Asia's current account surplus narrowed in the first half of 2017 as imports surged, and despite rising exports. In the PRC, a smaller trade surplus and higher spending by outbound tourists slashed the current account surplus substantially, but the overall balance of payments deficit nevertheless narrowed on lower capital outflows. Current account surpluses also narrowed in the Republic of Korea,

3.2.1 GDP growth, East Asia

2016　　2017　　2018

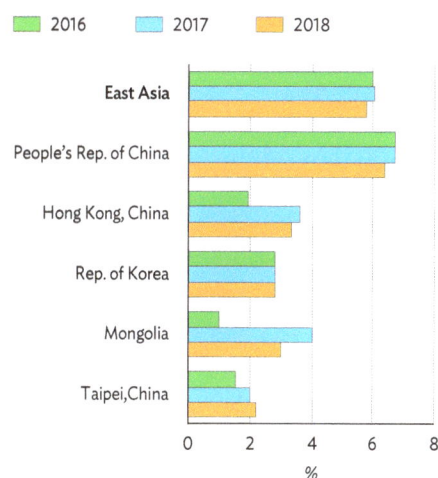

Source: Asian Development Outlook database.

The section on the PRC was written by Jurgen Conrad and Jian Zhuang, and the part on other economies by Cindy Castillejos-Petalcorin, Benno Ferrarini, Xuehui Han, Marthe Hinojales, Amar Lkhagvasuren, Declan Magee, Nedelyn Magtibay-Ramos, and Donghyun Park. Authors are in the East Asia and Economic Research and Regional Cooperation departments of ADB. Subregional assessment and prospects were written by Reza Vaez-Zadeh, consultant, Economic Research and Regional Cooperation Department.

Taipei,China, and—despite steadily increasing tourist arrivals, mainly from the PRC—Hong Kong, China. Mongolia bucked the trend. Its trade surplus improved significantly as coal exports surged, almost halving its current account deficit.

The rising trend in exports and higher market confidence will lift 2017 and 2018 growth rates in all East Asian economies beyond the previous forecasts. The subregional GDP will expand by 6.0% in 2017 and 5.8% in 2018, 0.2 percentage points higher than forecast in April (Figure 3.2.1). In the PRC, expansionary fiscal policy will push growth up by the same value, to 6.7% in 2017 and 6.4% in 2018, and other East Asian economies will see growth accelerate on higher demand from the PRC. Economy-specific factors will further support growth, including rising business confidence in Hong Kong, China and stimulus measures in the Republic of Korea. In Taipei,China, higher investment and rising government infrastructure spending will push up growth in 2017, but the forecast for 2018 is unchanged because of a negative base effect. In Mongolia, growth will benefit from rising coal production and mining-related services.

Inflation in East Asia will be lower than forecast in April, at 1.7% in 2017 and 2.3% in 2018 (Figure 3.2.2). The PRC will see prices rise by 1.7% in 2017 and 2.4% in 2018, less than previously forecast, with food prices having plummeted earlier this year and expected to rise only moderately next year. The forecast for Hong Kong, China is pared down from *ADO 2017* as recent price trends point to moderation and as wage growth slows. Mongolia's inflation forecast is also revised down because a hike in fuel taxes had less impact than expected, and fiscal policy is likely to be less expansionary, in line with the government's commitments under the reform program. Lagging recovery in oil prices will contain price pressures this year in Taipei,China below the earlier forecast, but the outlook for 2018 remains unchanged. In contrast, inflation forecasts for the Republic of Korea are revised up on higher growth, ongoing drought, and impending wage hikes.

The combined current account surplus of the East Asian economies will shrink from the equivalent of 3.0% of subregional GDP in 2016 to 2.0% in 2017 and 1.9% in 2018—both forecasts narrower than those in April (Figure 3.2.3). Exports will rise, but as imports strengthen to meet robust domestic demand the current account surpluses of the PRC, the Republic of Korea, and Hong Kong, China will be narrower than previously forecast, and Mongolia's current account deficit will be higher, both this year and the next. In Taipei,China, currency appreciation relative to trade partners in the first half of the year will accentuate the effect of strengthening domestic demand on imports, narrowing the current account surplus more than previously forecast.

A sustained improvement in global trade would harbor an upside risk to growth forecasts for East Asia. Volatile food prices—in Mongolia and the Republic of Korea, due to drought—and commodity price swings pose upside and downside risks to subregional forecasts depending on circumstances. Meanwhile, the main downside risks to growth are uncertainty regarding the impact of Brexit negotiations on trade, a feared rise in protectionism, fragile regional geopolitical security, and any unexpectedly abrupt monetary tightening in the US.

3.2.2 Inflation, East Asia

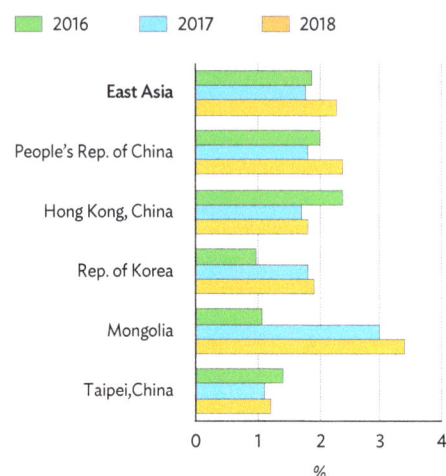

Source: Asian Development Outlook database.

3.2.3 Current account balance, East Asia

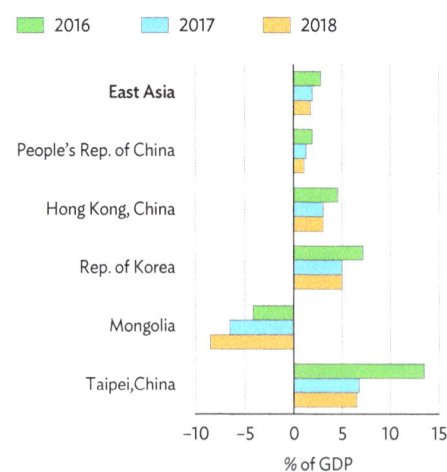

Source: Asian Development Outlook database.

People's Republic of China

The growth forecast is revised up to 6.7% for 2017 and 6.4% for 2018 in response to strong growth so far in 2017 buoyed by expansionary fiscal policy and unanticipated favorable external demand. Inflation will accelerate less than previously forecast, and the current account surplus will narrow faster. Supply-side reform is moving forward but eventual success hinges on a careful balancing of the role of the market and the state during the current economic transition.

Updated assessment

GDP growth accelerated to 6.9% in the first half of 2017 from 6.7% in 2016 (Figure 3.2.4). On the supply side, services remained the main driver, despite real estate and financial services weakening from a high base. Retail trade and transport services boomed, fueling growth in services at 7.7% year on year in the first half of 2017, slightly down from 7.8% in 2016. Industry expanded by 6.4%, up from 6.1% in 2016, despite weaker construction growth, as export- and consumer-oriented industries benefited from surges in demand. Agriculture grew by 3.5%, up from 3.3% in 2016, on better weather. The contribution of services to GDP growth slipped to 3.7 percentage points, that of industry climbed to 2.8 points, and that of agriculture edged up to 0.4 points (Figure 3.2.5). Heavy industry continued to report job losses, but the labor market remained tight nationwide with a stagnant or shrinking supply of labor and the creation of 7.4 million new urban jobs, which pushed the ratio of urban job openings to job seekers to its highest since 2014. The tight labor market has placed some upward pressure on wages.

Domestic demand growth was in line with *ADO 2017* projections in the first 6 months of 2017. Consumption held up well, contributing 4.4 percentage points to GDP growth (Figure 3.2.6). Strong consumption reflected wage growth and more generous social spending on health, education, and pensions, which pushed up household disposal income by 7.3%.

As anticipated in *ADO 2017*, investment growth weakened in the first half of this year, despite continued strong government support for infrastructure, and contributed only 2.3 percentage points to growth, down from 2.5 points in the first half of 2016. Manufacturing investment remained constrained by high corporate debt (Box 3.2.1). Another constraint was excess capacity, though capacity utilization improved to 76.4% in the first half of 2017 from 73.0% in the same period of 2016, owing to ongoing supply-side reform. Industry profits, particularly in upstream industries, have grown strongly since mid-2016 thanks to higher commodity prices, but the profits have gone primarily toward higher wages and debt service, not investment.

Real estate investment is still an important growth driver but less so than in 2016 because of purchase restrictions introduced gradually since September 2016 in many larger cities. However, real estate dodged a sharp downturn as demand rose in smaller cities and the government increased support for shantytown reconstruction. The floor space of newly started construction projects (a proxy for real estate investment in real terms) grew by 7.6% in the first 8 months of 2017, down from 12.2% a year earlier (Figure 3.2.7). Meanwhile, growth in housing sales

3.2.4 Economic growth

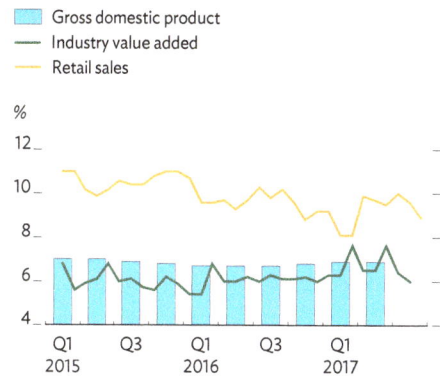

- Gross domestic product
- Industry value added
- Retail sales

Q = quarter.
Source: National Bureau of Statistics.

3.2.5 Supply-side contributions to growth

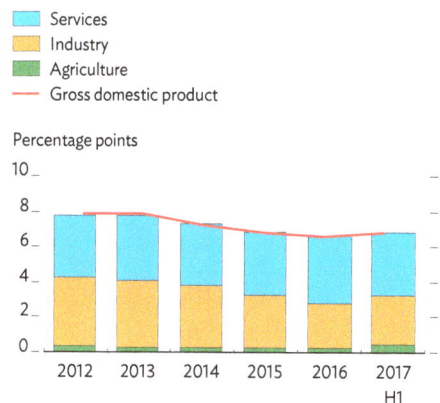

- Services
- Industry
- Agriculture
- Gross domestic product

H = half.
Source: National Bureau of Statistics.

3.2.6 Demand-side contributions to growth

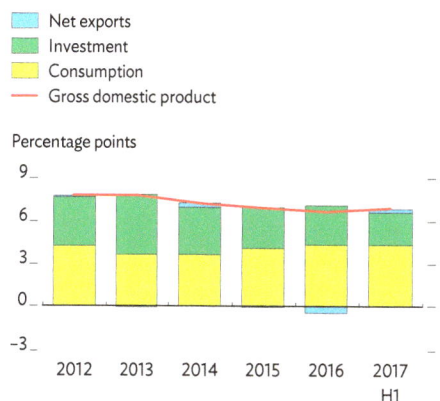

- Net exports
- Investment
- Consumption
- Gross domestic product

H = half.
Source: National Bureau of Statistics.

3.2.1 Evolution of corporate debt in the People's Republic of China

Domestic debt in the PRC rose further to equal 256% of GDP in 2016, with all debt components growing. Government debt rose to 46% of GDP, and household debt to 44%, but both remained moderate by global standards (box figure 1). However, the ratio of corporate debt to GDP increased from 96% in 2008 to 166% in 2016, surpassing that of the US at 73%, the United Kingdom at 77%, Japan at 94%, and the European Union and the Republic of Korea both at 104%. State-owned enterprises account for about 60% of corporate debt.

1 Domestic debt

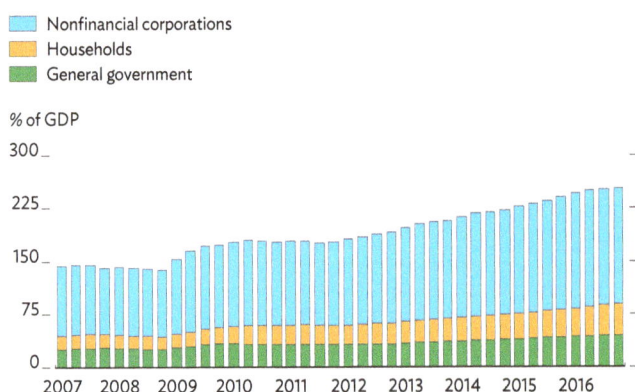

Source: Bank for International Settlements.

This ratio began to decline, however, in the third quarter of 2016 (box figure 2). Factors contributing to this decline include (i) lower corporate net borrowing from banks and nonbanks, partly reflecting greater reliance on equity finance; (ii) local governments borrowing less through local government financing vehicles, which are counted as corporate debt, and more through bond issuance; (iii) progress in resolving highly indebted "zombie" companies through bankruptcy and debt write-off, particularly in economically stronger coastal provinces; and (iv) higher enterprise profits and lower interest rates, which have since 2016 helped to make debt more affordable and enabled corporations to meet their repayment obligations

more easily. Profits surged by 21.2% in the first 7 months of 2017 after increasing by 8.5% in 2016 and declining by 2.3% in 2015, owing mainly to a sharp pickup in raw material prices. Further, the declining trend during 2011–2016 in industrial enterprises' return on assets and equity bottomed out in the first half of 2017, with return on assets increasing to 6.8% from 6.4% in 2016 and return on equity to 15.4% from 14.6%.

Despite these improvements, corporate debt remains a concern. First, some of the factors that mitigated debt problems over recent quarters, including rising profits and low interest rates, may not be sustained. Second, debt continues to be misallocated to sectors that are unproductive or suffer excess capacity, which undermines productivity and potential GDP growth and, over the medium to long term, raises questions about debt sustainability. Third, double-digit increases in credit growth are just too high to be sustainable and threaten to spark a proliferation of nonperforming loans. That said, the risk of a traditional debt crisis is low in the PRC because debt is predominantly in domestic currency, held by domestic investors, backed by a high savings rate, and used for asset-creating investment rather than consumption. Further, the government has capital controls in place and exercises pervasive control over borrowers and lenders.

2 Nonfinancial corporate debt

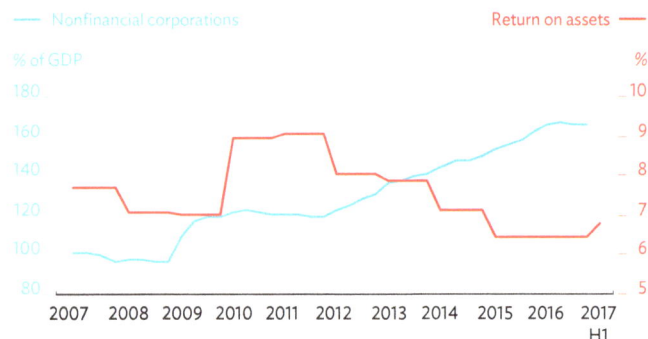

H = half.
Source: Bank for International Settlements.

lost steam but, sustained by mortgage loans and the government's purchase of apartments for transfer to low-income households, still outpaced housing completion. Unsold floor space was thus down by 12.0% year on year in the first 8 months, in line with a key objective of supply-side reform.

Net exports turned around to contribute 0.3 percentage points to GDP growth in the first half of 2017. The turnaround was caused by a surge in export demand from developed and developing economies alike for both capital- and labor-intensive goods. Demand was particularly pronounced from commodity-exporting economies as rising commodity prices and export volumes spurred their demand for imports, benefiting the PRC as the world's largest exporter and the nexus of an extensive and diverse trade network.

Inflation remained moderate. Rising on higher costs for services that reflected strong demand and ongoing price liberalization, core inflation, which excludes food and energy, increased from an average of 1.6% in 2016 to 2.1% in the first 8 months of 2017 (Figure 3.2.8). By contrast, headline inflation moderated to 1.5% from 2.0% in 2016 as pork and vegetable prices plummeted with oversupply. Food accounts for a third of the consumer price index. Administered energy prices were cut as oil prices eased. Purchase restrictions helped further moderate home price increases in the largest cities. Prices in the top 70 cities rose by an average of 4.3% year on year in the first 7 months of 2017, less than half the 10.1% rate in 2016, but many smaller towns registered solid increases. Average producer price inflation hit 6.4%, reversing 1.3% deflation in 2016, as industrial input costs—heavily weighted in the PRC producer price index—remained elevated with global commodity prices rising and capacity being rationalized in upstream industries such as steel and coal. Corporate profits and the ability to service debt improved, particularly in highly indebted heavy industries and state-owned enterprises, fulfilling another key objective of official supply-side reform.

Monetary policy continued its delicate balancing act of clamping down on speculative nonbank credit and containing public enterprise debt, while ensuring adequate financing to the rest of the economy to support the government's growth objective. To this end, the government employed a mix of monetary and regulatory policies. In September 2016, it started reducing its liquidity injections through open market operations, prompting domestic interest rates to rise across the yield curve, though bank deposit and loan rates were unchanged (Figure 3.2.9). Early this year, the People's Bank of China, the central bank, raised rates in several steps for its repurchase transactions and various medium- and long-term lending facilities. The authorities tightened regulations on bank lending to nonbank financial institutions to forestall regulatory arbitrage. With such lending sharply down as a result, nonbanks offered less credit and investment. This, together with higher yields, reduced the issuance of corporate bonds, a key investment vehicle for nonbank financial institutions.

As noted above, bank deposit and loan rates were kept unchanged, causing real rates to fall. This lowered financing costs for enterprises and sparked a surge in bank loans, particularly long-term loans to enterprises, which have been further facilitated by rising liquidity injections from the central bank since May 2017. Total social financing—a broad credit aggregate that comprises bank and some nonbank credit as well as equity finance—grew 13.2% year on year in the first 7 months of 2017, the same rate as in 2016 (Figure 3.2.10). Growth in domestic finance slowed a bit when taking into account nonbank credit not captured by total social financing, including finance provided by asset management companies and government bond issuance. In sum, movement in financial aggregates this year reconfirmed that the goal of central bank intervention is to make financial intermediation less opaque and to deleverage financial institutions, not to reduce bank liquidity.

3.2.7 Real estate market indicators

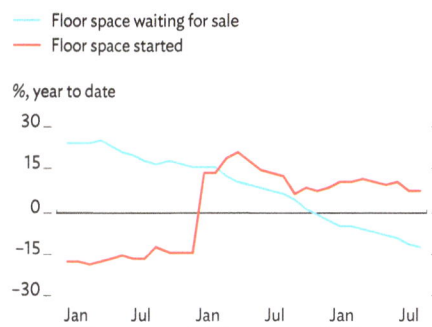

Sources: National Bureau of Statistics; National Development and Reform Commission; ADB estimates.

3.2.8 Monthly inflation

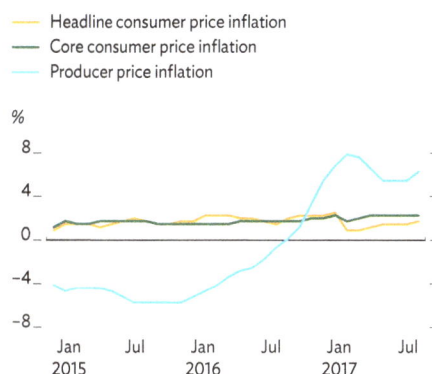

Source: National Bureau of Statistics.

3.2.9 Interest rates

Source: People's Bank of China.

Fiscal policy was expansionary in early 2017. The budget recorded a deficit equal to 2.4% of GDP in the first half of 2017, up from 1.1% in the corresponding period of 2016. The main reason was that the local government budget deficit before central government transfers rose to 10.2% of GDP from 8.1% in the first half of 2016. Revenues strengthened on higher land sales, corporate profits, and external trade, but higher income was more than offset by a sharp pickup in expenditure on education, health, and other social services. The widening budget deficit may reflect, aside from an expansionary fiscal stance, progress in accelerating heretofore back-loaded expenditure and in bringing off-budget spending on budget, though off-budget infrastructure spending remains sizeable.

The strong rebound of export growth in the first half of 2017 was outweighed by an even greater increase in imports, mostly a price effect, which narrowed the trade surplus. As higher spending by outbound tourists exacerbated a deficit in the services account, the current account surplus plummeted from the equivalent of 2.1% of GDP in the first half of 2016 to 1.3% a year later, or $71.3 billion.

Capital outflows slowed substantially thanks to capital controls and a shift in sentiment toward the renminbi on account of US dollar weakness, higher yields on domestic financial instruments, and an improved domestic growth outlook. This helped narrow the overall balance of payment deficit and ease its drain on official reserves. Taking into account the higher US dollar value of reserves held in other currencies, the central bank reported reserves rising by $90.7 billion in the first 8 months of 2017, climbing to $3.2 trillion. In May 2017, the authorities eased controls on capital and individual foreign exchange purchases. However, restrictions on offshore acquisitions, especially of enterprises outside of companies' core businesses, were further tightened.

Strong downward pressure on the renminbi since mid-2015 eased this year (Figure 3.2.11). Amid some volatility, the renminbi has appreciated by 4.8% against the US dollar but depreciated by 1.2% in nominal effective terms (against a trade-weighted basket of currencies) since the end of 2016. In real effective terms (taking inflation into account) it weakened by 3.2%, returning to its 2014 value.

Prospects

GDP growth forecasts are revised up to 6.7% for 2017 and 6.4% for 2018, reflecting growth that was higher than expected in the first half of 2017, though momentum weakened in July and August (Figure 3.2.12). Consumption will remain the main growth driver as incomes rise strongly and consumer confidence hits its highest on record.

Investment is on a decelerating trend and will likely remain so due to structural and cyclical factors. Real estate investment will support growth but less so than in 2016 because of new purchase restrictions in many municipalities and somewhat reduced access to mortgage loans (Figure 3.2.13). Investment growth in capital-intensive industries with excess capacity and high debt has been weak or negative for years. This cannot be fully compensated by strong investment in emerging industries, consumer-oriented industries, and services because they

3.2.10 Growth of money supply and total social financing

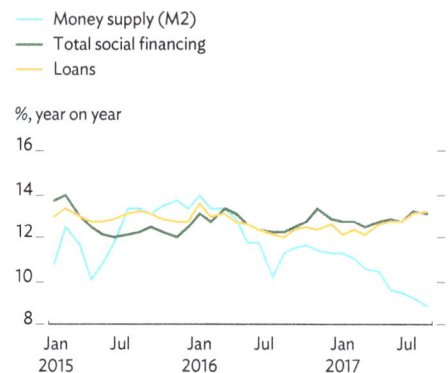

— Money supply (M2)
— Total social financing
— Loans

Sources: People's Bank of China; ADB estimates.

3.2.11 Exchange rates

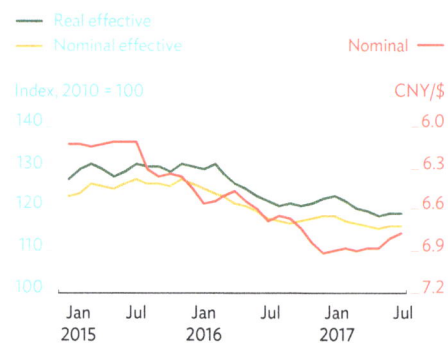

— Real effective
— Nominal effective
Nominal —

Sources: Bank for International Settlements; State Administration of Foreign Exchange.

3.2.12 GDP growth

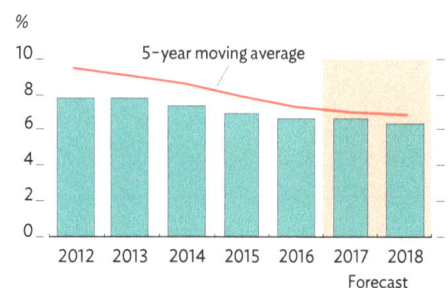

Source: Asian Development Outlook database.

are much less capital intensive. High corporate profit growth in recent months has not yet translated into higher investment and, in any case, has already begun to weaken along with the commodity price increases that generated it. Further, notwithstanding the recent surge in exports, the business outlook for export-oriented industries remains uncertain, inhibiting investment growth in them. Government investment in infrastructure cannot fully compensate for the falloff in investment elsewhere, as infrastructure outlays account for only one-fifth of total investment. Thus, the share of investment in GDP, though still high at above 40%, will continue to fall.

Net exports will recover to contribute to GDP growth in 2017 but subtract from it again in 2018 as, absent another upturn in global growth and trade, the boost to exports in 2017 runs its course. Further, strong import growth in US dollar terms will narrow the trade and current account surpluses more than projected in *ADO 2017*.

Inflation forecasts are revised down to 1.7% for 2017, as local food prices have fallen sharply, and to 2.4% for 2018, both well below the government ceiling of 3.0% (Figure 3.2.14). The key drivers remain strong consumer demand, higher wages, continued price deregulation, and spillover from global commodity price increases. Volatile food prices harbor a risk to the inflation forecast.

Monetary and financial policies will likely remain broadly unchanged over the forecast period. The National Financial Work Conference, which sets policy for the coming 5 years, reemphasized in July 2017 that the financial sector needs to serve the real economy and that corporate financing costs should be lowered. It also established a commission to better coordinate the activities of financial regulators and the central bank, which will play the leading role in macroprudential regulation and in maintaining stability in the financial sector. Hence, expectations over the forecast period are not for monetary tightening per se but for continued efforts to strengthen financial regulation to reduce risk while providing long-term lending to the economy.

The financial conference in July singled out state-owned enterprises (SOEs) as the main culprits for high corporate debt. As reform toward mixed ownership and SOE mergers offers only limited potential to ease their indebtedness, more far-reaching reform is expected in 2018. Reform could include allowing more bankruptcies and even privatization, but it should also aim to rationalize the close relationships among SOEs, state-owned or -controlled financial institutions, and local governments—relationships that created the SOE debt problem in the first place. Further, the conference urged that local government officials be held accountable for borrowings even after they leave their posts. This, together with additional regulatory constraints on off-budget borrowing in place since April 2017, should limit local government expenditure, thus making fiscal policy less expansionary and therefore likely to slow growth. A precondition for the success of reform hinges on a careful balancing of the role of the market and the state during the current economic transition. As lending rates remain low even as nominal GDP and profits increase, the environment for tackling corporate debt is now more favorable than it has been in recent years.

3.2.13 Growth of housing mortgage loans

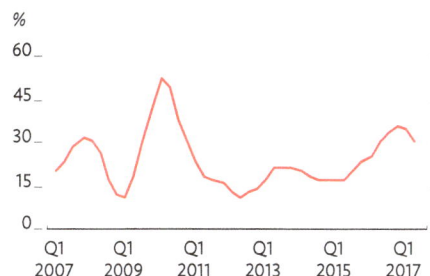

Source: People's Bank of China.

3.2.1 Selected economic indicators, People's Republic of China (%)

	2017		2018	
	ADO 2017	Update	ADO 2017	Update
GDP growth	6.5	6.7	6.2	6.4
Inflation	2.4	1.7	2.8	2.4
Current acct. bal. (share of GDP)	1.8	1.4	1.7	1.2

Source: ADB estimates.

3.2.14 Inflation

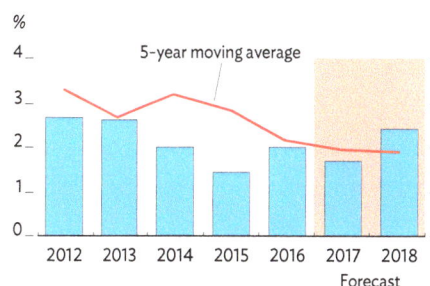

Source: Asian Development Outlook database.

The government used the July conference to reconfirm its commitment to its strategic objectives of exchange rate liberalization and capital account openness. Further exchange rate liberalization, such as widening the ±2% trading band for the renminbi, is possible in the forecast period, particularly if recent stability in foreign exchange markets and a favorable balance of payments are sustained. Such a move would further free up official reserves and allow monetary policy to focus on the domestic objectives of preserving price stability and supporting economic activity, make it easier for the government to manage larger capital flows, and prepare the ground for further easing of capital controls. It should also help to invigorate renminbi internationalization, which has been in retreat since mid-2015, with less than 1.7% of all international payments worldwide now settled in renminbi, down from nearly 3.0% in mid-2015. Experience with other international currencies has shown that exchange rates for a fully liberalized renminbi could be determined by market forces without causing economic or financial instability.

Sustained improvement in global trade would harbor an upside risk to the forecast, while a slower pace of commodity price increases would be a downside risk, as it could undercut recently strong export demand from commodity-exporting economies. Other downside risks are the specter of global trade protectionism and renewed large capital outflows triggered by large US interest rate increases and resulting US dollar strength. A domestic downside risk to the forecast would be a deepening slowdown in investment growth, perhaps enough to reset baseline growth forecasts for the next 2 years, though the government would have monetary and fiscal tools to push back if needed.

Another domestic risk is that regulatory tightening could cause liquidity shortages and the failure of weaker financial institutions, engendering a systemic crisis. The likelihood of such a risk materializing is low, however, as substantial progress has been made in reducing financial flows between banks and nonbanks and in making intermediation channels more transparent. Further, the central bank has acknowledged that removing risk from the financial sector would mean cutting credit availability and reducing liquidity in the banking system, which can hurt weaker banks. It stands ready to address liquidity shortages as needed. Once implemented, the decisions made at the National Financial Work Conference will further mitigate financial risks by providing an institutional framework for sector regulators to work together to head off incidents and contain their fallout.

Other economies

Hong Kong, China

Steadily strengthening demand, both local and external, pushed economic growth in the first half of 2017 to 4.0% from 1.4% a year earlier. Private consumption rose by 4.6%, helped by rising incomes, wealth effects from higher asset prices, and a strong labor market buoyed by low 3.2% unemployment. In line with market sentiment that improved in tandem with export demand, gross fixed capital formation rebounded by 7.0%, after contracting by 6.8% last year, as building and construction strengthened and as equipment acquisition picked up in the second quarter after 2 quarters of decline.

Export performance rebounded strongly from a disappointing result last year to expand in real terms by 7.4% year on year, driven by stronger regional trade. Exports of services rose by 2.6%, after a 5.8% drop last year, on growth in cross-border trade and finance. Despite an unsteady recovery in tourist arrivals, an uptick in the second quarter improved retail sales, the first such expansion after a long spell of contraction recorded in every quarter since early 2015. The current account surplus stood equal to 2.7% of GDP in the first half of 2017, similar to last year, even as import growth slightly outpaced export growth. Consumer prices reversed their 0.1% decline in February, which reflected mainly seasonal factors and electricity tariff reductions, to rise by 2.0% in the second quarter as transport costs and rents increased moderately. Over the first 8 months of 2017, inflation halved to 1.4% from a year earlier with smaller increases for food and rent, as well as easing external price pressures.

Growth forecasts are revised up markedly in light of robust growth in the first half and continuing strength in leading indicators. The latest business survey indicates rising optimism as favorable global trade dynamics buoy exports. The purchasing managers' index, though falling to 49.7 in August after a strong reading in July, also suggests that more firms expect higher output in the near-term. Further, domestic demand is likely to remain robust in the second half of 2017 even with growth in fixed investment moderating from its strong first half as base effects wane. Inflation forecasts are nevertheless pared by 0.3 percentage points from *ADO 2017* as price trends point to moderation and wage growth slows.

Current account surpluses are now expected to be narrower in both 2017 and 2018 than previously forecast as imports strengthen to meet robust domestic demand, outweighing an expected recovery in tourist arrivals and rising exports signaled by strengthening export orders. Risks to the forecast are uncertainties stemming from Brexit negotiations, regional geopolitical developments, and US monetary policy normalization, which could have implications for mortgage rates in the local property market.

3.2.2 Selected economic indicators, Hong Kong, China (%)

| | 2017 | | 2017 | |
	ADO 2017	Update	ADO 2017	Update
GDP growth	2.0	3.6	2.1	3.2
Inflation	2.0	1.7	2.1	1.8
Current acct. bal. (share of GDP)	3.1	2.9	3.1	2.9

Source: ADB estimates.

Republic of Korea

GDP grew by 2.8% in the first half of 2017, slower than in the same period of 2016, as export growth weakened. A resurgence of some merchandise exports, particularly of semiconductors and petrochemicals, is now in its eighth month but was outweighed by weak exports of car parts, electronic components, and services, which lowered export growth overall. Net exports declined in real terms as import growth surged on double-digit rises for machinery and mineral fuels, outpacing export growth. Domestic demand strengthened as investment growth accelerated to 12.0%. Outlays for equipment to manufacture semiconductors were their highest since late 2010, cushioning drag from falling government investment. Private consumption grew by 2.1% as purchases of durable goods and services increased, boosted by higher incomes and receding political tensions that helped to buoy consumer sentiment to a 78-month high in July.

On the supply side, industry propelled expansion in the first half of 2017, growing by 4.3%—its fastest in 6 years—on both construction and manufacturing. The Nikkei manufacturing purchasing managers' index rose briefly to 50.1 in June, and even as it subsided to 49.9 in August optimism held as new orders continued to rise. Services were less robust, rising by 1.8%, and agriculture declined as it reeled under an ongoing drought.

In the first 8 months of the year, consumer price inflation averaged 2.1%, a tad higher than the target of 1.9% for the year set by the Bank of Korea, the central bank, because of increases for agricultural products. Core inflation, which excludes food and energy, fell slightly to 1.5%. In view of minimal inflationary pressure, the central bank sought to stimulate demand by keeping the policy rate at its historic low of 1.25%, unchanged since June 2016. The new administration enacted a $10 billion supplementary budget allocated to job creation, support for local governments, and income subsidies for the elderly.

An upward revision to the growth forecast for 2017 hinges on an expected revival in consumer demand, the stimulus measures mentioned above, and an improved global outlook that promises continued bullish exports. A smaller upward revision for 2018 yields a sustained rate. Growth will be further supported by more rapid expansion in the PRC, higher consumption as temporary public workers acquire a regularized status, and a 16% boost to the minimum wage next year. It will be tempered by financial instability in response to rising US interest rates and by domestic concerns over mounting household debt.

The inflation forecast is revised up for both 2017 and 2018 owing to improved demand and economic growth, an anticipated oil price recovery, drought, and impending wage hikes.

As the expected rise in exports will likely be countered by the ongoing recovery for merchandise imports as domestic demand strengthens, forecasts are lowered for the current account surplus this year and next. Other downside risks to the growth forecast stem from a renegotiation of the free trade agreement with the US, trade tensions with the PRC, and sharpening geopolitical risks.

3.2.3 Selected economic indicators, Republic of Korea (%)

	2017		2018	
	ADO 2017	Update	ADO 2017	Update
GDP growth	2.5	2.8	2.7	2.8
Inflation	1.7	1.8	1.8	1.9
Current acct. bal. (share of GDP)	5.8	5.0	5.3	5.0

Source: ADB estimates.

Mongolia

The economy grew by 5.3% in the first half of 2017, recovering strongly from only 1.2% growth in 2016. Services lifted GDP by 4.3 percentage points, and agriculture by 1.0 point. Coal production soared, with coal exports increasing by more than fourfold. However, mining as a whole slumped as copper concentrate production languished, causing the larger industry sector to subtract marginally from growth. On the demand side, investment, mainly into mining, contributed 13.2 percentage points to growth, and consumption added 1.6 points. Net exports subtracted almost 9.6 points as imports rose by 37.4% in tandem with mining investment.

The fiscal deficit for the first half of the year plunged by 34.1%, to the equivalent of 5.8% of GDP, as a 41.1% surge in revenues stemming mainly from strong export performance dwarfed a 9.6% rise in expenditures. As coal exports surged in the first half, the trade surplus widened by 69.5% year on year, and the current account deficit narrowed by 42.8% to equal 5.6% of GDP. Gross reserves at the end of June remained unchanged from the end of 2016 at $1.3 billion, or cover for 2.6 months of imports. Reflecting these developments, the Mongolian togrog appreciated by 5.6% against the US dollar in the year to June.

Inflation averaged 3.0% in the first half of the year as togrog depreciation last year began to affect prices. In June, the Bank of Mongolia, the central bank, lowered its policy rate by 2.0 percentage points to 12.0% as terms of trade improved and short-term external debt pressures eased. Broad money surged by 21.1% in the first 6 months, mainly on the improved balance of payments. The ratio of loans past due declined slightly to 6.2%, but the nonperforming loan ratio remained at 8.8%.

Growth forecasts are raised in light of the rapid expansion in coal production, continued strong demand for coal in the PRC, and spillover to mining-related services. The government's reform plans, supported by a 3-year stabilization program approved by the International Monetary Fund in May, are also helping restore business confidence. Together with commitments from other development partners, the extended fund facility provides Mongolia with $5.5 billion. A recent review of its implementation showed that progress is being made under the program toward enabling sustainable inclusive growth without the boom–bust cycles of the past.

The inflation forecast is revised down as a higher excise tax on fuel did not push up fuel prices as expected. With strong imports set to continue in the second half, the current account deficit is now seen widening this year and next.

Downside risks to the growth forecasts are vulnerability to commodity price downswings, prevailing drought that may affect crop and livestock production, and political instability negatively affecting the implementation of the stabilization program. Important upside risks are stronger growth in the PRC, shocks affecting its domestic coal supply, and rising copper prices. The same factors could undermine forecasts for inflation and the current account balance.

3.2.4 Selected economic indicators, Mongolia (%)

	2017		2018	
	ADO 2017	Update	ADO 2017	Update
GDP growth	2.5	4.0	2.0	3.0
Inflation	3.5	3.0	3.9	3.4
Current acct. bal. (share of GDP)	−2.1	−6.4	−6.3	−8.5

Source: ADB estimates.

Taipei,China

GDP growth accelerated in the first half of 2017 to 2.4% year on year, up from 0.5% in the first half of 2016, on both external and domestic demand. Net exports contributed 0.5 percentage points to growth as exports rose in real terms by 6.1%, against a 6.0% rise in imports. Despite a small decrease in government consumption expenditure, domestic demand contributed 1.7 percentage points to growth, with equal contributions from consumption and investment. Rising wage growth supported private consumption, the increase in average monthly earnings reaching 6.6% year on year in May. Strong external demand boosted investment.

The GDP growth forecast for 2017 is revised up based on sustained exports of semiconductors above expectations, with total export orders rising by 11.2% in the first half of the year. Other factors are higher investment, mainly in machinery and equipment, and rising government infrastructure spending. The growth forecast for 2018 is unchanged as the base effect of higher 2017 growth could offset the positive impact of stronger growth forecast for the euro area this year and next.

Inflation returned, albeit less than anticipated in April in *ADO 2017*, as 0.1% deflation year on year in February reversed to reach 1.0% inflation in August. The trend mirrored a rise in food prices that accelerated as heavy rains destroyed vegetable crops, but the food price increase also fell short of the April forecast. Wholesale price inflation dropped steadily from 2.7% year on year in January to –1.8% in June, rising back to 1.0% in August. Reflecting these trends and a lagging recovery in oil prices, the inflation projection for 2017 is revised down slightly. Inflation is expected to accelerate modestly in 2018, for which the forecast is unchanged.

The current account surplus fell from the equivalent of 13.3% of GDP in the second quarter of 2016 to 12.8% a year later as import growth outpaced export growth, narrowing the trade surplus. Export demand surged in the second quarter of 2017, but local currency appreciation in the first half of the year, notably by 6.4% against the US dollar, will likely dampen the impact on the trade balance. Thus, the narrowing trend in the current account surplus is expected to continue this year and next, in line with forecasts in *ADO 2017*.

As expected at the beginning of the year, a forward-looking infrastructure investment program was enacted in July 2017, setting the stage for major infrastructure spending in the coming months. An unexpectedly rapid rise in the pace of expenditure is an upside risk to the forecast. The main downside risk is that continuing strong appreciation of the local currency against the US dollar may eventually harm exports, especially with the waning of current high demand from the PRC for semiconductors.

3.2.5 Selected economic indicators, Taipei,China (%)

	2017		2018	
	ADO 2017	Update	ADO 2017	Update
GDP growth	1.8	2.0	2.2	2.2
Inflation	1.3	1.1	1.2	1.2
Current acct. bal. (share of GDP)	6.8	6.8	6.5	6.5

Source: ADB estimates.

South Asia

Strong growth endures, but forecasts are downgraded from *ADO 2017* to 6.7% in 2017 (as in 2016), with acceleration to 7.0% in 2018. Revision reflects lower growth expectations for India in both years. Projections for inflation are lowered to 4.2% in 2017 and 4.7% in 2018 mainly because of reviving agriculture and despite an uptick in global commodity prices. The current account deficit is now forecast widening to 1.6% of subregional GDP in 2017 and 1.8% in 2018 as export growth underperforms the Asian norm.

Subregional assessment and prospects

This *Update* lowers GDP growth forecasts to 6.7% from 7.0% for 2017 and to 7.0% from 7.2% for 2018 (Figure 3.3.1). While slightly lower growth is expected in heavily weighted India, the outlook for most South Asian economies either meets or exceeds the April forecasts. Uncontrollable events such as bad weather affected the few exceptions.

In India, GDP growth slowed from the last quarter of FY2016 (ended 31 March 2017) to 5.7% in the first quarter of FY2017, with private consumption, agriculture, and industry weakening. Industry growth decelerated to 1.6% as manufacturers slashed production to clear inventories before the 1 July introduction of a goods and services tax (GST). The outlook for the remaining 3 quarters of FY2017 is positive. A new insolvency tribunal promises to curb stressed assets at commercial banks and free up new lending. At 7.0%, growth will be lower than forecast because of lingering effects from a currency exchange program late in 2016 that caused cash shortages in the first quarter, transitory disruption as firms adjusted to the GST, and muted private and state government investment. As government efforts to resolve nonperforming loans yield results, more credit will flow to industry, but growth in fixed investment will remain subdued. With teething issues resolved and the GST boosting growth and efficiency, growth is expected to improve to 7.4% in FY2018 but still underperform the earlier forecast.

In Bangladesh and Pakistan, estimated growth in FY2017 (ended 30 June 2017) exceeded forecasts on robust manufacturing and services and on revived agriculture. The growth forecast for Bangladesh in

3.3.1 GDP growth, South Asia

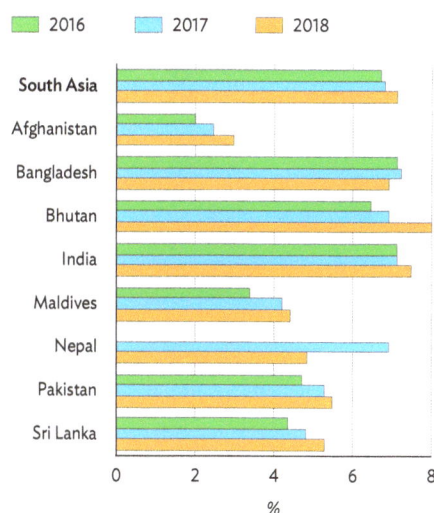

Source: *Asian Development Outlook* database.

The subregional assessment and prospects were written by Masato Nakane. The section on Bangladesh was written by Jyotsana Varma, Md. Golam Mortaza, and Barun K. Dey; India by Johanna Boestel and Abhijit Sen Gupta; Pakistan by Guntur Sugiyarto, Farzana Noshab, and Ali Khadija; and other economies by Tadateru Hayashi, Soon Chan Hong, Savindi Jayakody, Manbar Singh Khadka, David Oldfield, and Hasitha Wickremasinghe, as well as consultants Macrina Mallari and Remedios Baes-Espineda. Authors are in the Central and West Asia and South Asia departments of ADB.

FY2018 is maintained at 6.9%, slightly below the official estimate for the previous fiscal year, as income growth in agriculture and wage employment slows and as improvement in worker remittances remains slow. Marked expansion in infrastructure and energy investments will drive growth in Pakistan to 5.5%, unchanged from the *ADO 2017* forecast.

In Nepal, growth at 6.9% exceeded the forecast for FY2017 (ended 15 July 2017) on recovery from earthquakes in 2015 and consequent stagnation in FY2016. Nepal's growth forecast for FY2018 is downgraded to 4.7% as excessive rain along its southern tier depresses agriculture and implementation delays curb planned government capital expenditure.

Bhutan looks strong in FY2017 (ended 30 June 2017) and FY2018, but growth forecasts are downgraded to 6.9% for FY2017 and 8.0% for FY2018 as geological problems limit construction on two large hydropower projects.

In Sri Lanka, drought and floods depressed agriculture, and industry growth slowed, holding growth in the first half of 2017 to 3.9% year on year, unchanged from the 2016 outcome and dragging the forecast for the year down half a percentage point to 4.5%. The forecast for 2018 is maintained at 5.0% in light of an economic adjustment program agreed with the International Monetary Fund. In Maldives, stronger tourism poises GDP growth to beat *ADO 2017* forecasts. Afghanistan enjoyed a slight pickup in growth in the first half of 2017, but poor security continues to restrain investment and consumption; some progress on policy and governance reform sustains *ADO 2017* growth forecasts.

Inflation in the subregion is now forecast lower at 4.2% in 2017 and 4.7% in 2018, mainly reflecting slower growth and inflation expected in India (Figure 3.3.2). Forecasts for most other economies are maintained or only slightly revised because of weather-affected agriculture. In Sri Lanka, severe drought and flooding in the first half, combined with higher GST rates and currency depreciation, will push inflation higher in 2017, but a high base effect and firmer credit policy will reverse this trend in 2018. In Nepal, normalized trade flows and a bountiful harvest brought sharply lower inflation in FY2017, below the projection. Maldives has used price controls and subsidies to limit the pass-through of global commodity price increases and keep inflation low.

The combined current account deficit in South Asia is now forecast equal to 1.6% of aggregate GDP in 2017 and 1.8% in 2018, slightly wider than forecast in April (Figure 3.3.3). Deficit forecasts for India are maintained; for Pakistan widened from 2.1% of GDP to 4.0% in FY2017 and from 2.5% to 4.2% in FY2018, mainly on marked import expansion; and for Bangladesh slightly narrowed for FY2017 and widened for FY2018, with weak exports and remittances recovering but food restocking likely to buoy imports in FY2018. Deficit forecasts for Sri Lanka are widened to 3.5% of GDP in FY2017 and 2.5% in FY2018 as weak exports strengthen and a heavy oil bill moderates with less need for thermal electric power generation. In Nepal, worker remittances and travel receipts suffice to keep the deficit in check and narrow forecasts for FY2017 and FY2018. Forecasts for deficits in Bhutan are lowered

3.3.2 Inflation, South Asia

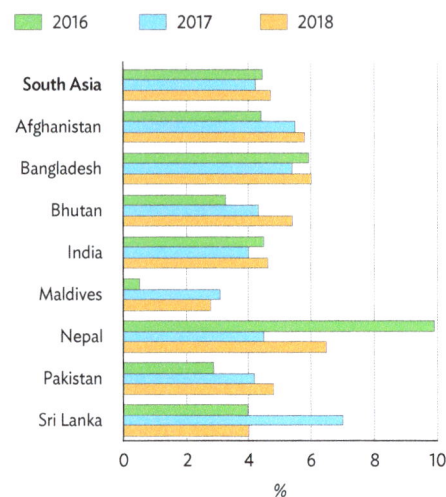

Source: *Asian Development Outlook* database.

3.3.3 Current account balance, South Asia

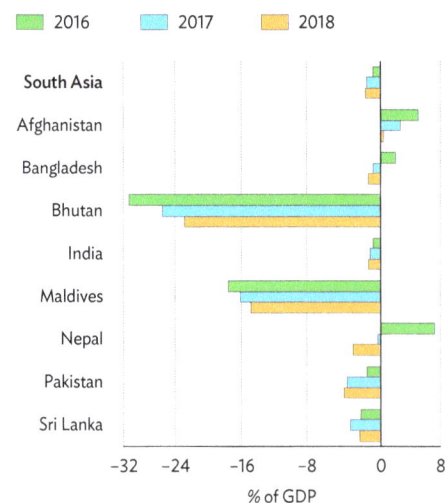

Source: *Asian Development Outlook* database.

for FY2017 as interrupted construction cuts import requirements. Maldives will have lower deficits on improved tourism earnings in both years. Grants keep the Afghanistan current account marginally in surplus.

Bangladesh

Growth in FY2017 (ended 30 June 2017) was higher than expected as consumption picked up in response to rising income, and as public investment strengthened. Inflation was lower than projected, and the current account moved into deficit, as expected, with a wider trade deficit and lower remittances. For FY2018, this *Update* retains the *ADO 2017* growth projection but anticipates slightly lower inflation and a larger current account deficit. Recent flooding is unlikely to affect growth, which could improve if infrastructure development accelerates. Mobilizing domestic revenue remains a priority.

Updated assessment

Preliminary official estimates put FY2017 GDP growth at 7.2%, slightly higher than 7.1% in FY2016 and the *ADO 2017* projection of 6.9% (Figure 3.3.4). A decline in remittances notwithstanding, higher farm and wage income lifted private consumption and growth, as did an uptick in public investment. Despite improved power supply, which is vital for investment, private investment slowed. Net exports subtracted from growth as the volume of exports stagnated and imports expanded. A significant statistical discrepancy in preliminary GDP estimates renders tentative any analysis of expenditure contributions to growth.

On the supply side, agriculture grew by 3.4% in FY2017, up from 2.8% a year earlier, as crop production responded to higher prices. At 6.5%, services growth was slightly stronger, mainly on advances in wholesale and retail trade, transport, and public services. Industry growth moderated to 10.5% from 11.1% as activity at large and medium-sized enterprises slowed, weighed down by a depressed garment industry.

Average inflation softened further to 5.4% in FY2017 from 5.9% in FY2016, coming in below the *ADO 2017* projection of 6.1% with lower global commodity prices and slower growth in money supply. Inflation rose to 5.9% year on year in June 2017 from 5.5% a year earlier (Figure 3.3.5). Food inflation accelerated over most of FY2017, broadly in line with developments in global food prices, and spiked to 7.5% in June as floods and landslides in parts of the country caused crop losses, marketing problems, and consequent rice shortages. Nonfood inflation trended lower from its peak in January 2016 following sizeable adjustments to administered prices for electricity and gas. With a high base effect ending in January 2017, nonfood inflation rose only slightly to 3.7% year on year in June 2017, substantially moderating overall inflation.

Broad money growth slowed to 10.9% in FY2017 from 16.4% a year earlier, well below a monetary program target of 15.5% (Figure 3.3.6). Growth in private credit slowed to 15.7% from 16.8%, falling short of the 16.5% program target. Bangladesh Bank, the central bank, provided

3.3.4 Demand-side contributions to growth

- Consumption
- Investment
- Net exports
- Statistical discrepancy
- Gross domestic product

Percentage points

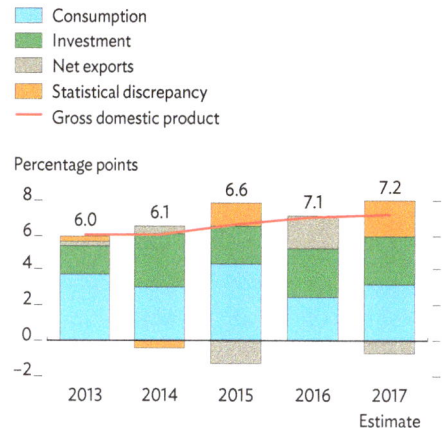

Note: Years are fiscal years ending on 30 June of that year.
Source: Bangladesh Bureau of Statistics; ADB estimates.

3.3.5 Monthly inflation

- Food
- Nonfood
- Overall

% change, year on year

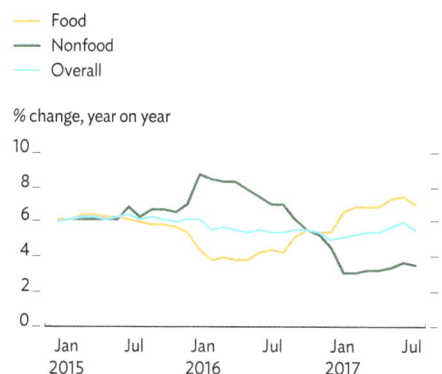

Source: Bangladesh Bank. 2017. *Monthly Economic Trends.* August. https://www.bb.org.bd

3.3.6 Contributions to broad money growth

- Credit to the private sector
- Net foreign assets
- Credit to the public sector
- Other domestic assets
- Broad money growth

Percentage points

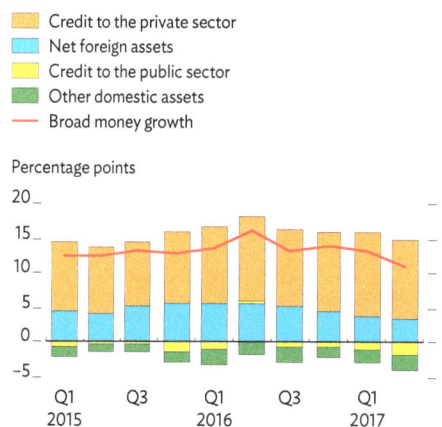

Q = quarter.

Sources: Bangladesh Bank. 2017. *Major Economic Indicators, Monthly Update.* August. https://www.bb.org.bd; ADB estimates.

ample bank liquidity to fully meet loan demand, and bank lending rates fell by 83 basis points to 9.6%.

Net credit to the public sector declined by 12.0% with a surge in nonbank borrowing through national savings certificates sold at fixed rates. Proceeds in excess of domestic budget requirements were used to repay less-costly bank borrowing. Notwithstanding eligibility requirements and purchase limits per buyer, private savers prefer these high-yielding instruments to savings accounts in banks, for which interest rates are falling. Meanwhile, rates on these popular certificates could be lowered in line with the market to save on interest costs and to keep them from inhibiting the development of corporate and government bond markets.

Revenue was again below budget in FY2017, though it rose to equal 11.2% of GDP from 10.0% a year earlier. Spending jumped to 16.2% from 13.8% as recurrent spending rose on higher payments for salaries and allowances, interest payments, and subsidies, and as development spending improved to 5.9% of GDP from 4.7% a year earlier. The budget deficit stayed within its target of 5.0% of GDP as recurrent expenditure was kept under control to compensate for the revenue shortfall. Domestic sources financed 70% of the deficit.

Among the 48 nonfinancial state-owned enterprises, 31 earned a combined profit of about $1.8 billion in FY2017 to 30 April, and the rest lost $980.9 million. The net profit of all such enterprises fell to $836.2 million as of 30 April 2017 from $1.4 billion in the whole of FY2016 (Figure 3.3.7). Bangladesh Petroleum Corporation net profits declined to $926.9 million from $1.2 billion as international oil prices rose, and those of the Bangladesh Telecommunications Regulatory Commission slid to $489.1 million from $528.6 million. The net profits of the Bangladesh Oil, Gas, and Mineral Resources Corporation rose to $116.7 million from $89.0 million with higher domestic gas prices. The net losses of the Bangladesh Power Development Board rose to $649.7 million (equal to 0.3% of GDP) from $494.0 million in FY2016, in part because of the higher cost of electricity purchased from oil-fired private rental power plants. These losses consumed just over a fifth of government subsidy spending for the year.

The government's subsidy bill rose to $3.0 billion in FY2017 (1.2% of GDP) from $2.3 billion in FY2016 with higher allocations for food and export subsidies (Figure 3.3.8). For the second consecutive year, the government did not have to subsidize Bangladesh Petroleum Corporation because it earned profits. The Bangladesh Power Development Board received a subsidy of $695.1 million, which was lower than the budgetary allocation of $758.2 million and the actual subsidy in the previous year of $702.7 million. Agriculture's share in the subsidy budget remained the largest as support to farmers for fertilizer, diesel, and electricity continued, though allocations declined to $758.2 million from $894.3 million in FY2016.

Exports grew by only 1.7% to $34 billion in FY2017, well below the 8.9% expansion a year earlier and the *ADO 2017* forecast of 6.0% (Figure 3.3.9). Garment exports, accounting for about 80% of total exports, grew by 0.2%, compared with 10.2% in FY2016. Garment demand weakened steadily through the year, with exports

3.3.7 Profits and losses at state-owned enterprises

- Bangladesh Power Development Board
- Bangladesh Petroleum Corporation
- Bangladesh Telecommunications Regulatory Commission
- Bangladesh Oil, Gas, and Mineral Resources Corporation
- Others
- Total

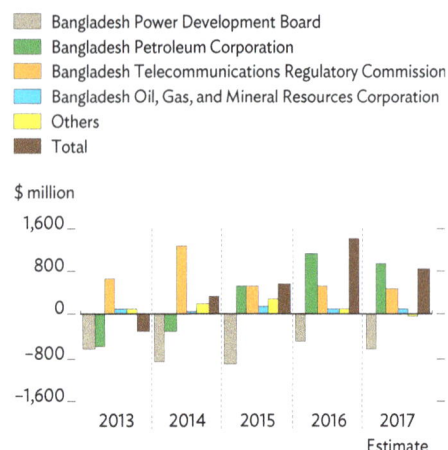

Note: Years are fiscal years ending on 30 June of that year.
Sources: Ministry of Finance. *Bangladesh Economic Review 2017*; ADB estimates.

3.3.8 Government subsidies

- Electricity (Bangladesh Power Development Board)
- Fuel (Bangladesh Petroleum Corporation)
- Export
- Agriculture
- Food
- Others
- Total subsidy

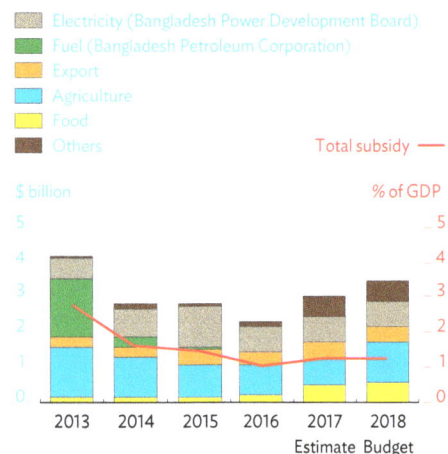

Note: Years are fiscal years ending on 30 June of that year.
Sources: Ministry of Finance; ADB estimates.

3.3.9 Contributions to export growth

- Garments
- Others
- Export growth

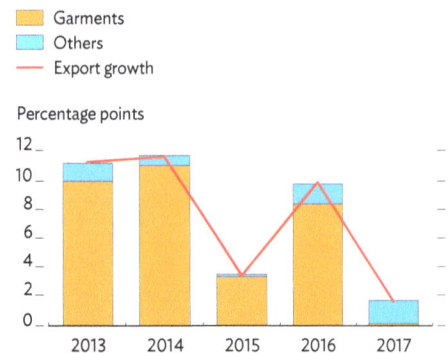

Note: Years are fiscal years ending on 30 June of that year.
Sources: Export Promotion Bureau; ADB estimates.

in June 2017 about 15% below those in June 2016. Demand fell in all major markets: the euro area, US, and United Kingdom. Infrastructure bottlenecks exacerbated lower export growth. Exports other than garments grew robustly by 8.5% following a 7.8% advance a year earlier.

Imports increased by 9.0% to $43.5 billion in FY2017, in line with expectations. Imports of wheat, other consumer foods, crude petroleum, and petroleum products grew robustly. Imports of capital goods and intermediates for manufacturing and construction rose broadly in line with growth, while growth was moderate for intermediates for the garment industry.

Remittances declined by 14.5% to $12.8 billion in FY2017, though the number of jobs held by Bangladeshi workers abroad rose by 32.2%. Persistently weak oil prices kept wages depressed in the Gulf, host to over 80% of Bangladeshi migrant workers. The rising cost of living in the Gulf left workers with less to remit, and weaker host country currencies further discouraged remittances. Finally, workers found it costlier to send money home because of higher bank fees and requirements introduced to counter money laundering and terror financing. Inflows fell by 23.5% from Saudi Arabia and by 23.0% from the United Arab Emirates, the two largest sources of remittances. The steepest decline, at 30.0%, was from the US, the third-largest source, possibly reflecting policy uncertainty there.

The trade deficit widened by $3.0 billion to $9.5 billion in FY2017 as higher import payments outpaced the increase in export earnings. The current account balance fell into a deficit of $1.5 billion, equal to 0.6% of GDP and a reversal from the $4.3 billion surplus in the previous year (Figure 3.3.10). The downturn reflected higher deficits in trade, services, and primary income—as well as the fall in remittances, the heretofore reliable mitigating factor for trade deficit.

Net inflows of capital and financing reached an estimated $4.5 billion in FY2017 with $2.3 billion in medium-term loans, $1.7 billion in foreign direct investment, and $0.5 billion in portfolio investment. Despite the current account deficit in FY2017, financing flows allowed a $3.2 billion increase in gross official foreign exchange reserves, which reached at the end of June $33.4 billion, or cover for 8.0 months of imports (Figure 3.3.11).

The nominal Bangladesh taka–US dollar exchange rate remained broadly stable in FY2017 as the central bank remained watchful for volatility (Figure 3.3.12). With export earnings growing only slightly and remittances falling sharply, the central bank allowed market forces to operate more freely toward the end of the year. The taka had depreciated by 2.7% against the dollar by the end of June 2017.

Prospects

GDP is expected to grow by 6.9% in FY2018, unchanged from *ADO 2017* but, because of weak domestic demand, slightly below the preliminary official estimate for FY2017. Private consumption will likely stay at the current level as income growth slows in agriculture and wage employment and as remittances continue to fall. Private investment will rise moderately with prevailing political stability and the authorities delivering economic reform and better infrastructure. The decline

3.3.10 Current account components

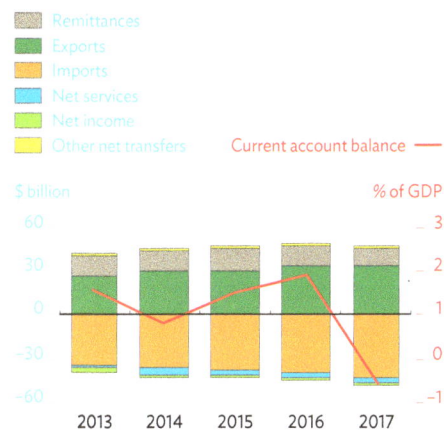

- Remittances
- Exports
- Imports
- Net services
- Net income
- Other net transfers
- Current account balance

Note: Years are fiscal years ending on 30 June of that year.
Sources: Bangladesh Bank. http://www.bb.org.bd; ADB estimates.

3.3.11 Foreign exchange reserves

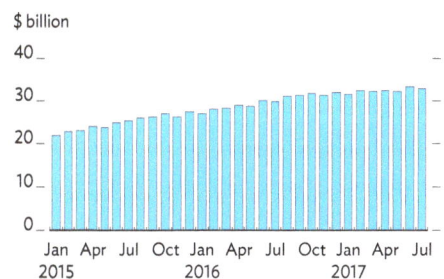

Source: Bangladesh Bank. 2017. *Major Economic Indicators, Monthly Update.* August. https://www.bb.org.bd

3.3.12 Exchange rate

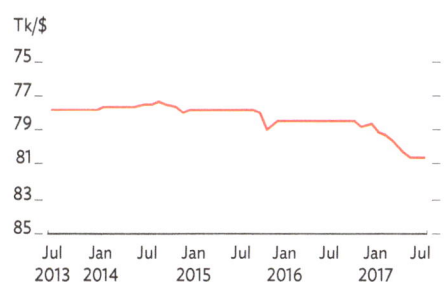

Source: Bangladesh Bank. 2017. *Monthly Economic Trends.* August. https://www.bb.org.bd

in remittances will slow and is unlikely to reverse in the near term. Some pickup in export growth is expected, and there is potential for an upside surprise if consumer confidence improves.

The government is implementing several transport and energy infrastructure projects to leverage private investment: upgrading rural roads in the southwest, developing the Elenga–Hatikumrul–Rangpur highway in the northwest to four lanes for better connectivity with Bhutan and India, and constructing and upgrading electricity transmission lines to prevent power interruptions. The Bangladesh Investment Development Authority, set up in 2016, is implementing reform to improve the business climate, including the expected launch by December 2017 of a one-stop business service center.

Agriculture growth is expected lower at 2.6% in FY2018 because of a higher base effect and prolonged flooding that hindered planting for the monsoon crop (Figure 3.3.13). Industry growth will moderate to 10.2% as falling remittances restrain domestic demand. Services growth will ease to 6.0% because of slower growth in agriculture and industry.

Inflation is expected to be higher at 6.0% in FY2018 but below the 6.3% projected in *ADO 2017*. Crops lost to the floods at the turn of the fiscal year may put further pressure on rice prices, to be partly offset by expected higher imports. Gas prices were raised in March 2017 with little immediate impact on inflation. However, further increases seem likely as prices remain below international levels, and because revenue will be needed to pay for the expected operation of a liquefied natural gas gasification terminal in 2018 and the planned awarding of gas exploration contracts. A likely rise in electricity prices and taka depreciation may add to price pressures. Nevertheless, expected moderation in global food prices and weak domestic demand should keep inflation in check.

In its monetary policy statement for the first half of FY2018, the central bank prioritized price stability while supporting growth and job creation. It thus kept its main policy, or repo, rate at 6.75%, unchanged since January 2016. Call money rates are likely to rise on some pickup in government borrowing (Figure 3.3.14). Policy support will continue for micro, small, and medium-sized enterprises with renewed emphasis on employment-focused manufacturing and services, and on expanding the availability of low-interest agricultural loans. The central bank is cooperating with capital regulators to encourage startup financing for entrepreneurs in Bangladesh.

The FY2018 budget aims to raise revenue to the equivalent of 13.0% of GDP, a marked boost from 11.2% in the previous year (Figure 3.3.15). Targeted public spending is also, at 18.0% of GDP, much higher than in FY2017, with the deficit again planned at 5.0% of GDP. The authorities project revenues to grow by 31.8%, implying high buoyancy at 2.3 times projected nominal GDP growth of 13.7%, and outpacing spending growth at 26.2%. Recurrent spending is to grow moderately by 16.3%, but the annual development program is slated to grow by 38.5% to accelerate the implementation of some large infrastructure projects.

The implementation of a new value-added tax scheduled for July 2017, after a delay of 1 year, was deferred again. The second deferment prompted the authorities to retain tax measures adopted

3.3.13 GDP growth

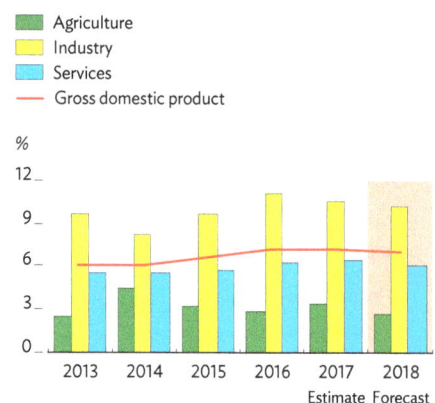

Note: Years are fiscal years ending on 30 June of that year.
Sources: Bangladesh Bureau of Statistics. 2017. *National Account Statistics*. May. http://www.bbs.gov.bd; ADB estimates.

3.3.14 Interest rates

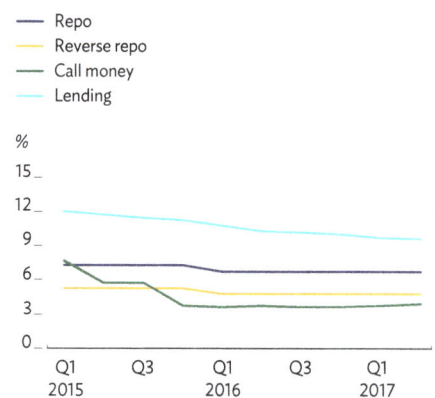

Q = quarter.
Source: Bangladesh Bank. 2017. *Major Economic Indicators, Monthly Update*. August.http://www.bb.org.bd

3.3.15 Fiscal indicators

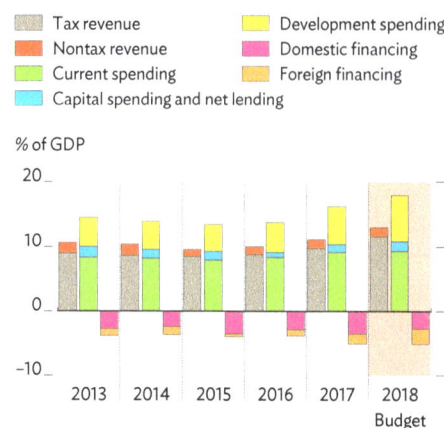

Note: Years are fiscal years ending on 30 June of that year.
Source: Asian Development Outlook database.

in the previous year to help sustain such revenue and to adopt other measures to enhance revenue. However, attaining the high revenue target will remain a major challenge, and some adjustments to expenditures may be required to meet the deficit objective.

Exports are projected to return to higher growth and rise by 6.0% in FY2018. This projection is underpinned by favorable growth in major markets, a shift in market share toward emerging countries that are projected to see faster growth, a reduction in the corporate tax from 20.0% to 12.0% for the garment industry, expanded export incentives to cover new items, and government efforts to improve transport logistics, cargo handling at ports, and customs procedures.

The import bill is expected to be higher by 10.0% in FY2018. Aided by duty reduction from 28.0% to 2.0% for rice, food grain imports are set to pick up to offset shortfalls in domestic production. Petroleum imports will rise to run rental power plants as demand for electricity increases. Imports of machinery and raw materials for infrastructure and liquefied natural gas projects will increase the import bill.

Remittance inflows will decline again in FY2018, albeit at a much slower rate of 3.0% as fiscal consolidation moderates in Middle East oil producers. The government is trying to encourage migrant workers to send remittances through official channels by cutting heretofore high bank fees for fund transfers, promoting the sale of bonds with higher yields, and offering attractive loans to home buyers. A higher trade deficit is expected to push the current account deficit to 1.5% of GDP in FY2018 (Figure 3.3.16).

Forecasts assume that domestic revenues rise in line with budget targets, which must be met to implement the public investment program, and that absorptive capacity improves toward effectively spending a large increase in external financing. They further assume the implementation of policy reform and the completion of ongoing power and transport projects vital to reviving private investment, as well as the maintenance of political stability as national elections approach in 2018.

3.3.1 Selected economic indicators, Bangladesh (%)

	2017		2018	
	ADO 2017	Update	ADO 2017	Update
GDP growth	6.9	7.2	6.9	6.9
Inflation	6.1	5.4	6.3	6.0
Current acct. bal. (share of GDP)	−1.0	−0.6	−0.7	−1.5

Note: Years are fiscal years ending on 30 June of that year.
Source: ADB estimates.

3.3.16 Current account balance

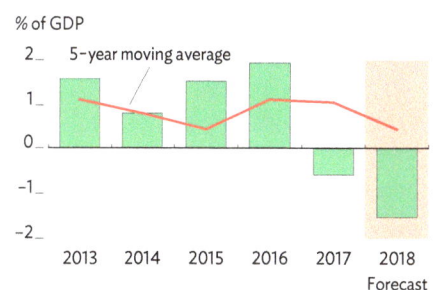

Note: Years are fiscal years ending on 30 June of that year.
Sources: Bangladesh Bank. http://www.bb.org.bd; ADB estimates.

India

Growth in FY2017 (ending 31 March 2018) is expected to be lower than forecast in *ADO 2017* as a new tax regime poses transitory challenges to firms and as investment by state governments and private investors remain muted. A pickup is envisaged in FY2018, aided by restructured bank balance sheets and efficiency gains from the new tax regime, but growth will again fall short of the April forecast. Stronger agriculture will ease inflation by more than expected in FY2017 and FY2108. Current account projections are unchanged.

Updated assessment

GDP growth slowed to 5.7% year on year in the first quarter of FY2017 from 6.1% in the previous quarter (Figure 3.3.17). The slowdown was broad, with private consumption, agriculture, and industry weakening compared with recent quarters. Government consumption and services were the mainstays of growth.

Private consumption, a pillar of growth in the last few quarters, slowed to 6.7%, its lowest in 7 quarters. The slowdown is partly attributable to waning consumption in rural areas, where incomes are vulnerable to falling agricultural prices. Urban consumption may have been similarly dented by weakening of job prospects in recent quarters and some lingering effects of a currency demonetization and exchange program announced in November 2016. Growth in government consumption was in double digits but still slower than in previous quarters. Although gross capital formation increased by a healthy 8.5%, the bulk of the increase was in valuables, mainly gold for personal holding, which grew by more than 200%. Fixed capital formation grew by only 1.6%.

A healthy winter crop helped agriculture increase by 2.3% in the first quarter of FY2017 (Figure 3.3.18). However, despite stronger volume growth, value addition was muted by lower output prices relative to input costs for some commodities like pulses and vegetables.

Growth in industry decelerated to 1.6% in the first quarter, its slowest in 5 years, the decline led by manufacturing and mining. Mining contracted by 0.7% as coal and crude oil production languished. Growth in manufacturing braked sharply to 1.2% as firms cut back on production to clear inventories built up before the introduction of a goods and services tax (GST) on 1 July 2017. Construction, a cash-intensive sector, modestly revived from the previous quarter as new currency became less scarce.

Growth in services strengthened to 8.7% on healthy retail, trade, and transportation services. Trade services benefitted from brisk sales and inventory destocking ahead of the implementation of the GST. Demand surged for consultant services as firms prepared for the GST, and new legislation to speed bankruptcy and insolvency proceedings helped financial services, real estate, and business services grow at a brisk 6.4% in the first quarter of FY2017. Public administration services grew by a robust 9.5%, helped by a strong growth in government current expenditure.

3.3.17 Demand-side contributions to growth

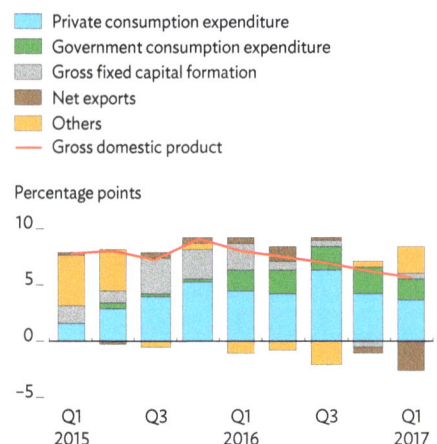

- Private consumption expenditure
- Government consumption expenditure
- Gross fixed capital formation
- Net exports
- Others
- Gross domestic product

Q = quarter.
Notes: Years are fiscal years ending on 31 March of the next year. "Others" includes valuables, changes in inventories, and statistical discrepancy.
Sources: Ministry of Statistics and Programme Implementation. http://www.mospi.nic.in; CEIC Data Company (accessed 1 September 2017).

3.3.18 Supply-side contributions to growth

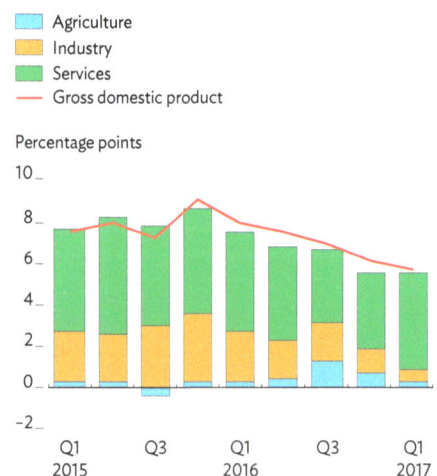

- Agriculture
- Industry
- Services
- Gross domestic product

Q = quarter.
Notes: Years are fiscal years ending on 31 March of the next year. Sectoral output valued at basic prices.
Sources: Ministry of Statistics and Programme Implementation. http://www.mospi.nic.in; CEIC Data Company (accessed 1 September 2017).

Inflation surprised on the downside in the first 4 months of FY2017, averaging only 2.2% (Figure 3.3.19). Food prices, a major factor in headline inflation, fell by 1.6 percentage points with a supply glut and sharp price decline for pulses and vegetables, bringing headline inflation down to 2.4% in July. Subdued demand under the lingering effects of demonetization helped keep prices benign. Fuel inflation inched up a bit as the government hiked subsidized prices for kerosene and cooking gas cylinders. Setting aside food and oil, core inflation still moderated as many retailers offered discounts to clear inventory before the GST. Inflation in August inched up to 3.4% as the glut cleared.

With headline inflation low through July, moderation in core inflation, and a healthy monsoon in the initial months, the Reserve Bank of India, the central bank, reduced policy rates by 25 basis points in August (Figure 3.3.20), bringing the repo rate to its lowest level in more than 6 years.

Credit growth remained anemic, growing by only 6.0% in the first quarter of FY2017 (Figure 3.3.21). The broad slowdown hit the pace of credit growth to most manufacturing and service enterprises. Part of the decline reflected corporations moving away from traditional banking channels toward overseas funds, institutional borrowing, housing finance companies, and mutual funds. Stress on banks remained elevated as their nonperforming loans (NPLs) inched up to 9.6% of gross advances in March 2017 from 9.2% in September 2016 (Figure 3.3.22). Encouragingly, the ratio of stressed assets to gross assets, which includes restructured assets apart from NPLs, declined marginally from 12.3% to 12.1% in the same period with improvement in stressed assets in agriculture, retail, and services—even as those in industry worsened.

The government has continued to focus on resolving NPLs. After creating a tribunal in May 2017 to speed bankruptcy and insolvency processes, the government passed an order that empowered the central bank to regulate bank NPLs. In June 2017, the central bank directed banks to file insolvency proceedings with the tribunal against 12 companies that accounted for about 25% of NPLs. Subsequently, it advised banks to resolve some of the accounts by December or initiate insolvency proceeding. While a time-bound mechanism has been established for dealing with NPLs, the prescribed pace could be hindered by a lack of experienced specialists in the area, reluctance to accept the large losses that bankruptcy may bring, and possible legal appeals.

The central government budget deficit is targeted to narrow to the equivalent of 3.2% of GDP in FY2017 (Figure 3.3.23). However, the deficit for April–July 2017 equaled 92.4% of the annual target, up from 73.7% the previous year. Part of the increase in the deficit through July came from the central government front-loading expenditure, especially capital expenditure, which was in the first 4 months of the fiscal year 34.4% higher than a year earlier.

Tax revenues remained buoyant in the first 4 months of FY2017, growing by 17.1%, well above their 12.2% target. Corporate taxes rose at a robust rate after remaining subdued over the last 4 years, while custom duties were bolstered by an uptick in merchandise imports.

3.3.19　Inflation

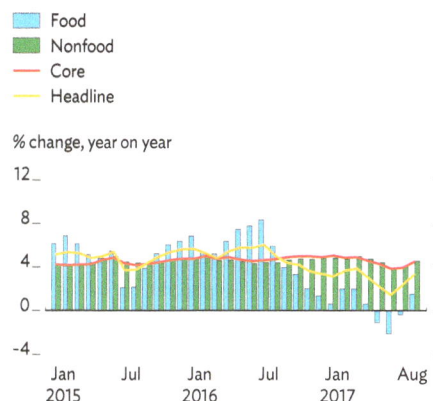

Legend: Food, Nonfood, Core, Headline

% change, year on year

Sources: CEIC Data Company (accessed 14 September 2017); ADB estimates.

3.3.20　Policy interest rates

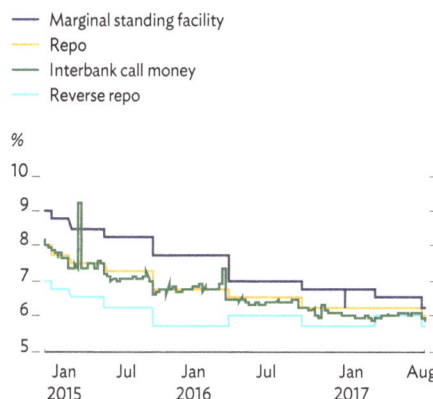

Legend: Marginal standing facility, Repo, Interbank call money, Reverse repo

%

Sources: Bloomberg; CEIC Data Company (both accessed 14 September 2017).

3.3.21　Bank credit to business

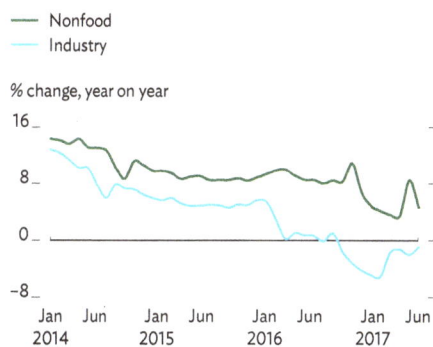

Legend: Nonfood, Industry

% change, year on year

Sources: Bloomberg; CEIC Data Company (both accessed 14 September 2017).

In contrast, nontax revenue remained sluggish as profits and dividends moderated for public enterprises and disinvestment got off to a slow start. Central bank dividends to the government fell by half from the previous year, squeezed by the cost of printing new banknotes and absorbing excess liquidity resulting from the currency exchange process.

The government successfully rolled out the GST on 1 July 2017. While GST collections in July were healthy, they are unlikely to be a reliable indicator for estimating collection over the full year. Collections in July could have been distorted by limited claims for an input tax credit, companies building up their inventories after earlier destocking, and the likely predating of sales to beat the GST.

The merchandise trade deficit widened in April–August 2017 to $63.1 billion, the highest since 2013 (Figure 3.3 24). Imports increased by 26.6% over the year-earlier period, the increase driven by higher oil import costs even as volumes were largely unchanged from FY2016. Gold and silver imports more than doubled from a year earlier as prices and volumes both rose. Robust consumption demand for these precious metals was enhanced by their allure as an alternative way to store value following the currency exchange. Other goods that boosted the import bill were electronics, minerals and ores, and some agricultural products.

Export growth in the period has been more sluggish, at 8.6%. An uptick in oil prices benefited the export of petroleum products, with export volume growing as well. Exports of iron, steel, and aluminum rose on improved external demand. The services trade surplus in April–July 2017 improved a bit to $23.2 billion, primarily due to a dip in imports of services.

Continued relaxation of regulations on foreign direct investment significantly increased net inflows from previous year to over $10.5 billion in April–July 2017, with telecom, cement, and electrical equipment attracting the bulk of it. Net portfolio inflows surged to $16.3 billion from April to mid-September 2017. Their concentration in the debt segment reflected both the low yields available in industrial economies and the view that India's economic fundamentals had markedly strengthened (Figure 3.3.25). Inflows to the equity segment were more subdued at $1.0 billion until mid-September despite the stock market being one of the best performers in Asia, with mostly domestic investors pushing prices up by 22.5% since the beginning of 2017 (Figure 3.3.26). Robust capital inflows have appreciated the Indian rupee by 1.6% against the US dollar from the beginning of FY2017 in April to mid-September 2017. The rupee has trended steadily higher in both nominal and real effective terms since January 2016, such that, in the first 7 months of 2017, it appreciated by 4.4% in real terms. This reduced export earnings in local currency and squeezed operating margins (Figure 3.3.27). Foreign exchange reserves increased by $33.8 billion in the first 6 months of FY2017, crossing $400 billion for the first time in mid-September (Figure 3.3.28).

3.3.22 Nonperforming loans

- Nonperforming loans
- Restructured assets

% of gross advances

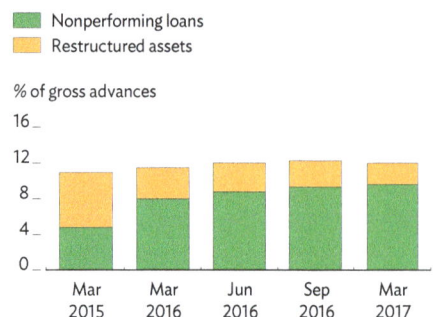

Source: Security and Exchange Board of India.

3.3.23 Federal budget indicators

- Tax revenue
- Nontax revenue
- Other revenue
- Current expenditure
- Capital expenditure
- Fiscal balance

% of GDP

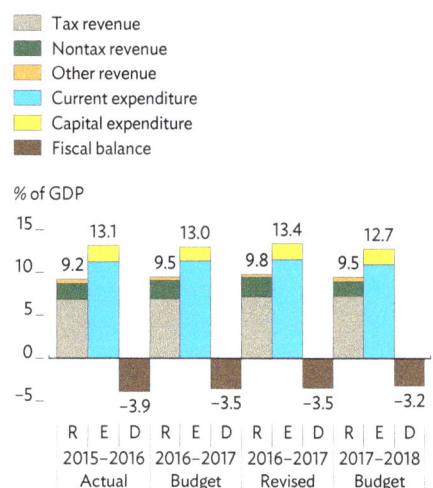

R = revenue, E = expenditure, D = deficit financing.
Note: Years are fiscal years ending on 31 March of the next year.
Source: Ministry of Finance Union Budget 2016–18. http://indiabudget.nic.in

3.3.24 Trade indicators

- Gold imports
- Oil imports
- Other imports
- Oil exports
- Other exports
- Trade balance

$ billion

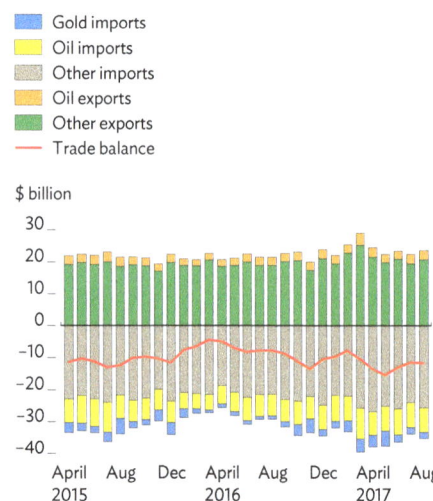

Sources: CEIC Data Company (accessed 20 September 2017); ADB estimates.

Prospects

Forecasts in *ADO 2017* assumed a healthy monsoon, revived consumption, some improvement in private investment, and modest growth recovery in the major industrial economies. This *Update* considers a stronger economic uptick in the industrial economies, the monsoon weakening a bit after a healthy start, some progress on structural reform, the lingering effects of demonetization, transitory disruptions from the introduction of the new tax system, and sluggish private investment.

Although growth in the first quarter of FY2017 was its slowest in 3 years, it is expected to pick up smartly in the remaining quarters of the year. Consumption is seen buoyed by low inflation and a strong currency. After the central government hiked government wages in 2016 at the recommendation of a committee that sits once every 10 years, several state governments are likely to announce similar increases. Moreover, central government employees will enjoy higher allowances that were deferred to FY2017. This will boost urban consumption. Rural consumption is likely to get a fillip from an uptick in procurement prices and rural wage growth trending above inflation rates.

Investment growth is likely to remain muted in FY2017. The central government attempted to jumpstart the investment cycle by front-loading its capital expenditure, but budgetary constraints will limit such expenditure for the rest of the year. State government investment is likely to be crowded out by pressures arising from higher staff salaries and the financing of farm loan waivers. Private capital expenditure continues to be challenged by weak growth in credit to industry, stressed corporate balance sheets after excessive investment several years ago, and continued low capacity utilization reflecting weak demand (Figure 3.3.29). However, private investment is expected to recover on lower borrowing costs stemming from the central bank's August rate cuts, an uptick in capacity utilization as consumer demand strengthens, and moderation in corporate financial stress.

A normal monsoon until the end of August 2017 ensured at least as much crop sown area as last year, which brought record grain harvests. However, the weakening of the monsoon in the first half of September may depress farm output a bit.

Manufacturing weakened briefly in July, with the Nikkei purchasing managers' index showing contraction (Figure 3.3.30). However, this was a result of temporary teething issues as firms adapted to the new GST, and the index moved back to expansion in August. Moreover, the outlook index of the same survey showed rising optimism as it climbed to its highest in almost a year. The central bank's industrial outlook survey similarly showed business sentiment higher than in the previous year with a better outlook for production and order books. The boost to affordable housing from interest rate subventions and the sector's new eligibility for cheap institutional credit is likely to boost construction.

Services growth is expected to remain robust as trade and transport services revive with the easing of cash constraints. Demand for consultant services is expected to remain healthy as firms transition to new business practices. An improvement in growth prospects for the industrial economies will benefit tradeable services. However, the

3.3.25 Portfolio capital flows

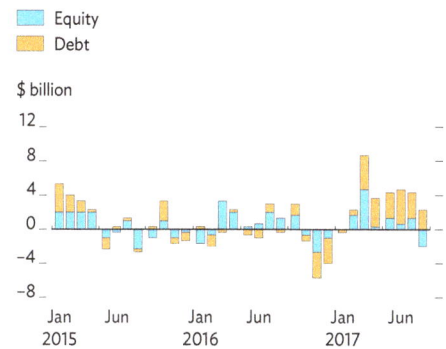

Source: Security and Exchange Board of India.

3.3.26 Stock prices

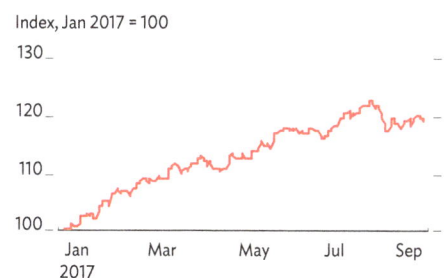

Source: Bloomberg (accessed 7 September 2017).

3.3.27 Exchange rates

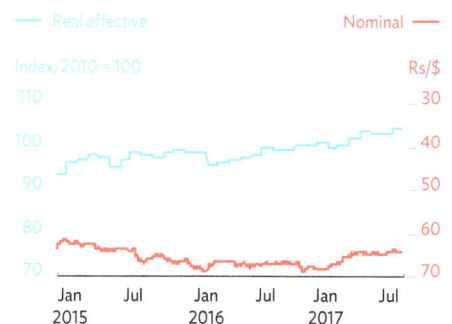

Source: Bloomberg (accessed 7 September 2017).

sharp increase in public administration services experienced in the first quarter of FY2017 is likely to taper off under the government's commitment to rein in the budget deficit.

With inflation within the central bank target range of 2%–6% and economic activity weakening in January–June 2017, the latter part of the fiscal year offers some scope for additional monetary easing. Fiscal stimulus, on the other hand, is less likely with the government having exhausted 92.4% of the full fiscal year deficit to cover slippage in nontax revenue due to slow progress in achieving disinvestment targets. Meanwhile, scope for cutting back expenditure is limited. GDP growth will thus be held to 7.0%, moderately lower than the 7.4% forecast in *ADO 2017* because of the lingering effects of cash constraint in the first quarter, transitory disruption as firms adjust to the GST, and muted investment. Downside risks to this revised estimate are the possible waning of consumer confidence, oil prices picking up faster than expected, and slower growth in the industrial economies.

As government efforts to resolve banks' NPLs yield results and corporations continue to deleverage, credit flow to industry and services is expected to increase. The expected uptick in consumption augurs well for capacity utilization and should attract fresh investment. With teething issues resolved, the GST is expected to boost growth and efficiency. On balance, growth is expected to edge up to 7.4% in FY2018, marginally lower than the *ADO 2017* forecast.

Very low inflation in the first quarter of FY2017 gave way to upward movement in July, a trend that is likely to continue at a moderate pace for the rest of the fiscal year. Food inflation is expected to strengthen on higher government procurement prices and a base effect. A possible uptick of global crude oil prices and periodic increases in prices for some subsidized fuel products will add to inflation. GST implementation may do the same with most services taxed at a higher rate. Moreover, some firms may raise prices on products for which GST increases the tax burden but retain benefits in cases of tax reduction. Improved purchasing power from higher salaries and allowances in urban areas and real wage growth in rural wages will likely augment demand and add to inflationary pressure. The easing of the cash constraint will aid recovery in demand and strengthen firms' pricing power, pushing up core inflation.

Inflation is thus expected to average 4.0% in FY2017, significantly lower than the *ADO 2017* forecast. Higher global food and fuel prices and improved aggregate demand are likely to push inflation to 4.6% in FY2018, though still below the earlier forecast.

Despite government efforts to map each product to the closest possible GST slab, changes in the tax levied on several products will introduce some fiscal uncertainty. However, tax collections are expected to pick up as firms adapt to the new regime and the economy grows. Income tax collections are expected to improve as well with legislative changes to improve compliance. Robust imports will boost customs revenue. Some of the current shortfall in nontax revenue will likely be made up later in the fiscal year with higher proceeds from disinvestment in public corporations aided by a rising stock market. Government expenditure will likely moderate from its current pace to

3.3.28 International reserves

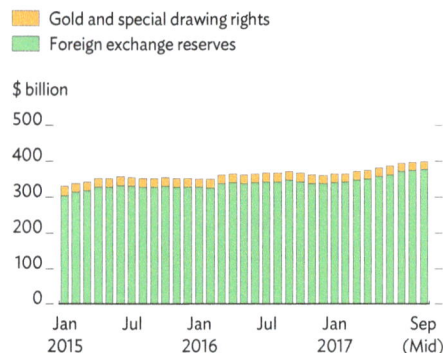

□ Gold and special drawing rights
□ Foreign exchange reserves

Source: CEIC Data Company (accessed 7 September 2017).

3.3.29 Manufacturing capacity utilization

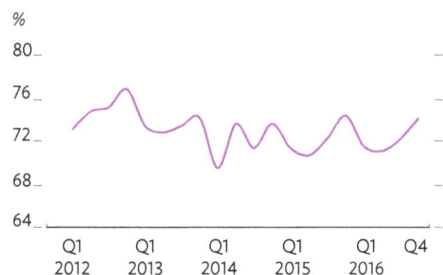

Q = quarter.
Note: Years are fiscal years ending on 31 March of the next year.
Source: Haver Analytics (accessed 6 September 2017).

3.3.30 Purchasing managers' indexes

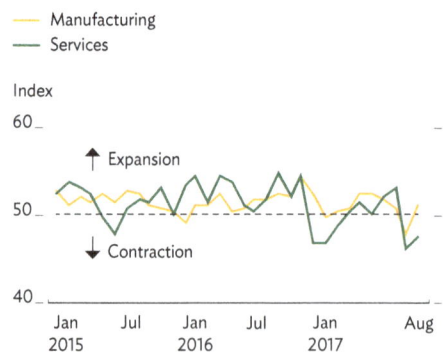

— Manufacturing
— Services

Note: Nikkei, Markit.
Source: Bloomberg (accessed 13 September 2017).

avoid breaching the spending target. The government looks able to meet its target of cutting the fiscal deficit to the equivalent of 3.2% of GDP in FY2017, despite downside risks.

The slowdown in monthly export growth year on year in the first 5 months of FY2017, from double digits in April to 8.6% in August, is likely to stabilize along with commodity prices, and with the gradual revival of global trade and the waning of disruption to the supply chain caused by the shift to the GST. However, further strengthening of the rupee against the currencies of trading partners could dent competitiveness and exports. Strong domestic consumption looks likely to fuel demand for imports of consumer goods. The currency exchange initiative may stimulate a change in investment patterns that raises demand for gold imports. Revived manufacturing as firms adjust to the new tax regime could raise demand for imports. The trade deficit is thus expected to widen in FY2017.

The invisible surplus is likely to widen as improved growth prospects in the advanced economies benefit exports of software and business services. An uptick in crude oil prices may bolster remittances from the oil-exporting economies. On balance, the current account deficit is expected to equal 1.3% of GDP in FY2017, as forecast in *ADO 2017*.

Strong growth in the industrial economies and measures taken to improve the ease of doing business will help exports grow at a faster clip in FY2018. At the same time, improvement in domestic demand as private investment picks up will spur imports to faster growth. The current account deficit is forecast to widen to 1.5% of GDP in FY2018, also as forecast.

Current account deficits in FY2017 and FY2018 are expected to be comfortably financed through stable capital flows. Government efforts to liberalize foreign ownership caps across sectors and measures to improve competitiveness and foster a climate friendly to investment have piqued foreign investors' interest in India. In its latest edition of policy on foreign direct investment, the government allowed startup businesses to raise funds from abroad, which should attract investors. Portfolio investment is expected to remain strong in FY2017. Portfolio debt flows are likely to be limited during the remaining months of FY2017, however, as investors have already filled more than 86% of the cap on foreign portfolio investment in government bonds and 92% of the cap for corporations. Portfolio equity flows, on the other hand, are expected to pick up with improved corporate earnings and growth prospects.

3.3.2 Selected economic indicators, India (%)

	2017		2018	
	ADO 2017	*Update 2017*	*ADO 2017*	*Update 2017*
GDP growth	7.4	7.0	7.6	7.4
Inflation	5.2	4.0	5.4	4.6
Current acct. bal. (share of GDP)	–1.3	–1.3	–1.5	–1.5

Note: Years are fiscal years ending on 31 March of the next year.
Source: ADB estimates.

Pakistan

Growth accelerated in FY2017 (ended 30 June 2017), mainly on recovery in agriculture and stronger manufacturing. With higher global prices for oil and other commodities, inflation slightly exceeded the forecast. The projection for the current account deficit was surpassed by a wide margin because of a very large increase in imports. Foreign exchange reserves were drawn down to fill a financing gap. For FY2018, projections for growth and inflation are maintained, but the current account deficit is expected to exceed the earlier forecast again by a wide margin.

Updated assessment

Provisional estimates indicate that GDP growth in FY2017 accelerated to 5.3% from a year earlier, led by revived agriculture and manufacturing (Figure 3.3.31). Better weather and input use improved yields for major crops, boosting agriculture growth to 3.5%. Growth in manufacturing strengthened markedly to 5.3% on strong upturns in steel, sugar, electronics, and automobiles, solid growth in pharmaceuticals and cement, but only slight expansion in the large textile and garment industry. Overall industrial growth slowed slightly to 5.0%, though, as construction growth eased to 9.0%. Strong wholesale and retail trade, finance and insurance, and general government services edged up growth in services to 6.0%.

On the expenditure side, private consumption, at 80% of GDP, increased by 8.6% to remain the largest contributor to growth (Figure 3.3.32). Increased consumption spending reflected rising middle class incomes, as average monthly household income in the three middle quintiles more than doubled in the past 10 years from PRs9,788 in FY2006 to PRs23,145 in FY2016. Faster growth in fixed capital formation, at 8.3%, reflected a 20.7% increase in public investment in large infrastructure programs. Private fixed investment, which varies from year to year and is markedly lower than elsewhere in Asia, grew by only 4.1%. Low private investment in recent years has many causes, but the main one is a substantial infrastructure deficit, especially in electric power supply. This deficit is being addressed by several new infrastructure projects including an economic corridor project called the CPEC approved in April 2015, which links Pakistan with the People's Republic of China. Many of these planned infrastructure projects are already under way, prioritizing power investments that are being financed by government development expenditure, multilateral development banks, and CPEC lending. Net exports substantially subtracted from growth as the volume of imports increased, especially of machinery, transport equipment, and intermediate goods.

Stronger domestic demand and reviving global prices for oil and other commodities pushed inflation higher to average 4.2% in FY2017 from only 2.9% a year earlier, the lowest rate in the past decade (Figure 3.3.33). Food inflation increased to average 3.8% despite improved supply as global prices strengthened, while nonfood inflation rose to 4.4%. Categories contributing to inflation were housing, education, perishable fruits, meat, medicine, and fuel.

3.3.31 Supply-side contributions to growth

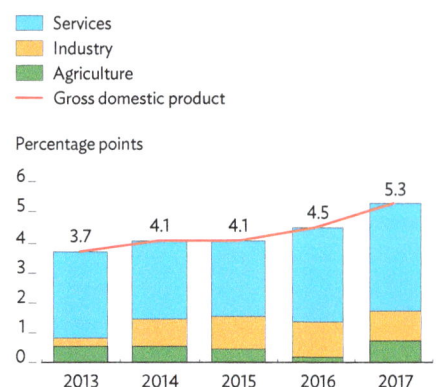

Services
Industry
Agriculture
— Gross domestic product

Percentage points

Note: Years are fiscal years ending on 30 June of that year.
Source: Ministry of Finance. Pakistan Economic Survey 2016–17. http://www.finance.gov.pk

3.3.32 Demand-side contributions to growth

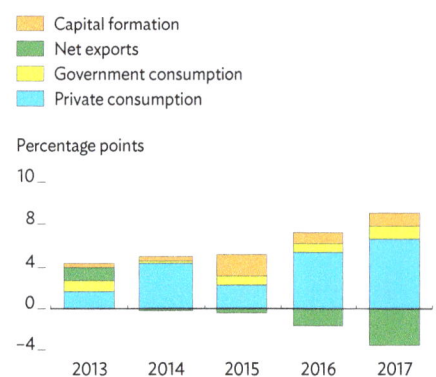

Capital formation
Net exports
Government consumption
Private consumption

Percentage points

Note: Years are fiscal years ending on 30 June of that year.
Source: Ministry of Finance. Pakistan Economic Survey 2016–17. http://www.finance.gov.pk

3.3.33 Inflation

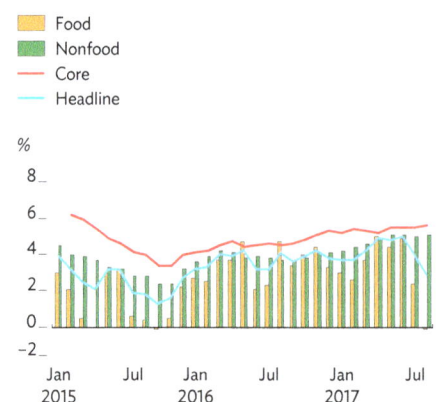

Food
Nonfood
— Core
— Headline

%

Source: State Bank of Pakistan. Economic Data. http://www.sbp.org.pk (accessed 24 August 2017).

Core inflation, leaving aside food and energy, rose by 1.0 percentage point to average 5.2% in FY2017. Year-on-year food inflation dropped sharply in June and July with a bountiful harvest to bring overall inflation down to 2.9%, the lowest in nearly 2 years.

To support growth, the State Bank of Pakistan, the central bank, maintained its policy rate at 5.75% in FY2017, allowing domestic credit to expand by 13.1%, slightly faster than a year earlier (Figure 3.3.34). The average rate on new lending was broadly stable at 7.25% through the fiscal year, and credit to the private sector grew by 67%, the strongest expansion in recent years, to PRs748 billion (Figure 3.3.35). The increase was notable in working capital and fixed investment, especially in food processing, construction, and consumer finance but in other sectors as well. Credit to public sector enterprises more than doubled to PRs355 billion, reflecting their weak financial position and the need for continued reform.

The deficit in the provisional general government budget, consolidating federal and provincial accounts, surged to PRs1.8 trillion, equaling 5.8% of GDP in FY2017, up from 4.6% a year earlier and much higher than the initial estimate of 4.2% (Figure 3.3.36). Revenues increased by only 0.2% of GDP over the previous year to reach 15.5% despite additional excise and customs taxes to cover emerging shortfalls in indirect taxes. Nontax revenue recovered after declining over the past 2 years, reaching 3.0% of GDP but not the budget target because of disappointing receipts from the Coalition Support Fund, the sale of 3G/4G telephone licenses, central bank profit transfers, and dividends from public sector enterprises.

Expenditure was, at 21.3% of GDP in FY2017, higher by 1.3% than in the previous year. Current expenditure grew by 0.4% of GDP, to 16.3%, with higher spending on defense and a fertilizer subsidy in a farm relief package. Electricity subsidies were higher than budgeted, but interest payments edged down. Development expenditures grew by 0.9% of GDP to 5.3%, mainly on increased infrastructure spending under the consolidated public sector development program.

The government financed a sharply higher fiscal deficit largely through domestic bank loans. Borrowing from the central bank reached PRs907 billion in FY2017, against net retirement of PRs486 billion in FY2016, to significantly reduce reliance on commercial banks. External borrowing increased by half to finance about 30% of the deficit.

The current account deficit widened to $12.1 billion, equal to 4.0% of GDP in FY2017 from 1.7% a year earlier (Figure 3.3.37). Imports rose sharply, especially in the final months, to grow by 17.5%, with just over half of the increase being petroleum, machinery, and transport equipment. A sharp rise in global prices was a major cause of a 26% higher petroleum bill, while imports of machinery and equipment increased by about 20%, following 40% expansion a year earlier, in part to supply the CPEC. Exports declined by 1.4%, slowing the 8.8% fall in FY2016 as all major export categories suffered lower earnings. While the trade deficit was the main factor widening the current account deficit, worker remittances, the major cushion to Pakistan's traditionally large trade deficit, widened it further with a 3% decline.

3.3.34 Interest rates

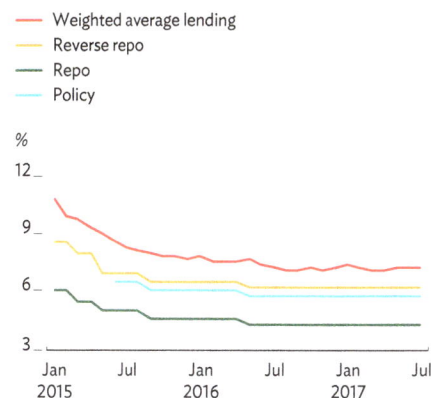

- Weighted average lending
- Reverse repo
- Repo
- Policy

Sources: State Bank of Pakistan. Economic Data. http://www.sbp.org.pk (accessed 24 August 2017); *Monetary Policy Information Compendium* January 2017.

3.3.35 Annual change in credit to the private sector

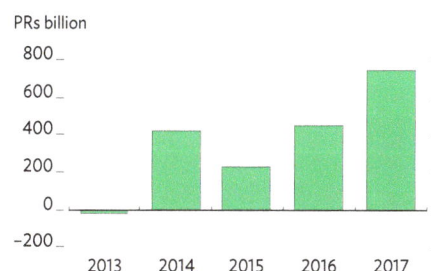

Note: Years are fiscal years ending on 30 June of that year.
Source: State Bank of Pakistan. 2017. *Monetary Statistical Bulletin.* August.

3.3.36 Government budget indicators

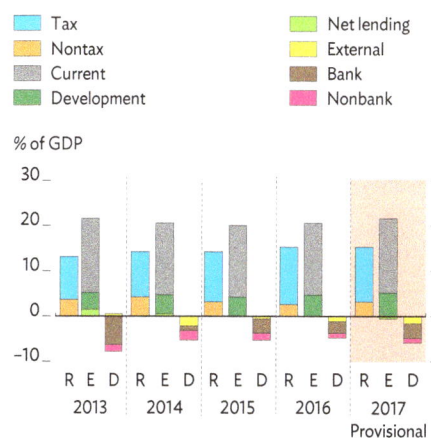

- Tax
- Nontax
- Current
- Development
- Net lending
- External
- Bank
- Nonbank

R = revenue, E = expenditure, D = deficit financing.
Notes: Years are fiscal years ending on 30 June of that year. Data refer to consolidated federal and provincial governments. Net lending includes statistical discrepancy. Nonbank includes privatization proceeds.
Source: Ministry of Finance. *Pakistan Economic Survey 2016–17.* http://www.finance.gov.pk

The capital and financial account surplus increased sharply by just over 40% to $10 billion in FY2017, mainly reflecting increased borrowing by the government, the private sector, and commercial banks as debt-free foreign direct investment stagnated from a year earlier at $2.3 billion (Figure 3.3.38). With the current account deficit at $12.1 billion, the gap was financed by a $2 billion draw on official foreign reserves, which declined to $16.1 billion at the end of FY2017 but still provided 3.7 months of cover for imported goods and services (Figure 3.3.39). External debt and liabilities are increased by an estimated $8.9 billion, with the government accounting for $4.8 billion of the rise, to bring Pakistan's estimated external debt, excluding currency valuation adjustments, to $82.8 billion in June 2017, or 27.2% of GDP, up from 26.4% a year earlier.

The Pakistan rupee remained largely stable in FY2017, buoyed by central bank open market operations, but subsequently depreciated by 0.6%, from PRs104.8 to the US dollar in June to PRs105.4 in July. In recent years, the currency has been on a rising trend in real effective exchange terms, eroding Pakistani competitiveness with appreciation by 3.6% in FY2017 on a widening inflation differential (Figure 3.3.40).

Prospects

GDP growth is expected to accelerate to 5.5%. This *Update* assumes better growth prospects in advanced and developing economies alike, a continued revival in world trade volumes, and continued improvement in the security and business environment. The main impetus for industry and services growth will be expanded CPEC infrastructure investments, other energy investments, and government development expenditure. Agriculture should expand by trend rates.

There are downside risks. Growth has improved, but the government needs to address fiscal and external sector vulnerabilities that have reappeared with the wider current account deficit, falling foreign exchange reserves, rising debt obligations, and consequently greater external financing needs. Political uncertainty heightened following the Supreme Court decision in August to disqualify for office the Prime Minister elected in 2013. Calm has returned, and his party will continue to lead the government until new Parliamentary elections due by the third quarter of 2018. Still, possible loss of momentum for making policy decisions may hamper growth prospects.

Rising domestic demand fueled by economic expansion is expected to stoke inflation in FY2018. However, the *ADO 2017* projection for 4.8% inflation could stand with continued central bank policy vigilance, a muted increase in global oil prices, and some expected easing of global food prices.

The general government budget for FY2018 sets the target deficit at 4.1% of GDP, significantly narrower than the 5.8% of GDP deficit of a year earlier. An 18.0% increase in tax collection and larger nontax revenues would boost total revenue to 17.2% of GDP. Further rationalization of current expenditure to the equivalent of 15.0% of GDP is envisioned to support a projected expansion in capital expenditures. Total expenditures are projected at 21.3% of GDP, reflecting an increase of 18.0% on significantly higher budgetary

3.3.37 Current account components

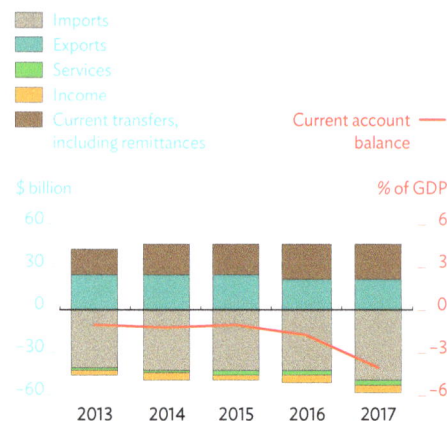

Note: Years are fiscal years ending on 30 June of that year.
Source: State Bank of Pakistan, *Economic Data* (accessed 27 August 2017); ADB estimates.

3.3.38 Capital and financial flows

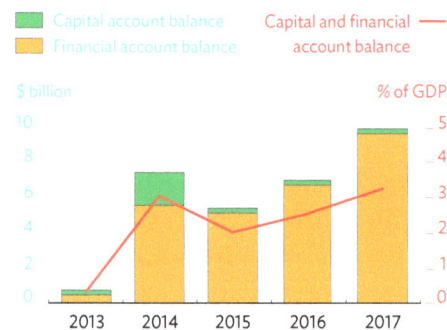

Note: Years are fiscal years ending on 30 June of that year.
Source: State Bank of Pakistan, *Economic Data* (accessed 27 August 2017); ADB estimates.

3.3.39 Gross international reserves

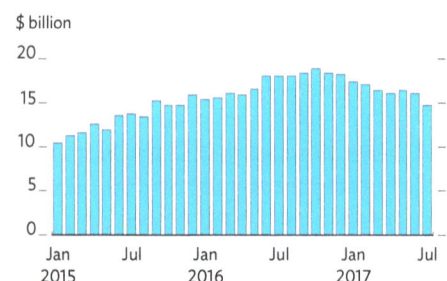

Source: State Bank of Pakistan. *Economic Data.* http://www.sbp.org.pk (accessed 24 August 2017).

allocations for development. Development expenditures are forecast to reach 6.3% of GDP after public sector development program allocations increased by half in FY2017, the year before an election. Notable areas for allocations are security, road transport, aid for less-developed areas and internally displaced people, health, and education.

The federal budget for FY2018 assumes two-thirds of deficit financing will come from domestic bank and nonbank sources with no borrowing from the central bank. Achieving such a large reduction in the general government budget deficit and this ambitious financing target appears to be very difficult, but a continued large deficit would again require very substantial foreign financing. There was a significant increase in government borrowing from the central bank in FY2017 to retire debt from commercial banks and nonbank sources such as Pakistan Investment Bonds. This government borrowing from the central bank helped increase commercial bank liquidity and extend credit to the private sector, but further large borrowing risks creating inflationary pressure. Accordingly, the central bank needs to vigilantly shape monetary policy to emerging circumstances in FY2018.

The current account deficit is expected to remain high in FY2018, projected at 4.2% of GDP, with rising imports, declining remittances, and stagnant exports. A key challenge will be to finance Pakistan's burgeoning trade deficit as remittance inflows, however substantial, continue to fall. The share of exports in GDP nearly halved from 13.0% in FY2006 to a dismal 7.1% in FY2017. Exports fell annually by 2.5% on average from FY2013 to FY2017 for lack of competitiveness or conditions for modernizing investment, leaving persistently low value addition to fetch low unit prices. Better prospects for global growth and trade are expected to further the recent improvement in export performance, however weak, in FY2017. Exports are likely to take off, though, only with adequate and reliable power supply and other supporting infrastructure and policy.

Imports are expected to continue to increase as growth spurs domestic demand that domestic production cannot meet. July 2017 imports were, though 8% less than the peak in June, 50.9% above a year earlier. Petroleum accounted for a quarter of the increase, while imports doubled for power generation machinery and construction, much of it apparently related to the CPEC. The continued large trade and current account deficits in July 2017 exceeded capital and financial account net inflows to create a gap that again was covered by drawing on foreign exchange reserves, which fell by $1.5 billion to $14.6 billion at the end of that month. Worker remittances have shown some unexpected improvement, however, in the first 2 months of FY2018, increasing by 13.2% from the same period in FY2017. If this rebound can be sustained for the rest of FY2018, it may ameliorate the projected deficit. In any case, the authorities may need to consider rapid currency depreciation at some point to rein in import growth, or increase foreign borrowing to finance the external gap, to prevent an undue weakening of foreign exchange reserves.

3.3.40 Exchange rates

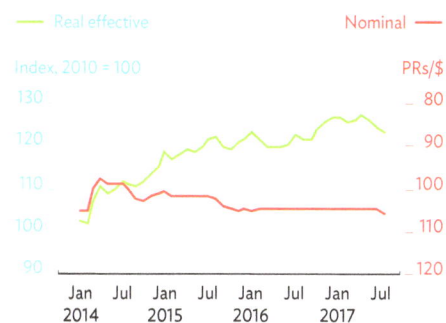

Source: State Bank of Pakistan. *Economic Data.* http://www.sbp.org.pk (accessed 24 August 2017).

3.3.3 Selected economic indicators, Pakistan (%)

	2017		2018	
	ADO 2017	Update 2017	ADO 2017	Update 2017
GDP growth	5.2	5.3	5.5	5.5
Inflation	4.0	4.2	4.8	4.8
Current acct. bal. (share of GDP)	-2.1	-4.0	-2.5	-4.2

Note: Years are fiscal years ending on 30 June of that year.
Source: ADB estimates.

Over the medium term, increasing government and CPEC-related repayment obligations highlight the need to carefully manage external debt, the balance of payments, and their financing requirements, while instituting macroeconomic and structural policies to support economic stability and make Pakistan more competitive.

Other economies

Afghanistan

Anecdotal evidence showed growth in Afghanistan picking up slightly in the first half of 2017, though the poor security situation continued to restrain investment and consumption and thus the economy. Rainfall below average in many parts of the country from March to May adversely affected the first harvest and so constrained growth in agriculture. Nonetheless, economic growth should continue its upward trend in the second half of the year, as ample precipitation more recently augurs for a better second harvest.

However, growth is contingent on several factors, such as recovery in industry and services, continued improvement in domestic revenue collection, sustained support from development partners, and the government's successful implementation of reform. Assuming these conditions, especially some progress in policy and governance reform, this *Update* maintains the growth forecast published in *ADO 2017* in April.

Inflation accelerated in the first half of 2017, averaging 6.0% and driven mainly by food price increases that averaged 8.2% in the period. Inflation peaked in June 2017 at 7.5% year on year but then easing to 5.1% in July on lower food inflation. Food inflation was also highest in June, reaching 10.9% from a year earlier as a border closure with Pakistan that lasted more than a month pushed up prices for cooking oil, fresh fruit, meat, vegetables, spices, sugar, and sweets, and as high external demand did the same for dried fruit. Food price inflation fell back to 7.4% in July on better supply.

Nonfood inflation increased to an average of 3.8% from January to July 2017, reflecting higher prices for tobacco, rent, transportation, and education services. Despite the increase in the first half, inflation remains within the central bank target range. Assuming a gradual rise in global commodity prices and increased demand from returning refugees, but stable agricultural prices in the second half of 2017 and throughout 2018, this *Update* maintains the April inflation forecasts.

The current account balance before grants is a large deficit, but the influx of foreign aid keeps it in balance or slightly in surplus. As the border closure with Pakistan in 2017 is likely to reduce imports for the year, this *Update* adjusts the forecast for the current account surplus in 2017 slightly higher. Assuming normal conditions for imports from Pakistan and constructive support from development partners, the forecast for the current account balance in 2018 is revised from a marginal deficit to an equally small surplus.

3.3.4 Selected economic indicators, Afghanistan (%)

	2017		2018	
	ADO 2017	Update	ADO 2017	Update
GDP growth	2.5	2.5	3.0	3.0
Inflation	5.5	5.5	5.8	5.8
Current acct. bal. (share of GDP)	1.4	2.2	−0.2	0.2

Source: ADB estimates.

Bhutan

Economic performance in FY2017 (ended 30 June 2017) and FY2018 will remain strong despite major problems at two large hydropower projects. Geological complications limited construction on these two hydropower projects in FY2017 and FY2018, such that the anticipated positive impact was not fully realized. GDP growth projections are thus revised down for both years.

In the absence of current indexes of production or quarterly national accounts estimates, various other indicators show buoyant economic activity. Hydropower generation grew by 4.1% in FY2017, and export earnings rose by 16.0%, mainly contributed by higher tariffs. Data on the balance of payments for the first 3 quarters, the latest available, show exports other than electricity up by 9.1% over the year-earlier period. Earnings from tourism, equal to 3.3% of GDP, grew by 12.1% in FY2017. A broad indicator of robust economic activity is a 15.6% increase in bank credit to the private sector in the first 11 months of the fiscal year, with expansion pronounced for services, tourism, transport, and manufacturing. Finally, the government continues to facilitate growth with budget expenditure up by an estimated 24.7% and capital expenditure up by 38.5%. Growth momentum is expected to continue in FY2018 with additional electricity generation enabled by the completion of a medium-sized hydropower project.

India's goods and services tax (GST), implemented in July 2017, may have an adverse impact on the Bhutanese economy in FY2017 through trade and revenue channels. Imports will likely increase as Indian exports are zero rated under the GST, making Bhutan's imports cheaper, while exports to India will be subject to GST, removing Bhutan's previous competitive edge over Indian producers. Moreover, rebates of Indian excise duties to the Government of Bhutan will end, as these taxes has been subsumed within the GST, implying a loss of budget revenue. The government has decided for the time being not to levy higher taxes on imports from India but to use credit policy to restrain import demand, especially for automobiles.

Inflation rose steadily in FY2017 but less than projected in April. Food inflation averaged 5.9% mainly because destructive rains that peaked in July 2016 damaged local crops and new restrictions on vegetable imports limited supply during the winter. Nonfood inflation averaged 3.3%. Inflation is expected to accelerate in FY2018 as projected—and in keeping with the historical rate differential with inflation in India, the predominant trade partner.

Exports in the first 3 quarters of FY2017 increased by 10.0% from the year-earlier period while imports declined by 2.0%, narrowing the trade and current account deficits. Gross international reserves fell slightly to $1.1 billion at the end of June 2017, but their Indian rupee component grew slightly to 5.2 months of merchandise imports, maintaining a good working balance. The current account deficit in FY2017 is estimated to be narrower than projected in April mainly because curtailed hydropower construction limited import requirements. The forecast for the FY2018 current account deficit is retained. On balance, gains from import restraint stemming from continued limits on hydropower construction, and from new electricity-generating capacity, will likely

3.3.5 Selected economic indicators, Bhutan (%)

	2017		2018	
	ADO 2017	*Update*	*ADO 2017*	*Update*
GDP growth	8.2	6.9	9.9	8.0
Inflation	4.9	4.3	5.4	5.4
Current acct. bal. (share of GDP)	−27.4	−25.5	−22.8	−22.8

Note: Years are fiscal years ending on 30 June of that year.
Source: ADB estimates.

offset curbs on Bhutan's other exports to India and higher imports of goods that now have lower price tags, especially major purchases like automobiles.

Maldives

An improved outlook for key sectors poise GDP growth to beat *ADO 2017* forecasts. Tourist arrivals grew by 6.1% in the first 6 months of 2017, more than triple 1.8% growth a year earlier, with large influxes from Europe only partly offset by continued declines from the People's Republic of China. Africa and the Americas recorded strong increases, albeit from small bases, to the credit of the Travel Trade Maldives marketing campaign. Growth in tourism earnings, measured as occupancy in bed nights, accelerated to 8.7% in the first 6 months. Further tourism gains are expected in 2018 with additional international and domestic flights anticipated and 30 resorts opening.

Construction remained strong in the first 6 months of the year, as indicated by rapid growth in imports of wood, cement, and machinery, and by expansion in bank loans for residences, real estate, and resort development and renovation. Enhanced prospects prompt this *Update* to revise GDP growth forecasts upward for both 2017 and 2018. Risks to the outlook are rising political tension that may worsen as the 2018 elections approach, untoward events affecting tourism, and an elevated ratio of public debt to GDP that is only thinly cushioned with foreign exchange reserves.

Inflation accelerated in the first quarter of 2017 before slowing in the second as the government cut staple food prices and set ceilings for imported staples. It climbed to an average of 3.8% year on year in the first half on steadily higher global commodity markets, pushing up local prices notably for food, housing, electricity, fuel, and transport. It subsided to 3.4% in June. An amendment to the Export Impact Act reduced the import duty on fuel, which lowered electricity rates starting in July. On balance, the forecast for inflation is revised up by 1.0 percentage point for 2017 but by only half as much for 2018 owing to the recent government price cuts and controls and to an expected easing of global commodity prices.

Imports grew by 11.5% year on year to $1.2 billion in the first 6 months of 2017. Exports rose by 56.2% to $171.2 million on much higher jet fuel re-exports and fish exports. The trade deficit rose by 6.3%, down from 17.5% expansion a year earlier. Auguring well for fisheries and exports is agreement likely this year with the People's Republic of China to remove duties on Maldivian fish products. The services balance markedly improved in the first 6 months on higher earnings from tourism and transportation services. Gross foreign exchange reserves increased by $136 million from the end of 2016 to $603 million in June 2017. Usable reserves rose from $200 million to $249 million, cover for 1.3 months of imports, after the government issued its first sovereign bond, for $200 million. Half of the gain was offset, however, by repayment on a $100 million foreign currency swap with India and by exchange market sales. The improved outlook for tourism and exports justifies lower forecasts for current account deficits.

3.3.6 Selected economic indicators, Maldives (%)

	2017		2018	
	ADO 2017	Update	ADO 2017	Update
GDP growth	3.8	4.2	4.1	4.4
Inflation	2.1	3.1	2.3	2.8
Current acct. bal. (share of GDP)	−18.9	−16.4	−19.1	−15.2

Source: ADB estimates.

Nepal

GDP growth exceeded the *ADO 2017* forecast for FY2017 (ended 15 July 2017) as the economy rebounded from stagnation in FY2016 caused by devastating earthquakes a year earlier. The robust performance in FY2017 mainly reflects a good monsoon and harvest, accelerated reconstruction, better electricity supply and management, and the normalization of disrupted foreign trade and supply, as well as base effects.

Agriculture, which accounts for nearly a third of GDP, bounced back from a poor monsoon to grow by 5.3% on a surge in rice production. Industry, providing 15% of GDP, expanded by 10.9% on strong rebounds in all subsectors—manufacturing, construction, utilities, and mining—from depressed output in FY2016. Services, at just over half of GDP, advanced by 6.9% after sluggish growth a year earlier, with strong performance across the sector and tourist arrivals returning to numbers recorded before the earthquake.

On the demand side, FY2017 saw a revival of consumption expenditure, which dominates spending, and fixed investment growth at 27.2%, to account for 25.1% of GDP, after falling by 12.3% a year earlier. Private fixed investment rose by over 30.7% after a deep fall a year earlier, and public fixed investment rose by 16.1% to 5.4% of GDP.

Inflation averaged 4.5%, below the 9.9% outturn a year earlier and the *ADO 2017* projection of 6.0%. It fell steadily year on year to bring average food inflation down to only 1.9% and other inflation to 6.5%. Moderation reflected higher domestic agricultural production, the normalization of trade, and subdued inflation in neighboring India. Markups over Indian prices shrank to 1.1% from 4.7% a year earlier as scarcities abated.

Merchandise imports surged by 29.0%, and exports rose by 9.7%. As imports are 10 times exports, the trade deficit soared to $8.4 billion, equal to 34.5% of GDP, despite unexpectedly strong offset by worker remittances at $6.6 billion and travel receipts at $0.6 billion. The current account balance reversed from a $1.3 billion surplus in FY2016 to a $95.7 million deficit, which, at 0.4% of GDP, was smaller than the *ADO 2017* projection. Continued capital and financial inflows boosted gross foreign exchange reserves by 7.8% to $10.4 billion.

The growth forecast for FY2018 is revised down because excessive rain along the southern tier of Nepal will depress farm output and hamper growth, and continuing project implementation delays indicate a substantial shortfall in FY2018 capital expenditure relative to the budget allocation.

Inflation is expected to rise moderately in FY2018 in line with the *ADO 2017* forecast. Flood damage may push food prices higher than expected but will be offset by lower projections for inflation in India and petroleum products.

The current account deficit is expected to widen in FY2018 from the year earlier, but by less than projected in *ADO 2017*. Imports will increase as in FY2017, but exports will not for lack of competitiveness. Meanwhile, growth in remittances will drop following a decline in the number of workers going abroad in FY2017, especially to Middle East oil producers, the main destination countries.

3.3.7 Selected economic indicators, Nepal (%)

	2017		2018	
	ADO 2017	Update	ADO 2017	Update
GDP growth	5.6	6.9	5.4	4.7
Inflation	6.0	4.5	6.5	6.5
Current acct. bal. (share of GDP)	−1.6	−0.4	−3.2	−2.2

Note: Years are fiscal years ending on 15 July of that year.
Source: ADB estimates.

Sri Lanka

GDP grew by 3.8% in the first quarter of 2017 and 4.0% in the second to hold growth in the first half of 2017 to 3.9% year on year, unchanged from the 2016 outcome. Agriculture was hit in the first quarter by continuing drought, causing a 3.2% decline. Rice production fell by 53%, and there were significant declines in tea and rubber, major exports crops. Floods in the second quarter shrank agriculture by 2.9% with further rice loses, even as tea and rubber rebounded.

Industry grew by 6.3% in the first quarter and 5.2% in the second to bring first-half expansion to 5.8%. Garment production strengthened slightly in the second quarter but was offset by a marked slowing in construction, to 9.3% from 16.1% in the first quarter. Services expanded by 3.5% in the first quarter and 4.5% in the second for 4.0% growth in the first half. An increase in financial services including insurance and in government services offset slippage in wholesale and retail trade and in hospitality. Faster growth in the large service sector in the second quarter provided lift for 4.0% GDP growth in the period despite slackening agriculture and industry.

While global trade growth augurs well for industry in the second half, the forecast for GDP growth in 2017 is revised down by 0.5 percentage points. The higher forecast for 2018 is maintained as Sri Lanka pursues economic adjustment agreed with the International Monetary Fund.

Food inflation peaked in April at 11.8% but remained high at 8.2% in July, when headline inflation softened to 6.3%. Despite this moderation, higher-than-expected food inflation, on top of currency depreciation and higher value-added taxes, prompts a 1.0 percentage point upgrade to the 2017 inflation forecast. Inflation is forecast to slow in 2018 in the wake of monetary tightening and a high base effect, downgrading the forecast by 2.0 percentage points.

Exports grew by 5.2% year on year in the first half of 2017, rebounding from a 5.8% fall in 2016 as better global prices spurred agricultural exports. Garment exports fell by 5.2%, stunting growth in industry exports, which are 3 times larger. Imports expanded by 8.9%, with crude oil and petroleum products accounting for more than 40% of the rise because of higher prices and drought-induced thermal generation of electricity. The trade deficit widened by nearly $600 million even as offsetting tourism earnings slowed markedly and worker remittances fell. Although garment exports may improve in the second half, the forecast for the current account deficit in 2017 is revised up by more than half. The deficit is now expected to shrink in 2018 but remain wider than forecast in April.

A $1.5 billion sovereign bond issue and a $450 million syndicated loan to the government helped to sustain gross international reserves at $7.0 billion in June 2017. Sri Lankan rupee depreciation against the US dollar in the first 8 months of 2017 was modest at 2.9%.

3.3.8 Selected economic indicators, Sri Lanka (%)

	2017		2018	
	ADO 2017	Update	ADO 2017	Update
GDP growth	5.0	4.5	5.0	5.0
Inflation	6.0	7.0	6.0	4.0
Current acct. bal. (share of GDP)	−2.2	−3.5	−2.2	−2.5

Source: ADB estimates.

Southeast Asia

Growth in the subregion is now forecast at 5.0% in 2017 and 5.1% in 2018, both projections slightly higher than in *ADO 2017*. Higher growth will be accompanied by slightly lower inflation both this year and next because international petroleum prices are rising at a slower pace than was foreseen in April. Meanwhile the subregion's current account surplus will shrink more than earlier envisaged.

Subregional assessment and prospects

Growth is picking up faster than forecast in *ADO 2017*. Combined GDP is now seen to expand by 5.0% in 2017, or 0.2 percentage points faster than reported in April. Integral to regional and global production networks and supply chains, Southeast Asia is benefiting from revived global electronics trade. A rebound in agriculture, strong inflows of foreign direct investment (FDI), and ambitious public infrastructure investment are country-specific factors additionally boosting growth.

Yet growth prospects vary across the 10 economies. Malaysia, the Philippines, and Singapore are now expected to post higher growth this year than earlier forecast, while Brunei Darussalam and Viet Nam will register slightly lower growth. Growth in Cambodia, Indonesia, the Lao People's Democratic Republic (Lao PDR), Myanmar, and Thailand is still forecast in line with *ADO 2017* (Figure 3.4.1). The largest upward revision is 1.0 percentage point for Malaysia, followed by 0.5 points for Singapore and 0.1 points for the Philippines. Forecasts are revised down by 1.0 percentage point for Brunei Darussalam and 0.2 percentage points for Viet Nam.

Broad expansion in demand, both external and domestic, underpins faster growth in Malaysia and the Philippines, while stronger exports spur growth in Singapore. Strengthening investment and exports helped Indonesia sustain growth in line with earlier forecasts, as did exports and FDI inflows for Cambodia, the Lao PDR, and Myanmar. Declining GDP in Brunei Darussalam and slightly softer growth in Viet Nam largely reflect continued doldrums in global demand for fuel and minerals.

As global electronics trade turned around, domestic production of semiconductors, home appliances, and electric and other consumer goods got a fillip in Malaysia, the Philippines, Singapore, Thailand, and Viet Nam. In the first half of this year, Malaysia's merchandise exports

3.4.1 GDP growth, Southeast Asia

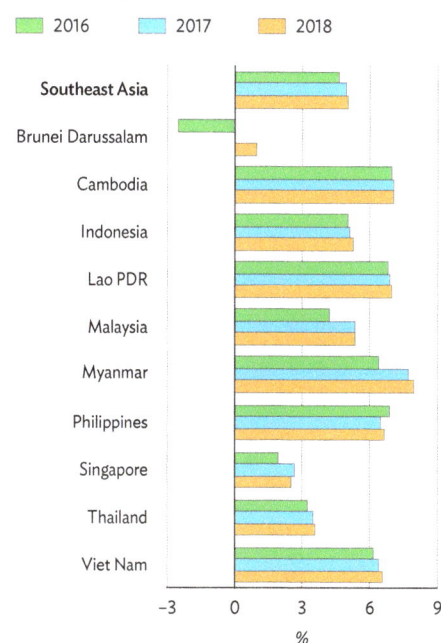

Lao PDR = Lao People's Democratic Republic.
Source: Asian Development Outlook database.

The subregional assessment and prospects were written by Kwang Jo Jeong and Dulce Zara. The section on Indonesia was written by Priasto Aji and Emma Allen; Malaysia by Valerie Mercer-Blackman and Shiela Camingue-Romance; the Philippines by Aekapol Chongvilaivan and Teresa Mendoza; Thailand by Luxmon Attapich; Viet Nam by Aaron Batten, Nguyen Luu Thuc Phuong, and Chu Hong Minh; and other economies by Poullang Doung, Jan Hansen, Minsoo Lee, Soulinthone Leuangkhamsing, Rattanatay Luanglatbandith, Pilipinas Quising, Yumiko Tamura, and Mai Lin Villaruel. Authors are in the Southeast Asia and Economic Research and Regional Cooperation departments of ADB.

recovered strongly from contraction last year. Philippine merchandise exports were up by a hefty 18.0% in the first half, and Thailand's merchandise exports grew by 7.4%, with agriculture and industry both benefiting. Coupled with higher international commodity prices, stronger exports enabled Indonesia, Southeast Asia's largest economy, to turn in robust 5.0% growth in the first half.

As external demand and exports gathered pace, private consumption, the largest component of GDP, supported growth in domestic demand in much of Southeast Asia, especially Indonesia, Malaysia, the Philippines, Thailand, and Viet Nam. The contribution of government consumption was more varied, notably up in Malaysia.

Trends in investment have been mixed. In Indonesia, higher allocations for public infrastructure investment and measures to enhance the ease of doing business lifted investment. In Malaysia, higher public and private investment boosted growth in total investment into double digits. Public and private investment alike in the Philippines helped drive the ratio of investment to GDP to a record high. Investment remained vibrant in Viet Nam, helped by strong FDI inflows. In contrast, public investment remained anemic in Thailand. Meanwhile, buoyant FDI and easy domestic monetary and credit conditions boosted investment in Cambodia, the Lao PDR, and Myanmar.

Growth momentum should continue next year, with combined GDP growth edging up to 5.1%. Malaysia's 2018 growth forecast is revised up the most, from 4.6% to 5.4%. Singapore's 2018 growth forecast is higher by 0.4 percentage points, and that of the Philippines by 0.1 points. Growth next year is seen slightly lower in Viet Nam and more so in Brunei Darussalam but still positive. Other economies are on track to meet April forecasts.

Even as growth picks up, subregional inflation is now foreseen lower than in *ADO 2017*. Low international petroleum prices, and domestic food prices subdued by recovery in agriculture, will help contain inflation at 3.1% this year and next, revised down from 3.3% and 3.5%. Exceptions are Malaysia and Viet Nam. Continued upward adjustment of some administered prices, notably for education and health care fees, and a raised minimum wage underpin higher inflation in Viet Nam. In Malaysia, rationalization of the domestic fuel pricing mechanism largely explains the higher inflation forecast (Figure 3.4.2).

Stronger growth is narrowing the subregion's current account surplus this year and next, faster than foreseen. As a share of GDP, it is now expected at 3.0% this year, a tad lower than the 3.1% forecast in *ADO 2017*. The widest forecast deficit is 17.5% in the Lao PDR, and the biggest surplus is 19.5% in Singapore. Brunei Darussalam, Malaysia, the Philippines, Thailand, and Viet Nam expect current account surpluses this year, and Cambodia, Indonesia, and Myanmar deficits.

The combined current account surplus is now expected to equal 2.8% of GDP in 2018, narrower than the April forecast of 3.0%. Thailand and Viet Nam are likely to see surpluses shrink more than anticipated, while Indonesia and Cambodia will see deficits widen slightly more than in the April forecast. The Lao PDR deficit in 2018 will be narrower than earlier forecast, while Brunei Darussalam and Malaysia will likely experience higher current account surpluses. Forecasts are unchanged for Myanmar, the Philippines, and Singapore (Figure 3.4.3).

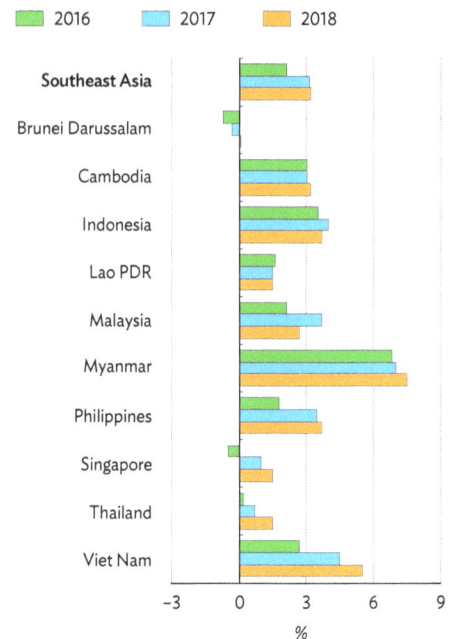

3.4.2 Inflation, Southeast Asia

■ 2016   ■ 2017   ■ 2018

Lao PDR = Lao People's Democratic Republic.
Source: Asian Development Outlook database.

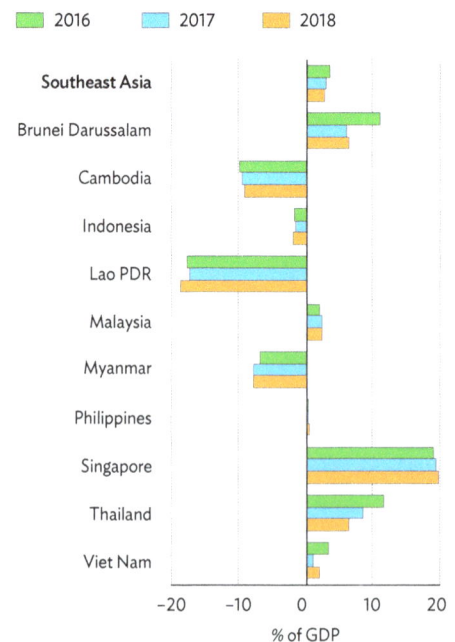

3.4.3 Current account balance, Southeast Asia

■ 2016   ■ 2017   ■ 2018

Lao PDR = Lao People's Democratic Republic.
Source: Asian Development Outlook database.

Indonesia

Strengthening investment and exports enabled Southeast Asia's biggest economy to grow by 5.0% in the first half of 2017. GDP growth is likely to come in at 5.1% this year and 5.3% next year, in line with *ADO 2017* forecasts in April. The current account deficit is likely to narrow slightly this year, as forecast, but is now expected to widen next year. Recent trends indicate that inflation will be lower than envisaged in April both this year and next.

Updated assessment

GDP grew by 5.0% in the first half of this year, only marginally slower than in the same period of 2016. Buoyant fixed investment and net exports underpinned growth as these two components of aggregate demand accounted for nearly 50% of growth in the first half (Figure 3.4.4). Fixed investment increased by 5.1% in the first half, up from 4.4% a year earlier and contributing 1.6 percentage points to growth. Expansion was driven by higher allocations for public infrastructure investment. Partly aided by higher international commodity prices, exports rose faster than imports in the first half. Net external demand thus contributed 0.7 percentage points to GDP growth.

From the demand side, private consumption rose by 4.9% in the first half of this year, slightly down from 5.0% in the corresponding period of 2016 but contributing more than half of GDP growth. Despite the rollback of the government's energy subsidy, which saw electricity prices for richer households more than double in the first half, private consumption remained strong. Meanwhile, the postponed disbursement of this year's bonus for civil servants to the second half of the year slowed government consumption in the first half.

By sector, agriculture, construction, and services grew faster than manufacturing. Benefiting from buoyant commodity prices and improved weather, agriculture grew by 5.1% in the first half, doubling from 2.5% in the same period last year. Helped by government efforts to accelerate public infrastructure investment, construction registered solid 6.5% growth in the first half of the year, up from 5.9% a year earlier.

Services expanded by 5.4% in the first half, providing nearly half of GDP growth (Figure 3.4.5). Within the sector, information and communications posted growth above 5%, as did transport and storage, while retail trade and real estate services remained subdued. Retail trade expanded by only 4.4%, with car sales sluggish and motorbike sales contracting in the first half. At 3.8%, growth in real estate services was similarly subdued. A survey of realtors reported high mortgage interest rates as a key reason for slower growth in home sales.

Growth in manufacturing slowed to 3.9% in the first half of this year from 4.7% in the same period last year, partly reflecting weakness in regional demand arising from moderating activity in Asia's international supply chain and production network in the second quarter of the year. Purchasing managers' indexes in Asia picked up earlier in the year but had moderated by midyear, with adverse effects on regional demand for parts and components from supplying countries such as

3.4.4 Demand-side contributions to growth

- Private consumption
- Gross fixed capital formation
- Net exports
- Government consumption
- Change in stocks
- Statistical discrepancy
- Gross domestic product

Percentage points

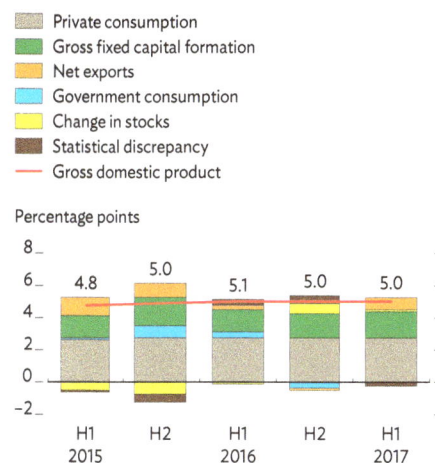

H = half.
Source: CEIC Data Company (accessed 11 September 2017).

3.4.5 Supply-side contributions to growth

- Agriculture
- Industry
- Services
- Gross domestic product

Percentage points

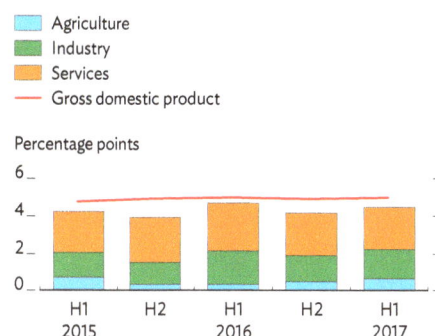

H = half.
Source: CEIC Data Company (accessed 11 September 2017).

3.4.6 Manufacturing purchasing managers' index

- Indonesia manufacturing PMI
- PRC manufacturing PMI
- ASEAN manufacturing PMI

Index

ASEAN = Association of Southeast Asian Nations, PMI = purchasing managers' index, PRC = People's Republic of China.
Source: Bloomberg (accessed 11 September 2017).

Indonesia (Figure 3.4.6). As growth in manufacturing slowed, so did growth in industry demand for energy, sending electricity sales in the first half below expectations.

Despite a lowered subsidy and consequent hike in the domestic electricity price, inflation was milder than anticipated, averaging 3.9% in the first 8 months of 2017, which was within the annual inflation target range of 4% ± 1 percentage point set by Bank Indonesia, the central bank (Figure 3.4.7). Although inflation reached a 15-month high of 4.4% year on year in June, it subsequently moderated to 3.8% in August. Food prices were subdued in the first 8 months of the year, thanks largely to better weather and buoyant food production. Core inflation, which in Indonesia excludes administered and volatile prices, has also trended down, from 3.4% in January to 3.0% in August.

The positive trend in merchandise trade that began in the fourth quarter of 2016 has continued in 2017, with merchandise exports growing at 15.3% in the first half and imports at 10.4% (Figure 3.4.8). The merchandise trade surplus reached $10.4 billion in the first half, up from $6.4 billion in the same period last year. This narrowed the current account deficit to 1.5% of GDP in the first half from 2.2% a year earlier (Figure 3.4.9).

A surplus in the financial account of the balance of payments more than offset the current account deficit. With investor confidence strong following an upgrade to the Standard & Poor's sovereign rating for Indonesia to investment grade in May, capital inflows strengthened. Foreign direct investment soared by 40% in the first half of the year. As Indonesia became more attractive to foreign investors, direct investment flowed into manufacturing, trade, agriculture, and finance. Net inflows of portfolio capital also strengthened on higher investments in Indonesia's bonds and stocks. The financial account climbed to a surplus of $13.8 billion in the first half of 2017 from $11.0 billion in the corresponding period last year.

The balance of payments surplus thus more than doubled in the first half to $5.3 billion, up from $1.9 billion 12 months earlier. International reserves strengthened, reaching $128.8 billion at the end of August 2017 and providing cover for 8.6 months of imports and repayment of official debt (Figure 3.4.10). Meanwhile, the Indonesian rupiah has been stable, appreciating against the US dollar by only 0.6% in the first 8 months of 2017.

With inflation slowing and the current account deficit narrowing, the central bank lowered at the start of July 2017 reserve requirements for commercial banks from 6.5% to 5.0%. On 22 August, it cut for the first time in 10 months its policy interest rate, the 7-day reverse repo, by 25 basis points to 4.50% and made equivalent adjustments to deposit and lending facility rates. On 22 September, it further lowered the reverse repo rate to 4.25%, while also lowering the deposit rate to 3.5% and the lending facility rate to 5.0%.

Revenue collection in the first 7 months of 2017 rose by 12.5% over the same period last year, to meet 48.8% of the original budget for the full year (Figure 3.4.11). Meanwhile, government expenditure was higher by 5.7% in the first 7 months, or 51.1% of the original budget for the year. The fiscal deficit in the first 7 months is estimated to equal

3.4.7 Inflation

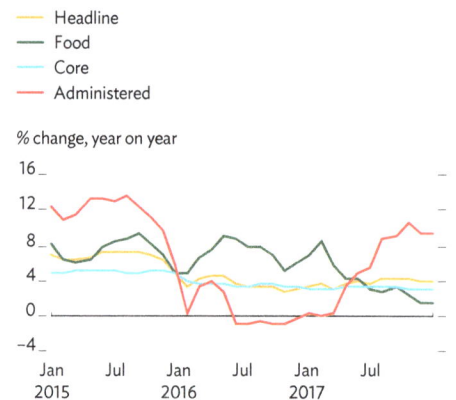

Source: CEIC Data Company (accessed 11 September 2017).

3.4.8 Merchandise trade

Source: CEIC Data Company (accessed 11 Sep 2017)

3.4.9 Current account components

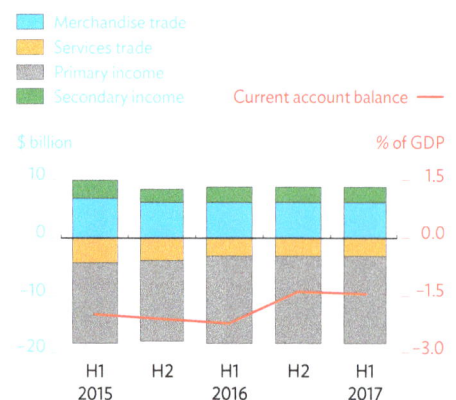

H = half.
Source: CEIC Data Company (accessed 11 September 2017).

1.5% of GDP. The 9-month tax amnesty introduced in July 2016 to elicit better tax compliance and widen the tax base brought in $10.2 billion. Regarding expenditure, capital spending was stronger in the first half on the implementation of public investment projects that had been delayed in 2016, while public consumption spending was weaker. A recently initiated program to reform government subsidies focused in the first half of the year on better targeting the electricity subsidy and on replacing the price subsidy for rice with food vouchers for qualified households.

Prospects

Looking forward, economic growth is expected to be supported by higher allocations for public investment and the gradually improving climate for private investment. Encouragingly, the government is pursuing further reform to improve the business environment. In late August, it released a 16th economic policy package that featured the development of an integrated online licensing system to make it easier for private investors to obtain various licenses and government approvals. Government consumption is also expected to boost growth in the second half of 2017.

Private consumption should remain robust in the near term. Consumer confidence is seen to hold up well, benefitting from expectations of tamer inflation (Figure 3.4.12). Despite steady consumer lending rates, demand has increased for property and consumer loans. Leading indicators for vehicle sales show consumer spending up in July. Private consumption should receive a boost in the remaining half of the year as the government accelerates its new food assistance program.

Private investment is expected to expand gradually over the forecast period as it benefits from policy reform to improve the business environment, and the Standard & Poor's rating upgrade should accelerate capital inflows including foreign direct investment. A 2017 business survey conducted by the United Nations Conference on Trade and Development ranked Indonesia in the top four destinations for investors—after the US, the People's Republic of China, and India— up from eighth place only a year earlier. Reflecting this, several Indonesian e-commerce firms recently received substantial foreign equity investments.

A survey in the second quarter showed business tendency improving but unevenly across sectors. Business confidence was up in finance, transport, and storage but subdued in manufacturing and mining, where weaker international orders are expected in the third quarter.

Fiscal policy continues to support growth. The revised budget for this year, approved by the legislature in July, raises the budget deficit to the equivalent of 2.9% of GDP from 2.4%. As tax revenues excluding petroleum grew slightly slower than envisaged in the original budget, total revenues are likely to be lower by 0.3% of GDP. Meanwhile, the revised budget foresees total expenditures somewhat higher, notably with higher allocations for public infrastructure, health care, and education. Higher government spending and a larger budget deficit should support domestic demand and economic growth. The government

3.4.10 Gross international reserves and exchange rate

Sources: Bloomberg; CEIC Data Company (both accessed 11 September 2017).

3.4.11 Fiscal performance, 2017

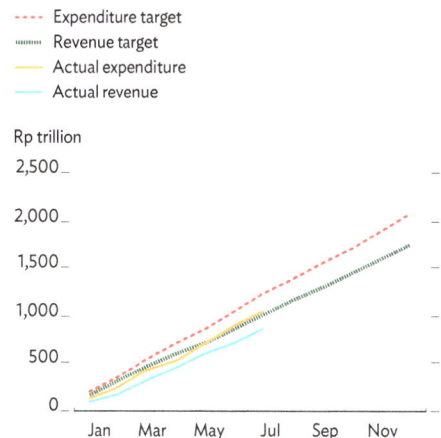

Source: CEIC Data Company (accessed 11 September 2017).

3.4.12 Consumer confidence

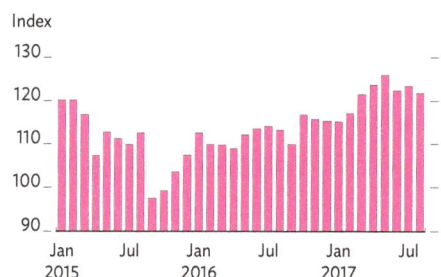

Note: A score above 100 means that respondents are optimistic and vice versa.
Source: CEIC Data Company (accessed 16 September 2017).

is currently preparing a comprehensive medium-term revenue strategy promising significant reform to tax policy and administration.

On balance, economic growth is seen to come in at the earlier forecast rates of 5.1% this year and 5.3% next year. Growth in 2018 should find support from the 2018 Asian Games in Jakarta and Palembang, regional elections, and preparations for national elections the following year.

Inflation is now seen averaging 4.0% in 2017, revised down from the 4.3% forecast *ADO 2017*, and slowing to 3.7% next year. Underpinning this downward trend is a new government effort to restrain food prices by better managing logistics and regional food distribution centers. With the national election planned for 2019, major upward adjustments to administered prices are unlikely this year or next.

Credit growth should improve gradually following recent central bank rate cuts and measures to allow banks more flexibility to manage liquidity. However, the course of monetary policy in the coming months is difficult to predict and will depend on domestic inflationary pressures and the pace of global interest rate tightening. Moreover, bank credit expansion is not expected to exceed 10% this year, with many midsized banks now focused on improving asset quality more than on increasing the size of their loan portfolios (Figure 3.4.13).

Indonesia's trade prospects are mixed, with recovery and growth among its trading partners uneven and international prices for coal and palm oil still declining. On a more positive note, the manufacturing purchasing managers' indexes of key trading partners such as the People's Republic of China and India have bounced back since mid-2017, promising to lift demand for Indonesian exports. Imports are still expected to grow more slowly than exports in the second half of this year. This *Update* retains the April forecast for a current account deficit equal to 1.7% of GDP this year, but the deficit is now expected to widen to 2.0% in 2018, not narrow further to 1.6% as forecast in *ADO 2017*. This is because imports are expected to outpace exports to supply several large public investment projects. Capital inflows are expected to be more than sufficient to finance the current account deficit, thus adding to foreign exchange reserves.

External risks to the outlook tilt to the downside as they stem from weakening global commodity prices, volatility in international financial markets, geopolitical fragility in East Asia, and policy uncertainty in the advanced economies, notably with regard to US monetary normalization. These risks underscore the need for Indonesia to maintain a flexible exchange rate and open trade and capital accounts. Domestic risks to the outlook include shortfalls in tax revenue. With a fiscal deficit for the year approaching a legal limit equal to 3.0% of GDP, any further slippage in revenue collection would require lower government expenditure, including development expenditure. That could hurt growth, employment, and wages. In addition, slow implementation of structural reform and policy uncertainty as elections near may see private investors, both domestic and foreign, adopt a wait-and-see approach.

3.4.1 Selected economic indicators, Indonesia (%)

	2017		2018	
	ADO 2017	Update	ADO 2017	Update
GDP growth	5.1	5.1	5.3	5.3
Inflation	4.3	4.0	4.5	3.7
Current acct. bal. (share of GDP)	–1.7	–1.7	–1.6	–2.0

Source: ADB estimates.

3.4.13 Credit growth

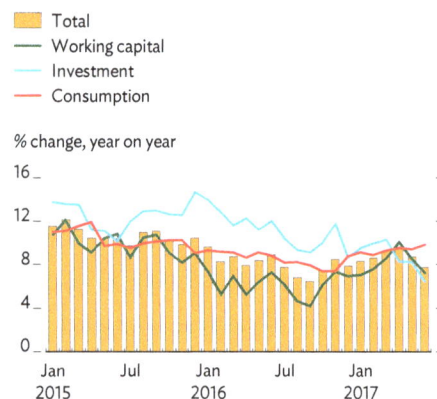

- Total
- Working capital
- Investment
- Consumption

% change, year on year

Source: CEIC Data Company (accessed 11 September 2017).

Malaysia

With GDP growth better than expected in the first half of 2017, the economy is experiencing a healthy resurgence. Driven by broadly expanding demand, annual GDP growth this year and next is now seen to accelerate to 5.4%, or 1.0 percentage point higher for 2017 than forecast in *ADO 2017*, the forecast raised almost as much for 2018. Accelerating growth is likely to be accompanied by slightly higher inflation this year, slowing in 2018 as earlier forecast. The 2016 current account surplus should be sustained both years, beating *ADO 2017* forecasts.

Updated assessment

GDP grew by an impressive 5.7% in the first half of this year, up from 4.0% expansion in the corresponding period of 2016. Growth was broadly supported by both domestic and external demand.

Private consumption rose by 6.9%, higher than the 6.2% figure for the first half of last year on account of higher incomes, expanded employment, and government measures to support incomes (Figure 3.4.14). Real wages have risen on account of a tighter labor market that saw the unemployment rate dip to 3.4% in June 2017 and job vacancies triple from a year earlier. Private investment picked up sharply, posting a 10.0% increase in the first half of the year, or more than double the 4.8% increase in the corresponding period of last year (Figure 3.4.15).

Government consumption gathered momentum on an upward adjustment to government salaries and higher pension payments, rising by 5.3% in the first half of the year. However, public investment contracted by 0.9% mainly because investment by Petronas, the state oil and gas producer, was softer in response to the subdued global hydrocarbon demand.

Strengthening domestic demand in a highly trade-dependent economy such as Malaysia's can reflect an upswing in foreign trade. In the first half of this year, the volume of goods and services exports registered a 9.7% rise, up from the meager 0.8% increase in the first half of last year, while real imports picked up faster, at 15.3%, reflecting strong import demand for export production and imports for domestic infrastructure projects.

Economic expansion has also been broad across sectors. Agriculture registered solid recovery with a 7.1% rise in production in the first half of 2017, reversing 5.9% contraction in the same period last year as palm oil and rubber performed particularly well. Manufacturing growth edged up from last year's rate of 5.8%. The service sector posted 6.1% growth in the first half of the year as higher exports and domestic production lifted transportation and storage, finance and real estate, and retail trade. However, oil and gas production fell as global markets for petroleum products remained weak.

Annual inflation climbed to 4.0% in the first 7 months of 2017 from 2.5% in the same period last year (Figure 3.4.16). The major impetus to inflation seems to have been a one-time jump in domestic fuel and transport prices. In March 2017, the government replaced its managed float mechanism for pricing fuel—which adjusted prices monthly using

3.4.14 Demand-side contributions to growth

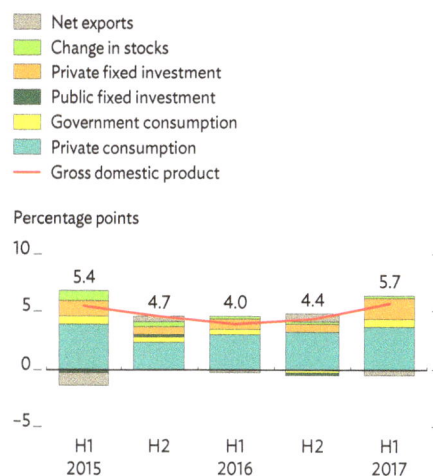

Legend:
- Net exports
- Change in stocks
- Private fixed investment
- Public fixed investment
- Government consumption
- Private consumption
- Gross domestic product

Percentage points

H = half.
Sources: Haver Analytics; Bank Negara Malaysia. 2017. *Monthly Statistical Bulletin.* July. http://www.bnm.gov.my (both accessed 15 September 2017).

3.4.15 Investment indicators

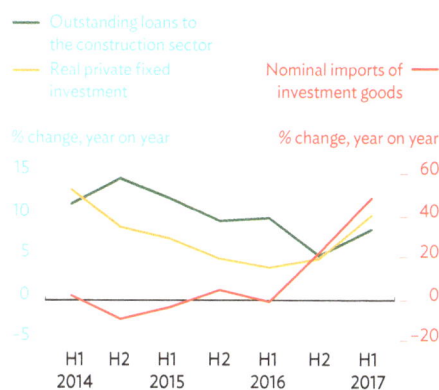

- Outstanding loans to the construction sector
- Real private fixed investment
- Nominal imports of investment goods

% change, year on year

H = half.
Source: Haver Analytics (accessed 15 September 2017).

3.4.16 Monthly inflation

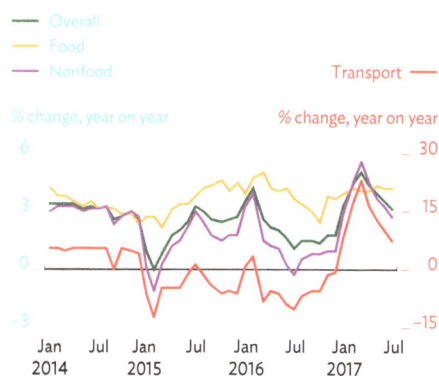

- Overall
- Food
- Nonfood
- Transport

% change, year on year

Source: Haver Analytics (accessed 15 September 2017).

a formula that included the average domestic price in the preceding 10 days and the operational costs of domestic fuel suppliers—with a new floating pricing system. Under the new system, domestic prices are adjusted weekly to reflect changes in international prices. This change caused a sharp jump in domestic fuel prices, especially for diesel, the fuel commonly used for commercial transport in the country. As a result, the transport component of the consumer price index rose by 5.1% in March and 4.4% in April. However, after this one-off inflationary jolt, sluggish international oil prices reversed the rising trend for domestic fuel and transport prices, especially since June. Moreover, bank credit to the private sector grew at an annual rate of 5.9%, lower than the 6.5% pace a year earlier and thus another factor helping to ease inflationary pressures. Bank Negara Malaysia, the central bank, has kept its monetary stance unchanged since July 2016, with the overnight policy rate at 3.0%.

Fiscal policy in 2017 was expansionary, perhaps causing the deficit to come in slightly wider than planned in the original budget. Buoyant tax revenues from both individual income tax and general sales tax pushed fiscal revenues slightly higher than expected despite a continued downward trend in revenues from oil and gas that began in 2009. Meanwhile, government expenditures rose in the first half of 2017 by only 1.6%, much less than either budgeted growth or the 5.4% rise in the same period in 2016 (Figure 3.4.17). This slowdown came despite government efforts to fast-track major public infrastructure projects under the Eleventh Malaysia Plan, its 2016–2020 public spending agenda. The net result was a budget deficit equal to 5.2% of GDP, slightly lower than the 5.6% figure for last year but much higher than the original government target of 3.0% for this year. The government is thus likely to miss its fiscal deficit target for this year and will need to raise tax revenues before long to meet its medium-term target. Although federal government debt will remain manageable at the equivalent of 52.0% of GDP, public loan guarantees, estimated at 18% of GDP in 2016, point to significant contingent liabilities for the government.

Turning to the external account, the US dollar value of merchandise exports rose by 12.9% in the first half of the year, reversing mild contraction in the first half of last year. The pickup in exports was broad-based, featuring double-digit expansion for high-tech manufactures, in particular the intermediate electrical and electronic products that comprise about 15% of Malaysia's total exports. By destination, exports to the PRC, the European Union, Japan, and the US grew markedly, reflecting buoyant external demand and a pickup in commodity prices. Merchandise imports rose even faster, by 16.5%, driven by imports of parts and components for domestic manufacturing and imports of capital equipment for infrastructure projects already under way.

The trade surplus came in at $11.9 billion, slightly higher than last year. Net receipts from services fell slightly. Consequently, the current account surplus of $3.4 billion in the first half of the year, equal to 2.3% of GDP, was higher than the 1.6% recorded in the corresponding period last year (Figure 3.4.18). With net capital inflows slightly positive,

3.4.17 Fiscal performance

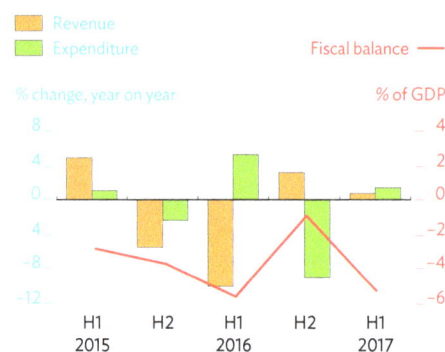

Source: Haver Analytics (accessed 15 September 2017).

3.4.18 Current account balance

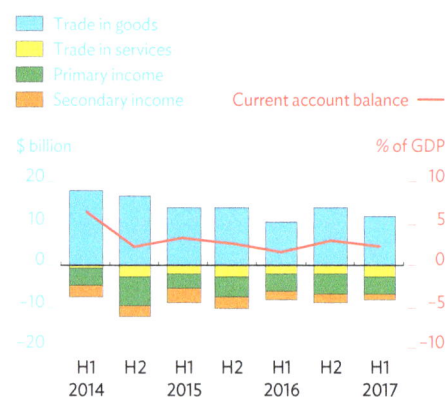

Source: Haver Analytics (accessed 15 September 2017).

3.4.19 GDP growth

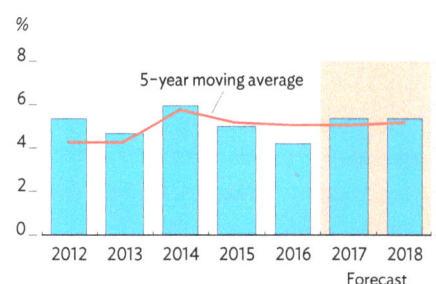

Source: Asian Development Outlook database.

foreign exchange reserves rose. These reserves stood at $97.4 billion in June 2017, which is more than the country's short-term external debt and sufficient to finance 6.6 months of imports.

Prospects

Growth in the second half of the year is likely to hold up well at around 5.0%, albeit somewhat lower than in the first half. The full-year growth forecast is thus revised up to 5.4%, as is the growth forecast for next year (Figure 3.4.19). Both these forecasts are higher than *ADO 2017* projections of 4.4% growth in 2017 and 4.6% in 2018. As in the first half of this year, growth will be broadly-based. Malaysia's export prospects should hold up well, assuming continued strength in external demand.

Private consumption is expected to remain robust in the near term, boosted by higher incomes, positive employment prospects, and optimistic consumer sentiment. Manufacturing wages in nominal terms, which increased by 3.2% in the first half of 2017, should continue to post gains for the rest of this year and in 2018. Meanwhile, growth in government consumption may see a modest pickup as the government seeks to balance its goal of controlling spending while providing financial assistance to poorer households and salary increments to government employees.

Business confidence started gathering strength in late 2016 and continues to be high, which bodes well for private investment (Figure 3.4.20). The business conditions index remained upbeat, rising above 100 in the second quarter of 2017, its highest in 3.5 years. The recovery in private investment in the first half of this year, particularly in export-oriented sectors, should continue in the near term. A double-digit surge in outstanding loans for construction year on year to June 2017 further suggests that the recent pickup in domestic private investment will continue. Further, firms are expanding their workforces in response to a rise in industrial production by 6.0% year on year in July 2017, the highest pace since December 2016.

Public investment, which contracted in the first half of this year, is expected to pick up steam, albeit slowly, with the resumption of government projects initiated since the second half of last year. Major ongoing public investment projects that could see faster implementation are the Pan-Borneo Highway, West Coast Expressway, Sungai Besi–Ulu Kelang Elevated Expressway, and Damansara–Shah Alam Elevated Expressway. Moreover, the construction of the Kuala Lumpur–Singapore High Speed Rail, slated to begin in 2018, could support higher public investment next year.

External demand for Malaysia's exports is likely to maintain its recent gains. In particular, as the rebound in the global electronics trade firms up, exports of semiconductors and related items are expected to continue to benefit in 2017 and 2018. Malaysia's export base is quite diversified, with machinery and transport equipment accounting for 42% of total exports (Figure 3.4.21).

Growth is similarly likely to remain broadly based across sectors, given Malaysia's diverse production base, with both agriculture and manufacturing expanding. Manufacturing, which accounts for a quarter of GDP, is expected to perform well in line with healthy export

3.4.20 Business and consumer confidence

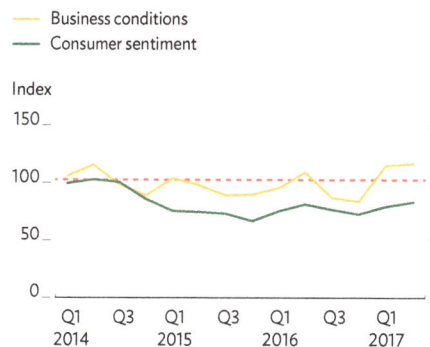

Note: Above 100 indicates improvement in business conditions and rising consumer confidence.
Source: CEIC Data Company (accessed 18 September 2017).

3.4.21 Exports and manufacturing base, first half 2017

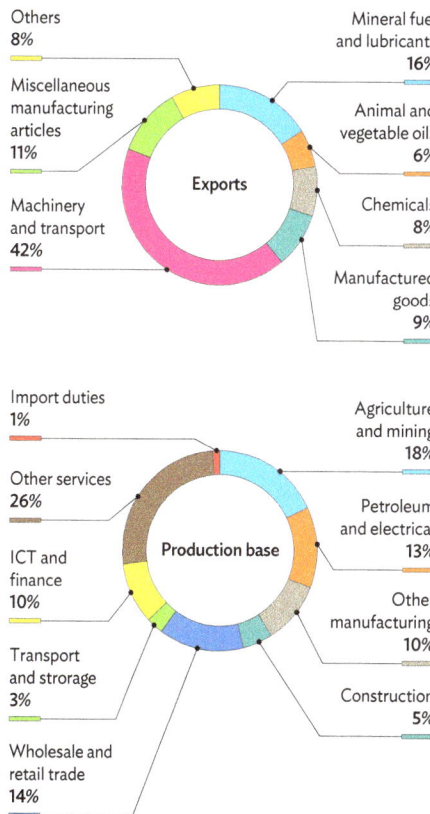

Sources: Haver Analytics and CEIC Data Company (accessed 15 September 2017).

demand, particularly for electronics. The service sector, which provides more than half of GDP, will continue to grow. Tourism, though a small contributor, will see a modest pickup on increasing tourist arrivals from the People's Republic of China, India, and the US despite a new tourist tax implemented in July 2017.

Hydrocarbon production, accounting for about 7% of GDP, should improve slightly. Following its withdrawal from some joint ventures overseas, Petronas still has many domestic investments. While greenfield exploration has temporarily halted in Malaysia, domestic gas and oil production is projected to rise this year and next as natural gas fields in Kanowit and oil fields in Malikai have started production and as efforts continue to improve production efficiency in existing fields. Current investments in refineries should support better growth in the medium term, despite the subdued international market for fuel.

Higher wages and rising incomes may put upward pressure on prices. There are already some signs that the labor market is tightening, as evident from the continued rise in average manufacturing wages since March. However, since the spike in inflation in the first half of this year was caused by a one-off hike to previously administered fuel prices, some respite from supply-side pressures on inflation can be expected. On balance, inflation in this year as a whole is likely to be 3.7%, higher than the *ADO 2017* projection of 3.3%, which will require inflation to slow more in 2018 to reach the unchanged forecast of 2.7% for that year (Figure 3.4.22).

Regarding the external payments position, two sets of forces are at work. On the one hand, the recovery in exports should improve the current account balance. On the other, given that a large chunk of production for exports is highly dependent on imports, and that higher growth and rising incomes will raise demand for consumer imports, imports should rise almost in tandem with exports. This *Update* therefore projects that the current account surplus will hold at the equivalent of 2.4% of GDP both this year and next. This is upward revision for both years from *ADO 2017* forecasts.

External risks to the outlook include backsliding in the global electronics trade and possible volatility in international financial markets. On the domestic front, a national election scheduled for 2018 could prompt political standoffs and even instability.

3.4.2 Selected economic indicators, Malaysia (%)

	2017		2018	
	ADO 2017	Update	ADO 2017	Update
GDP growth	4.4	5.4	4.6	5.4
Inflation	3.3	3.7	2.7	2.7
Current acct. bal. (share of GDP)	1.8	2.4	2.0	2.4

Source: ADB estimates.

3.4.22 Inflation

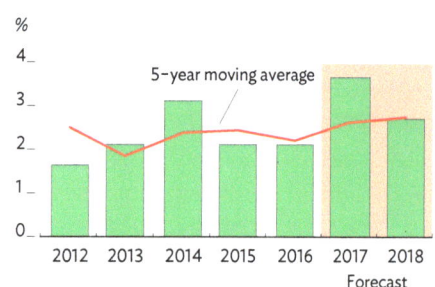

Source: Asian Development Outlook database.

Philippines

Driven by broad expansion in domestic demand, the Philippine economy continued to perform strongly in the first half of 2017. GDP is now seen to grow at a slightly faster pace than was forecast in *ADO 2017* both this year and next. Inflation will be higher than last year but lower than anticipated in April, while the current account surplus is likely to be in line with the earlier forecast.

Updated assessment

GDP grew by 6.4% year on year in the first half of 2017, moderating from the 7.0% pace in the same period last year but in line with the average 6.3% annual expansion since 2010. The Philippines remains among the fastest growing Southeast Asian economies this year.

Broad-based strength in domestic demand underpinned growth in the first half of this year (Figure 3.4.23). Fixed investment sustained strong momentum, rising by 12.1% in the first half of this year on top of hefty 29.3% growth in the corresponding period last year. As a result, fixed investment now constitutes 25.8% of GDP, its highest share in over a decade and comparable to its regional peers (Figure 3.4.24). Private investment remained brisk, driven by investment in construction and larger capital spending, notably on machinery and transport equipment. Public investment in construction also continued to expand, by 9.0% in the first half of the year.

Household consumption, which accounts for two-thirds of GDP, rose by 5.8% in the first half. Although easing from 7.3% expansion in the first half of last year, the pace of consumption growth was in line with its 5.7% annual average from 2010 to 2016. Remittances from overseas Filipinos provided strong support to private consumption, which rose by 5.5% in the first half, up from 4.4% growth in the same period last year. Growth in remittances picked up to 8.7% year on year in July. Merchandise export growth improved, though net exports remained negative.

By sector, services and industry were the key drivers of growth in the first 6 months of this year, while a rebound in agriculture gave an additional boost to the economy. The service sector remained buoyant with 6.4% growth in the first half (Figure 3.4.25). Within the service sector, growth spread across business process outsourcing (BPO), trade, tourism, finance, and real estate.

Industrial production grew by a robust 6.8% in the first half of this year, albeit moderating from 8.4% in the same period in 2016. Manufacturing, which occupies about 70% of the sector, rose by 7.7% in the first 6 months of 2017, higher than the 7.1% increase in the corresponding period last year (Figure 3.4.26). Buoyant domestic demand and higher exports drove manufacturing with strong gains in food processing (the biggest subsector), construction materials, furniture, communication, transportation, and office equipment (Figure 3.4.27).

Construction turned in 7.4% growth in the first 6 months of this year, following a 13.8% rise in the first half of last year, as public and private projects alike remained strong. Agriculture recovered from a dry spell associated with weather disruption from El Niño last year, growing by 5.6% in the first half of 2017, adding support to the economy.

3.4.23 Demand-side contributions to growth

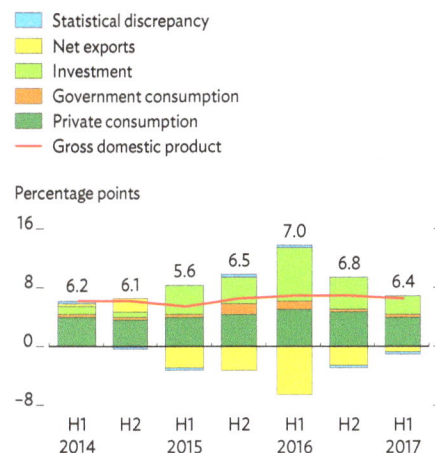

Statistical discrepancy
Net exports
Investment
Government consumption
Private consumption
— Gross domestic product

Percentage points

H = half.
Source: CEIC Data Company (accessed 25 August 2017).

3.4.24 Fixed investment

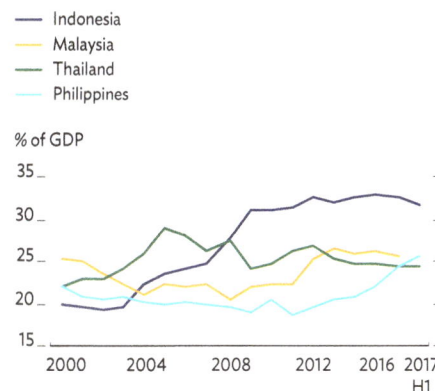

— Indonesia
Malaysia
Thailand
Philippines

% of GDP

H = half.
Source: CEIC Data Company (accessed 3 September 2017).

3.4.25 Supply-side contributions to growth

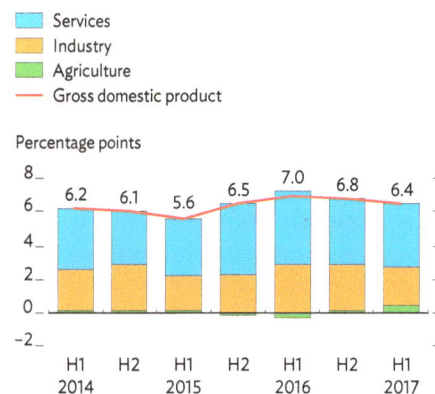

Services
Industry
Agriculture
— Gross domestic product

Percentage points

H = half.
Source: CEIC Data Company (accessed 25 August 2017).

Inflation averaged 3.1% in the first 8 months of the year, doubling from 1.5% in the same period last year. Buoyant demand, higher fuel prices, and a hike in public transport fares largely drove inflation. Despite edging upwards, inflation remained within the inflation target range of 2%–4% set by Bangko Sentral ng Pilipinas, prompting the central bank to keep the overnight reverse repurchase rate unchanged at 3.0%.

Reflecting the accommodative policy, bank credit to the private sector went up by 18.8% in the year to July 2017, an acceleration from 15.8% growth a year earlier. The corresponding figures for growth in money supply (M3) were 13.5% in the year to July 2017, marginally up from 13.4% a year earlier.

On the fiscal front, government expenditure excluding interest payments increased by 10.5% in the first half of this year, with a significant increase in the allocation for infrastructure. Tax collections, which supply about 90% of government revenues, rose by 8.8%. The net result of these budgetary trends was a fiscal deficit equal to 2.1% of GDP in the first half of 2017, somewhat higher than the 1.7% figure in the same period last year.

The current account deficit stood at the equivalent of 0.2% of GDP in the first half of 2017, narrowing the 0.3% deficit in the same period last year (Figure 3.4.28). The current account turned from a deficit in the first quarter of the year to a surplus in the second quarter supported by strong remittances and earnings from BPO and tourism. Even as merchandise exports rebounded with 18.0% expansion in the first half, strong growth in imports widened the trade deficit. The merchandise trade deficit reached the equivalent of 12.9% of GDP in the first half of 2017, deepening from 11.8% in the first 6 months of last year.

Inflows of foreign direct investment amounted to $3.6 billion in the first half of 2017, coming on top of hefty inflows worth $8.0 billion in the whole of 2016. These investments were channeled mainly into finance, real estate, manufacturing, and trade. The balance of payments recorded a small deficit equal to 0.5% of GDP, reversing a surplus of 0.4% in the same period last year, partly because of higher portfolio capital outflows. Nevertheless, gross international reserves totaled $81.7 billion in August 2017, cover for 8.6 months of imports of goods and services and income payments. The Philippine peso depreciated by 2.7% against the US dollar in the year to mid-September. External debt as a share of GDP steadily declined to 23.5% in the first half of 2017, indicating a comfortable external payments position.

Prospects

GDP growth is projected to strengthen in the rest of the year and in 2018 as domestic demand is likely to continue to expand in the near term. Growth can expect a push from higher public spending, particularly on infrastructure and social services. Forecasts for growth in this year and next are thus revised up marginally from *ADO 2017* projections, from 6.4% to 6.5% for 2017 and from 6.6% to 6.7% for 2018 (Figure 3.4.29).

Besides strong remittances from overseas Filipinos, household consumption is expected to get a boost from a proposed reduction in personal income tax rates. A recent central bank survey showed that the

3.4.26 Contributions to industry growth

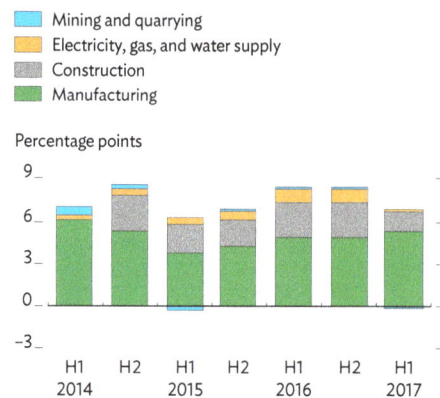

Mining and quarrying
Electricity, gas, and water supply
Construction
Manufacturing

Percentage points

H = half.
Source: CEIC Data Company (accessed 13 September 2017).

3.4.27 Contributions to manufacturing growth

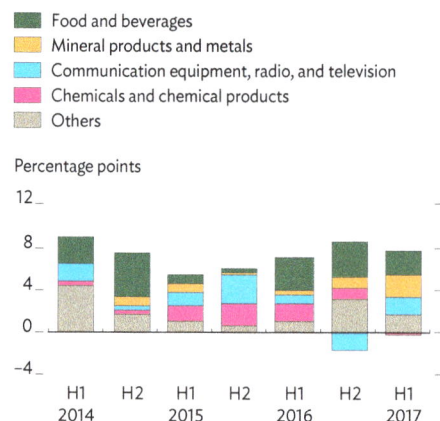

Food and beverages
Mineral products and metals
Communication equipment, radio, and television
Chemicals and chemical products
Others

Percentage points

H = half.
Source: CEIC Data Company (accessed 13 September 2017).

3.4.28 Current account balance

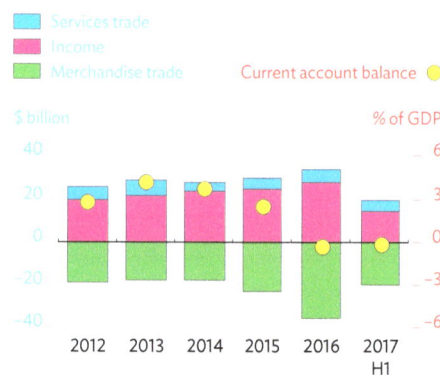

Services trade
Income
Merchandise trade   Current account balance

$ billion   % of GDP

H = half.
Source: CEIC Data Company (accessed 15 September 2017).

consumer outlook for the year ahead remained favorable (Figure 3.4.30). The survey also showed optimistic business sentiment, citing buoyant domestic demand and the rollout of public infrastructure projects as among the major positive factors. Fixed investment is seen to remain upbeat. Rising imports of capital goods and sustained expansion in credit to business, which rose by 18.8% year on year in July, suggest that private investment will maintain solid growth. Acceleration in public infrastructure investment will improve the country's investment climate.

Concerted government efforts to improve budget execution in terms of project preparation and implementation, procurement, and financial management systems should help ensure that the budget and public investment programs are implemented effectively and on time. There is already some evidence that this is occurring. For example, in the first 7 months of 2017, both total public spending and public infrastructure investment were on track to achieve their full year targets. This improves on earlier years when actual public expenditures fell short of original budget targets.

Moreover, in the proposed budget for 2018, public spending is 12.4% higher than the 2017 budget, boosting allocations for infrastructure and social programs. Nearly 40.0% of overall budgetary spending will go to social services, including support for national health insurance, immunization programs, cash transfers to poor families, and universal basic education. Government infrastructure development focuses on national roads, railways, ports, health-care facilities, school buildings, and agricultural works. The government has begun implementing an ambitious infrastructure development program called "Build Build Build," under which public infrastructure spending is targeted to increase from less than the equivalent of 3.0% of GDP during 2010–2016 to 5.3% in 2017, 6.3% in 2018, and 7.4% by 2022 (Figure 3.4.31). The government estimates the total funding requirement for the infrastructure program to be $160 billion–$180 billion in the 6 years from 2017 to 2022.

To help finance higher public investment, the government is proposing comprehensive tax reform. The first package of the tax reform program, likely to be approved in late 2017, includes proposals to raise excise taxes on automobiles and petroleum products and to broaden the base for the value-added tax by eliminating a number of exemptions, while reducing personal income tax rates. The expected net increase in revenue from these reforms, together with some measures to improve tax administration, will support infrastructure and social spending programs. At the same time, the lower personal income tax rate is seen to boost domestic demand and economic growth.

By sector, services will continue to be the lead driver of growth, with BPO, tourism, and trade expected to perform well. Revenues from BPO are estimated to reach $25.5 billion this year, employing about 1.4 million workers. Prospects for manufacturing remain robust. The composite purchasing managers' index in July 2017 remained firmly above the 50-point threshold, indicating expansion ahead. Factories that produce cement, glass, and metal products are benefitting from brisk construction and in particular from public infrastructure projects.

3.4.29 GDP growth

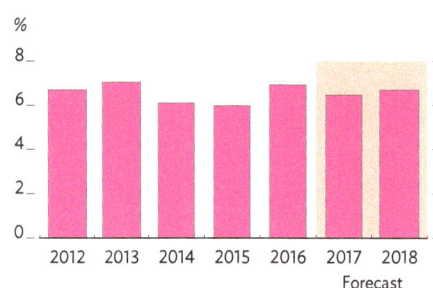

Source: Asian Development Outlook database.

3.4.30 Consumer and business confidence

Q = quarter.
Note: A positive index indicates a favorable view.
Source: Bangko Sentral ng Pilipinas.

3.4.31 Government infrastructure spending program

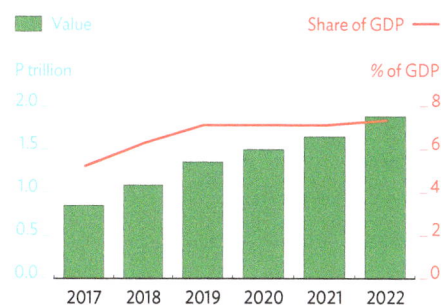

Source: Department of Budget and Management.

Also boding well for investment in manufacturing are sustained growth in credit to manufacturers, which rose by 12.3% year on year in July, and high utilization of manufacturing capacity. Private construction is likely to be supported by demand for office and retail space, as well as housing.

Inflation forecasts are now revised down to 3.2% from 3.5% for 2017 and to 3.5% from 3.7% for 2018 (Figure 3.4.32). Fuel price inflation is likely to be lower than earlier projected as international oil prices stay subdued. The rebound in agriculture and resulting augmentation of food supply will help contain food prices. At these projected rates, inflation will be higher than in 2016 but still within the central bank target range of 2%–4%, allowing the continuation of accommodative monetary policy. A new central bank governor, who assumed office in July 2017, announced that the bank will continue to fine-tune its execution of monetary policy to make it more market oriented and further strengthen governance and risk-management practices in banks and other financial institutions.

Despite a small deficit in the first half of this year, the current account surplus is projected to equal a modest 0.2% of GDP in 2017 and a somewhat less modest 0.5% in 2018, as forecast in the April. Upward pressure on imports will persist as domestic investment and growth strengthen, causing the merchandise trade balance to continue to be negative. Yet, strength in remittances and net services exports, notably income from BPO and tourism, are likely to help the country keep its current account balances in surplus both this year and next.

Possible volatility in global financial markets and persistent uncertainty about the trade policies of major industrial economies pose risks to the outlook. On the domestic front, further progress in improving budget execution and expediting tax policy reform will be crucial. The timely passage of tax reform packages is vital for financing the planned increases in investment into much-needed infrastructure and social services. The government aims to raise the ratio of tax to GDP from 14.2% in the first half of 2017 to 15.3% in 2018. On the expenditure side, the government is pushing for approval of a budget reform bill in the legislature that seeks to institutionalize reform that will accelerate budget execution, improve service delivery, and enhance transparency and accountability. In view of the ambitious public investment program, government agencies need to expand their absorptive capacity and their ability to prepare, implement, and manage infrastructure projects.

3.4.3 Selected economic indicators, Philippines (%)

	2017		2018	
	ADO 2017	Update	ADO 2017	Update
GDP growth	6.4	6.5	6.6	6.7
Inflation	3.5	3.2	3.7	3.5
Current acct. bal. (share of GDP)	0.2	0.2	0.5	0.5

Source: ADB estimates.

3.4.32 Inflation

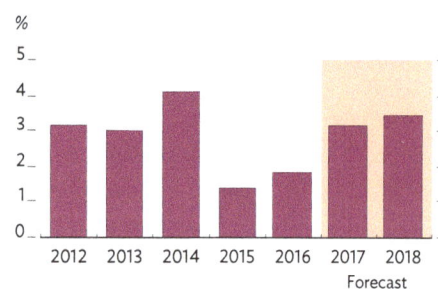

Source: Asian Development Outlook database.

Thailand

The economy expanded by 3.5% in the first half of 2017. Surprisingly robust growth in agriculture and exports offset subdued investment to sustain a GDP growth rate in line with the *ADO 2017* forecast in April. The current account surplus is now seen to come in at 8.5% of GDP and inflation at 0.7%, both lower than the April forecasts. Growth and inflation are likely to edge up in 2018, and the current account surplus to shrink.

Updated assessment

GDP expanded by 3.5% in the first half of 2017, marginally higher than in the first half of 2016. Continued favorable weather pushed agricultural production up by an impressive 10.3% in the first half. Major crops such as rice, oil palm, sugarcane, and fruits registered large gains, as did fisheries. Services expanded by a strong 4.9% in the first 6 months of the year, while manufacturing and construction were almost flat (Figure 3.4.33). Within the service sector, buoyant tourist arrivals gave a major fillip to hotels and restaurants and to transport, storage, and communication, but construction posted a 1.9% decline. Within the manufacturing sector, production expanded well for electronic components and parts, computers and computer parts, and machinery and equipment. The manufacturing production index for semiconductors climbed by 12.3% in the first half of the year, and that for hard disk drives by 10.2%.

On the demand side, private consumption rose by a modest 3.1% in the first half of this year, slightly slower than the 3.4% pace in the same period last year. Private consumption was supported by higher farm incomes that followed the turnaround in agriculture and a program offering subsidized small personal loans that the government launched in February 2017 through state-owned banks.

Investment remained subdued largely because of lackluster interest from private investors as fragility in the country's business environment and political situation persisted. Private investment grew by a meager 1.0% in the first half of the year, down from 1.4% in the same period of 2016 (Figure 3.4.34). Private construction investment hardly grew at all in the first half of the year, though it seems to have picked up somewhat in more recent months on higher residential demand along mass rapid transit lines in Bangkok. Meanwhile, the construction of commercial buildings, industrial plants, and industrial estates continued its declining trend. Government investment was similarly anemic, growing by only 1.1% in the first half of the year, though investment by the state enterprises posted robust growth at 6.0%.

Sluggish investment in the first half of the year was partly offset by exports that exceeded expectations. Helped by a recovery in global demand, merchandise exports increased by 7.4% in the first half, with both agriculture and industry accelerating. Rice exports rose by 4.5%, and rubber exports jumped by an eye-catching 57.7%. Electronics exports rose by 13.4% in the period, driven by recovery in the global electronics trade. Exports of petroleum products increased by 39.6%, and exports of chemicals by 18.5%. Imports of merchandise, meanwhile, rose by 14.8% in the first half of the year, partly on the

3.4.33 Supply-side contributions to growth

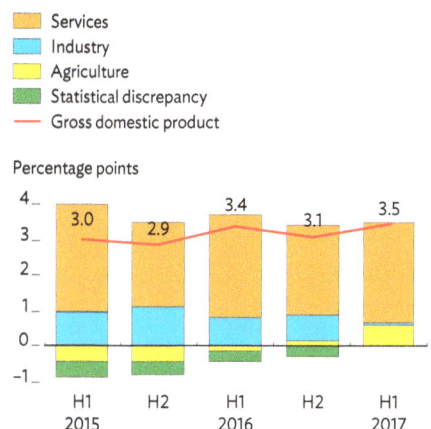

H = half.
Source: Office of the National Economic and Social Development Board, http://www.nesdb.go.th (accessed 29 August 2017).

3.4.34 Fixed investment growth

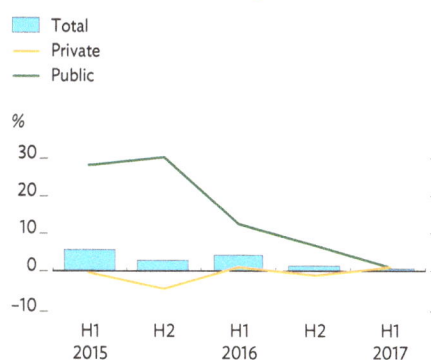

H = half.
Source: Office of The National Economic and Social Development Board, http://www.nesdb.go.th (accessed 29 August 2017).

3.4.35 Trade indicators

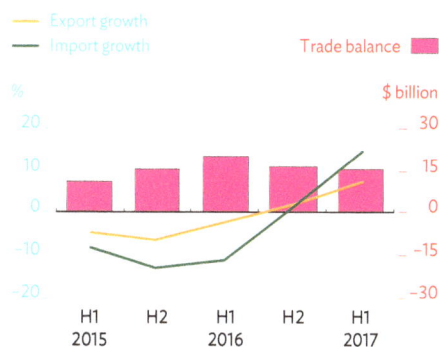

H = half.
Source: Bank of Thailand, http://www.bot.or.th (accessed 7 September 2017).

importation of raw materials, parts, and components for export-oriented manufacturing. The net result was a trade surplus of $15.4 billion, equal to 7.1% of GDP, down from the $20.2 billion trade surplus in the corresponding period last year (Figure 3.4.35).

Receipts from net exports of services were $8.1 billion in the first half of 2017, higher than the $6.1 billion recorded in the first half of the previous year. The current account surplus in the first half thus came to $23.5 billion, equal to 10.9% of GDP. Although tourism revenues posted a robust rise, the number of foreign tourist arrivals grew by only 4.1% in the first half of 2017, just a third of the 12.0% rise in the corresponding period in 2016 (Figure 3.4.36). This was largely because of a crackdown by the government on so-called "zero dollar" budget tours from the People's Republic of China last year, as well as flooding in southern Thailand in early 2017.

The capital account in the balance of payments registered a net outflow of $13.7 billion, narrowing the current account surplus somewhat. The overall balance of payments was still positive, enabling Thailand to add to its foreign exchange reserves. At the end of July 2017, reserves stood at $190.4 billion, or cover for 9.5 months of imports. With external debt equal to 33.1% of GDP, of which only 39.5% had a maturity of less than a year, the country's overall external payments position continued to be comfortable. The Thai baht therefore strengthened by around 7% against the US dollar in the first half of 2017.

Inflationary pressures eased with continued slack in investment, higher agricultural production, and the appreciating baht. It averaged 1.3% in the first quarter, partly from higher international fuel prices, but only 0.1% in the second quarter as international fuel prices softened again and improved farm output forced food prices to decline. The average in the first half was, at 0.7%, much lower than the April projection and far below the inflation target of 1.5%–2.5% set by the Bank of Thailand, the central bank (Figure 3.4.37).

With slowing inflation, sluggish private investment, and lackluster expansion of bank credit to business in the first half of 2017, the central bank has ample grounds for easing monetary policy. However, it has kept its policy interest rate unchanged at 1.50% since April 2015 in line with its continued perception that the economy is on the path to recovery despite global uncertainty. Credit to business expanded by 2.0% in the first quarter of 2017 and by 2.7% in the second.

Fiscal policy has continued to be expansionary. The fiscal deficit in the first 9 months of FY2017 (ending 30 September 2017) amounted to B473.9 billion, equal to 4.2% of GDP and slightly down from 4.4% in the first half of last year. Government revenue in the first 9 months of FY2017 was 0.4% above its projection but 3.1% below revenue collected in the year-earlier period. Meanwhile, expenditure reached 71.1% of the FY2017 annual budget, putting it largely on track with the government's budget projection. With the country's public debt manageable at the equivalent of 32.3% of GDP at the end of July 2017, up only marginally from 31.2% a year earlier, fiscal expansion can proceed for some time without endangering public debt sustainability.

3.4.36 Tourist arrivals

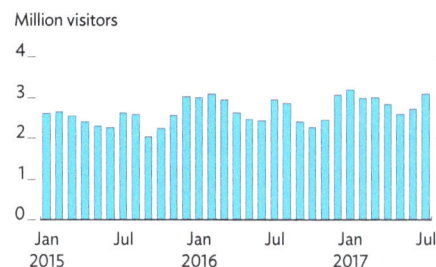

Source: CEIC Data Company (accessed 7 September 2017).

3.4.37 Inflation and policy interest rate

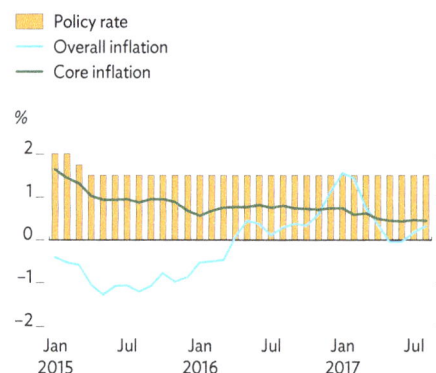

Source: CEIC Data Company (accessed 7 September 2017).

3.4.38 GDP growth

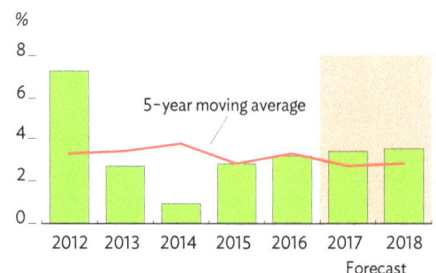

Source: Asian Development Outlook database.

Prospects

Trends in the first half of the year indicate that GDP growth for the full year 2017 is likely to come in at the *ADO 2017* forecast of 3.5%. With exports continuing to gather momentum and the government prioritizing the stepped-up implementation of public investment projects, growth next year will likely edge up to 3.6%, as anticipated in April (Figure 3.4.38).

Agriculture should be able to build on its solid recovery in the first half of the year and expand at a robust pace both this year and next, notwithstanding recent flooding in the northeast. Manufacturing is seen to improve only gradually, with electronics and chemicals expected to outperform other industries.

On the demand side, private consumption should stay robust, growing at an annual rate of 3.0%–3.5% in the rest of this year and in 2018 (Figure 3.4.39). However, a recent downward trend in consumer confidence, perhaps reflecting uncertainty over commodity prices, sounds a cautionary note, as do high household debt, equal to 78.6% of GDP at the end of the first quarter of 2017, and its adverse effect on consumption (Figure 3.4.40).

Although the pace of public investment slowed in the first half of this year, it is expected to pick up again in the coming months as the government fast-tracks the implementation of public infrastructure projects, both ongoing projects and new ones to expand mass rapid transit, airports, electricity distribution systems, and expressways. Moreover, a strong 20.5% rise in construction investment by state enterprises in the second quarter of 2017 bodes well for public investment, as most of the large public infrastructure projects are within the purview of state enterprises.

A mild recovery in private investment in the second quarter of this year—by 3.2% after contracting in the preceding 3 quarters—indicates that a gradual recovery is under way. Faster implementation of public investment projects should spur otherwise sluggish private investment. Moreover, a program to develop the Eastern Economic Corridor has attracted attention from foreign investors but has yet to be fully approved. The Eastern Economic Corridor Act is expected to be cleared by the national legislature by the end of 2017.

Inflation in the first half of this year was much lower than anticipated earlier. Inflation for the year as a whole is now seen to come to only 0.7%, less than half of the *ADO 2017* projection of 1.8%. Even if prices pick up somewhat next year, inflation in 2018 is more likely to come in at around 1.5%, somewhat lower than the April forecast of 2.0% (Figure 3.4.41).

Merchandise exports, having turned around in the first half of this year, should continue to contribute significantly to growth both this year and next. Exports are expected to grow by 5% in 2017 as a whole and improve further in 2018. Those of electronic and chemical products in particular are projected to expand well in the rest of the forecast period. Exports of agricultural products such as rice, rubber, and sugar are also likely to expand well, unless international commodity prices suddenly dip and dampen global trade in agriculture.

3.4.39 Private consumption and investment

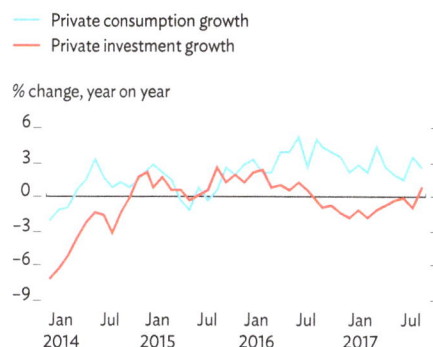

Note: Seasonally adjusted 3-month moving average.
Source: CEIC Data Company (accessed 7 September 2017).

3.4.40 Consumer confidence and business sentiment indexes

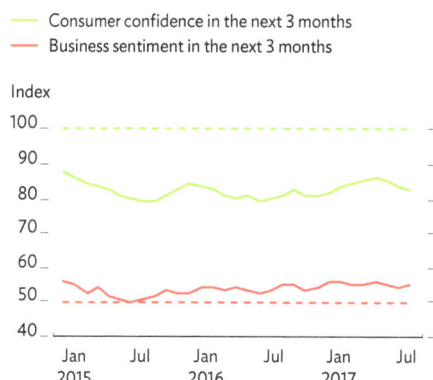

Note: A reading of less than 50 denotes a deterioration in business sentiment, while a reading of less than 100 denotes deterioration in consumer confidence.
Sources: CEIC Data Company; Bank of Thailand. http://www.bot.or.th (both accessed 7 September 2017).

3.4.41 Inflation

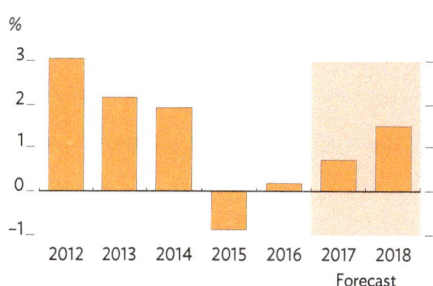

Source: *Asian Development Outlook* database.

As in the first half of this year, imports will grow strongly for the rest of this year and in 2018, mainly to meet domestic demand for raw materials, intermediate goods, and parts and components for export-oriented manufacturing. Imports of capital goods are also likely to rise faster with the launch of large infrastructure projects, both public and private. Merchandise imports are thus projected to expand by around 10% in 2017 and accelerate further in 2018. The trade balance is likely to narrow this year and next but will remain in surplus.

Net exports of services look set to post robust growth, especially as receipts from tourism continue to be buoyant. The increase in foreign tourist arrivals in 2017 is projected to be about 7.5%, taking the number of tourist arrivals in the full year to about 35 million. With modest remittances, the current account surplus is nevertheless likely to narrow somewhat this year and next, to 8.5% of GDP in 2017 and 6.5% in 2018, both figures half a percentage point lower than forecast in April (Figure 3.4.42).

While monetary policy is unlikely to ease, the government has reiterated that fiscal policy will continue to support growth, using public infrastructure spending as the key lever. Although actual government spending in FY2017 may come in slightly lower than the budgeted figure, investment by state enterprises is proceeding at a brisk pace. The fiscal deficit for the year as a whole is therefore likely to be close to the budgeted B390 billion. The budget for FY2018 is set at B2.9 trillion, with the fiscal deficit targeted at B450 billion, equal to 2.8% of projected GDP. Government capital expenditure for FY2018 is set at 22.7% of the total budget, for a similar share as in the FY2017 budget.

Risks to the economic outlook for 2018 are volatility in international financial markets and the fragile domestic political situation. Thailand's next general election is scheduled for the second half of 2018. If the election brings unexpected political standoffs or clashes, it could weaken the country's fragile business and investment climate.

3.4.4 Selected economic indicators, Thailand (%)

	2017		2018	
	ADO 2017	Update	ADO 2017	Update
GDP growth	3.5	3.5	3.6	3.6
Inflation	1.8	0.7	2.0	1.5
Current acct. bal. (share of GDP)	9.0	8.5	7.0	6.5

Source: ADB estimates.

3.4.42 Current account balance

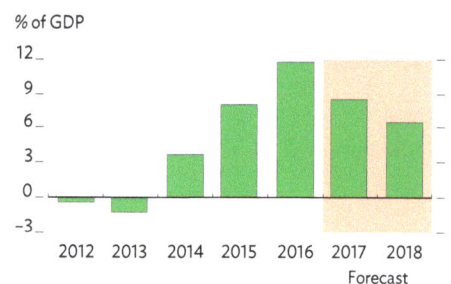

Source: Asian Development Outlook database.

Viet Nam

Economic growth in 2017 is now expected to come in at 6.3%, marginally lower than forecast in *ADO 2017*. Inflation is projected slightly higher than foreseen in April, and the current account surplus is likely to shrink faster than earlier envisaged.

Updated assessment

GDP expanded at 5.7% in the first half of 2017, marginally higher than in the first half of 2016 (Figure 3.4.43). While agriculture and services turned in higher growth, construction posted milder growth and mining contracted.

Driven by buoyant tourism, services expanded by 6.9% in the first half of this year, improving upon 6.5% growth in the corresponding period in 2016. International tourist arrivals jumped by 30%, boosting tourism-related services by 8.9%. Banking and financial services also posted higher growth, at 7.7% in the first half, up from 6.9% a year earlier.

Better weather contributed to 2.7% growth in agricultural production in the first half of 2017, marking a turnaround from 0.2% contraction in the same period last year. Farm production grew by 2.0%, reversing 0.8% contraction, while growth in fisheries and aquaculture accelerated to 5.1% from 1.2% in the first half 2016.

Industrial output growth weakened to 5.3% in the first half from 7.0% a year earlier. Mining output contracted by 8.2% as international coal prices fell, domestic production costs rose, and oil and coal reserves became depleted—as well as from the effect of a natural resource tax hike introduced in July 2016 (Figure 3.4.44). Construction softened, with the sector posting growth at 8.5% in the first half of this year, down from 9.3% in the corresponding period in 2016, largely the result of constrained public spending.

On the demand side, private consumption expanded by 7.0% in the first half of 2017, and public consumption by 7.2%. Gross domestic capital formation grew by 9.5%, comparable with its 9.6% growth rate in the first half of last year. Using data from the General Statistics Office, disbursements of foreign direct investment in the first 8 months of 2017 were estimated to reach $10.3 billion, up 5.1% from a year earlier (Figure 3.4.45).

Net exports of goods and services continued to drag on economic growth. Exports performed strongly on robust demand from Viet Nam's major export markets in Europe and the US. Merchandise exports climbed by 19% in the first 6 months of this year on impressive gains for manufactured products, including electronics, mobile phones, garments, and footwear.

Rapid import growth more than offset export growth, however, forcing down net exports in the first half of the year. Imports grew strongly to supply the expansion of import-intensive domestic manufacturing of electronics, telecommunications, and home appliances.

Average inflation edged up in the first 8 months of 2017 but remained modest at 3.8%, though core inflation rose sharply to 6.9% year on year in the same period on a hike in administered prices and fees for health care and education (Figure 3.4.46). The upward adjustment in

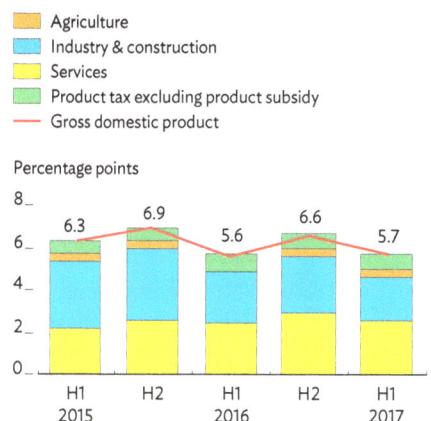

3.4.43 Supply-side contributions to growth

H = half.
Source: General Statistics Office of Viet Nam.

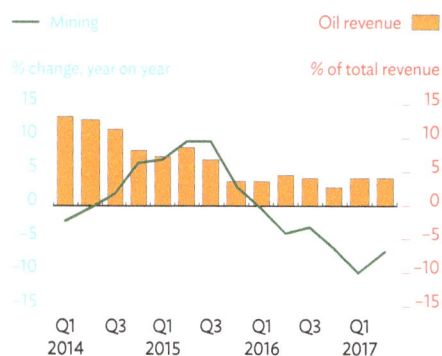

3.4.44 Mining growth and oil revenue

Sources: General Statistics Office of Viet Nam; Ministry of Finance.

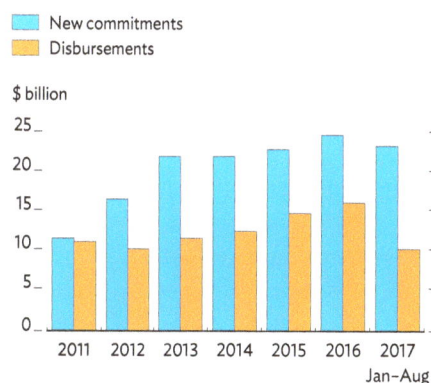

3.4.45 Foreign direct investment

Source: General Statistics Office of Viet Nam.

administered prices was, however, offset by moderation in prices for food, energy, and transportation. Recent months have seen the pace of inflation slow. The consumer price index posted in August a rise of only 3.4% year on year, much lower than the 5.2% posted at the beginning of 2017.

As inflation moderated, the State Bank of Viet Nam, the central bank, responded on 10 July 2017 by cutting its policy interest rates by 25 basis points, taking the refinancing rate down to 6.25% and the discount rate to 4.25%. The preferential lending rate for priority sectors such as agriculture and rural development was also reduced, from 7.0% to 6.5%, to stimulate recovery in drought-affected rural areas. Credit growth increased by an estimated 19.6% year on year in the first half of 2017, putting it on track to reach the government's target of 18%–20% growth for the full year. Broad money supply rose by an estimated 14.3% in the first half, similarly in line with the government's target of 16%–18% for the year (Figure 3.4.47).

Turning to government finances, the budget deficit narrowed in the first half of the year to the equivalent of 0.9% of GDP, down from 3.0% in the first half of 2016. Strong growth in government revenue and a more modest increase in government expenditure helped to narrow the budget deficit.

Government revenue grew by 18.2% in the first half of the year to reach the equivalent of 27.4% of GDP. Among revenue categories, nontax revenues rose by 23.0% on proceeds from the sale of state assets including equity in state-owned enterprises. Tax revenues increased by 16% thanks to the natural resource tax hike introduced in 2016. The collection of personal income tax rose by 20.8% in the first half of the year along with strong employment growth. Meanwhile, government expenditure grew at a more modest pace of 9.5% in the first half. Current expenditure increased by 9.2%, while capital expenditure rose by 11.2%.

The trade surplus narrowed faster than expected as surging imports outpaced strong export growth (Figure 3.4.48). In the first 6 months of the year, the trade surplus shrank to equal an estimated 1.5% of GDP from 8.1% in the first half of 2016. The narrowing trade surplus and lower net service receipts generated a current account deficit equal to an estimated 1.2% of GDP in the first half 2017, reversing a 6.2% surplus a year earlier (Figure 3.4.49). The overall balance of payments nevertheless remained in surplus, estimated to equal 2.7% of GDP, thanks to a surplus in the capital account estimated at 5.7% and derived mostly from stable remittances, large net foreign direct investment, and a modest rise in net inflows of portfolio capital. Foreign exchange reserves in June 2017 provided 2.5 months of cover for goods and service imports, marginally up from 2.4 months at the end of 2016.

Rising foreign portfolio inflows and a growing domestic financial market boosted the stock market. Continuing its strong run over the past 3 years, the Viet Nam share price index rose by 17.0% in the year to July 2017. By the end of that month, stock market capitalization had reached the equivalent of 56.4% of GDP, up from 42.0% at the end of 2016.

3.4.46 Monthly inflation

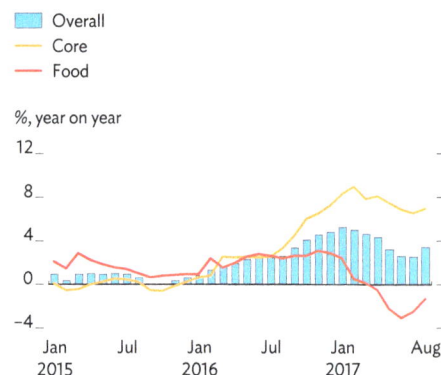

Note: Core inflation excludes only food.
Source: General Statistics Office of Viet Nam.

3.4.47 Credit and money supply growth

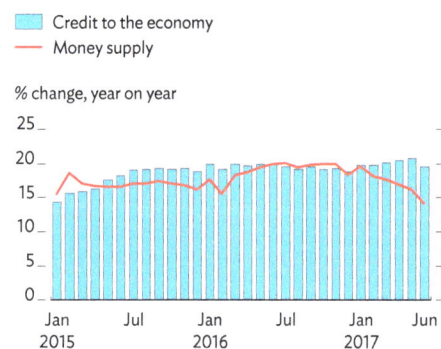

Sources: State Bank of Viet Nam; ADB estimates.

3.4.48 Trade indicators

H = half.
Sources: State Bank of Viet Nam; International Monetary Fund; ADB estimates.

Progress on structural reform has continued but at a modest pace. Of 45 state-owned enterprises to be equitized in 2017, only 22 had begun selling equity by the end of August and only 6 had achieved their target for the full year. Nevertheless, revenue generation from these sales remained broadly on track, allowing the government to collect in the first half of the year $510 million in divestment receipts, equal to 0.5% of GDP. The target for the whole of 2017 is 1.0%.

Progress in bank restructuring and the resolution of nonperforming loans (NPLs) was limited. While NPLs were reported at 2.6% of all outstanding loans at the end of March 2017, total NPLs—including reported NPLs, unresolved NPLs warehoused with the Viet Nam Asset Management Company, and loans deemed at risk of becoming NPLs—were estimated at 10.1% of outstanding loans in the whole banking system. Moreover, despite government plans to further consolidate the banking sector, not a single bank merger or acquisition was completed in the first half of 2017.

Prospects

Growth is likely to hold up fairly well in the second half of 2017, though continued contraction in mining will drag on the economy. This *Update* trims Viet Nam's growth forecasts to 6.3% for 2017 and 6.5% in 2018, taking 0.2 percentage points off each forecast in *ADO 2017* (Figure 3.4.50).

A modest recovery in mining output is foreseen as declines in mineral and crude oil output bottom out later this year or early next year.

Other economic indicators also point to strong growth next year. The manufacturing purchasing managers' index continues its rising trend. New orders have risen steadily since December 2015 to signal improving business conditions for manufacturers (Figure 3.4.51). Backlogs of work orders rose in July at the fastest pace in over 6 years, while inventories of finished products fell, suggesting that firms will be looking to increase their output in the coming months. Continued buoyancy in foreign direct investment inflows should add impetus to growth in the coming months, as should the recent easing of monetary and credit conditions.

The service sector is likely to maintain its current growth momentum. Aided by simplified visa procedures since February 2017, tourist arrivals are forecast by the government to reach 15 million by the end of 2017. Tourist revenues should get a further boost as Viet Nam hosts Asia-Pacific Economic Cooperation leaders' meetings from August to November 2017.

The recovery in agriculture is projected to remain on track, assuming that improved weather and current strength in demand for aquaculture exports are maintained in the coming months. Growth in the sector is expected to reach around 3% in the whole of 2017.

On the demand side, the outlook for private consumption remains stable as it benefits from strong growth in manufacturing employment. Acceleration in public capital expenditure in the second half of the year is expected to boost growth in investment. With only about 26% of planned capital outlays for the full year completed by the end of June 2017, efforts are being made to speed up the implementation of public

3.4.49 Current account indicators

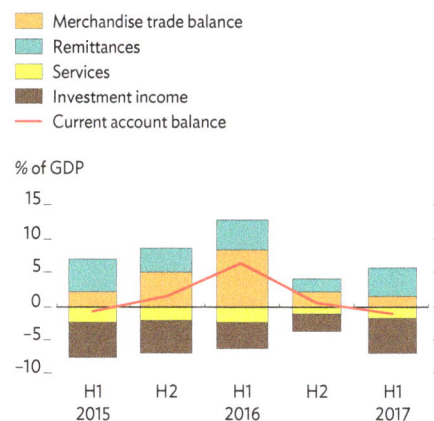

- Merchandise trade balance
- Remittances
- Services
- Investment income
- Current account balance

H = half.
Sources: State Bank of Viet Nam; International Monetary Fund; ADB estimates.

3.4.50 GDP growth

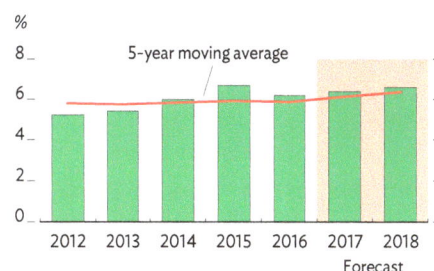

Source: Asian Development Outlook database.

3.4.51 Purchasing managers' index

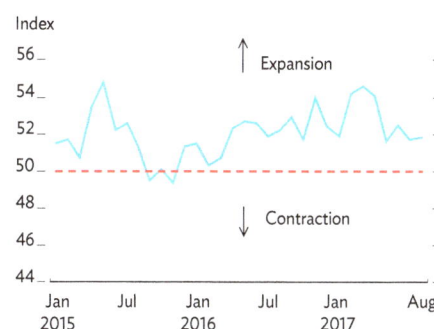

Note: Nikkei, Markit.
Source: Bloomberg (accessed 5 September 2017).

infrastructure projects in the remainder of the year. Prospects for private investment also look bright, with the number of new companies registered in January–August 2017 rising by 16.3% and additional support coming from high inflows of foreign direct investment.

Inflation is projected to continue its upward trend of recent months, fueled by the recent interest rate cuts, buoyant domestic demand, and strong GDP growth. Planned increases in fees for public education and health care will exert additional upward pressure on inflation, as will a recently announced 6.5% increase in the minimum wage that will take effect in 2018, building on a 7.0% rise in 2017. In this year as a whole, average inflation is now expected to reach 4.5%, rising further to 5.5% in 2018, in each case half a percentage point higher than forecast in April (Figure 3.4.52).

As revenue growth exceeds expectations, the government's target of trimming the budget deficit to the equivalent of 3.5% of GDP in 2017 and 4.0% in 2018 looks broadly attainable. This will depend, however, on further efforts to enhance revenue collection and on stricter control of spending on wages and salaries and other recurrent expenditures. After 3 years of lower infrastructure spending, redirecting the 2017 budget toward capital outlays should help achieve this badly needed adjustment to public expenditure.

Viet Nam's export performance is expected to remain strong with continued support from new foreign-invested factories and an upturn in commodity prices. A free trade agreement with the European Union that will come into effect in January 2018 should boost export prospects. Meanwhile, the economy's heavy reliance on imported capital goods and intermediate inputs for manufactures will keep imports buoyant. As a result, the current account surplus is expected to shrink to the equivalent of 1.0% of GDP in 2017 before expanding again to 2.0% in 2018. Both of these projections are lower than the April forecasts.

The main external risk to the outlook is the continued fragility of economic recovery in the advanced economies. A domestic risk is the possibility that the government may decide to stimulate growth by excessively loosening monetary and fiscal policies. With public debt now reaching its legislated limit at the equivalent of 65% of GDP, any weakening of budget discipline would derail fiscal consolidation and debt sustainability. Similarly, any continued loosening of monetary policy would compound the already serious problem of bad loans and nonperforming assets in the banking system.

A recent National Assembly resolution has correctly identified measures to address several legal obstacles to effective NPL resolution. Further, the government is imposing more stringent regulation on the banking system through its adoption of Basel II standards. Toward ensuring that these measures yield significant benefits, it is critical to relax current tight controls on foreign ownership.

3.4.5 Selected economic indicators, Viet Nam (%)

	2017		2018	
	ADO 2017	Update	ADO 2017	Update
GDP growth	6.5	6.3	6.7	6.5
Inflation	4.0	4.5	5.0	5.5
Current acct. bal. (share of GDP)	2.0	1.0	2.5	2.0

Source: ADB estimates.

3.4.52 Inflation

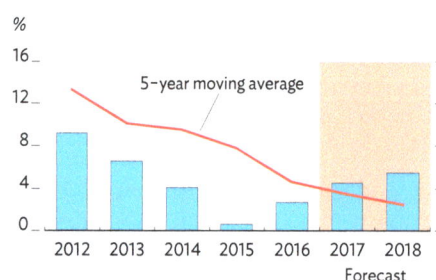

Source: Asian Development Outlook database.

Other economies

Brunei Darussalam

Recent economic trends in Brunei Darussalam indicate that the economy is unlikely to post positive growth in 2017, as earlier envisaged, because it has not yet fully adjusted to subdued global demand for oil and gas.

Although the value of oil and gas exports increased in the first 5 months of 2017, the decline in their volume persisted. The value of crude oil exports was up by 39.0% in US dollar terms in the first 5 months of the year, but the volume was down by 5.7%. Meanwhile, gas exports fell 1.3% by value and 3.8% by volume. Moreover, in May 2017, Brunei reiterated its commitment to continue cutting domestic oil production until March 2018, as agreed in December last year with the Organization of the Petroleum Exporting Countries and eight other hydrocarbon exporters that are not members of the cartel.

Thus, trends in the first half of this year suggest that GDP growth this year will underperform the *ADO 2017* forecast, but Brunei Darussalam may nevertheless manage to leave behind 4 years of contraction. Positive growth is still forecast for 2018, albeit rather less than projected in April.

The earlier forecast that prices would stop declining by the end of this year now seems optimistic. The consumer price index fell by 0.4% in the first half of the year. Deflation was present across the board, with the exception of transportation and education. It is thus more likely that this year will end up showing mild deflation for a fourth year running, with marginal inflation still forecast for next year.

Merchandise exports rose by 10.8% in the first 5 months of the year, while imports grew by an anemic 1.6%, generating a trade surplus in the period of $1.3 billion. The current account surplus for this year as a whole is now forecast higher than envisaged in *ADO 2017*. The surplus is likely to widen further in 2018, exceeding the projection made in April, as weakness in the economy keep imports subdued.

A monetary policy linking the Brunei dollar to the Singapore dollar has helped Brunei Darussalam to maintain monetary stability in the face of adverse external conditions in recent years. The government budget continued to be under pressure in the first half of the year, however, as a persistent slump in the global oil and gas market caused revenues to weaken further. The fiscal deficit for the year may thus turn out to be somewhat higher than the *ADO 2017* forecast, which projected a narrowing from a 2016 deficit that equaled an estimated 20% of GDP.

Cambodia

In the absence of quarterly or half-yearly GDP data, other evidence suggests that the economy is on track to grow strongly this year, as anticipated in April in *ADO 2017*. Improved weather supported farm and fishery output in the first half of the year. The government approved construction projects worth nearly $5 billion in the first 6 months, up by 27% year on year. Indicating strong growth in the service sector, international tourist arrivals reached 2.3 million in the first 5 months.

3.4.6 Selected economic indicators, Brunei Darussalam (%)

	2017		2018	
	ADO 2017	Update 2017	ADO 2017	Update 2017
GDP growth	1.0	0.0	2.5	1.0
Inflation	0.1	−0.3	0.1	0.1
Current acct. bal. (share of GDP)	5.3	6.0	5.5	6.5

Source: ADB estimates.

3.4.7 Selected economic indicators, Cambodia (%)

	2017		2018	
	ADO 2017	Update 2017	ADO 2017	Update 2017
GDP growth	7.1	7.1	7.1	7.1
Inflation	3.4	3.0	3.5	3.2
Current acct. bal. (share of GDP)	−9.4	−9.7	−9.0	−9.3

Source: ADB estimates.

This meant 12.5% growth year on year, more than quadrupling meager 2.4% growth in arrivals in the previous 12-month period.

Inflation averaged 3.3% in the first 7 months of 2017, higher than the 2.8% average a year earlier. Inflation has trended down, however, since a fuel price hike in March, almost halving from an annual rate of 4.2% in that month to 2.3% in July as fuel prices subsequently softened, along with food prices. Average inflation in 2017 is now forecast to come in somewhat lower than the *ADO 2017* projection and edge up marginally in 2018 but still below the forecast.

Customs data indicate that merchandise exports rose by 7.7% and imports by 8.1% in the first half of 2017. Balance of payments data, on the other hand, show merchandise exports up by 20.7% in the first half, much higher than the 12.3% figure a year earlier, and imports up by 11.1%, improving on year-earlier 7.3% growth. The current account deficit for the full year excluding official transfers is now seen narrowing from the 10.8% of GDP recorded in 2016 but still slightly exceeding the *ADO 2017* forecast. The current account deficit is forecast to narrow further in 2018 but remain wider than projected in April. In June 2017, gross foreign exchange reserves stood at $7.9 billion, providing close to 6 months of import cover.

Fiscal trends in the first 6 months of 2017 remained broadly supportive of growth, as envisaged in the 2017 budget. Government revenues grew faster than public expenditures. Domestic revenues collected in the first 6 months of the year amounted to 53.6% of the budget target for the year. Meanwhile, public spending in the first 6 months was only 35.5% of the full year budget target. Past experience shows, however, that public spending will likely pick up in the second half of the year and take the fiscal deficit for 2017 close to the budget target, the equivalent of 4.3% of GDP.

In June 2017, money supply (M2) was growing at 19.7% year on year, slightly higher than the 18.0% pace set a year earlier. Bank credit to the private sector slowed to 16.5% from 28.1%. For construction, real estate, and mortgages, however, bank credit continued to rise, recording whopping 33.3% growth year on year in June, in line with the pace a year earlier.

Lao People's Democratic Republic

Economic growth is on track to meet April forecasts in *ADO 2017*. Growth in the first half of the year was 6.8%, driven mainly by strong electricity exports, the construction of a couple of large infrastructure projects, and a surge in cash crop production and exports.

In the first half, electricity generation rose by an impressive 34.8% year on year, and cement production by a sturdy 14.6%. By the middle of 2017, the $3 billion Xayaburi hydropower project was 70% completed, with commercial operation expected by 2019. A $6 billion project building a rail connection with the PRC has progressed well since its start in December 2016, stimulating economic activity along its route. Meanwhile, the country's special economic zones attracted in the first half an additional 50 companies whose combined investments came to $54 million.

3.4.8 Selected economic indicators, Lao People's Democratic Republic (%)

	2017		2018	
	ADO 2017	Update 2017	ADO 2017	Update 2017
GDP growth	6.9	6.9	7.0	7.0
Inflation	2.5	1.5	3.0	1.5
Current acct. bal. (share of GDP)	−19.0	−17.5	−20.0	−19.0

Source: ADB estimates.

Rice prospered under favorable weather. Agriculture in general is benefiting from higher public and private investment in recent years that has supported commercialization. Services are likely to record slightly lower growth than foreseen after tourist arrivals declined by 9.8% in the first half of 2017, notably from Viet Nam and Europe. The decline reflected the government's stricter control over illegal migrants and a weak tourism publicity campaign. Although gold exports rose by 14.5% in the period, continuing slack in international markets held total mining output nearly flat.

With exports increasing by 9.3% in the first half but outpaced by imports at 10.7%, this *Update* revises down the forecast for the current account deficit this year. Net foreign reserves rose from $767 million at the end of 2016 to $887 million at the end of June 2017, providing cover for 1.7 months of imports. The current account deficit is seen to resume widening in 2018, albeit less than earlier forecast, as imports of machinery, construction materials, and fuel rise to supply the construction of the railway project and seven new hydropower plants.

Largely because prices for oil and food remained subdued, inflation in the first 7 months of 2017 was, at 1.2%, lower than foreseen in April, even hitting a record 0.03% deflation in July. The inflation forecasts for this year and next are both revised down by about half.

With inflation low and growth in bank credit at only 7.0% year on year in the first half—and assuming no abrupt worsening of the external payments position—there is scope for easing monetary policy in the near term. Government revenues reached in the first 6 months 44% of the budget for the year, and the corresponding figure for expenditure was 39%. As this yielded a budget deficit of $381 million, or 2.8% of GDP, current trends suggest that the government should be able to hold the 2017 fiscal deficit to the budget target of 5.0% of GDP. Recently announced measures to curtail spending, including suspending the construction of new government office buildings, should facilitate fiscal consolidation.

Downside risks to the outlook are a sustained worsening of the international market for mining products, an unexpected slowdown in Thailand, its vital electricity market, and, as always, bad weather affecting agriculture.

Myanmar

This economy looks set to become the fastest growing in Southeast Asia in FY2017 (ends 31 March 2018), as anticipated in *ADO 2017*. With the return of normal weather this year, agriculture is recovering from flooding last year. Crop production is benefiting as well from higher demand and strong international prices for agricultural commodities. Industry growth continues to accelerate with higher investment, both public and private, in garments and other light manufacturing, while services are getting a boost from buoyant tourism and expansion in the nascent telecommunications industry.

On the demand side, investment remains strong on higher inflows of external development assistance for infrastructure and buoyant private capital investment. Strong growth and rising incomes support private consumption. Foreign trade continues to grow at a brisk pace.

In the first quarter of FY2017, the US dollar value of merchandise exports grew by 17%, and merchandise imports accelerated even faster, by 22%.

Although annual inflation halved to 3.9% in the first quarter of FY2017 from 7.6% in the fourth quarter of FY2016, inflation for the year as a whole is still forecast at the much higher rate projected in *ADO 2017* because the first quarter decline came largely from a one-time drop in food prices. Slightly higher inflation is still forecast for FY2018. Continued demand pressure from strong growth and rising incomes will keep inflation elevated.

Exports are benefiting from robust global demand for garments and other light manufactures, but natural gas exports are subdued by soft international energy prices. Meanwhile, imports are growing strongly to meet the import requirements of a fast-growing economy. In the first quarter of FY2017, imports of consumer goods surged by 54% and those of intermediate goods by 20%. In the rest of the fiscal year, high imports of capital goods are expected to support infrastructure projects. The current account deficit is thus likely to widen this year, as forecast in April.

In the budget for FY2017, the government is pursuing a prudent fiscal policy. In response to a declining ratio of revenue to GDP, it recently passed a new tax law with significant changes to commodity and commercial tax rates. In tandem with prudent management of public expenditures, such revenue reform should help the government contain the fiscal deficit for FY2017 within the budget target, equal to 4.4% of GDP. The country's nascent banking system got a fillip when the Central Bank of Myanmar granted operating rights to four foreign banks, bringing the number of foreign bank branches in the country to 13.

The government plans to pass an investment law to attract more foreign direct investment and a new company law to allow foreign investors to operate in the stock market. While these initiatives could help achieve steady growth in the near term, inclusive and sustainable development require national peace and stability. An international risk to the outlook is possible volatility in financial markets.

Singapore

GDP grew by 2.7% in the first half of 2017. While manufacturing posted solid growth at 8.3%, services grew by a meager 1.9%, and construction contracted by 6.0%. Within the manufacturing sector, semiconductor and equipment output and exports expanded particularly strongly on recovery in the global electronics trade. Contraction in construction largely reflected weak investment, both public and private.

Domestic demand grew by 3.7%, driven primarily by a larger buildup of inventories and modest fiscal stimulus. Gross fixed investment fell by 5.6%, however, weighed down by declines in both private and public investment, and household consumption declined by 0.3%. The fiscal measures that supported domestic demand and firmed up economic recovery were higher budgetary spending on health care and targeted transfers, as well as workforce retraining that began a few years ago.

3.4.9 Selected economic indicators, Myanmar (%)

	2017		2018	
	ADO 2017	Update	ADO 2017	Update
GDP growth	7.7	7.7	8.0	8.0
Inflation	7.0	7.0	7.5	7.5
Current acct. bal. (share of GDP)	−8.0	−8.0	−8.0	−8.0

Source: ADB estimates.

In the first half of this year, the volume of merchandise exports grew by 4.2% (9.0% by value) and that of imports somewhat more, by 4.7% (11.6% by value). Strong net service exports nevertheless drove Singapore's current account surplus from $26 billion in the first half of 2016 up to $29 billion, equal to a high 19.5% of GDP.

As anticipated in *ADO 2017*, a deflationary trend in recent years reversed with the firming of domestic growth and slightly higher international fuel prices. Inflation averaged 0.7% in the first 7 months, with prices rising across a wide range of products and services, including food, fuel, automobiles, and transportation. As inflation was still low, however, monetary and fiscal policy remained accommodative.

Taking into account macroeconomic developments in the first half of the year, the forecasts for GDP growth in 2017 and 2018 are revised up. Manufacturing and services should benefit as global trade accelerates in the coming months. Meanwhile, the start next year of work on the Kuala Lumpur–Singapore High Speed Rail, and on an additional terminal at Singapore's Changi Airport, should boost the sagging construction sector. Inflation is expected to edge up for the whole of this year and next, in line with April forecasts.

This *Update* retains the earlier forecast for further widening of the current account surplus this year and next. From a medium-term perspective, policy makers should consider placing a high priority on reining in persistent current account surpluses, which are primarily the product of an unusually high savings rate. Even a modest adjustment to this perennial macroeconomic imbalance would boost domestic demand and raise the economy's potential growth rate. To this end, the government has ample resources for fiscal expansion, bringing forward public investment in infrastructure and further expanding public spending on health care and skills development.

3.4.10 Selected economic indicators, Singapore (%)

	2017		2018	
	ADO 2017	Update	ADO 2017	Update
GDP growth	2.2	2.7	2.3	2.7
Inflation	1.0	1.0	1.5	1.5
Current acct. bal. (share of GDP)	19.5	19.5	19.8	19.8

Source: ADB estimates.

The Pacific

The 2017 growth projection for the subregion is retained from *ADO 2017*, mainly because the outlook for Papua New Guinea is unchanged. Other prospects are mixed. Public investments and tourism are set to stimulate some economies but hamper growth in others. A slight revision down is made for growth in 2018. Inflation is seen to accelerate, despite weak global food and fuel prices, as supply constraints push up prices in some economies. The current account surplus will likely widen on higher earnings from tourism, exports, and fishing license fees.

Subregional assessment and prospects

Economic growth in the Pacific is still projected to average 2.9% in 2017, held steady mainly by an unchanged growth outlook for Papua New Guinea (PNG), the subregion's largest economy (Figure 3.5.1). This forecast is a slight uptick from 2.7% growth in 2016. In PNG, mining and agricultural output are expected to recover from climate-related and other constraints experienced in recent years. Growth in Timor-Leste will likely continue to be driven by public spending in the near term, with higher wages and purchases of goods and services offsetting a planned slowdown in capital expenditure.

Elsewhere, some growth estimates have been revised down from *ADO 2017*, mostly in the North Pacific and small island economies. Constraints on the implementation of public investment projects are seen to drag on growth in the Federated States of Micronesia and in Palau in FY2017 (ending 30 September 2017). Growth in Palau has been further dampened by continuing declines in tourist arrivals. In Nauru, the base effect from higher growth estimates for FY2016 (ended 30 June 2016) and the impact of lower prices for phosphates, the country's main export, are key reasons for a lower growth estimate for FY2017.

These downward revisions are offset by reports of higher growth in the South Pacific economies in FY2017 (ended 30 June 2017) and in Fiji. Agriculture and nonfood manufacturing outpaced expectations to help the Samoan economy exceed the *ADO 2017* forecast, and the Fijian economy benefitted from public investment, steady growth in tourism, and unexpectedly strong sugar production. In Tonga, the economy expanded on increased tourism receipts and export earnings. There and in Vanuatu, post-disaster reconstruction and the implementation of new projects supported economic growth.

3.5.1 GDP growth, the Pacific

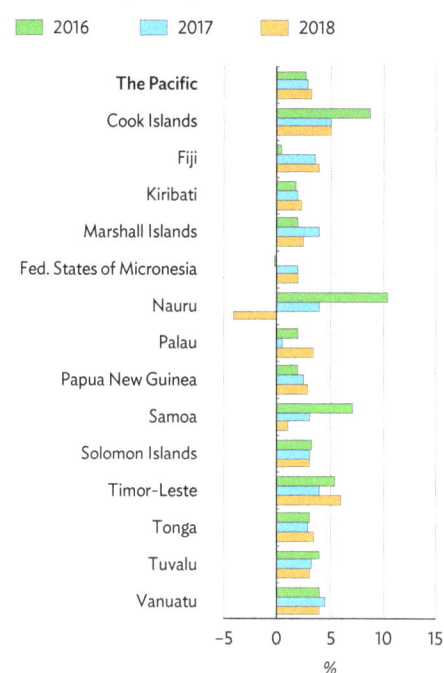

Source: Asian Development Outlook database.

The writeup on the Pacific economies was prepared by Yurendra Basnett, David Freedman, Rommel Rabanal, Shiu Raj Singh, Cara Tinio, Laisiasa Tora, and Norio Usui of the Pacific Department of ADB, and by Prince Cruz and Noel Del Castillo, consultants to the Pacific Department.

The subregional growth projection for 2018 is adjusted to 3.2%, a slight reduction from the 3.3% projected in *ADO 2017*. This comes from a downward revision for Fiji that takes into account updated forecasts for lower sugar production. Declines in the output of manufactures other than food are likely to have a similar effect on the Samoan economy in this fiscal year.

Constraints on the implementation of public investment projects are expected to continue hampering growth in the Federated States of Micronesia and Palau in FY2018, prompting projections downgraded from *ADO 2017*. By contrast, stimulus from the implementation of such projects is forecast to continue boosting growth in Tonga and Vanuatu.

In PNG, the expected commencement of large mining investments in late 2018, particularly a new liquefied natural gas project, are offsetting the downside risk posed mainly by uncertainty regarding public infrastructure investments. Although the outlook for Timor-Leste is maintained, it could be affected by any changes in fiscal policy instituted by the new government formed following parliamentary elections in July 2017.

Average inflation in the subregion is now seen to accelerate from 4.5% in 2016 to 5.3% in 2017, or 0.1 percentage points higher than projected in April (Figure 3.5.2). Price rises have been milder than expected in the Republic of the Marshall Islands and in Solomon Islands—and the Cook Islands even experienced deflation—but developments in other economies have caused significant supply constraints that push up the subregional inflation outlook. Unfavorable weather has forced up food prices in Fiji, and increased economic activity is raising prices in Tuvalu and Vanuatu. Inflation in Nauru exceeded *ADO 2017* projections in FY2017 as imports from Australia, the country's main trading partner, were more costly than anticipated.

The aggregate current account balance in the Pacific is expected to remain in surplus, almost tripling to the equivalent of 2.8% of subregional GDP in 2017 from 1.0% in 2016 (Figure 3.5.3). However, this projection is 0.2 percentage points lower than in *ADO 2017*. The change partly reflects a reversal in the projection for Fiji, from a surplus to a deficit equal to 4.2% of GDP, arising from increased foreign exchange outflows as controls are relaxed and Fiji Airways upgrades its fleet.

Developments elsewhere in the Pacific are expected to boost surpluses and narrow deficits, keeping the subregion's current account balance positive. In FY2017, unexpectedly high tourism receipts caused a larger current account surplus in the Cook Islands and narrowed the deficit in Samoa. The Marshall Islands is seen to widen its surplus with higher revenues from fishing license fees, as Solomon Islands narrows its deficit with higher mining-related export earnings and Timor-Leste does the same with petroleum income that exceeds expectations.

3.5.2 Inflation, the Pacific

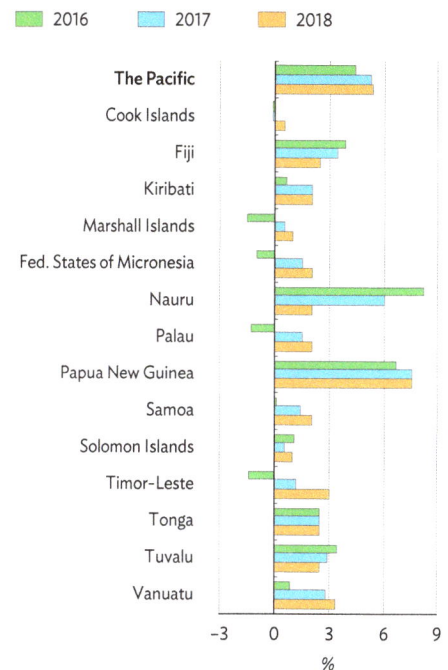

Source: *Asian Development Outlook* database.

3.5.3 Current account balance, the Pacific

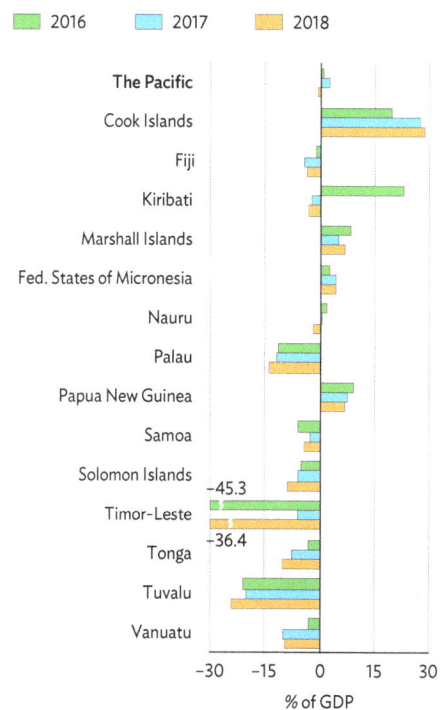

Source: *Asian Development Outlook* database.

Fiji

As expected in *ADO 2017*, growth continues to be supported by fiscal stimulus, public investment, higher visitor arrivals, and continuing reconstruction after Cyclone Winston in 2016—all supported by low interest rates and a sound external position. Standard & Poor's affirmed in July its ratings for Fiji of B+ for the long term and B for the short. Meanwhile, Moody's upgraded Fiji's rating from B to Ba3 and changed the outlook from positive to stable. This upgrade recognizes Fiji's improved institutional framework and effective policies for economic growth.

With recovery in sugarcane and sugar production outpacing expectations, the growth forecast is revised marginally up for 2017. Government infrastructure investment continues to be implemented with assistance from development partners. For 2018, the growth forecast is lowered slightly, reflecting base effects from the strong sugar output this year. Risks to the outlooks include higher oil prices, volatility in financial markets, and the possibility of another disaster, counterbalanced by potentially higher tourism and remittance receipts with an improving global economy.

Tourist arrivals have grown at a steady pace, as expected, increasing by 6.3% year on year in the first 7 months of 2017. Arrivals from New Zealand and the US grew strongly, and arrivals from Asia grew by 7.7%, though this market still accounted for only 11.3% of arrivals. Fiji Airways enhanced connections to Australia with twice-weekly flights from Adelaide. From San Francisco, it regularized its twice-weekly flights and added a third flight in the high season, announcing its ambition to fly the route daily.

Commercial bank lending to services—largely tourism and wholesale and retail trade—leapt by 27.6% year on year in the first 7 months of 2017, while lending for consumption increased by 8.4%. Investment loans, notably for real estate, surged by 58.1%. Total credit to the private sector grew by 15.2% in July over the same month in 2016. Foreign exchange reserves at the end of August were estimated to cover 5.8 months of retained imports of goods and nonfactor services.

A 19.3% increase in the public sector wage bill in the FY2018 budget (ending 31 July 2018) will contribute to an 18.8% rise in total operating expenditure. Although revenues are projected to increase more rapidly, higher capital spending means that the net fiscal deficit is projected at the equivalent of 4.6% of GDP. This includes the rollover of reconstruction and capital projects that were delayed in FY2017, when an estimated fiscal deficit equal to 2.0% of GDP fell far short of a planned 7.2% deficit. As the projection for FY2018 also factors in the planned sale of shares in state-owned enterprises, the deficit could be higher if these sales are delayed and the budget nears full implementation.

Higher taxes on alcoholic beverages and tobacco have had greater impact than expected and, together with higher fuel prices, contributed to average inflation reaching 4.1% in the 12 months to August. The full-year inflation forecast for 2017 is now revised up, but for 2018 it remains unchanged.

3.5.1 Selected economic indicators, Fiji (%)

	2017		2018	
	ADO 2017	Update	ADO 2017	Update
GDP growth	3.5	3.6	4.0	3.9
Inflation	2.5	3.5	2.5	2.5
Current acct. bal. (share of GDP)	3.5	−4.2	3.0	−3.6

Source: ADB estimates.

The current account deficit, estimated to equal 1.5% of GDP in 2016, is now expected to deepen in 2017 and ease only moderately in 2018, rather than post surpluses in both years. These revisions from *ADO 2017* take into account ongoing fleet upgrades by Fiji Airways and the central bank's relaxation of foreign exchange controls in response to healthy reserves.

Papua New Guinea

The economy is still projected to grow in 2017 as forecast in *ADO 2017*. Growth will revive from 2.0% in 2016 as mining returns to nearly full production after shutdowns in 2015 and 2016 caused by bad weather and operational issues. Agricultural output is forecast to increase as the production of cash crops returns to levels that existed before the recent El Niño weather disturbances.

The economic growth forecast for 2018 likewise remains unchanged. The hosting of the Asia-Pacific Economic Cooperation (APEC) Summit 2018 in Port Moresby is expected to provide a limited upside boost for construction, services, and other sectors related to consumption. The impact of hosting the APEC Summit is likely to be observed in economic performance for 1 or 2 quarters but not sustained over the whole year. Moreover, the possibility that public infrastructure investment may not be maintained at levels seen in the past 5 years poses a significant downside risk to the 2018 forecast.

The limited impact of the APEC Summit could be augmented by anticipated large investments in mining, in particular the start of construction on the next liquefied natural gas (LNG) project. While the precise starting date for the new LNG project has yet to be confirmed, the market currently assumes it to be in the third or fourth quarter of 2018. If the size of the investment is anything like that of the first LNG project, economic growth could reach double digits, as observed in 2011 when construction started, and again in 2014 when operations commenced. In any case, previous experience teaches that any such growth spurt is unlikely to be inclusive or sustainable, highlighting the need for appropriate policy to manage growth swings.

Inflation is still projected to accelerate in 2017 from 6.7% in 2016 and to remain stable in 2018. This reflects loose monetary policy and can be expected to further weaken the kina, the national currency. The release later in 2017 of the biannual monetary policy statement from the Bank of Papua New Guinea, the central bank, will provide new data for reassessing inflation projections.

Current account projections are similarly unchanged from earlier forecasts. As expected, output from the Ok Tedi gold and copper mine and the Ramu nickel mine has increased. However, the 2018 current account surplus could end up lower than foreseen if the rises in mining and agriculture exports are not sustained. Further, spending on the APEC Summit is likely to spur increased imports. Debt repayment for the first LNG project and overseas dividend payments will perpetuate the capital account deficit.

3.5.2 Selected economic indicators, Papua New Guinea (%)

	2017		2018	
	ADO 2017	Update	ADO 2017	Update
GDP growth	2.5	2.5	2.8	2.8
Inflation	7.5	7.5	7.5	7.5
Current acct. bal. (share of GDP)	7.7	7.7	6.7	6.7

Source: ADB estimates.

In its midyear economic and fiscal outlook for 2017, the Department of Treasury revised its revenue forecast for this year to K10.9 billion—short of budget projections by K514.0 million—as company tax revenue and dividend payments disappoint expectations. Weak company tax revenue reflects cost-cutting by companies in the wake of lower global commodity prices.

Public revenue remains well below the peak of K11.5 billion collected in 2014, despite the economy registering average annual growth of 7.4% in 2014–2017. Year-on-year growth in public revenue has been lower than increases in inflation. This disconnect between public revenue and macroeconomic indicators seems to stem from the Papua New Guinea LNG project. Although the investment, estimated at $18 billion, propelled the economy to high growth rates, subsequent mining and petroleum tax revenues from exports have been minimized by provisions for accelerated debt payment and depreciation that favor the operators of the project.

Solomon Islands

Growth is still forecast to slow in 2017 from 3.2% in 2016, consistent with the forecast in *ADO 2017*, as current growth drivers fade. In 2018, logging output is expected to decline further, but mining investment and exports are expected to increase, pushing up the growth projection. Construction on the Tina River Hydropower Project is also expected to boost investment and growth in 2018.

A supplementary appropriations bill filed in August seeks to increase total expenditure by 14.4% from the 2017 budget. If approved, planned spending in 2017 would be 4.5% higher than in 2016. This would reverse an earlier plan under the 2017 budget to reduce spending by 6.7% from 2016. Even with the supplemental budget approved, actual expenditure in 2017 may end up lower than in 2016 because of lingering problems with cash flow management and budget execution. Actual expenditures in the first half of 2017 were lower by 2.1% than in the same period last year.

Log production fell by 2.0% in the first half of 2017 from the same period last year. Total logging output in 2017 is expected to be lower than the 2.7 million cubic meters in 2016 but still way above the sustainable rate of 250,000 cubic meters per year, as estimated in 2005. This raises concern about the impact of logging on the environment and local communities. In March 2017, the Ministry of Forestry stopped issuing new logging licenses or reissuing licenses to companies not in the Solomon Forest Association. Further, it proposes higher fines and penalties for overharvesting.

The value of mineral exports in the first quarter of 2017 exceeded those in the whole of 2016, largely with the shipment of the bauxite stockpile following the resolution of legal obstacles. Mining output is expected to increase further with a new bauxite mining permit granted to one company in January and a prospecting license granted to another in August. After the license of the Gold Ridge Mine was reinstated in March, new funding for the country's only gold mine was secured in August from a group of investors that includes local landowners.

3.5.3 Selected economic indicators, Solomon Islands (%)

	2017		2018	
	ADO 2017	Update	ADO 2017	Update
GDP growth	3.0	3.0	2.8	3.0
Inflation	1.8	0.5	2.2	1.0
Current acct. bal. (share of GDP)	-8.3	-6.0	-10.7	-9.0

Source: ADB estimates.

The funds will be used to repair, rehabilitate, and upgrade the mine to allow operations to resume by 2019. Gold Ridge had closed in 2014 after Cyclone Pam heightened the risk of toxic mine tailings overflow. Mine-related industries such as transportation and storage, quarrying, and construction are expected to benefit from the resumption of bauxite and gold mining.

Despite a lag, the impact of low international commodity prices on domestic prices has been stronger than expected, prompting downward revisions to forecasts for inflation in 2017 and 2018. Average deflation at 1.3% was registered in the first half of 2017, mainly from lower prices for imported goods.

Forecasts for the current account deficit are revised down for 2017 and 2018 due to lower prices for international goods and because export earnings from minerals and agricultural commodities such as palm oil are now expected to be higher.

Timor-Leste

The outlook for growth and inflation is unchanged from *ADO 2017*, but unexpectedly strong petroleum income and an updated GDP series prompt lower projections for current account deficits.

While public spending remains the key economic driver, presidential and parliamentary elections have had little evident impact on budget execution in 2017. Government spending excluding development partner grants was down by 11.2% year on year in January–July, but this was largely a planned slowdown in disbursements for capital works. In the same period, expenditures on salaries and wages rose by 12.0%, and expenditures on goods and services by 33.1%. Transfer payments fell by 34.9% because of lower transfers to the Special Administrative Region of Oe-Cusse Ambeno. Excluding them, transfers including pensions and other social assistance rose by 7.4%.

Disbursements for publicly financed capital works fell by 10.7% year on year in January–July and are likely to remain far below 2016 levels. One reason is early payments from the government for some projects, notably for Tibar Bay port a payment of $130.4 million, equal to 7.8% of GDP excluding the large offshore petroleum sector. A groundbreaking ceremony was held for the port in June, but construction may not commence until 2018.

A range of indicators suggests that steady budget execution has contributed to favorable business conditions. Electricity use by business was up by 15.2% year on year in the first quarter of 2017, while residential electricity consumption rose by 13.2%. Motorcycle registrations climbed by 10.9% in the period, and all vehicle registrations by 11.6%.

Consumer prices have risen moderately in 2017, reversing recent deflation. Consumer prices were up by 0.9% year on year in May as costs rose for food, alcohol and tobacco, and recreational goods and services. Increases have been concentrated in Dili, however, with little change in the rest of the country. The *ADO 2017* forecasts for inflation in 2017 and 2018 are unchanged.

Negotiations with Australia to delineate permanent maritime boundaries and agree on terms for developing the Greater Sunrise oil and

3.5.4 Selected economic indicators, Timor-Leste (%)

	2017		2018	
	ADO 2017	Update	ADO 2017	Update
GDP growth	4.0	4.0	6.0	6.0
Inflation	1.2	1.2	3.0	3.0
Current acct. bal. (share of GDP)	−12.2	−5.9	−40.2	−36.4

Source: ADB estimates.

gas field reached an important milestone. On 1 September, the Permanent Court of Arbitration in The Hague announced that the two countries had achieved a consensus on key principles. The formal agreement expected in October should define the ownership of Greater Sunrise, the road to developing it, and arrangements for sharing revenues.

Oil and gas revenues exceeded expectations in the first half of 2017, with tax and royalty income of $200.0 million equaling 75.9% of the budget forecast for the whole of 2017. The Petroleum Fund investment portfolio performed strongly in the first 2 quarters, generating $178.2 million in cash income, $716.5 million in asset appreciation, and an overall return of 5.6%. The Petroleum Fund balance rose from $15.8 billion at the beginning of 2017 to $16.5 billion at the end of the second quarter, equal to 9.4 times non-oil GDP.

Updated national accounts were published in 2017 with revised GDP statistics for 2010–2014 and new figures for 2015. The revisions rebase the GDP series, benchmark against new data such as the Timor-Leste Living Standards Survey as well as the 2015 National Census, and reflect other methodological improvements. These adjustments and unexpectedly strong petroleum revenues require new, lower projections for current account balances in 2017 and 2018.

The outlook for growth and inflation in 2018 and beyond could change with clarification of prospects for future revenues from Greater Sunrise and with any new fiscal policy following parliamentary elections.

Vanuatu

The economy is now expected to expand in 2017 slightly more than forecast in *ADO 2017*. The upgrade mainly reflects higher investments for reconstruction after Cyclone Pam, which struck in March 2015, and new projects funded by development partners and private businesses. In addition, the forecast for growth in 2018 is also adjusted upward as the completion of several projects was delayed.

Originally targeted for completion in 2016, the Luganville Port Rehabilitation and Extension Project and the Vanuatu Tourism Infrastructure Project are now nearing completion. Other major projects in the capital, Port Vila, that were originally planned for completion this year but delayed to 2018 include the Port Vila Urban Development Project and the Lapetasi International Multi-Purpose Wharf. The Vanuatu Interisland Shipping Support Project is also set to be completed in 2018.

Visitor arrivals by air in the first half of 2017 are estimated to have been at least 20% higher than in the same period last year, and the increase in the whole year is expected to be even greater. Qantas Airways resumed its codeshare agreement with Air Vanuatu in June 2017 following the completion of emergency repairs to the runway of Bauerfield International Airport in Port Vila. Arrivals by air in 2017 may exceed 100,000 for the first time since 2014.

Although arrivals by cruise ship dropped by 11.9% in the first half of 2017, the total for the year is still expected to exceed last year's 254,489 with the completion of the Luganville Port and Vanuatu Tourism Infrastructure projects. Total visitor arrivals in 2017 are projected to grow by 5.0%, in line with previous forecasts.

3.5.5 Selected economic indicators, Vanuatu (%)

	2017		2018	
	ADO 2017	Update 2017	ADO 2017	Update 2017
GDP growth	4.3	4.5	3.8	4.0
Inflation	2.4	2.8	2.6	3.3
Current acct. bal. (share of GDP)	−17.7	−10.0	−15.0	−9.5

Source: ADB estimates.

Further rehabilitation and upgrading of Bauerfield International Airport are expected following a contract award in April. Airports in Luganville, Vanuatu's second-largest city, and on the southern island of Tanna are expected to be upgraded starting in late 2017 or early 2018.

Inflation in the first quarter of 2017 was 2.1%, largely reflecting higher prices for education, transportation, and food. With aggregate demand now expected to accelerate in the second half of 2017 and into next year, inflation forecasts are adjusted upward for both 2017 and 2018.

Forecasts for current account deficits, on the other hand, are narrowed in expectation of higher tourism services income and increased grants from development partners.

Risks to the forecasts notably include further construction delays. With several major infrastructure projects under way simultaneously, absorptive capacity is a constraint on project implementation, as is the challenge of adhering to the national debt strategy while supporting the incumbent government's prioritized projects.

North Pacific economies

Growth projections for FY2017 (ending 30 September 2017) are revised down for two of the three North Pacific economies. Palau continues to suffer lower tourist arrivals, and the delayed implementation of public investment projects has further hampered growth. Economic growth in the Federated States of Micronesia (FSM) was temporarily constrained by a suspension of infrastructure grants under its Compact of Free Association with the US. The growth forecasts for the Republic of the Marshall Islands are unchanged, but long-term prospects remain weak. Although rapidly rising revenue from fishing license fees generates fiscal surpluses in the North Pacific economies, medium-term fiscal challenges persist.

Marshall Islands

Economic growth in FY2017 appears set to meet the *ADO 2017* forecast, with public investments funded by development partners and infrastructure grants under the compact with the US progressing in accordance with expectations. Growth in FY2018 is expected to slow in line with the forecast as project implementation suffers under capacity constraints. Inflation projections are revised down for both FY2017 and FY2018, in line with the outlook for global food and fuel prices.

Despite a 26.0% increase in expenditure, FY2016 recorded a fiscal surplus equal to 4.0% of GDP on soaring revenues from fishing license fees. Subsidies to state-owned enterprises (SOEs) exceeded $11.0 million, reaching 5.9% of GDP that year. Revenues from fishing license fees have continued to increase in FY2017 and are expected to remain high in FY2018. However, large increases in expenditure and the slow implementation of SOE reform suggest a fiscal deficit equal to 2.0% of GDP in FY2017, with the same deficit projected for FY2018. On top of continued subsidies to SOEs, social security transfers weigh heavily on the deficit. SOE reform and the restructuring of the social security system remain core challenges to putting government finances on a sustainable path.

3.5.6 Selected economic indicators, Marshall Islands (%)

	2017		2018	
	ADO 2017	Update	ADO 2017	Update
GDP growth	4.0	4.0	2.5	2.5
Inflation	1.5	0.5	1.5	1.0
Current acct. bal. (share of GDP)	4.0	5.0	4.5	7.0

Source: ADB estimates.

The current account surplus is expected to narrow from the equivalent of 8.5% of GDP in FY2016, as inflows of fishing license revenues are increasing more slowly than imports of construction materials and fuel for public investment projects. The surplus will likely finish the fiscal year slightly higher than projected in *ADO 2017*, however, and the projection for the surplus in FY2018 is revised up more substantially.

Federated States of Micronesia

Economic data released after *ADO 2017* was published in April show that the economy contracted by 0.1% in FY2016. Growth is projected to return in FY2017 but below the *ADO 2017* forecast. The downward revision partly reflects the temporary suspension of infrastructure grants for new projects under the compact with the US after the FSM failed to establish an adequate project management system. Limited capacity in national and state governments is a longstanding constraint on project implementation. Bilateral discussions to clarify appropriate channels for infrastructure grants resulted in a transitional agreement under which the FSM would engage the US Army Corps of Engineers to assist in managing and implementing infrastructure projects. This agreement facilitated the resumption of grants. The agreed technical assistance is subject to periodic review, with the FSM expected to depend on it less as local capacity for project development strengthens.

Inflation in FY2017 has been in line with *ADO 2017* projections, with prices for fuel imports and domestic power stable. The forecast for FY2018 also remains unchanged.

Soaring fishing license revenues have supported fiscal surpluses since 2012 and current account surpluses since 2014, and will continue to do so in the coming years. This *Update* retains *ADO 2017* forecasts for the current account surplus in FY2017 and FY2018.

Palau

The growth forecast for FY2017 is revised sharply down because tourist arrivals declined in the latter part of the fiscal year and public investment projects suffered implementation delays. Growth is still forecast to accelerate in FY2018, but that projection is similarly revised down.

Tourist arrivals in the first 9 months of FY2017, mostly from the People's Republic of China and Taipei,China, dropped by an estimated 16.5% from a year earlier. Arrivals from Japan have not recovered since tourist attractions were affected by drought in 2016. The jellyfish lake, one of Palau's main attractions, has been closed for most of FY2017. Meanwhile, ongoing projects for water supply and wastewater treatment funded by development partners have left an acute shortage of construction materials. This has significantly impeded the implementation of other projects and slowed economic growth.

Inflation has remained low in FY2017, in line with *ADO 2017* projections, with food prices stable and fuel prices lower. A slight acceleration is still projected for FY2018.

3.5.7 Selected economic indicators, Federated States of Micronesia (%)

	2017		2018	
	ADO 2017	Update	ADO 2017	Update
GDP growth	2.5	2.0	2.5	2.0
Inflation	1.5	1.5	2.0	2.0
Current acct. bal. (share of GDP)	4.5	4.5	4.5	4.5

Source: ADB estimates.

3.5.8 Selected economic indicators, Palau (%)

	2017		2018	
	ADO 2017	Update	ADO 2017	Update
GDP growth	3.0	0.5	5.5	3.5
Inflation	1.5	1.5	2.0	2.0
Current acct. bal. (share of GDP)	–12.5	–12.0	–15.0	–14.0

Source: ADB estimates.

The government projects a fiscal surplus equal to 4.0% of GDP in FY2017, down from the 4.7% surplus realized in FY2016 largely because of declining tourism receipts. However, the fiscal surplus is expected to hit 5.0% of GDP in FY2018 with an expected recovery in visitor arrivals and a planned increase in the departure tax to be implemented in 2018.

The current account deficit is expected to widen marginally in FY2017, partly because of lower tourism receipts, but slightly less than anticipated in *ADO 2017* with a smaller increase in imports of project construction materials and stable fuel imports. The continued implementation of these projects in the near term is expected to widen the deficit further in FY2018, but less than forecast in April.

South Pacific economies

Economic performance in the Cook Islands, Samoa, and Tonga in FY2017 (ended 30 June 2017) reflects stable economic conditions. Growth continues to derive from tourism, particularly in the Cook Islands, as well as from agriculture in Samoa and public investment projects in Tonga. Inflation has generally been low, in keeping with international commodity price movements, with deflation persisting in the Cook Islands. Sustained tourism inflows and remittances have bolstered current account balances in the South Pacific economies but are being offset in Tonga by rising imports for public investment projects.

Cook Islands

Estimated economic growth in the Cook Islands in FY2017 was in line with the April forecast in *ADO 2017*. This marked the sixth straight year of economic expansion in the country. The positive performance reflected a continued rise in visitor arrivals, which accelerated to 14.9% in FY2017 from 11.0% in FY2016 on large increases from the Americas, Asia, and New Zealand. Visitor arrivals are expected to continue growing in FY2018, as forecast earlier, and the projection for GDP growth is unchanged.

Costs for housing and household operations were lower than foreseen, keeping average annual inflation marginally negative in FY2017 and well below the forecast in *ADO 2017*. In light of this, the inflation projection is revised down for FY2018 but remains in positive territory.

The government has revised its estimate of the FY2017 fiscal outcome from a budget deficit equal to 3.9% of GDP to a surplus of 1.4%. This reflects public investment spending significantly below expectations. A deficit equal to 6.0% of GDP is budgeted for FY2018. Gross public debt, excluding the debt service reserve, is expected to reach the equivalent of 33.6% of GDP in FY2018. Subtracting cash reserves held for debt service yields a net debt of 29.7%.

Private sector credit declined by 5.7% year on year in the first 3 quarters of FY2017. Despite this and low 2.1% growth in broad money, interest rates were maintained.

3.5.9 Selected economic indicators, Cook Islands (%)

	2017		2018	
	ADO 2017	Update 2017	ADO 2017	Update 2017
GDP growth	5.0	5.0	5.0	5.0
Inflation	0.5	−0.1	1.2	0.5
Current acct. bal. (share of GDP)	24.5	27.6	21.0	28.7

Source: ADB estimates.

The current account surplus in FY2017 is estimated to have surpassed both the FY2016 outcome and the *ADO 2017* projection. It was fueled by growth in tourism receipts, which outpaced expectations and are expected to continue rising in FY2018. The forecast for the current account balance in FY2018 is revised up accordingly.

Samoa

Growth in FY2017 is estimated to have risen higher than the *ADO 2017* projection. Data for the first 3 quarters of the fiscal year show the economy growing by 3.4% year on year as agricultural and nonfood manufacturing output exceeded expectations, but growth is thought to have slowed in the last quarter. Visitor arrivals declined by 1.2% in the first 8 months of the fiscal year. Nonfood manufacturing is expected to decline in FY2018, prompting a downward revision to the forecast that now foresees growth slowing by two-thirds.

Prices rose in FY2017 by somewhat less than the projection in *ADO 2017* because price increases for imports were less than anticipated. The forecast for inflation in FY2018 remains unchanged.

The fiscal deficit in FY2017 is estimated to have stayed within the budget target, equal to 3.5% of GDP, as expenditures did not exceed allocations. Public debt, which has been declining for the past 2 fiscal years, was the equivalent of 48.6% of GDP at the end of March 2017. A deficit of 3.5% is budgeted again for FY2018.

The Central Bank of Samoa is maintaining its accommodative monetary policy to support economic growth. Private sector credit in March 2017 was 9.9% higher than in March 2016.

The current account deficit was low in the first half of FY2017 as tourism inflows and remittances outperformed expectations. Accordingly, the estimated current account deficit for the full year is revised down from *ADO 2017*. Foreign exchange reserves at the end of June 2017 were sufficient to cover 3.6 months of goods and services imports. For FY2018, the current account deficit is forecast to widen more than foreseen in April, after projections for tourism earnings and remittances were revised down.

Tonga

The economy is estimated to have grown in FY2017 somewhat faster than forecast in *ADO 2017*. This result was driven by increases in tourism receipts and agricultural production. Growth was further accelerated by construction, notably reconstruction in Ha'apai in the wake of Cyclone Winston in February 2016.

The growth projection for FY2018 is revised sharply higher than forecast in April in response to a stronger rebound in agriculture, enhanced domestic demand, a more vibrant financial sector, and ongoing reconstruction. Further, the government has announced an expansionary FY2018 budget.

Average annual inflation in FY2017 is in line with the *ADO 2017* forecast. Steady inflation this past year is attributed to higher prices for alcohol, tobacco, and kava. Inflation is still projected to remain at this rate in FY2018, as international prices for fuel and food begin to increase.

3.5.10 Selected economic indicators, Samoa (%)

	2017		2018	
	ADO 2017	Update	ADO 2017	Update
GDP growth	2.0	3.0	1.5	1.0
Inflation	2.0	1.4	2.0	2.0
Current acct. bal. (share of GDP)	−4.9	−2.9	−2.8	−4.2

Source: ADB estimates.

3.5.11 Selected economic indicators, Tonga (%)

	2017		2018	
	ADO 2017	Update	ADO 2017	Update
GDP growth	2.6	2.8	2.6	3.5
Inflation	2.5	2.5	2.5	2.5
Current acct. bal. (share of GDP)	−7.7	−7.7	−11.9	−10.0

Source: ADB estimates.

Government operating expenditures in FY2017 are estimated to be lower than initially budgeted, narrowing the fiscal deficit from a target equal to 1.3% of GDP to 0.4%. The FY2018 budget increases operating expenditure by 17.0% over previous government assumptions. The increase is to meet government commitments to improve sports facilities, maintain existing roads and buildings, and commence repayment on a large loan received a decade ago from a state-owned bank in the People's Republic of China. Expenditures are intended to be financed from increased tax collections and disbursements from development partners. The projected fiscal deficit is equal to 1.4% of GDP. Public debt at the end of FY2017 is estimated to be equivalent to half of GDP.

Bank lending in May 2017 was 14% higher than a year earlier. The increase reflects a rise in household loans by 23.3%.

Although Tonga will no longer host the Pacific Games in 2019, imports in FY2017 remained elevated to supply stepped-up construction and the commencement of major projects to be financed by development partners. The resulting FY2017 current account deficit was in line with the *ADO 2017* projection. The projection for the current account deficit in FY2018 is revised down from the April forecast by 1.9 percentage points because higher imports projected for the games will no longer be needed.

Small island economies

Prospects for the small island economies have varied since the April forecasts in *ADO 2017*, with growth forecasts now maintained for Kiribati, raised for Tuvalu, and downgraded for Nauru.

Kiribati has enjoyed several consecutive years of economic growth, which averaged 2.9% from 2011 to 2015. The forecast for 2017 remains unchanged, with growth spurred largely by continuing investments in airports, roads, solid waste management, and sanitation financed by development partners. However, recent developments suggest that growth in 2018 will be higher than projected in *ADO 2017*. In August, Solomon Airlines commenced flights linking Kiribati's capital, Tarawa, to Brisbane via Honiara in Solomon Islands under its recent agreement with Air Kiribati. Further, a new $50 million water supply project in South Tarawa and a $30 million infrastructure development project to upgrade roads, marine landings, and airfields on outer islands are expected to start in the next few months.

The fiscal deficit is now expected to rise to the equivalent of 9.2% of GDP in 2017, the increase caused by government wages and subsidies to copra producers on the outer islands.

Tuvalu, meanwhile, is now expected to grow by more than forecast in *ADO 2017* because fishing license revenue has exceeded projections. By the end of August, actual receipts from fishing license fees had reached 84% of the 2017 budgeted amount of A$24.9 million, equal to 51.8% of GDP. At this rate, receipts are projected to exceed the 2017 budget projection by as much as 18%. The growth forecast for 2018 is maintained as fishery revenue receipts are projected to decline. Despite this, new sources of climate financing and the ongoing

3.5.12 Selected economic indicators, Kiribati (%)

	2017		2018	
	ADO 2017	*Update 2017*	*ADO 2017*	*Update*
GDP growth	2.0	2.0	1.5	2.3
Inflation	2.0	2.0	2.0	2.0
Current acct. bal. (share of GDP)	−2.4	−2.4	−1.5	−3.0

Source: ADB estimates.

3.5.13 Selected economic indicators, Tuvalu (%)

	2017		2018	
	ADO 2017	*Update 2017*	*ADO 2017*	*Update*
GDP growth	3.0	3.2	3.0	3.0
Inflation	2.0	2.9	2.0	2.5
Current acct. bal. (share of GDP)	−20.8	−20.2	−25.4	−24.4

Source: ADB estimates.

implementation of projects financed by development partners will keep growth well above its long-term average. In July, for example, the Green Climate Fund released the first tranche of a $36 million contribution toward making Tuvalu resilient under climate change.

Nauru is now estimated to have grown less in FY2017 (ended 30 June 2017) than projected in *ADO 2017*. The revision partly reflects updated growth figures for FY2016 and lower prices for phosphate, Nauru's main export. GDP growth in FY2016 is now estimated to have been 10.4%, up from an earlier estimate of 7.2%, mainly because of higher contributions from phosphate exports and government expenditure. Economic contraction is still expected in 2018 in line with the planned scaling down or closure of the Regional Processing Centre for asylum seekers and refugees. Contraction is now projected to be less severe than forecast in *ADO 2017*.

All three economies use the Australian dollar as their currency, and this has provided some price stability in conjunction with continued softness in international food and commodity prices. Inflation forecasts remain unchanged for Kiribati in both 2017 and 2018 but are upgraded for Tuvalu in line with developments in its economy. The inflation estimate for Nauru in FY2017 is higher than the April forecast, as is the revised forecast for FY2018, mainly reflecting supply constraints, higher transaction costs, and perhaps pass-through of inflation from Australia.

Forecasts for current account balances are revised to take into account changes in projected prices and flows of goods and services, as well as country-specific developments. The forecast for Kiribati's current account deficit in 2017 is unchanged, but the deficit is now seen widening in 2018 instead of narrowing. Although the recently signed aviation agreement may boost tourism and so improve the current account balance, a projected decline in fishing revenue and an expected increase in imports of capital goods for ongoing infrastructure projects may outweigh this development. In Tuvalu, the current account deficit is still projected to widen sharply in 2017, and widen again in 2018, but by somewhat less than forecast in April. The forecasts for both years reflect increased public expenditure and imports for consumption, as well as the expected fall in fishing license revenue.

In Nauru, the current account surplus (not forecast in *ADO 2017*) is estimated to have fallen from the equivalent of 1.7% of GDP in FY2016 to 0.5% in FY2017 with higher imports of goods and services. The current account is expected to cross into deficit in FY2018 as exports of services drop significantly in line with the scaling down of Regional Processing Centre operations. How this unfolds is a risk to the outlook. An agreement between Australia and the US to resettle in the US refugees currently in Nauru is now expected to stand despite some uncertainty early in the new US administration. Vetting for the first batch of refugees to be resettled has been completed, and their transfer is expected to commence later this year, though the exact timing and number of refugees involved remains unclear.

Another risk to the outlook is uncertainty over phosphate prices.

3.5.14 Selected economic indicators, Nauru (%)

	2017		2018	
	ADO 2017	Update	ADO 2017	Update
GDP growth	4.3	4.0	−4.5	−4.0
Inflation	5.7	6.0	1.8	2.0
Current acct. bal. (share of GDP)	...	0.5	...	−1.8

... = data not available.
Source: ADB estimates.

STATISTICAL
APPENDIX

Statistical notes and tables

This statistical appendix presents selected economic indicators for the 45 developing member economies of the Asian Development Bank (ADB) in three tables: gross domestic product (GDP) growth, inflation, and current account balance as a percentage of GDP. The economies are grouped into five subregions: Central Asia, East Asia, South Asia, Southeast Asia, and the Pacific. The tables contain historical data for 2014–2016 and forecasts for 2017 and 2018.

The data are standardized to the degree possible to allow comparability over time and across economies, but differences in statistical methodology, definitions, coverage, and practices make full comparability impossible. The national income accounts section is based on the United Nations System of National Accounts, while the data on balance of payments are based on International Monetary Fund accounting standards. Historical data are obtained from official sources, statistical publications, ADB estimates, and databases, as well as from documents of ADB, the International Monetary Fund, and the World Bank. Projections for 2017 and 2018 are generally ADB estimates made on the bases of available quarterly or monthly data, though some projections are from governments.

Most countries report by calendar year. The following record their government finance data by fiscal year: Armenia; Azerbaijan; Brunei Darussalam; the Cook Islands; Fiji; Hong Kong, China; Kazakhstan; the Kyrgyz Republic; the Lao People's Democratic Republic; Samoa; Singapore; Taipei,China; Tajikistan; Thailand; and Uzbekistan. The Federated States of Micronesia, Nauru, the Republic of Marshall Islands, and Palau report government finance and balance-of-payments data by fiscal year. South Asian countries (except for Maldives and Sri Lanka), Myanmar, Samoa, and Tonga report all variables by fiscal year.

Regional and subregional averages are provided in the three tables. The averages are computed using weights derived from gross national income (GNI) in current US dollars following the World Bank Atlas method. The GNI data for 2014–2015 are obtained from the World Bank's World Development Indicators Online. Weights for 2015 are carried over through 2018. The GNI data for the Cook Islands and Taipei,China were estimated using the Atlas conversion factor.

The following paragraphs discuss the three tables in greater detail.

Table A1: Growth rate of GDP (% per year). The table shows annual growth rates of GDP valued at constant market price, factor cost, or basic price. GDP at market price is the aggregation of value added by all resident producers at producers' prices including taxes less subsidies on imports plus all nondeductible value-added or similar taxes. Constant factor cost measures differ from market price measures in that they exclude taxes on production and include subsidies. Basic price valuation is the factor cost plus some taxes on production, such as those on property and payroll taxes, and less some subsidies, such as those on labor-related subsidies but not product-related subsidies. Most countries use constant market price valuation. Pakistan uses constant factor cost, while Fiji, Maldives, and Nepal use basic prices.

Table A2: Inflation (% per year). Data on inflation rates are period averages. The inflation rates presented are based on consumer price indexes. The consumer price indexes of the following economies are for a given city or group of consumers only: in Cambodia for Phnom Penh, in the Marshall Islands for Majuro, in Solomon Islands for Honiara, and in Nepal for urban consumers.

Table A3: Current account balance (% of GDP). The current account balance is the sum of the balance of trade for merchandise, net trade in services and factor income, and net transfers. The values reported are divided by GDP at current prices in US dollars. In the case of Cambodia, the Lao People's Democratic Republic, and Viet Nam, official transfers are excluded from the current account balance.

Table A1 Growth rate of GDP (% per year)

	2014	2015	2016	2017		2018	
				ADO2017	Update	ADO2017	Update
Central Asia	5.2	3.1	2.2	3.1	3.3	3.5	3.9
Armenia	3.6	3.2	0.2	2.2	3.8	2.5	3.0
Azerbaijan	2.8	1.1	–3.8	–1.1	–1.3	1.2	1.0
Georgia	4.6	2.9	2.7	3.8	4.2	4.5	4.5
Kazakhstan	4.2	1.2	1.1	2.4	2.7	2.2	3.0
Kyrgyz Republic	4.0	3.9	3.8	3.0	4.0	3.5	4.0
Tajikistan	6.7	6.0	6.9	4.8	5.0	5.5	5.5
Turkmenistan	10.3	6.5	6.2	6.5	6.5	7.0	6.5
Uzbekistan	8.1	8.0	7.8	7.0	6.8	7.3	7.5
East Asia	6.6	6.1	6.0	5.8	6.0	5.6	5.8
China, People's Rep. of	7.3	6.9	6.7	6.5	6.7	6.2	6.4
Hong Kong, China	2.6	2.4	2.0	2.0	3.6	2.1	3.2
Korea, Rep. of	3.3	2.8	2.8	2.5	2.8	2.7	2.8
Mongolia	7.9	2.4	1.0	2.5	4.0	2.0	3.0
Taipei,China	4.0	0.7	1.5	1.8	2.0	2.2	2.2
South Asia	6.9	7.3	6.7	7.0	6.7	7.2	7.0
Afghanistan	1.3	0.8	2.0	2.5	2.5	3.0	3.0
Bangladesh	6.1	6.6	7.1	6.9	7.2	6.9	6.9
Bhutan	4.0	6.1	6.4	8.2	6.9	9.9	8.0
India	7.5	8.0	7.1	7.4	7.0	7.6	7.4
Maldives	6.0	2.8	3.4	3.8	4.2	4.1	4.4
Nepal	5.7	3.0	0.0	5.6	6.9	5.4	4.7
Pakistan	4.1	4.1	4.5	5.2	5.3	5.5	5.5
Sri Lanka	5.0	4.8	4.4	5.0	4.5	5.0	5.0
Southeast Asia	4.6	4.6	4.6	4.8	5.0	5.0	5.1
Brunei Darussalam	–2.5	–0.4	–2.5	1.0	0.0	2.5	1.0
Cambodia	7.1	7.0	7.0	7.1	7.1	7.1	7.1
Indonesia	5.0	4.9	5.0	5.1	5.1	5.3	5.3
Lao People's Dem. Rep.	7.5	6.7	6.8	6.9	6.9	7.0	7.0
Malaysia	6.0	5.0	4.2	4.4	5.4	4.6	5.4
Myanmar	8.0	7.0	5.9	7.7	7.7	8.0	8.0
Philippines	6.1	6.1	6.9	6.4	6.5	6.6	6.7
Singapore	3.6	1.9	2.0	2.2	2.7	2.3	2.7
Thailand	0.9	2.9	3.2	3.5	3.5	3.6	3.6
Viet Nam	6.0	6.7	6.2	6.5	6.3	6.7	6.5
The Pacific	9.4	8.4	2.4	2.9	2.9	3.3	3.2
Cook Islands	3.2	3.2	8.8	5.0	5.0	5.0	5.0
Fiji	5.6	3.8	0.4	3.5	3.6	4.0	3.9
Kiribati	0.4	3.5	1.8	2.0	2.0	1.5	2.3
Marshall Islands	–0.8	–0.4	1.9	4.0	4.0	2.5	2.5
Micronesia, Fed. States of	–2.2	4.9	–0.1	2.5	2.0	2.5	2.0
Nauru	36.5	2.8	10.4	4.3	4.0	–4.5	–4.0
Palau	4.8	10.9	1.9	3.0	0.5	5.5	3.5
Papua New Guinea	13.3	12.0	2.0	2.5	2.5	2.8	2.8
Samoa	1.2	1.6	7.1	2.0	3.0	1.5	1.0
Solomon Islands	2.0	2.9	3.2	3.0	3.0	2.8	3.0
Timor-Leste	4.2	4.0	5.4	4.0	4.0	6.0	6.0
Tonga	2.1	3.7	3.1	2.6	2.8	2.6	3.5
Tuvalu	2.2	2.6	4.0	3.0	3.2	3.0	3.0
Vanuatu	2.3	1.6	4.0	4.3	4.5	3.8	4.0
Developing Asia	6.4	6.0	5.8	5.7	5.9	5.7	5.8
Developing Asia excluding the NIEs	6.8	6.6	6.3	6.3	6.4	6.2	6.3

Note: The newly industrialized economies (NIEs) are the Republic of Korea, Singapore, Taipei,China, and Hong Kong, China.

Table A2 Inflation (% per year)

	2014	2015	2016	2017		2018	
				ADO2017	Update	ADO2017	Update
Central Asia	5.9	6.3	11.0	7.8	8.9	7.3	7.8
Armenia	3.0	3.7	–1.4	1.2	1.2	1.8	1.8
Azerbaijan	1.4	4.0	12.4	9.0	14.0	8.0	10.0
Georgia	3.1	4.0	2.1	4.2	5.7	4.5	4.0
Kazakhstan	6.7	6.6	14.6	8.0	8.0	7.0	7.0
Kyrgyz Republic	7.5	6.5	0.4	5.0	3.5	4.0	5.0
Tajikistan	6.1	5.1	6.1	8.0	8.0	7.0	7.5
Turkmenistan	6.0	6.4	6.0	6.0	5.7	6.0	5.5
Uzbekistan	9.1	8.5	8.0	9.5	11.5	10.0	12.0
East Asia	1.9	1.3	1.9	2.3	1.7	2.6	2.3
China, People's Rep. of	2.0	1.4	2.0	2.4	1.7	2.8	2.4
Hong Kong, China	4.4	3.0	2.4	2.0	1.7	2.1	1.8
Korea, Rep. of	1.3	0.7	1.0	1.7	1.8	1.8	1.9
Mongolia	12.8	6.6	1.1	3.5	3.0	3.9	3.4
Taipei,China	1.2	–0.3	1.4	1.3	1.1	1.2	1.2
South Asia	6.3	4.9	4.5	5.2	4.2	5.4	4.7
Afghanistan	4.7	–1.5	4.4	5.5	5.5	5.8	5.8
Bangladesh	7.3	6.4	5.9	6.1	5.4	6.3	6.0
Bhutan	9.6	6.6	3.3	4.9	4.3	5.4	5.4
India	6.0	4.9	4.5	5.2	4.0	5.4	4.6
Maldives	2.1	1.0	0.5	2.1	3.1	2.3	2.8
Nepal	9.1	7.2	9.9	6.0	4.5	6.5	6.5
Pakistan	8.6	4.5	2.9	4.0	4.2	4.8	4.8
Sri Lanka	3.3	3.8	4.0	6.0	7.0	6.0	4.0
Southeast Asia	4.1	2.8	2.1	3.3	3.1	3.5	3.1
Brunei Darussalam	–0.2	–0.4	–0.7	0.1	–0.3	0.1	0.1
Cambodia	3.9	1.2	3.0	3.4	3.0	3.5	3.2
Indonesia	6.4	6.4	3.5	4.3	4.0	4.5	3.7
Lao People's Dem. Rep.	4.2	1.3	1.6	2.5	1.5	3.0	1.5
Malaysia	3.1	2.1	2.1	3.3	3.7	2.7	2.7
Myanmar	5.9	11.4	6.8	7.0	7.0	7.5	7.5
Philippines	4.1	1.4	1.8	3.5	3.2	3.7	3.5
Singapore	1.0	–0.5	–0.5	1.0	1.0	1.5	1.5
Thailand	1.9	–0.9	0.2	1.8	0.7	2.0	1.5
Viet Nam	4.1	0.6	2.7	4.0	4.5	5.0	5.5
The Pacific	3.5	4.0	4.5	5.2	5.3	5.4	5.3
Cook Islands	1.6	3.0	–0.1	0.5	–0.1	1.2	0.5
Fiji	0.6	1.4	3.9	2.5	3.5	2.5	2.5
Kiribati	2.1	0.6	0.7	2.0	2.0	2.0	2.0
Marshall Islands	1.1	–2.3	–1.5	1.5	0.5	1.5	1.0
Micronesia, Fed. States of	0.7	0.0	–1.0	1.5	1.5	2.0	2.0
Nauru	3.0	11.4	8.2	5.7	6.0	1.8	2.0
Palau	4.0	2.2	–1.3	1.5	1.5	2.0	2.0
Papua New Guinea	5.2	6.0	6.7	7.5	7.5	7.5	7.5
Samoa	–1.2	1.9	0.1	2.0	1.4	2.0	2.0
Solomon Islands	5.2	–0.5	1.1	1.8	0.5	2.2	1.0
Timor-Leste	0.7	0.6	–1.4	1.2	1.2	3.0	3.0
Tonga	2.5	–1.0	2.5	2.5	2.5	2.5	2.5
Tuvalu	1.1	3.2	3.5	2.0	2.9	2.0	2.5
Vanuatu	1.0	2.5	0.8	2.4	2.8	2.6	3.3
Developing Asia	3.0	2.2	2.5	3.0	2.4	3.2	2.9
Developing Asia excluding the NIEs	3.2	2.4	2.7	3.2	2.5	3.5	3.1

Note: The newly industrialized economies (NIEs) are the Republic of Korea, Singapore, Taipei,China, and Hong Kong, China.

Table A3 Current account balance (% of GDP)

	2014	2015	2016	2017		2018	
				ADO2017	*Update*	ADO2017	*Update*
Central Asia	2.1	–3.5	–6.2	–3.0	–3.4	–1.7	–2.0
Armenia	–7.6	–2.6	–2.3	–2.3	–2.5	–2.0	–2.3
Azerbaijan	13.9	–0.4	–3.6	5.9	5.6	11.4	11.0
Georgia	–10.6	–11.9	–13.5	–12.0	–12.0	–11.5	–11.5
Kazakhstan	2.8	–2.8	–6.3	–3.4	–4.5	–3.0	–3.5
Kyrgyz Republic	–17.2	–15.2	–10.0	–13.0	–13.0	–13.5	–13.5
Tajikistan	–9.1	–5.9	–4.8	–5.5	–5.5	–6.0	–6.0
Turkmenistan	–6.7	–12.3	–18.5	–15.0	–12.8	–13.0	–12.4
Uzbekistan	1.4	0.3	0.1	0.2	0.1	0.4	0.5
East Asia	3.3	3.7	2.8	2.5	2.0	2.3	1.8
China, People's Rep. of	2.6	2.7	1.8	1.8	1.4	1.7	1.2
Hong Kong, China	1.4	3.3	4.5	3.1	2.9	3.1	2.9
Korea, Rep. of	6.0	7.7	7.0	5.8	5.0	5.3	5.0
Mongolia	–15.8	–8.1	–4.0	–2.1	–6.4	–6.3	–8.5
Taipei,China	11.7	14.3	13.6	6.8	6.8	6.5	6.5
South Asia	–1.1	–0.9	–0.9	–1.4	–1.6	–1.6	–1.8
Afghanistan	2.4	4.7	4.4	1.4	2.2	–0.2	0.2
Bangladesh	0.8	1.5	1.9	–1.0	–0.6	–0.7	–1.5
Bhutan	–26.4	–28.3	–31.4	–27.4	–25.5	–22.8	–22.8
India	–1.3	–1.1	–1.0	–1.3	–1.3	–1.5	–1.5
Maldives	–3.8	–8.6	–22.3	–18.9	–16.4	–19.1	–15.2
Nepal	4.6	5.1	6.2	–1.6	–0.4	–3.2	–2.2
Pakistan	–1.3	–1.0	–1.7	–2.1	–4.0	–2.5	–4.2
Sri Lanka	–2.5	–2.3	–2.4	–2.2	–3.5	–2.2	–2.5
Southeast Asia	3.1	3.2	3.7	3.1	3.0	3.0	2.8
Brunei Darussalam	30.7	16.0	11.0	5.3	6.0	5.5	6.5
Cambodia	–11.7	–11.3	–10.8	–9.4	–9.7	–9.0	–9.3
Indonesia	–3.1	–2.0	–1.8	–1.7	–1.7	–1.6	–2.0
Lao People's Dem. Rep.	–25.0	–20.3	–18.0	–19.0	–17.5	–20.0	–19.0
Malaysia	4.4	3.0	2.4	1.8	2.4	2.0	2.4
Myanmar	–3.3	–5.2	–7.0	–8.0	–8.0	–8.0	–8.0
Philippines	3.8	2.5	0.2	0.2	0.2	0.5	0.5
Singapore	19.7	18.1	19.0	19.5	19.5	19.8	19.8
Thailand	3.7	8.0	11.7	9.0	8.5	7.0	6.5
Viet Nam	4.9	0.5	3.3	2.0	1.0	2.5	2.0
The Pacific	10.1	9.4	1.0	3.0	2.8	–0.5	–0.8
Cook Islands	26.1	18.8	19.5	24.5	27.6	21.0	28.7
Fiji	–7.6	–1.5	–1.2	3.5	–4.2	3.0	–3.6
Kiribati	54.0	51.1	22.8	–2.4	–2.4	–1.5	–3.0
Marshall Islands	1.9	16.5	8.5	4.0	5.0	4.5	7.0
Micronesia, Fed. States of	1.3	2.2	2.8	4.5	4.5	4.5	4.5
Nauru	–13.4	–9.4	1.7	...	0.5	...	–1.8
Palau	–14.5	–3.4	–11.3	–12.5	–12.0	–15.0	–14.0
Papua New Guinea	3.7	13.4	9.4	7.7	7.7	6.7	6.7
Samoa	–6.9	–3.1	–6.1	–4.9	–2.9	–2.8	–4.2
Solomon Islands	–5.4	–3.5	–5.1	–8.3	–6.0	–10.7	–9.0
Timor-Leste	73.3	14.9	–45.3	–12.2	–5.9	–40.2	–36.4
Tonga	–7.9	–11.7	–3.2	–7.7	–7.7	–11.9	–10.0
Tuvalu	12.8	9.9	–21.0	–20.8	–20.2	–25.4	–24.4
Vanuatu	–0.3	–8.8	–3.2	–17.7	–10.0	–15.0	–9.5
Developing Asia	2.6	3.0	2.3	1.9	1.5	1.7	1.4
Developing Asia excluding the NIEs	1.8	2.0	1.1	1.1	0.7	0.9	0.5

... = data not available.

Note: The newly industrialized economies (NIEs) are the Republic of Korea, Singapore, Taipei,China, and Hong Kong, China.

www.ingramcontent.com/pod-product-compliance
Lightning Source LLC
Chambersburg PA
CBHW061219270326
41926CB00032B/4778